Constitutional
Debate in Action

Constitutional Debate in Action

Governmental Powers

H. L. POHLMAN

Dickinson College

◆

■ HarperCollinsCollegePublishers

EDITOR-IN-CHIEF: Marcus Boggs
DEVELOPMENTAL EDITOR: Jennifer Goebel
PROJECT EDITOR: Andrew Roney
TEXT DESIGN: Nancy Sabato
COVER DESIGN: Kay Petronio
COVER PHOTOGRAPH: Barbara Maslen
PHOTO RESEARCHER: Nina Page
ELECTRONIC PRODUCTION MANAGER: Valerie A. Sawyer
DESKTOP ADMINISTRATOR: Sarah Johnson
MANUFACTURING MANAGER: Helene Landers
ELECTRONIC PAGE MAKEUP: RR Donnelley Barbados
PRINTER AND BINDER: RR Donnelley & Sons Company
COVER PRINTER: RR Donnelley & Sons Company

Constitutional Debate in Action: *Governmental Powers*

Library of Congress Cataloging-in-Publication Data

Pohlman, H. L., 1952–
    Constitutional debate in action. Governmental powers / H.L.
    Pohlman.
        p. cm.
    ISBN 0–06–500514–7
    1. Separation of powers--United States--Cases   I. Title.
II. Title: Governmental powers.
KF4565.A7P64 1995
342.73'041--dc20
[347.30241]   94–19166
                                                     CIP

94 95 96 97 9 8 7 6 5 4 3 2 1

*To Ken, Jim, Ron, and Don
and the memory of Tony*

C O N T E N T S

PREFACE

The standard textbook on constitutional law assumes that the United States Constitution is best understood as a set of Supreme Court decisions. *Constitutional Debate in Action* is a series of textbooks that adopts a different premise without denying the value of the traditional approach. At a minimum, the orthodox casebook insightfully shows how the Constitution, from 1789 to the present, has evolved as Supreme Court justices have transformed constitutional doctrine. Yet, it is indisputable that such a text does not capture all the aspects of the U.S. Constitution that deserve to be considered. It is not, for example, especially illuminating in regard either to the process of constitutional adjudication itself or to the surrounding political context of any particular case. The Constitution is presented as what the justices say it is, but the political and intellectual forces that directly shape Supreme Court decisions are often ignored or deemphasized. The result is that doctrinal sophistication is often purchased at the expense of the student's understanding of the nature of constitutional adjudication. The student knows a lot of constitutional law, but he or she knows less about how and why it has grown. *Constitutional Debate in Action* tries to rectify this imbalance by viewing constitutional interpretation as an institutionalized form of debate by which certain litigants and their lawyers press their political demands and arguments upon the Supreme Court. It is in this fashion, in the wider context of human wants, passions, and values, that judges interpret the Constitution and thereby transform the basic framework of our government and society.

The more political and process-oriented view of the Constitution that is articulated in *Constitutional Debate in Action* has several distinctive features. First, breadth is sacrificed for depth. A case-study approach is used, and therefore each volume explores in depth only five landmark decisions. Second, each chapter begins with an introduction that describes the legal background as well as the political context. Relevant out-of-courtroom discussions of the constitutional issue in question are excerpted and highlighted in "boxes" set off from the text. Newspaper headlines from the period are also included. These materials will help the student appreciate the political context in which the Supreme Court is operating and assess the degree to which political factors are influencing constitutional adjudication.

The series, however, does not ignore the relevant legal arguments. Rather, it gives a great deal of attention to the process of constitutional argumentation by including sources that deserve more attention than traditional casebooks have given to them: the legal briefs filed in landmark cases and the corresponding oral arguments made before the Supreme Court. These materials, if properly presented, are pedagogically useful.[1] First, the adversarial character of the briefs and

---

[1]Overly technical discussions and the large number of citations that are often found in legal briefs have been eliminated from the excerpts that follow. In addition, for the sake of producing a readable text, stylistic usages peculiar to legal briefs, as well as small grammatical errors and typos, have been adapted to standard English or corrected. The same policy was followed in regard to the "boxes" and the Supreme Court opinions.

oral argument awakens student interest. Students want to figure out for themselves which side has the better argument. And, in general, the time spent reading the briefs is time well spent. The adversarial character of the American approach to constitutional adjudication more or less assumes that the best legal arguments find their way into the actual briefs of the cases, and, in the main (though not always), this assumption is borne out by the quality of the arguments found in the briefs.

However, even in the unlikely event that the briefs and oral argument of a particular case are not of the highest caliber, they nonetheless have pedagogical value. As students compare the validity of the opposing arguments, they are, in effect, preparing themselves for what comes next: a critical evaluation of the edited Supreme Court opinion. In each chapter, the opinion follows the briefs and oral argument. The students, in short, have done a lot of thinking about the issues before they have to consider what the Court has said. They are, for this reason, more inclined to analyze, dissect, and digest the opinion than merely to read and summarize it. In this way, reading the briefs and oral arguments not only provides insight into the process of constitutional adjudication but also encourages students to adopt a more critical perspective on the role that the Supreme Court plays in our constitutional democracy. Is it a court of law? Is it a political policymaker? Is it a little of both? *Constitutional Debate in Action* is designed to underline the significance of these questions by including materials that reveal the important but ambiguous role of the Supreme Court.

Each chapter ends with a postscript that briefly describes important developments of constitutional doctrine since the Court decided the landmark case. They are not meant to be comprehensive or detailed discussions. Instead, their primary purpose is to reaffirm the significance of the landmark decision itself. They show how such cases illustrate important moral, constitutional, and philosophical issues that will, in various guises, constantly reappear in our constitutional democracy.

Though *Constitutional Debate in Action* embodies a somewhat novel approach to teaching constitutional law, it is intended not to replace the more orthodox casebook approach but rather to complement it. It is possible to use the series as the main text in a course on American constitutional law, but any particular volume of the series can also function as a supplemental text for a course taught in the traditional manner. The virtue of such a supplement is that it gives students a different perspective from that of the main text. Most casebooks challenge the best students and frequently intimidate the rest. Page after page of abstract and complicated judicial reasoning is often too much for them. A change of pace is at times useful if not necessary. This series was designed with this need in mind. It will enable any class on constitutional law, no matter what major text is being used, to pause occasionally throughout the term to take a closer look—a look from a different perspective—at a landmark case. Such a supplement can improve student morale in a pedagogically valuable way.

The assumption of this text is that constitutional argumentation before the Supreme Court takes place within a broad political context. In many of the cases that come before the Court, litigants representing distinct political agendas press their claims and arguments. However, not just anyone can litigate before the Court because there are rules that limit access to all courts. Rules governing *ripeness* and *mootness* concern the nature of the "case or controversy" under litigation, whereas *standing* has more to do with the nature of the parties. Courts, including the Supreme Court, will address only "live" controversies. If a dispute has not yet "ripened" or if it has, for whatever reason, resolved itself (become "moot"), then courts—including the Supreme Court—will refuse to hear it. In the same way, the criteria of standing ask whether the litigant has "a sufficient personal interest" in the issue before the Court. Physical injury or economic damage clearly suffices for standing, but courts can deny access to others, not on the ground that the issue is not a "live" one, but rather because the person initiating the suit has not shown that he or she has been sufficiently harmed. The law governing ripeness, mootness, and standing is composed of complicated rules that limit the character of judicial policymaking, including the sort of policymaking inherent in constitutional adjudication.[2] Nevertheless, many litigants representing distinct political agendas satisfy the criteria of these rules, thereby insuring that the Supreme Court plays a political role in the process of constitutional argumentation.

For practical purposes, constitutional argumentation before the Court begins with "the rule of four." Whether the case is coming from the lower federal courts or from a high state court, the party appealing to the Supreme Court must convince four justices to review the case. Throughout most of its history, the Supreme Court has had no lack of cases from which it could pick and choose. At the present time, approximately 5,500 cases are appealed to the Supreme Court each year, and the Court hands down decisions with full opinions in only 120 to 150 cases. Therefore, because the Court has so many cases to choose from, it controls its own docket. Though political and institutional factors at times limit the Court's discretion, it is nonetheless true that the Court decides only those cases that four justices want it to decide.

Once the case is accepted for review, the petitioner (who filed the case at the Supreme Court) and the respondent (who answers) submit their constitutional arguments in written briefs. Soon thereafter both sides present their arguments orally in front of the justices of the Supreme Court. In addition, the Court often permits "friends of the court" (*amici curiae*) to submit briefs and participate in oral argument. These "friends" are individuals, groups, or organizations that are interested in the litigation. The number of *amici* briefs filed varies enormously from case to case and the degree to which they influence the Court is largely unknown. However, the fact that American constitutional adjudication tolerates, if it does not encourage, the participation of interested third parties is not without significance. It highlights the political aspect of the constitutional process.

After reading the briefs and listening to the oral argument, the justices discuss the case at a weekly conference and cast their initial votes. Each justice has one vote. If the chief justice votes with the majority, he or she has the privilege of deciding which member of the majority should write the majority opinion. If the chief justice votes in the minority, then the most senior judge in the majority makes the opinion assignment. However, not all decisions produce a majority opinion. If a

---

[2]For a more thorough discussion of these rules and others that limit access to courts, see Henry Abraham, *The Judicial Process,* 6th ed. (New York: Oxford University Press, 1993), Chapter 9.

majority of the justices decide in favor of the petitioner but cannot agree upon an opinion, the result is a plurality opinion or opinions. Moreover, any justice who agrees with the majority can also write his or her own concurring opinion. Justices who disagree with the majority or the plurality can either join a dissenting opinion or dissent separately.

In short, every individual justice is free to join any opinion or write one of his or her own. Therefore, the initial vote at conference is not decisive. The justices are perfectly free to change their minds. Hence there is often a great deal of fluidity in the voting as justices circulate, revise, and recirculate opinions and dissents. What started out as a majority opinion may end up as a dissenting opinion; a dissent can become the majority opinion. Consequently, the meaning and significance of a decision depends not upon the initial vote but rather upon how the justices vote when the decision (with any concurring and dissenting opinions) is handed down. The more consensus there is on the Court, the more definite the meaning of the decision and the greater its potential significance.

An analysis of a Supreme Court case, including those that follow in this series, requires paying attention to a number of different factors. First, the facts of a case should be noted: who did what to whom, when, why, how, and where. What were the political, social, and economic contexts of the litigation? Second, who are the parties to the litigation: Who initiated the lawsuit against whom? How did the lawsuit fare in the lower courts? Who is appealing to the Supreme Court? Third, what are the legal issues of the case and the arguments on both sides of the question? Which side has the better argument? Why? Fourth, are there any political influences operating on the Court? What are they? Are they permissible influences, or do they undermine the legal character of constitutional adjudication? Fifth, which side does the Supreme Court favor, and what is the breakdown of the vote? How many concurring and dissenting opinions are there? Sixth, how do the different justices justify their respective positions? Which justification is best? Finally, what is your general evaluation of how the Supreme Court has performed in the particular case under consideration?

Keeping these sorts of questions in mind while reading the following chapters, but at the same time keeping them distinct, will focus attention on the relevant issues. The present volume is entitled *Governmental Powers*. It discusses five landmark cases concerning the power of judicial review, the commerce power, the war power, executive emergency (or inherent) power, and the power of executive privilege. Any number of cases could have been used to explore these important areas of constitutional law. I chose *Marbury v. Madison, NLRB v. Jones & Laughlin Steel Corporation, Korematsu v. United States, Youngstown Sheet & Tube Co. v. Sawyer,* and *United States v. Nixon* because they reveal, in an insightful way, how the American system of constitutional adjudication involves the constant interplay of politics and law. Other cases, it is true, could probably have served this purpose just as well, but this fact is not overly significant. The underlying assumption of *Constitutional Debate in Action* is that the question of which cases deserve attention is less important than a deeper awareness of the process of constitutional adjudication itself.

Acknowledgments

I want to express my appreciation to Dickinson College for all the support that I received while working on *Constitutional Debate in Action*. I especially thank George Allan, the Dean of the College, along with Susan Nichols, Leon Fitts, Jeff Niemitz, Kim Lacy Rogers, and Sue Norman. The staffs at Dickinson Law School Library and Dickinson College Library, especially Tina Maresco and Natalia Chromiak, also provided invaluable assistance. Tina and Natalia processed my numerous interlibrary-loan requests with cheerful efficiency. I am also very grateful to my students, especially those who took an interest in this project. In particular, I would like to thank Bruce Butler (class of 1990), Cindy Mather (class of 1991), and Michelle Quinn (class of 1991). These students helped me put the initial sample chapter together and were wonderful sounding boards at a time when I was unsure of what exactly I was trying to accomplish. I will always be in their debt. For many hours of typing and proofing that went into this series of textbooks, I gratefully recognize the contributions of Jennifer Williams (class of 1992), Richard Schirmer (class of 1992), Ann Marie Branson (class of 1994), Marc Snyderman (class of 1994), and Tim Grieco (class of 1994). They did excellent work in a job that is as important as it is thankless. Finally, I am happy that I have this opportunity to express my gratitude to my student research assistant, Daniel DeArment (class of 1993). For the past year, Dan has been at my side helping me separate the wheat from the chaff, giving me the benefit of his perspective as a student. In this capacity, Dan gave me many valuable suggestions, especially in regard to the material set off in "boxes" throughout the series. I owe Dan a great deal for all the energy and insight that he has infused into this series. I am also indebted to the Mellon and the Dana foundations for their support of the student work that went into *Constitutional Debate in Action*.

A number of colleagues and friends deserve mention here for tolerating my obsession with this project over the past couple of years. Eugene Hickok, who is a fellow member of Dickinson's Political Science Department, has been an invaluable associate. I have used his books, his ideas, and his time. I want to thank him for all that he has done for me without promising that I will never ask for his help again. Gary Gildin, a member of the faculty of the Dickinson Law School, also patiently suffered my pleas for advice, giving me a number of valuable suggestions. When I was contemplating whether to begin this project, D. Grier Stephenson, from Franklin and Marshall College, gave me the necessary encouragement to get started. Last, I want to thank Victoria Kuhn, my departmental secretary, who put more time and energy into this series than anyone save myself. Never have I seen a person have so much fun working so hard tracking down permissions for copyrighted material. I owe Victoria so much because, as she knows, I would have been buried in frustration and despair by the job that she pursued with efficiency and good humor.

I also want to thank Philip B. Kurland and Gerhard Casper, the editors of *Landmark Briefs and Arguments of the Supreme Court of the United States*, published by University Publications of America. I often used this series while working on my project. It was an invaluable resource. Moreover, the editors and University

Publications of America have graciously allowed me to use their designations of which justices asked what questions during oral argument. In my opinion, having the names of justices linked to specific questions is a valuable pedagogical aid, and I am grateful to the editors and the press for letting me use their work. In the same vein, I want to thank all those who gave me permission to use copyrighted material. I use the material because I think, rightly or wrongly, that it will make the difficult task of teaching constitutional law somewhat easier. I am grateful because they care enough about education to give my textbook a chance to make a difference in the crucible of the classroom.

Marcus Boggs, Jennifer Goebel, Andrew Roney, and Paula Soloway, my editors at HarperCollins, have done a wonderful job ushering this project through the various stages of the publication process.

Last, I wish to apologize for the many mistakes that I have made in this series of constitutional law textbooks. I only wish to add, by way of explanation, how difficult it was for me to write and edit these fifteen chapters. Given the publication deadlines, I found it to be very much like trying to square fifteen circles in as many months. The task was one that made for some long days and short nights. I can only hope that the reader irritated with one of my lapses will understand if not forgive.

H. L. Pohlman

The Power of Judicial Review

MARBURY V. MADISON
1 CRANCH 137 (1803)

✦

In 1801, Thomas Jefferson, the newly elected president of the United States, made a decision that has had an enormous impact upon American constitutionalism. He denied to William Marbury (and three others) the job to which John Adams, Jefferson's immediate predecessor, had appointed him before leaving office. Marbury, a Federalist opponent of the new Republican administration, filed suit against James Madison, Jefferson's secretary of state, claiming that his legal rights had been violated. In an opinion written by Chief Justice John Marshall, the Supreme Court declined to come to Marbury's aid. Although Marbury was legally entitled to the job, Marshall reasoned, the law granting the Court jurisdiction in the case was unconstitutional and therefore not judicially enforceable. It was this proclamation by the Supreme Court of the doctrine of judicial review—the doctrine that judges could declare statutes and executive actions unconstitutional—that gave *Marbury v. Madison* its significance. All the groundbreaking Supreme Court decisions that followed during the nineteenth and twentieth centuries implicitly relied upon its authority; they could not be legally valid unless it was also. And as American constitutional law came to be equated with these opinions, *Marbury*'s status, along with that of the Supreme Court, climbed ever higher. In effect, Jefferson's decision to deny Marbury his position inadvertently gave the Supreme Court the opportunity to become, in time, the "ultimate" interpreter of the U.S. Constitution.

In varying degrees, many countries have imitated the U.S. model of judicial review, but no country except the United States gives every judge in the country the power to declare laws and executive actions unconstitutional.[1] The reason why most, if not all, countries refuse to implement fully the doctrine of judicial review is simple; they fear that judicial review transfers power from politically account-able bodies to politically insulated judges. What happens, they ask, if the judges exercise the power of judicial review in a political fashion, injecting their own po-litical biases into their interpretation of the constitution? The orthodox U.S. re-sponse to this question, one that is indirectly expressed in Marshall's opinion in *Marbury,* is that the political game needs an umpire. A written constitution, limit-ing the legislature's power, can be effective only if some other body besides the legislature defines individual rights and interprets what powers the constitution has given to the legislature. An independent judiciary is best able to fulfill this role because its "peculiar" function is to interpret law, including the law of the consti-tution. In sum, according to orthodox U.S. constitutionalism, the rule of law can be meaningfully achieved only by making the judiciary into a constitutional umpire.

Balancing the desire for limited government and the rule of law against the fear of politically insulated judges wielding unchecked power has always been at the center of the American debate concerning judicial review. At the time of the founding, the legal background favored judicial review, though political support for it was far from unanimous. During the colonial period, some of the colonies had practiced judicial review at the local level, and the English Privy Council had prepared the way for the institution of judicial review at the national level by in-validating colonial legislation that conflicted with English law. Hence, most of the delegates to the Constitutional Convention of 1787 supported some form of judi-cial review. Alexander Hamilton set forth the reasons for it in *Federalist #78,* one of the eighty-five newspaper articles published in New York during the ratification debates on the new Constitution (1787–88). Hamilton insisted that the judiciary, because it had neither the power of the sword nor that of the purse, was the "least dangerous" branch of government. It had "neither FORCE nor WILL but merely judgment." Accordingly, no danger arose if courts functioned as "an intermediate body between the people and the legislature, in order, among other things, to keep the latter within the limits assigned to their authority." Not only were courts relatively harmless, but their "proper and peculiar province" consisted of inter-preting law, including the "fundamental law" of the Constitution. (See Box 1.1.) Hamilton therefore concluded, as Marshall did later, that courts had the power and the duty to exercise the power of judicial review.

Not everyone agreed with Hamilton's analysis. One of the foremost critics of both the new Constitution and judicial review was Robert Yates, a delegate to the convention who opposed the Constitution's ratification under the name of Brutus. Yates rejected the new federal Constitution because, in his view, the federal judi-ciary, and especially the Supreme Court, would not exercise the power of judicial review in an impartial manner. The Court would favor the national government over the states and its own power over those of the executive and the legislature. Judicial review would therefore allow political power to gravitate toward the na-tional judiciary. (See Box 1.2.)

---

[1]For a brief description of judicial review in other countries, see Henry Abraham, *The Judicial Process,* 6th ed. (New York: Oxford University Press, 1986), Chapter 7.

Who do you think has the better argument: Hamilton or Yates? Is the judiciary the "least dangerous branch"? Can it be an impartial umpire? Is judicial review the only meaningful way to limit the legislature? Can the rule of law be attained without it? Is the rule of law worth the risk of an unchecked judiciary?

BOX 1.1

FEDERALIST #78

. . . Whoever attentively considers the different departments of power must perceive that, in a government in which they are separated from each other, the judiciary, from the nature of its functions, will always be the least dangerous to the political rights of the Constitution; because it will be least in a capacity to annoy or injure them. The executive not only dispenses the honors but holds the sword of the community. The legislature not only commands the purse but prescribes the rules by which the duties and rights of every citizen are to be regulated. The judiciary, on the contrary, has no influence over either the sword or the purse; no direction either of the strength or of the wealth of the society, and can take no active resolution whatever. It may truly be said to have neither FORCE nor WILL but merely judgment; and must ultimately depend upon the aid of the executive arm even for the efficacy of its judgments. . . .

There is no position which depends on clearer principles than that every act of a delegated authority, contrary to the tenor of the commission under which it is exercised, is void. No legislative act, therefore, contrary to the Constitution, can be valid. To deny this would be to affirm that the deputy is greater than his principal; that the servant is above his master; that the representatives of the people are superior to the people themselves; that men acting by virtue of powers may do not only what their powers do not authorize, but what they forbid.

If it be said that the legislative body are themselves the constitutional judges of their own powers and that the construction they put upon them is conclusive upon the other departments it may be answered that this cannot be the natural presumption where it is not to be collected from any particular provisions in the Constitution. It is not otherwise to be supposed that the Constitution could intend to enable the representatives of the people to substitute their *will* to that of their constituents. It is far more rational to suppose that the courts were designed to be an intermediate body between the people and the legislature in order, among other things, to keep the latter within the limits assigned to their authority. The interpretation of the laws is the proper and peculiar province of the courts. A constitution is, in fact, and must be regarded by the judges as, a fundamental law. It therefore belongs to them to ascertain its meaning as well as the meaning of any particular act proceeding from the legislative body. If there should happen to be an irreconcilable variance between the two, that which has the superior obligation and validity ought, of course, to be preferred; or, in other words, the Constitution ought to be preferred to the statute, the intention of the people to the intentions of their agents.

Nor does this conclusion by any means suppose a superiority of the judicial to the legislative power. It only supposes that the power of the people is superior to both, and that where the will of the legislature, declared in its statutes, stands in opposition to that of the people, declared in the Constitution, the judges ought to be governed by the latter rather than the former. They ought to regulate their decisions by the fundamental laws rather than by those which are not fundamental. . . .

Source: Clinton Rossiter, ed., *The Federalist Papers* (New York: Mentor, 1961), pp. 465–68.

The facts and circumstances of *Marbury* provide a useful context in which to consider the need for a political umpire and to explore the question whether judges can fulfill this role in a neutral, nonpolitical way. Some may find that the case produces no problems for the orthodox theory; others, that it proves that judicial review all too quickly degenerates into an abuse of power; and still others, that it shows that politics is a game that needs an umpire but that, unfortunately, none is available. In any event, however the above questions are answered, students should consider the nature and legitimacy of judicial review. It may be true that judicial review is now, after almost 200 years, a permanent feature of American political life, but a consideration of the political and legal context of the very case that established the doctrine will contribute to a deeper understanding of the fundamentals of American constitutionalism.

The background of *Marbury v. Madison* is an almost inseparable weave of political and legal elements. The case would never have arisen without the victory of Thomas Jefferson's newly formed Republican Party (a party, of course, different from today's Republican Party) in the election of 1800. In this election, the American people decisively rejected the older Federalist Party, whose policies favored the wealthy commercial classes and encouraged the growth of the federal government. Having lost control of the presidency and both houses of Congress, the Federalists enacted in February 1801, before the Republicans came to power in March, two laws: the Judiciary Act and the District of Columbia Act. The first law, which created sixteen new federal circuit judgeships and reduced the number of Supreme Court justices from six to five, had considerable merit. Under the old system, Supreme Court justices, in addition to their duties on the country's highest court, had sat on regional circuit courts—intermediate courts between the local district courts and the Supreme Court. Hence, the justices were overburdened with travel and reviewed cases on the Supreme Court that they had already decided while "riding circuit." The future odd number of justices, of course, would reduce the possibility of tie votes. The second law, the less important District of Columbia Act, expanded local government in the District by creating three additional circuit judgeships and a number of minor positions, including dozens of justices of the peace.

BOX 1.2

BRUTUS #11

The judicial power will operate to effect, in the most certain, but yet silent and imperceptible manner, what is evidently the tendency of the constitution:—I mean, an entire subversion of the legislative, executive and judicial powers of the individual states. Every adjudication of the supreme court, on any question that may arise upon the nature and extent of the general government, will affect the limits of the state jurisdiction. In proportion as the former enlarge the exercise of their powers, will that of the latter be restricted.

That the judicial power of the United States, will lean strongly in favour of the general government, and will give such an explanation to the constitution, as will favour an extension of its jurisdiction, is very evident from a variety of considerations.

1st. The constitution itself strongly countenances such a mode of construction. Most of the articles in this system, which convey powers of any considerable importance, are conceived in general and indefinite terms, which are either equivocal, ambiguous, or which require long definitions to unfold the extent of their meaning. . . .

This constitution gives sufficient colour for adopting an equitable construction, if we consider the great end and design it professedly has in view—these appear from its preamble to be, "to form a more perfect union, establish justice, insure domestic tranquility, provide for the common defense, promote the general welfare, and secure the blessings of liberty to ourselves and posterity." The design of this system is here expressed, and it is proper to give such a meaning to the various parts, as will best promote the accomplishment of the end; this idea suggests itself naturally upon reading the preamble, and will countenance the court in giving the several articles such a sense, as will most effectually promote the ends the constitution had in view. . . .

2d. Not only will the constitution justify the courts in inclining to this mode of explaining it, but they will be interested in using this latitude of interpretation. Every body of men invested with office are tenacious of power; they feel interested, and hence it has become a kind of maxim, to hand down their offices, with all its rights and privileges, unimpaired to their successors; the same principle will influence them to extend their power, and increase their rights; this of itself will operate strongly upon the courts to give such a meaning to the constitution in all cases where it can possibly be done, as will enlarge the sphere of their own authority. Every extension of the power of the general legislature, as well as of the judicial powers, will increase the powers of the courts; and the dignity and importance of the judges, will be in proportion to the extent and magnitude of the powers they exercise. I add, it is highly probable the emolument of the judges will be increased, with the increase of the business they will have to transact and its importance. From these considerations the judges will be interested to extend the powers of the courts, and to construe the constitution as much as possible, in such a way as to favour it; and that they will do it, appears probable. . . .

This power in the judicial, will enable them to mould the government, into almost any shape they please. . . .

Source: Herbert Storing, ed., *The Complete Anti-Federalist,* 7 vols. (Chicago: University of Chicago Press, 1981), II, pp. 420–22.

Notwithstanding the merits of these laws, their timing convinced the Republicans that the Federalists were enlarging the federal judiciary and the local administration of Washington, D.C., for political reasons, including the particularly unsavory one of patronage. "They have retired into the Judiciary as a stronghold," Jefferson wrote to John Dickinson. "There the remains of federalism are to be preserved and fed from the Treasury, and from that battery all the works of republicanism are to be beaten down and destroyed."[2] Jefferson's fear of a politically inspired Federalist judiciary was not just paranoia. During the 1790s, a number of Federalist judges had been quite politically active. They had campaigned for Federalist candidates, supported prosecutions under the Sedition Act of leading Republicans for their public criticisms of the Adams administration, and lectured grand juries in ways that had explicit political overtones. In 1798, Republican opposition to the Federalists, including the Federalist judiciary, crystalized in the Kentucky and Virginia Resolutions written, respectively, by Thomas Jefferson and James Madison. In its resolution, the Kentucky legislature condemned the Sedition Act and proclaimed that state legislatures had the power to "nullify" unconstitutional federal laws. (See Box 1.3.) It therefore appears that, though Republicans had earlier argued that federal judges should declare the Sedition Act unconstitutional, by 1798, they no longer trusted the federal judiciary and therefore switched their constitutional allegiance, at least somewhat, to state legislatures.

Accordingly, as they took office in 1801, the Republicans had reason to fear what an enlarged Federalist judiciary would do. They could draw little or no consolation from the fact that the new law reduced the likelihood of deadlocks on the Supreme Court. For them, the more important implication of the reduction of the number of Supreme Court justices was that Jefferson would be unable to make an appointment to the Supreme Court until two justices had retired. The Supreme Court's decisiveness had been purchased, it would seem, at the expense of the Republicans.

Republican patience finally snapped in December 1801 when William Marbury requested a writ of mandamus (a special court order to a public official) from

---

[2]Cited in Henry Adams, *History of the United States,* 2 vols. (New York: The Library of America, 1986), I, p. 175.

BOX 1.3

KENTUCKY RESOLUTION
(November 10, 1798)

1. *Resolved,* That the several states composing the United States of America, are not united on the principle of unlimited submission to their general government; but that by compact, under the style and title of a Constitution for the United States, and of amendments thereto, they constituted a general government for special purposes, delegated to that government certain definite powers, reserving, each state to itself, the residuary mass of right to their own self-government; and that whensoever the general government assumes undelegated powers, its acts are unauthoritative, void, and of no force: That to this compact each state acceded as a state, and is an integral party, its co-states forming as to itself, the other party: That the government created by this compact was not made the exclusive or final *judge* of the extent of the powers delegated to itself; since that would have made its discretion, and not the Constitution, the measure of its powers; but that, as in all other cases of compact among parties having no common judge, each party has an equal right to judge for itself, as well of infractions, as of the mode and measure of redress. . . .

   3. *Resolved,* That it is true as a general principle, and is also expressly declared by one of the amendments to the Constitution, that "the powers not delegated to the United States by the Constitution, nor prohibited by it to the states, are reserved to the states respectively, or to the people;" and that no power over the freedom of religion, freedom of speech, or freedom of the press, being delegated to the United States by the Constitution, nor prohibited by it to the states, all lawful powers respecting the same did of right remain, and were reserved to the states, or to the people; that thus was manifested their determination to retain to themselves the right of judging how far the licentiousness of speech and of the press may be abridged without lessening their useful freedom, and how far those abuses which cannot be separated from their use, should be tolerated rather than the use be destroyed; and thus also they guarded against all abridgment by the United States of the freedom of religious opinions and exercise, and retained to themselves the right of protecting the same, as this state by a law passed on the general demand of its citizens, had already protected them from all human restraint or interference: and that in addition to this general principle and express declaration, another and more special provision has been made by one of the amendments to the Constitution, which expressly declares, that "Congress shall make no law respecting an establishment of religion, or prohibiting the free exercise thereof, or abridging the freedom of speech, or of the press," thereby guarding in the same sentence, and under the same words, the freedom of religion, of speech, and of the press, insomuch, that whatever violates either, throws down the sanctuary which covers the

others, and that libels, falsehoods, and defamations, equally with heresy and false religion, are withheld from the cognizance of federal tribunals: that therefore the act of the Congress of the United States, passed on the 14th day of July, 1798, entitled, "an act in addition to the act for the punishment of certain crimes against the United States," which does abridge the freedom of the press, is not law, but is altogether void and of no effect. . . .

Source: Melvin I. Urofsky, *Documents of American Constitutional & Legal History,* 2 vols. (New York: Knopf, 1989), I, pp. 160–62.

the Supreme Court compelling James Madison, Jefferson's secretary of state, to deliver the commission that named him as one of the justices of the peace established by the District of Columbia Act. Such a commission existed, according to Marbury, or at least had existed in early 1801, even though it had not been delivered to him. The matter was scheduled for argument at the next term of the Supreme Court in June 1802. Though it is possible that Marbury initiated this litigation as part of a Federalist attempt to discourage the Republicans from tampering with the Judiciary Act of 1801, its effect was the exact opposite. It became an excuse for the Republicans to begin what some of them had been aching to do throughout 1801: repeal the Judiciary Act of 1801 and deprive the sixteen Federalist circuit judges (who had been appointed under the act) of their positions. On January 6, 1802, Kentucky's John Breckenridge, who had earlier supported the Kentucky Resolution, entered a motion in the Senate to repeal the Judiciary Act of 1801, and a similar motion soon followed in the House of Representatives.

A great constitutional debate immediately erupted. The Federalists objected that the repeal would be unconstitutional because the Constitution granted life tenure to federal judges during good behavior. Federal judges, in their view, could only be impeached from office; the office itself could not be abolished. Nonsense, cried the Republicans. Because Congress had created the lower federal courts by statute, it could abolish them as well, relieving the occupants of their judicial responsibilities. The Repeal Act, in their view, was as constitutional as the Judiciary Act of 1801, which had also abolished some judicial offices.

In this congressional debate, the Republicans attacked the legitimacy of judicial review itself because the Federalists suggested that the federal courts would invalidate the Repeal Act if it were passed. In the Senate, Breckenridge hotly contended with Gouverneur Morris, a former Pennsylvania delegate to the Constitutional Convention who had become a prominent member of the Federalist Party. (See Box 1.4.) Breckenridge emphasized that the Constitution did not grant the power of judicial review—it was an "inferred" power, and therefore "dangerous in the extreme." In contrast, because the Constitution explicitly gave Congress the "law-making" power, it had the responsibility to decide upon its "proper exercise." In response, Morris claimed that judicial review was derived from the "constitution of man" and that it was necessary if Congress was not to become an unlimited sovereign.

BOX 1.4

Senate Debate on Judicial Review (1802)

MR. Breckenridge:

. . . I did not expect, sir, to find the doctrine of the power of the courts to annul the laws of Congress as unconstitutional, so seriously insisted on. I presume I shall not be out of order in replying to it. It is said that the different departments of Government are to be checks on each other, and that the courts are to check the Legislature. If this be true, I would ask where they got that power, and who checks the courts when they violate the Constitution? Would they not, by this doctrine, have the absolute direction of the Government? To whom are they responsible? But I deny the power which is so pretended. If it is derived from the Constitution, I ask gentlemen to point out the clause which grants it. I can find no such grant. Is it not extraordinary, that if this high power was intended, it should nowhere appear? Is it not truly astonishing that the Constitution, in its abundant care to define the powers of each department, should have omitted so important a power as that of the courts to nullify all the acts of Congress, which, in their opinion, were contrary to the Constitution?

Never were such high and transcendent powers in any Government (much less in one like ours, composed of powers specially given and defined) claimed or exercised by construction only. The doctrine of constructions, not warranted by the letter of an instrument, is dangerous in the extreme. Let men once loose upon constructions, and where will you stop them? Is the *astutia* of English judges, in discovering the latent meanings of law-makers, meanings not expressed in the letter of the laws, to be adopted here in the construction of the Constitution? Once admit the doctrine, that judges are to be indulged in these astute and wire-drawn constructions, to enlarge their own power, and control that of others, and I will join gentlemen of the opposition in declaring that the Constitution is in danger.

To make the Constitution a practical system, this pretended power of the courts to annul the laws of Congress cannot possibly exist. My idea of the subject, in a few words, is, that the Constitution intended a separation of the powers vested in the three great departments, giving to each exclusive authority on the subject committed to it. That these departments are co-ordinate, to revolve each within the sphere of their own orbits, without being responsible for their own motion, and are not to direct or control the course of others. That those who made the laws are presumed to have an equal attachment to, and interest in the Constitution; are equally bound by oath to support it, and have an equal right to give a construction to it. That the construction of one department of the powers vested in it, is of higher authority than the construction of any other department; and that, in fact, it is competent to that department to which powers are confided exclusively to decide upon the proper exercise of those powers: that therefore the Legislature have the exclusive right to interpret the Constitution, in what regards the law-making power, and the judges are bound to execute the laws they make. . . .

MR. MORRIS:

. . . The honorable member tells us the Legislature have the supreme and exclusive right to interpret the Constitution, so far as regards the making of laws; which, being made, the judges are bound to execute. And he asks where the judges got their pretended power of deciding on the constitutionality of laws. If it be in the Constitution (says he) let it be pointed out. I answer, they derived that power from authority higher than this Constitution. They derive it from the constitution of man, from the nature of things, from the necessary progress of human affairs. When you have enacted a law, when process thereon has been issued, and suit brought, it becomes eventually necessary that the judges decide on the case before them, and declare what the law is. They must, of course, determine whether that which is produced and relied on, has indeed the binding force of law. The decision of the Supreme Court is, and, of necessity, must be final. This, Sir, is the principle, and the source of the right for which we contend. But it is denied, and the supremacy of the Legislature insisted on. Mark, then, I pray, the result. The Constitution says, no bill of attainder, or *ex post facto* law shall be passed, no capitation or other direct tax shall be laid, unless in proportion to the census or enumeration to be taxed; no tax or duty shall be laid on articles exported from any State; no preference shall be given by any regulation of commerce or revenue to the ports of one State over those of another. Suppose that, notwithstanding these prohibitions, a majority of the two Houses should (with the President) pass such laws. Suppose, for instance, that a capitation tax (not warranted by the Constitution) or a duty on exports were imposed. . . . [T]he honorable member last up has told us in so many words, that the Legislature may decide exclusively on the Constitution, and that the judges are bound to execute the laws which the Legislature enact. Examine then the state to which we are brought. If this doctrine be sustained, (and it is the fair logical deduction from the premises laid down) what possible mode is there to avoid the conclusion that the moment the Legislature of the Union declare themselves supreme, they become so? The analogies so often assumed to the British Parliament, will then be complete. The sovereignty of America will no longer reside in the people, but in the Congress, and the Constitution is whatever they choose to make it. . . .

Source: Annals, 7th Cong., 1st Session, pp. 178–81.

An even more strident and sarcastic discussion occurred between James A. Bayard, the Federalist leader in the House, and John Randolph, his Republican counterpart. (See Box 1.5.) Although Bayard admitted that the ultimate arbiter of the validity of laws was the American people, he argued that judges must also have this power if the American people were to be saved from "the gallows." If judges did not have the power to declare laws unconstitutional, constitutional limitations

BOX 1.5

HOUSE DEBATE ON JUDICIAL REVIEW (1802)

MR. BAYARD:

. . . It was once thought by gentlemen who now deny the principle, that the safety of the citizen and of the State rested upon the power of the judges to declare an unconstitutional law void. How vain is a paper restriction, if it confers neither power nor right! Of what importance is it to say, Congress are prohibited from doing certain acts, if no legitimate authority exists in the country to decide whether an act done is a prohibited act? Do gentlemen perceive the consequences which would follow from establishing the principle, that Congress have the exclusive right to decide upon their own powers? This principle admitted, does any Constitution remain? Does not the power of the Legislature become absolute and omnipotent? Can you talk to them of transgressing their powers when no one has a right to judge of those powers but themselves? They do what is not authorized, they do what is inhibited, nay, at every step they trample the Constitution under foot; yet their acts are lawful and binding, and it is treason to resist them. How ill, sir, do the doctrines and professions of these gentlemen agree ! . . .

. . . Let me now ask if the power to decide upon the validity of our laws resides with the people? Gentlemen cannot deny this right to the people. I admit that they possess it. But if, at the same time, it does not belong to the courts of the United States, where does it lead the people? It leads them to the gallows. Let us suppose that Congress, forgetful of the limits of their authority, pass an unconstitutional law. They lay a direct tax upon one State and impose none upon the others. The people of the State taxed contest the validity of the law. They forcibly resist its execution. They are brought by the Executive authority before the courts upon charges of treason. The law is unconstitutional, the people have done right, but the court[s] are bound by the law, and obliged to pronounce upon them the sentence which it inflicts. Deny to the courts of the United States the power of judging upon the constitutionality of our laws, and it is vain to talk of its existence elsewhere. . . .

. . . There is the case of the privilege of habeas corpus, which cannot be suspended but in times of rebellion or of invasion. Suppose a law prohibiting the issuing of the writ at a moment of profound peace. If in such [a] case the writ were demanded of a court, could they say, it is true the Legislature were restrained from passing the law, suspending the privilege of this writ, at such a time as that which now exists, but their mighty power has broken the bonds of the Constitution, and fettered the authority of the court. I am not, sir, disposed to vaunt, but standing on this ground I throw the gauntlet to any champion upon the other side. I call upon them to maintain, that in a collision between a law and the Constitution, the judges are bound to support the law, and annul the Constitution. Can the gentlemen relieve themselves from this dilemma? Will they say, though a judge has no power to pronounce a law void, he has a power to declare the Constitution invalid?. . .

I humbly trust, Mr. Chairman, that I have given abundant proofs from the nature of our Government, from the language of the Constitution, and from Legislative acknowledgement, that the judges of our courts have the power to judge and determine upon the constitutionality of our laws. . . .

. . . I say, in the nature of things, the dependence of the judges upon the Legislature, and their right to declare the act of the Legislature void, are re-pugnant and cannot exist together. The doctrine, sir, supposes two rights— first, the right of the Legislature to destroy the office of the judge, and the right of the judge to vacate the act of the Legislature. You have a right to abolish, by a law, the offices of the judges of the circuit court; they have a right to declare the law void. It unavoidably follows, in the exercise of these rights, either that you destroy their rights, or that they destroy yours. This doctrine is not an harmless absurdity, it is a most dangerous heresy. It is a doctrine which cannot be practiced without producing not discord only, but bloodshed. If you pass the bill upon your table the judges have a Constitu-tional right to declare it void. I hope they will have courage to exercise that right; and if, sir, I am called upon to take my side, standing acquitted in my conscience and before my God, of all motives but the support of the Consti-tution of my country, I shall not tremble at the consequences. . . .

MR. RANDOLPH:

. . . [I do] not rise for the purpose of assuming the gauntlet which has been so proudly thrown by the Goliath of the adverse party; . . .[I do not be-lieve my] feeble powers, armed with the simple weapon of truth, a sling and a stone, capable of prostrating on the floor that gigantic boaster, armed cap-a-pie as he was. . . .

. . . [I]f you pass the law, the judges are to put their veto upon it by de-claring it unconstitutional. Here is a new power, of a dangerous and uncon-trollable nature, contended for. The decision of a Constitutional question must rest somewhere. Shall it be confided to men immediately responsible to the people, or to those who are irresponsible? for the responsibility by impeachment is little less than a name. From whom is a corrupt decision most to be feared? To me it appears that the power which has the right of passing, without appeal, on the validity of your laws, is your sovereign. But an extreme case is put; a bill of attainder is passed; are the judges to support the Constitution or the law? Shall they obey God or Mammon? Yet you can-not argue from such cases. But, sir, are we not as deeply interested in the true exposition of the Constitution as the judges can be? With all the defer-ence to their talents, is not Congress as capable of forming a correct opinion as they are? Are not its members acting under a responsibility to public opinion, which can and will check their aberrations from duty? Let a case, not an imaginary one, be stated: Congress violate the Constitution by fetter-ing the press; the judicial corrective is applied to; far from protecting the liberty of the citizen, or the letter of the Constitution, you find them outdo-ing the Legislature in zeal; pressing the common law of England to their service where the sedition law did not apply. Suppose your reliance had been altogether on this broken staff, and not on the elective principle. Your press might have been enchained till doomsday, your citizens incarcerated for life, and where is your remedy? But if the construction of the Constitution is left with us, there are no longer limits to our power, and this would be true if an appeal did not lie through the elections, from us to the nation, to whom alone, and not a few privileged individuals, it belongs to decide, in the last resort, on the Constitution. Gentlemen tell us that our doctrine will carry the people to the gallows if they suffer themselves to be misled into the belief that the judges are not the expositors of the Constitution. Their practice has carried the people to infamous punishment, to fine and imprisonment; and had they affixed the penalty of death to their unconstitutional laws, judges would not have been wanting to conduct them to the gibbet. . . .

. . . No, sir, you may invade the press; the courts will support you, will outstrip you in zeal to further this great object; your citizens may be imprisoned and amerced, the courts will take care to see it executed; the helpless foreigner may, contrary to the express letter of your Constitution, be deprived of compulsory process for obtaining witnesses in his defense; the courts, in their extreme humility, cannot find authority for granting it; but touch one cent of their salaries, abolish one sinecure office which the judges hold, and they are immediately arrayed against the laws, as the champions of the Constitution. Lay your hands on the liberties of the people, they are torpid, utterly insensible; but affect their peculiar interest, and they are all nerve. They are said to be harmless, unaspiring men. Their humble pretensions extend only to a complete exemption from Legislative control; to the exercise of an inquisitorial authority over the Cabinet of the Executive, and the veto of the Roman Tribunate upon all your laws, together with the establishing any body of laws which they may chose to declare a part of the Constitution. . . .

Source: Annals, 7th Cong., 1st Session, pp. 645–62.

on legislative power were mere "paper restriction[s]." Moreover, because it was obvious that judges had to apply the Constitution if and when it conflicted with a law, it was "heresy" to assert that the legislature, by way of the Repeal Act, could abolish judicial offices. If the law passed, Bayard called upon judges to perform their constitutional duty and declare it unconstitutional. Answering Bayard for the Republicans, Randolph argued that constitutional questions must be left with those who are "immediately responsible to the people," not to those who are "irresponsible." Public opinion and elections would check any legislative abuse, while unchecked judges would trample the Constitution and lead the American people "to the gibbet [gallows]." A good example, according to Randolph, of judicial tyranny was the Federalists' "overzealous" prosecution during the 1790s of the unconstitutional Sedition Act. These actual historical events, rather than some imaginary instance of legislative abuse, showed that judges were unworthy of the awesome power of judicial review.

Morris's and Bayard's arguments in favor of judicial review, echoing what Hamilton had argued earlier, later found shelter in Marshall's opinion in *Marbury*. The Republican criticisms of judicial review, in contrast, like Yates's earlier complaints, have largely been ignored. Is there much significance to Breckenridge's point that judicial review is a power not expressly given to judges by the Constitution? After all, if judges can infer their power to declare laws unconstitutional, what do we mean by the rule of law, the ideal that orthodox supporters of judicial review hold most dear? Both Breckenridge and Randolph emphasized that members of Congress were, compared with judges, equally able and entitled to interpret the Constitution. Indeed, Randolph argued that congressmen were better qualified to perform this function because they were subject to election. If congressional interpretations of the Constitution were mistaken, the people could solve the problem by voting their representatives out of office. Is there any validity to this argument? What of Randolph's discussion of how Federalist judges during the 1790s invaded the liberties of the American people, especially the liberty of the press, by enforcing the English common law's definition of seditious libel in prosecutions brought under the controversial Sedition Act? An independent judiciary, one insulated from public opinion by life tenure, might very well be more of a danger to liberty, he concluded, than a legislature that interpreted its own constitutional powers. Was Randolph clearly wrong? Was it a close call? Or was he obviously correct?

The congressional debate of 1802 reveals, at a minimum, that certain elements of the Republican Party were willing to reject judicial review to protect or secure their immediate political objectives. They were not deeply committed to this emerging feature of American constitutionalism. At the time, of course, the Supreme Court was not a prestigious institution. Indeed, when the federal government moved to Washington in the autumn of 1800, no accommodation had been made for the Supreme Court. The president had the White House and Congress its Capitol, but the Supreme Court had no home. It was not until January, 23, 1801, after Marshall had been appointed chief justice, that both houses of Congress agreed to let the Court sit in one of the first-floor committee rooms in the new capitol.[3] Other factors, some of which were of the Court's own making, also diminished the Court's stature at the turn of the nineteenth century. Before Marshall was appointed to the Court, justices delivered their opinions *seriatim,* with each justice writing and signing his own opinion. Accordingly, no opinion had the full backing of the entire Court. In addition, given the available means of transportation, the necessity of circuit riding made the job of being a justice rather unattractive. A justice spent much of his time bumping along on a horse or in a carriage.

---

[3]See George Lee Haskins and Herbert A. Johnson, *The Foundations of Power: John Marshall, 1801–1815,* Vol. 2 of *Oliver Wendell Holmes Devise History of the Supreme Court of the United States* (New York: Macmillan, 1981), pp. 79–84.

John Jay, co-author of *The Federalist Papers*, a prominent diplomat, and the first chief justice of the United States, summed up the status of the Supreme Court in a letter to President Adams. In this letter, written in January 1801, Jay declined reappointment as chief justice (which kept the position open for John Marshall), explaining that he was "perfectly convinced that under a system so defective it [the Supreme Court] would not obtain the energy, weight, and dignity which are essential to its affording due support to the national government, nor acquire the public confidence and respect which, as the last resort of the justice of the nation, it should possess."[4] Although Jay was wrong about the Supreme Court's future, his words can be taken as an accurate representation of the status of the Court in 1801.

It was against this historical background that the Republican Senate in February passed the Repeal Act of 1802, which abolished the sixteen circuit court judgeships. The House of Representatives followed suit in March. Thus, the judges Adams had appointed to the bench during the last month of his administration were stripped of their offices. For good measure, Congress also canceled the 1802 term of the Supreme Court. The Court could not therefore consider *Marbury* or the constitutionality of the Repeal Act until February of 1803. The Republican tactic, something of a *fait accompli*, forced the Supreme Court justices to ride circuit during 1802 before they could decide whether the Repeal Act that reintroduced circuit riding was constitutional. In the spring of 1802, a few Supreme Court justices considered whether they should refuse to "ride circuit," on the theory that the Repeal Act was unconstitutional, but in the end they acquiesced to congressional will. However, while the justices rode their circuits in 1802, the Federalist Party initiated in lower federal courts several challenges to the constitutionality of the Repeal Act, including *Stuart v. Laird*, a case that the Supreme Court decided soon after *Marbury v. Madison* in 1803. At the time, of course, *Stuart* was the more important case. It dealt with the constitutionality of the Repeal Act, whereas *Marbury* concerned only a few minor judicial appointments in the District of Columbia. But because *Marbury* came first on the Supreme Court's docket, attention focused on it. How the Court resolved the earlier case might show how it intended to handle the later one.

In February 1803, when *Marbury* finally came up for oral argument before the Court, Charles Lee, Marbury's attorney and the attorney of record in *Stuart v. Laird*, faced serious practical and theoretical problems. His basic argument was that Jefferson and Madison were legally obliged to deliver Marbury's commission because Adams had appointed Marbury; the Senate had confirmed the appointment; Adams had signed the commission; and the commission had been sealed, though not delivered. Accordingly, the crucial fact that Lee had to prove was that there had been a commission, signed and sealed, with Marbury's name on it. This was not an easy undertaking because the now Republican-controlled Senate had refused to provide any documentation of Marbury's confirmation by the earlier

---

[4]Cited in Albert J. Beveridge, *The Life of John Marshall*, 4 vols. (Boston: Houghton Mifflin, 1919), III, p. 55.

Federalist-controlled Senate. Madison, the new secretary of state, also declined to provide the commission or any evidence of its existence. Indeed, Madison did not even show up for the oral argument. Deeming *Marbury* unworthy of its attention, the Republican administration snubbed the Court.

Lee's only option was to subpoena minor officials who had been working in the secretary of state's office during the time when the appointments were made, including James Marshall, the chief justice's brother. He also subpoenaed Levi Lincoln, Jefferson's attorney general, who had been in temporary charge of the office of the secretary of state during the first few days of Jefferson's administration—the time when the commission had disappeared. This subpoena truly irritated Jefferson and his administration. Lincoln's testimony (see p. 25) shows that he did not like being hauled in front of a court of Federalists to answer questions about what he took to be his official executive duties.[5]

The irony was that John Marshall, sitting as chief justice on the court deciding the facts of the dispute, knew all about the commissions. Both he and Lee had been high-ranking Federalists in John Adams's administration; Lee had been attorney general, and Marshall had been secretary of state, even after he accepted the office of chief justice in early February 1801. As secretary of state in the Adams administration, he had been primarily responsible for sealing and delivering the commissions. In a letter written in March 1801, Marshall admitted that he would have made sure that the commissions were sent out except for "the extreme hurry of the time" and his inability to foresee that Jefferson would withhold the commissions.[6] Marshall, therefore, could have been a perfect witness for Lee and Marbury, but instead he was, paradoxically, deciding the case. Accordingly, Lee had to tread very delicately in the way he attempted to prove that the commissions had been signed and sealed. Because Marshall's brother was appearing as a witness and Marshall himself had personal knowledge of the facts of the case, the Republicans already had grounds for believing that Marshall should disqualify himself from the decision. Lee did not want to exacerbate the situation by reminding the Court and the nation that the chief justice had been a participant in the activities that had produced the litigation.

Another problem confronting Lee concerned jurisdiction—the right of a particular court to hear a particular case. The Supreme Court's jurisdiction was, and still is, primarily *appellate,* having as its main responsibility the correction of legal errors made by lower courts. However, exceptional cases in which the Court has *original jurisdiction*—that is, jurisdiction to decide the facts of a case—are spelled out in Article III of the Constitution itself: "In all Cases affecting Ambassadors,

---

[5]Whether *Marbury* constituted an unjustified judicial intrusion into the executive branch is an important aspect of the litigation even though it is subordinate to the main question of the legitimacy of judicial review. In Chapter 5 of this volume, the issue of judicial intrusions into the executive branch will be directly addressed in the context of *United States v. Nixon.* At that time, a review of the relevant facts of *Marbury* is suggested.

[6]Letter from John Marshall to James Marshall, March 18, 1801, John Marshall Correspondence and Papers, Vol. I, Library of Congress, cited in Leonard Baker, *John Marshall: A Life in Law* (New York: Macmillan, 1974), p. 394.

other [foreign] public Ministers and Consuls, and those in which a State shall be Party, the Supreme Court shall have original jurisdiction." Obviously, *Marbury* was not one of these kinds of cases, which raises the question of why Lee brought the case immediately to the Supreme Court. Of course, a Supreme Court decision compelling Jefferson to hand over the commission would be, more so than a lower court decision, a Federalist political victory. Moreover, a long delay in the lower courts might make the case moot because Marbury's appointment as a justice of the peace was for only a five-year period, ending in early 1806. Nonetheless, despite these political and practical considerations for going to the Supreme Court immediately, the Court lacked the constitutional jurisdiction to hear the case as a court of first instance.

Lee's only option was to base the Court's jurisdiction on a statute, rather than on the Constitution. Unfortunately for Lee, the statutory basis for original jurisdiction was, arguably, quite weak. He claimed that Section 13 of the Judiciary Act of 1789 gave the Supreme Court original jurisdiction to issue writs of mandamus "in cases warranted by the principles and usages of law, to any courts appointed, or persons holding office, under the authority of the United States." According to Lee, this language meant that anyone who wanted a judicial order against a federal official could bring the case immediately to the Supreme Court. A different interpretation maintained that Section 13 was not a grant of jurisdiction at all. It gave the Supreme Court only the remedial power to issue such writs in cases in which it already had jurisdiction, whether the jurisdiction was original in character (granted in the Constitution) or appellate in character (also granted by the Constitution but subject to the control of Congress). If so, then Section 13 would give the Supreme Court the power to issue the writ of mandamus in *Marbury* if the Court had jurisdiction, but it would not itself give the Court the right to decide the case.

Despite the vulnerability of his argument in favor of the Court's original jurisdiction, Lee never suggested in *Marbury* that the Court should exert the extraordinary power of judicial review as a means of establishing its jurisdiction. In his view, once the existence of Marbury's commission and the Court's jurisdiction was conceded, the Court had to recognize only that Madison was violating a "ministerial" duty by withholding Marbury's commission—a legally mandated duty over which President Jefferson had no control. Only when the duty had such a character, only when it was totally independent of the president, Lee argued, were courts empowered to issue a writ of mandamus compelling its performance. If any duty of the secretary of state was within presidential control, then the duty was "political," and courts had to refrain from interfering. But because Marbury's commission had been signed and sealed, Lee insisted that Madison's duty was a "ministerial" one subject to a writ of mandamus. Based upon the jurisdiction provided by Section 13 of the Judiciary Act, the Court had the power and the legal duty to remedy the wrong done to Marbury by issuing a writ of mandamus compelling Madison to deliver the commission.

The case was far more troublesome, especially in a political sense, for Chief Justice John Marshall, Lee's friend and former colleague. One problem was that if the Court gave Lee and Marbury what they wanted, the Jefferson administration would likely ignore the writ, thereby humiliating the Supreme Court. On the other hand, if he denied the request for the writ, many would think that the Supreme Court had caved in to Republican political pressure, failing to fulfill the essential function of an independent judiciary—to protect the legal rights of an individual. Marshall, in *Marbury*, was therefore truly between a rock and a hard place.

Marshall's way of resolving his dilemma surely bears the mark of political genius. He decided against Marbury, which satisfied the Republicans, but he also proclaimed the doctrine of judicial review, which comforted the Federalists. Though prominent Republicans had condemned this doctrine in the congressional debate of 1802, Marshall undermined the practical force of their arguments by exercising the power in a way that favored their immediate political goals. As the beneficiaries of the very doctrine that they had condemned the year before, the Republicans were therefore largely uncritical of *Marbury*. Marshall's opinion also soothed the disappointed Federalists by lecturing the Jefferson administration and by establishing judicial review. Marbury's legal rights had been violated by Jefferson and Madison, Marshall insisted, and Madison had a legal "ministerial" duty to deliver the commission. It was therefore unfortunate that the Supreme Court could not give Marbury the relief he deserved because the law granting the Court jurisdiction was unconstitutional. This proclamation of the doctrine of judicial review consoled the Federalists even though Marbury did not get his job. Many of them perceived judicial review as an institution by which the predominantly Federalist judiciary could defend its constitutional principles and policies. More than one Federalist must have wondered whether Marshall had deliberately lost a minor political skirmish to increase the likelihood of victory in the larger political/constitutional war.

Though Marshall's political acumen in *Marbury* cannot be faulted, it is less easy to justify what he did from a professional and legal point of view. As noted earlier, Lee's interpretation of Section 13 of the Judiciary Act of 1789 was highly questionable. This provision may not have increased the Court's original jurisdiction, as Lee argued, but only granted the Court a specific remedial power when it already had jurisdiction. If Marshall had interpreted Section 13 in this fashion, then he would have reached the same result in the case, dismissing it for want of jurisdiction, but he would have done so without declaring Section 13 unconstitutional and without exercising judicial review. Marbury would still have lost his case, but on the simple ground that neither the Constitution nor Congress had given the Supreme Court the power to decide the case as a court of first instance.

Instead of deciding the case on this basis, Marshall opted for Lee's interpretation of Section 13 as an independent grant of original jurisdiction to the Supreme Court, a grant of jurisdiction to decide all cases involving writs of mandamus against federal officials. Can Marshall be faulted for choosing what appears to be the more strained interpretation of the law? Did he let his desire to proclaim the doctrine of judicial review dictate his understanding of Section 13? If so, the case should cause concern. If the chief justice of the United States, in the very case that established the doctrine of judicial review, adopted an indefensible interpretation of a statute so as to deepen, if not broaden, the judiciary's power, then should judges have the power to declare laws unconstitutional?

A similar question arises with Marshall's assessment that a new and independent grant of original jurisdiction violated the Constitution. In other words, even if one assumes that Marshall and Lee's interpretation of Section 13 was correct, even if the law did give the Supreme Court the power to hear (as a court of first instance) all cases involving writs of mandamus against federal officials, why did such a law violate the Constitution? Marshall's argument relied heavily upon certain language in Article III of the Constitution: "In all Cases affecting Ambassadors, other public Ministers and Consuls, and those in which a State shall be Party, the Supreme Court shall have original jurisdiction. In all the other Cases before mentioned, the Supreme Court shall have appellate Jurisdiction. . . ." Marshall claimed that if the "affirmative words" giving the Court original jurisdiction were to have any meaning, they had to be taken in a "negative" sense, implying that Congress could not give original jurisdiction where the Constitution granted appellate.

Once again Marshall's reasoning is not above criticism. The foregoing constitutional language granting original jurisdiction need not be meaningless if read in a non-negative sense. It could mean that the Court had original jurisdiction, specified by the Constitution, in certain cases; that Congress could, if it wanted to, *increase* this original jurisdiction; but that Congress could not, even if it tried to, *decrease* the Court's original jurisdiction granted by the Constitution. Article III provides some textual support for this interpretation because, after granting the Court appellate jurisdiction, it says, "with such Exceptions, and under such Regulations as the Congress shall make." In *Marbury,* Marshall ignored this language even though it seemed to have a direct bearing upon his argument. If Congress can make exceptions to the Supreme Court's appellate jurisdiction, then Marshall's conclusion that Congress cannot give "original jurisdiction where the constitution has declared it shall be appellate" seems somewhat vulnerable. After all, if Congress can take away from the Court's appellate power, if it can deprive the Court of appellate jurisdiction in a certain kind of case, then why can it not give that case to the Court to decide as a court of first instance?

Skeptics may wonder whether Marshall's interpretation of the Constitution was in good faith. Did he bend the Constitution, just as he purportedly bent the statute, to ensure that the two would come into conflict?[7] If so, is the judiciary a proper repository of the awesome power of judicial review?

In his opinion in *Marbury,* Marshall's basic argument in favor of judicial review was that a statute that conflicted with the Constitution had to be invalid if written constitutionalism meant anything at all. At the time, few Americans dis-

---

[7]It is interesting to note that Marshall himself later admitted that his argument in *Marbury* may have gone too far. In *Cohens v. Virginia,* 6 Wheat. 264 (1821), Marshall rejected Virginia's arguments against the Supreme Court's appellate jurisdiction. Virginia's position was that, because a state was involved, the Court had missed its chance to hear the case. The rationale in *Marbury,* Virginia insisted, implied that the Court could hear a case involving a state only as a court of original jurisdiction. Marshall, however, ruled in *Cohens* that it was permissible for a case that fit the Supreme Court's original jurisdiction to be first heard in a lower court and then be reviewed on appeal by the Supreme Court. But if a case within the Court's original jurisdiction could be reviewed by the Supreme Court on appeal, why (as in *Marbury*) could a case within the Court's appellate jurisdiction *not* be heard by the Court as a court of first instance?

puted this contention. The real issue was who decided whether a law was constitutional or not. Marshall, following the path laid down by Hamilton, Morris, and Bayard, argued that it could not be the legislature because the Constitution was meant to limit the legislature's power. Giving such a power to the legislature would, in effect, give it the power to alter the Constitution at will. Moreover, according to Marshall, it was "emphatically the province and duty of the judicial department to say what the law is." Because the Constitution was law, it was the "essence of judicial duty" for judges to decide, in the cases that properly came before them, what the Constitution required. What if, Marshall asked, Congress enacted an *ex post facto* law, a law that imposed criminal liability for an act previously done? Was it not obvious that Courts were obliged to strike such a law down?

The Constitution itself, Marshall insisted, hinted at the power of judicial review, if it did not establish it explicitly. Article III clearly stated that the judicial power extended to all cases "arising under the Constitution," which implied, in Marshall's opinion, that judges had the duty to interpret the Constitution as they decided such cases. Furthermore, the judicial oath of office required that judges discharge their duties "agreeably to the Constitution." And finally, the Constitution said that only laws made "pursuant" to the Constitution were a part of the "supreme law of the land," suggesting that judges had the power to decide if laws were made "pursuant" to the Constitution. Marshall's conclusion was that judicial review, in the American constitutional order, was an inherent duty imposed upon the judiciary.

Marshall's argument for judicial review, of course, was not original. The basic issues had been hashed and rehashed in the congressional debate of 1802, and Hamilton had earlier sketched out the arguments that Marshall later amplified. Even Marshall's examples of clearly unconstitutional laws were not new. Former arguments about the validity of judicial review had referred to *ex post facto* laws, bills of attainder, and other clearly unconstitutional laws. The interesting question was whether such examples were at all similar in character to the law that Marshall declared unconstitutional in *Marbury*.

Nor was the exercise of judicial review in *Marbury* unprecedented. Although *Marbury* was the first time that the Supreme Court invalidated any portion of a federal law, it had previously reviewed the constitutionality of a federal law in 1796, upholding its validity.[8] Moreover, lower federal courts had already rejected both federal and state laws, and a number of state courts had already invalidated state laws.[9] Accordingly, judicial review had wide support in the late-eighteenth- and early-nineteenth-century United States, especially on the bench and in the legal profession.

---

[8]See *Hylton v. United States* 3 Dallas 171 (1796).

[9]See summary of *Hayburn's Case,* an unreported decision, at 2 Dallas 409 (1792); *Van Hornes's Lessee v. Dorrance,* 2 Dallas 304 (1795). For a complete discussion of the early history of judicial review, see Julius Goebel, Jr., *Antecedents and Beginnings to 1801,* Vol. 1 of *Oliver Wendell Holmes Devise History of the Supreme Court of the United States* (New York: Macmillan, 1971); William E. Nelson, "Changing Conceptions of Judicial Review: The Evolution of Constitutional Theory in the States, 1790–1860," *University of Pennsylvania Law Review* 120 (1972), pp. 1166–85.

The depth of this support, however, is difficult to gauge. In *Marbury*, the Court exercised judicial review in a way that supported the dominant Republican Party. In *Stuart v. Laird*, the case in which the Supreme Court reviewed, soon after *Marbury*, the constitutionality of the Repeal Act of 1802, the Court found the law constitutional. Once again, in other words, the Court acted in a way that favored the dominant political party. Is it likely that the Court would have been ignored if it had decided either of these cases against the wishes of the Republican Party? If so, if a politically powerful group will ignore a Supreme Court decision, then in what sense is judicial review legitimate? How can it be justified on the ground of limited government if politics ultimately controls its use? And how important is judicial review if its exercise is dictated by the balance of political forces?

It should never be forgotten, however, when examining the historical circumstances of *Marbury v. Madison*, that Marbury's commission was signed and sealed. Did this mean that Jefferson abused his presidential powers when he refused to give Marbury his job? Jefferson thought that Marbury had no legal right to the position because, in his opinion, delivery was essential to the commission's validity. Whether or not he was correct that delivery was essential for the validity of a commission, Jefferson was especially incensed that Marshall addressed this issue in a case in which he admitted that he had no jurisdiction. This feature of Marshall's opinion bothered Jefferson more than any other, even more than its assertion of the power of judicial review. In his view, Marshall's opinion was composed primarily of *obiter dicta*, statements by the Court that were irrelevant to its decision denying jurisdiction in the case. If the Court had no right to decide the case, then why was it addressing the merits of the legal issues? In Jefferson's opinion, such "travelling out" of the case was "very irregular and very censurable." (See Box 1.6.)

It seems that Marshall, both for personal and political reasons, could not pass up the opportunity to lecture Jefferson on his legal duties. First, though they were cousins, it is well known that Jefferson and Marshall, by the time of *Marbury*, had disliked each other for many years. Similarly, in 1803, Marshall, a prominent Federalist, and Jefferson, the leader of the Republican Party, represented the opposite sides of the American political spectrum. Therefore, Jefferson quite naturally suspected that the *obiter dicta* in *Marbury* were a Federalist attempt to embarrass his administration politically and him personally. Accordingly, in his view, *Marbury* was an example of judicial indiscretion, not of presidential abuse of power.

The political context of *Marbury v. Madison* provides a useful perspective from which to evaluate the merits of judicial review, but not even a tentative conclusion is possible without a historical sketch of judicial review. After *Marbury*, the Supreme Court did not declare unconstitutional a federal law, or any part thereof, for fifty-four years. But in 1857, the Court took the ill-fated step of declaring the Missouri Compromise Act unconstitutional in *Dred Scott v. Sandford*.[10] The decision, denying that black slaves could be citizens of the United States, set the stage for the Civil War. A later chief justice of the Supreme Court, Charles

---

[10]19 Howard 393 (1857).

BOX 1.6

Thomas Jefferson on *Marbury v. Madison*

... This practice of Judge Marshall, of travelling out of his case to prescribe what the law would be in a moot case not before the court, is very irregular and very censurable. I recollect another instance, and the more particularly, perhaps, because it in some measure bore on myself. Among the midnight appointments of Mr. Adams, were commissions to some federal justices of the peace for Alexandria. These were signed and sealed by him, but not delivered. I found them on the table of the Department of State, on my entrance into office, and I forbade their delivery. Marbury, named in one of them, applied to the Supreme Court for a mandamus to the Secretary of State, (Mr. Madison) to deliver the commission intended for him. The Court determined at once, that being an original process, they had no cognizance of it; and therefore the question before them was ended. But the Chief Justice went on to lay down what the law would be, had they jurisdiction of the case, to wit: that they should command the delivery. The object was clearly to instruct any other court having the jurisdiction, what they should do if Marbury should apply to them. Besides the impropriety of this gratuitous interference, could anything exceed the perversion of law? For if there is any principle of law never yet contradicted, it is that delivery is one of the essentials to the validity of a deed. Although signed and sealed, yet as long as it remains in the hands of the party himself, it is *in fieri* only, it is not a deed, and can be made so only by its delivery. In the hands of a third person it may be made an escrow. But whatever is in the executive offices is certainly deemed to be in the hands of the President; and in this case, was actually in my hands, because, when I countermanded them, there was as yet no Secretary of State. Yet this case of Marbury and Madison is continually cited by bench and bar, as if it were settled law, without any animadversion on its being merely an *obiter* dissertation of the Chief Justice. ...

Source: From a letter by Jefferson to William Johnson, June 12, 1823, in A. E. Bergh, ed., *The Writings of Thomas Jefferson,* 20 vols. (Washington: Thomas Jefferson Memorial Association, 1904), XV, pp. 447–48.

Evans Hughes, described the ruling as a "great self-inflicted wound." Certainly *Dred Scott* showed that the Supreme Court was hardly infallible. The Court could abuse its power of judicial review or exercise it in a profoundly unwise way.

Beginning in the late nineteenth century, the Supreme Court invoked judicial review primarily to protect the rights of property. This trend did not end until the New Deal, when President Franklin D. Roosevelt perhaps intimidated the Court by threatening it with a court-packing plan—the subject of the next chapter. Since the New Deal, the Court has concentrated its energies on protecting, outside the socioeconomic area, the rights and liberties of individual Americans. In this regard, its most impressive accomplishment was probably *Brown v. Board of Education* (1954),[11] the decision that ended segregation in public education and ushered in a new era of race relations in the United States. But in any event, regardless of how *Brown* is viewed, the past fifty years suggest that it is possible for the Court, using the power of judicial review, to play a progressive role in the American polity.

Over the course of its history, the Court has declared 140 provisions of federal law unconstitutional and invalidated 110 federal executive orders. In addition, approximately 1,200 state laws and constitutional provisions have been set aside by the Court.[12] Most of these instances of judicial review have occurred over the past hundred years. History therefore shows that the Court has used the power of judicial review both for good and for ill, but that it uses it more now than ever before.

The orthodox theory of American constitutionalism, crystalized in Marshall's opinion in *Marbury,* insists that the political game needs a neutral umpire to apply the rules and that the judiciary is best suited to fulfill this role. Does *Marbury v. Madison* and the foregoing historical sketch substantiate or undermine this claim? Does Jefferson's flagrant disregard of Marbury's rights, if that was what it was, prove that American politics needs an umpire? Does the case show that the judiciary can function as the referee, as Marshall, Morris, and Bayard claim? Or do the circumstances show that the judiciary is one of the political players, as Jefferson, Breckenridge, and Randolph suggest? What about the contrasting implications of the *Dred Scott* case and *Brown v. Board of Education?* Is giving the power of judicial review to judges equivalent to making certain players of a game referees? Or, more tragically, does *Marbury* and the historical sketch show that the American game of politics needs an impartial umpire, but that unfortunately none is available? Whatever the answers to these questions may be, our understanding of a very important and most distinctive aspect of American constitutionalism requires that these questions be asked and their implications explored. *Marbury v. Madison,* the fountainhead of judicially created constitutional law, can admirably serve to put these issues into sharp focus.

BIBLIOGRAPHY

Clinton, Robert L. *Marbury v. Madison and Judicial Review.* Lawrence: University Press of Kansas, 1989.

Corwin., Edward S. "*Marbury v. Madison* and the Doctrine of Judicial Review," *Michigan Law Review* 12 (1914), pp. 538–72.

Dewey, Donald O. *Marshall v. Jefferson: The Political Background of Marbury v. Madison.* New York: Knopf, 1970.

Ellis, Richard E. *The Jeffersonian Crisis: Courts and Politics in the Young Republic.* New York: Oxford University Press, 1971.

---

[11]347 U.S. 483 (1954).

[12]See Abraham, *The Judicial Process,* p. 272.

Van Alstyne, William. "A Critical Guide to *Marbury v. Madison,*" *Duke Law Journal* (1969), pp. 1–47.

Wolfe, Christopher. *The Rise of Modern Judicial Review.* New York: Basic Books, 1986.

ORAL ARGUMENT[13]

Mr. Lee [William Marbury's attorney] . . . observed that it was important to know on what ground a justice of peace in the district of Columbia holds his office, and what proceedings are necessary to constitute an appointment to an office not held at the will of the president. However notorious the facts are . . . the applicants have been much embarrassed in obtaining evidence of them. Reasonable information has been denied at the office of the department of state. Although a respectful memorial has been made to the senate praying them to suffer their secretary to give extracts from their executive journals respecting the nomination of the applicants to the senate, and of their advise and consent to the appointments, yet their request has been denied, and their petition rejected. They have therefore been compelled to summon witnesses to attend court, whose voluntary affidavits they could not obtain. . . .

Mr. Lee observed that to show the propriety of examining these witnesses, he would make a few remarks on the nature of the office of the secretary of state. His duties are of two kinds, and he exercises his functions in two distinct capacities; as a public ministerial officer of the United States, and as agent of the President. In the first his duty is to the United States or its citizens; in the other his duty is to the President; in the one he is an independent, an accountable officer; in the other he is dependent upon the President, is his agent, and accountable to him alone. In the former capacity he is compellable by mandamus to do his duty; in the latter he is not. . . .

. . . Most of the duties assigned by this act [a law enacted September 15, 1789, that made the secretary of state responsible for the safekeeping of the records and the seal of the United States] are of a public nature, and the secretary is bound to perform them, without the control of any person. The President has no right to prevent him from receiving the bills, orders, resolutions and votes of the legislature, or from publishing and distributing them, or from preserving or recording them. While the secretary remains in office the President cannot take from his custody the seal of the United States, nor prevent him from recording, and affixing the seal to civil commissions of such officers as hold not their offices at the will of the President, after he has signed them and delivered them to the secretary for that purpose. By other laws he is to make out and record in his office patents for useful discoveries, and patents of lands granted under the authority of the United

---

[13]What follows is not from a transcript of the oral argument but from a summary of it made by William Cranch, the official reporter of the Supreme Court in 1803.

States. In the performance of all these duties he is a public ministerial officer of the United States. And the duties being enjoined him by law, he is, in executing them, uncontrollable by the President; and if he neglects or refuses to perform them, he may be compelled by mandamus, in the same manner as other persons holding offices under the authority of the United States. The President is no party to this case. The secretary is called upon to perform a duty over which the President has no control, and in regard to which he has no dispensing power, and for the neglect of which he is in no matter responsible. The secretary alone is the person to whom they are entrusted, and he alone is answerable for their due performance. The secretary of state, therefore, being in the same situation, as to these duties, as every other ministerial officer of the United States, and equally liable to be compelled to perform them, is also bound by the same rules of evidence. These duties are not of a confidential nature, but are of a public kind, and his clerks can have no exclusive privileges. There are undoubtedly facts, which may come to their knowledge by means of their connection with the secretary of state, respecting which they cannot be bound to answer. Such are the facts concerning foreign correspondences, and confidential communications between the head of the department and the President. This, however, can be no objection to their being sworn, but may be a ground of objection to any particular question. Suppose I claim title to land under a patent from the United States. I demand a copy of it from the secretary of state. He refuses. Surely he may be compelled by mandamus to give it. But in order to obtain a mandamus, I must shew that the patent is recorded in his office. My case would be hard indeed if I could not call upon the clerks in the office to give evidence of that fact. Again, suppose a private act of congress had passed for my benefit. It becomes necessary for me to have the use of that act in a court of law. I apply for a copy. I am refused. Shall I not be permitted, on a motion for a mandamus, to call upon the clerks in the office to prove that such an act is among the rolls of the office, or that it is duly recorded? Surely it cannot be contended that although the laws are to be recorded, yet no access is to be had to the records, and no benefit to result from them.

The court ordered the witnesses to be sworn and their answers taken in writing, but informed them that when the questions were asked they might state objections to answering each particular question, if they had any. . . .

[Mr. Wagner and Mr. Brent, both clerks in the office of the secretary of state in 1801 when Marbury's commission disappeared, then testified that they were unsure about which commissions were signed and sealed. After their testimony, Levi Lincoln, Jefferson's attorney general, was called to the stand.]

Mr. Lincoln, attorney general, having been summoned, and now called, objected to answering. He requested that the questions might be put in writing, and that he might afterwards have time to determine whether he would answer. On the one hand he respected the jurisdiction of this court, and on the other he felt himself bound to maintain the rights of the executive. He was acting as secretary of state at the time when this transaction happened. He was of opinion, and his opinion was supported by that of others whom he highly respected, that he was not bound, and ought not to answer, as to any facts which came officially to his knowledge while acting as secretary of state.

The questions being written were then read and handed to him. He repeated the ideas he had before suggested, and said his objections were of two kinds.

1st. He did not think himself bound to disclose his official transactions while acting as secretary of state; and
2nd. He ought not to be compelled to answer any thing which might tend to criminate himself.

Mr. Lee, in reply, repeated the substance of the observations he had before made in answer to the objections of Mr. Wagner and Mr. Brent. He stated that the duties of a secretary of state were two-fold. In discharging one part of those duties he acted as a public ministerial officer of the United States, totally independent of the President, and that as to any facts which came officially to his knowledge, while acting in this capacity, he was as much bound to answer as a marshal, a collector, or any other ministerial officer. But that in the discharge of the other part of his duties, he did not act as a public ministerial officer, but in the capacity of an agent of the President, bound to obey his orders, and accountable to him for his conduct. And that as to any facts which came officially to his knowledge in the discharge of this part of his duties, he was not bound to answer. He agreed that Mr. Lincoln was not bound to disclose any thing which might tend to criminate himself.

Mr. Lincoln thought it was going a great way to say that every secretary of state should at all times be liable to be called upon to appear as a witness in a court of justice, and testify to facts which came to his knowledge officially. He felt himself delicately situated between his duty to this court, and the duty he conceived he owed to an executive department; and hoped the court would give him time to consider of the subject.

The court said, that if Mr. Lincoln wished time to consider what answers he should make, they would give him time; but they had no doubt he ought to answer. There was nothing confidential required to be disclosed. If there had been he was not obliged to answer it; and if he thought that any thing was communicated to him in confidence he was not bound to disclose it; nor was he obliged to state any thing which would criminate himself; but that the fact whether such commissions had been in the office or not, could not be a confidential fact; it is a fact which all the world have a right to know. If he thought any of the questions improper, he might state his objections.

Mr. Lincoln then prayed time till the next day to consider of his answers under this opinion of the court.

The court granted it and postponed further consideration of the cause till the next day.

At the opening of the court the next morning, Mr. Lincoln said he had no objection to answering the questions proposed, excepting the last which he did not think himself obliged to answer fully. The question was, what had been done with the commissions. He had no hesitation in saying that he did not know that they ever came to the possession of Mr. Madison, nor did he know that they were in the office when Mr. Madison took possession of it. He prayed the opinion of the court whether he was obliged to disclose what had been done with the commissions.

The court were of the opinion that he was not bound to say what had become of them; if they never came to the possession of Mr. Madison, it was immaterial to the present cause, what had been done with them by others.

To the other questions he answered that he had seen commissions of justices of the peace of the district of Columbia, signed by Mr. Adams, and sealed with the seal of the United States. He did not recollect whether any of them constituted Mr. Marbury, col. Hooe, or col. Ramsay, justices of the peace; there were when he went into the office several commissions for justices of the peace of the district made out; but he was furnished with a list of names to be put into a general commission, which was done, and was considered as superseding the particular commissions; and the individuals whose names were contained in this general commission were informed of their being thus appointed. He did not know that any one of the commissions was ever sent to the person for whom it was made out, and did not believe that any one had been sent.

Mr. Lee then read the affidavit of James Marshall [Chief Justice John Marshall's brother], who had been also summoned as a witness. It stated that on the 4th of March, 1801, having been informed by some person from Alexandria that there was reason to apprehend riotous proceedings in that town on that night, he was induced to return immediately home, and to call at the office of the secretary of state, for the commissions of the justices of the peace; that as many as 12, as he believed, commissions of justices for that county were delivered to him for which he gave a receipt, which he left in the office. That finding he could not conveniently carry the whole, he returned several of them, and struck a pen through the names of those, in the receipt, which he returned. Among the commissions so returned, according to the best of his knowledge and belief, was one for colonel Hooe, and one for William Harper.

Mr. Lee then observed, that having proved the existence of the commissions, he should confine such further remarks as he had to make. . . .

1st Whether the supreme court can award the writ of mandamus in any case.

2d Whether it will lie to a secretary of state in any case whatever.

3d Whether in the present case the court may award a mandamus to James Madison, secretary of state. . . .

[As to the first issue,] Congress, by a law passed at the very first session after the adoption of the constitution, have expressly given the supreme court the power of issuing writs of mandamus. The words [from Section 13 of the Judiciary Act of 1789] are "The supreme court shall also have appellate jurisdiction from the circuit courts, and the courts of the several states, in the cases herein after specially provided for; and shall have power to issue writs of prohibition to the district courts, when proceeding as courts of admiralty and maritime jurisdiction; and writs of *mandamus,* in cases warranted by the principles and usages of law, to any courts appointed, or *persons holding office,* under the authority of the United States."

Congress is not restrained from conferring original jurisdiction in other cases than these mentioned in the constitution. . . .

The second point is, can a mandamus go to a secretary of state in any case? It certainly cannot in *all* cases; nor to the President in *any* case. It may not be proper to mention this position; but I am compelled to do it. An idea has gone forth, that a mandamus to a secretary of state is equivalent to a mandamus to the President of the United States. I declare it to be my opinion, grounded on a comprehensive view of the subject, that the President is not amenable to any court of judicature for the exercise of his high functions, but is responsible only in the mode pointed out in the constitution. The secretary of state acts, as before observed, in two capacities. As the agent of the President, he is not liable to a mandamus; but as a recorder of the laws of the United States; as keeper of the great seal; as recorder of deeds of land, of letters patent, and of commissions, &c. he is a ministerial officer of the people of the United States. As such he has duties assigned him by law, in the execution of which he is independent of all control, but that of the laws. It is true he is a high officer, but he is not above law. It is not consistent with the policy of our political institutions, or the manners of the citizens of the United States, that any ministerial officer having public duties to perform, should be above the compulsion of the law in the exercise of those duties. As a ministerial officer he is compellable to do his duty, and if he refuses, is liable to indictment. A prosecution of this kind might be the means of punishing the officer, but a specific civil remedy to the injured party can only be obtained by a writ of mandamus. If a mandamus can be awarded by this court in any case, it may issue to a secretary of state; for the act of congress expressly gives the power to award it, "in cases warranted by the principles and usages of law, *to any persons holding offices under the authority of the United States.*"

Many cases may be supposed, in which a secretary of state ought to be compelled to perform his duty specifically. . . . [For example,] copies under seal of the office of the department of state are made evidence in courts of law, and fees are given for making them out. The intention of the law must have been, that every person needing a copy should be entitled to it. Suppose the secretary refuses to give a copy, ought he not to be compelled? Suppose I am entitled to a patent for lands purchased of the United States; it is made out and signed by the President who gives a warrant to the secretary to affix the great seal to the patent; he refuses to do it; shall I not have a mandamus to compel him? Suppose the seal is affixed, but the secretary refuses to record it; shall he not be compelled? Suppose it recorded, and he refuses to deliver it; shall I have no remedy?

In this respect there is no difference between a patent for lands, and the commission of a judicial officer. The duty of the secretary is precisely the same.

Judge Patterson enquired of Mr. Lee whether he understood it to be the duty of the secretary to deliver a commission, unless ordered so to do by the President.

Mr. Lee replied, that after the President has signed a commission for an office not held at his will, and it comes to the secretary to be sealed, the President has done with it, and nothing remains, but that the secretary perform those ministerial acts which the law imposes upon him. It immediately becomes his duty to seal, record, and deliver it on command. In such a case the appointment becomes complete by the signing and sealing; and the secretary does wrong if he withholds the commission.

The third point is, whether in the present case a writ of mandamus ought to be awarded to James Madison, secretary of state.

The justices of the peace in the district of Columbia are judicial officers, and hold their office for five years. The office is established by the act of Congress passed the 27th of Feb. 1801. . . . They are authorized to hold courts and have cognizance of personal demands of the value of 20 dollars. The act of May 3d, 1802 considers them as judicial officers, and provides the mode in which execution shall issue upon their judgements. They hold their offices independent of the will of the president. The appointment of such an officer is complete when the President has nominated him to the senate, and the senate have advised and consented, and the President has signed the commission and delivered it to the secretary to be sealed. The President has then done with it; it becomes irrevocable. An appointment of a judge once completed, is made forever. He holds under the constitution. The requisites to be performed by the secretary are ministerial, ascertained by law, and he has no discretion, but must perform them; there is no dispensing power. In contemplation of law they are as if done.

These justices exercise part of the judicial power of the United States. They ought therefore to be independent. Mr. Lee begged leave again to refer to the Federalist Nos. 78 and 79, as containing a correct view of this subject. They contained observations and ideas which he wished might be generally read and understood. They contained the principles upon which this branch of our government was constructed. It is important to the citizens of this district that the justices should be independent; almost all the authority immediately exercised over them is that of the justices. They wish to know whether the justices of this district are to hold their commissions at the will of a secretary of state. This cause may seem trivial at first view, but it is important in principle. It is for this reason that this court is now troubled with it. The emoluments or the dignity of the office, are no objects with the applicants. They conceive themselves to be duly appointed justices of the peace, and they believe it to be their duty to maintain the rights of their office, and not to suffer them to be violated by the hand of power. The citizens of this district have their fears excited by every stretch of power of a person so high in office as the secretary of state.

[James Madison and Thomas Jefferson declined to offer any argument in *Marbury v. Madison.*]

THE OPINION

Opinion of the Court [by Chief Justice John Marshall]. . . .

The first object of enquiry is,

1st. Has the applicant a right to the commission he demands?

His right originates in an act of congress passed in February, 1801, concerning the district of Columbia. . . .

It appears, from the affidavits, that in compliance with this law, a commission for William Marbury as a justice of peace for the county of Washington, was signed by John Adams, then president of the United States; after which the seal of the United States was affixed to it; but the commission has never reached the person for whom it was made out. . . .

This is an appointment made by the President, by and with the advice and consent of the senate, and is evidenced by no act but the commission itself. In such a case therefore the commission and the appointment seem inseparable; it being almost impossible to show an appointment otherwise than by proving the existence of a commission; still the commission is not necessarily the appointment; though the conclusive evidence of it.

But at what stage does it amount to this conclusive evidence?

The answer to this question seems an obvious one. The appointment being the sole act of the President, must be completely evidenced, when it is shown that he has done everything to be performed by him. . . .

The last act to be done by the President, is the signature of the commission. He has then acted on the advice and consent of the senate to his own nomination. The time for deliberation has then passed. He has decided. His judgment, on the advice and consent of the senate concurring with his nomination, has been made, and the officer is appointed. This appointment is evidenced by an open unequivocal act; and being the last act required from the person making it, necessarily excludes the idea of its being, so far as it respects the appointment, an inchoate and incomplete transaction. . . .

The commission being signed, the subsequent duty of the secretary of state is prescribed by law, and not to be guided by the will of the President. He is to affix the seal of the United States to the commission, and is to record it.

This is not a proceeding which may be varied, if the judgment of the executive shall suggest one more eligible; but is a precise course accurately marked out by law, and is to be strictly pursued. It is the duty of the secretary of state to conform to the law, and in this he is an officer of the United States, bound to obey the laws. He acts, in this respect, as has been very properly stated at the bar, under the authority of law, and not by the instructions of the President. It is a ministerial act which the law enjoins on a particular officer for a particular purpose.

If it should be supposed, that the solemnity of affixing the seal, is necessary not only to the validity of the commission, but even to the completion of an appointment, still when the seal is affixed the appointment is made, and the commission is valid. No other solemnity is required by law; no other act is to be performed on the part of government. All that the executive can do to invest the person with his office, is done. . . .

. . . [I]t has been conjectured that the commission may have been assimilated to a deed, to the validity of which, delivery is essential.

This idea is founded on the supposition that the commission is not merely *evidence* of an appointment, but is itself the actual appointment; a supposition by no means unquestionable. . . .

It may have some tendency to elucidate this point, to enquire, whether the possession of the original commission be indispensably necessary to authorize a person, appointed to any office, to perform the duties of that office. If it was necessary, then a loss of the commission would lose the office. Not only negligence, but accident or fraud, fire or theft, might deprive an individual of his office. In such a case, I presume it could not be doubted, but that a copy from the record of the office of the secretary of state, would be, to every intent and purpose, equal to the original. The act of congress has expressly made it so. To give that copy validity, it would not be necessary to prove that the original had been transmitted and afterwards lost. The copy would be complete evidence that the original had existed, and that the appointment had been made, but, not that the original had been transmitted. If indeed it should appear that the original had been mislaid in the office of state, that circumstance would not affect the operation of the copy. When all the requisites have been performed which authorize a recording officer to record any instrument whatever, and the order for that purpose has been given, the instrument is, in law, considered as recorded, although the manual labor of inserting it in a book kept for that purpose may not have been performed.

In the case of commissions, the law orders the secretary of state to record them. When therefore they are signed and sealed, the order for their being recorded is given; and whether inserted in the book or not, they are in law recorded. . . .

. . . It is therefore decidedly the opinion of the court, that when a commission has been signed by the President, the appointment is made; and that the commission is complete, when the seal of the United States has been affixed to it by the secretary of state.

Where an officer is removable at the will of the executive, the circumstance which completes his appointment is of no concern; because the act is at any time revocable; and the commission may be arrested, if still in the office. But when the officer is not removable at the will of the executive, the appointment is not revocable, and cannot be annulled. It has conferred legal rights which cannot be resumed. . . .

Mr. Marbury, then, since his commission was signed by the President, and sealed by the secretary of state, was appointed; and as the law creating the office, gave the officer a right to hold for five years, independent of the executive, the appointment was not revocable; but vested in the officer legal rights, which are protected by the laws of his country.

To withhold his commission, therefore, is an act deemed by the court not warranted by law, but violative of a vested legal right.

This brings us to the second enquiry; which is,

2dly. If he has a right and that right has been violated, do the laws of his country afford him a remedy?. . .

The government of the United States has been emphatically termed a government of laws, and not of men. It will certainly cease to deserve this high appellation, if the laws furnish no remedy for the violation of a vested legal right.

If this obloquy is to be cast on the jurisprudence of our country, it must arise from the peculiar character of the case.

It behooves us then to enquire whether there be in its composition any ingredient which shall exempt it from legal investigation, or exclude the injured party from legal redress. In pursuing this enquiry the first question which presents itself, is, whether this can be arranged with that class of cases which come under the description of *damnum absque injuria*—a loss without an injury. . . .

. . . Is the act of delivering or withholding a commission to be considered as a mere political act, belonging to the executive department alone, for the performance of which, entire confidence is placed by our constitution in the supreme executive; and for any misconduct respecting which, the injured individual has no remedy.

That there may be such cases is not to be questioned; but that every act of duty, to be performed in any of the great departments of government, constituted such a case, is not to be admitted. . . .

[For instance,] By the act passed in 1796, authorizing the sale of the lands above the mouth of the Kentucky river, the purchaser, on paying his purchase money, becomes completely entitled to the property purchased; and on producing to the secretary of state, the receipt of the treasurer upon a certificate required by law, the president of the United States is authorized to grant him a patent. It is further enacted that all patents shall be countersigned by the secretary of state, and recorded in his office. If the secretary of state should choose to withhold this patent; or the patent being lost, should refuse a copy of it; can it be imagined that the law furnishes to the injured person no remedy?

It is not believed that any person whatever would attempt to maintain such a proposition.

It follows then that the question, whether the legality of an act of the head of the department be examinable in the court of justice or not, must always depend on the nature of that act.

If some acts be examinable, and others not, there must be some rule of law to guide the court in the exercise of its jurisdiction.

In some instances there may be difficulty in applying the rule to particular cases; but there cannot, it is believed, be much difficulty in laying down the rule.

By the constitution of the United States, the President is invested with certain important political powers, in the exercise of which he is to use his own discretion, and is accountable only to his country in his political character, and to his own conscience. To aid him in the performance of these duties, he is authorized to appoint certain officers, who act by his authority and in conformity with his orders.

In such cases, their acts are his acts; and whatever opinion may be entertained of the manner in which executive discretion may be used, still there exists, and can exist, no power to control that discretion. The subjects are political. They respect the nation, not individual rights, and being entrusted to the executive, the decision of the executive is conclusive. The application of this remark will be perceived by adverting to the act of congress for establishing the department of foreign affairs. This officer, as his duties were prescribed by that act, is to conform precisely to the will of the President. He is the mere organ by whom that will is communicated. The acts of such an officer, as an officer, can never be examinable by the courts.

But when the legislature proceeds to impose on that officer other duties; when it is directed peremptorily to perform certain acts; when the rights of individuals are dependent on the performance of those acts; he is so far the officer of the law; is amenable to the laws for his conduct; and cannot at his discretion sport away the vested rights of others.

The conclusion from this reasoning is, that where the heads of departments are the political or confidential agents of the executive, merely to execute the will of the President, or rather to act in cases in which the executive possesses a constitutional or legal discretion, nothing can be more perfectly clear than that their acts are only politically examinable. But where a specific duty is assigned by law, and individual rights depend upon the performance of that duty, it seems equally clear that the individual who considers himself injured, has a right to resort to the laws of his country for a remedy.

If this be the rule, let us enquire how it applies to the case under the consideration of the court.

The power of nominating to the senate, and the power of appointing to the person nominated, are political powers, to be exercised by the President according to his own discretion. When he has made an appointment, he has exercised his whole power, and his discretion has been completely applied to the case. If, by law, the officer be removable at the will of the President, then a new appointment may be immediately made, and the rights of the officer are terminated. But as a fact which has existed cannot be made never to have existed, the appointment cannot be annihilated; and consequently if the officer is by law not removable at the will of the President; the rights he has acquired are protected by the law, and are not resumable by the President. They cannot be extinguished by executive authority, and he has the privilege of asserting them in like manner as if they had been derived from another force. . . .

The doctrine, therefore, now advanced, is by no means a novel one.

It is true that the mandamus, now moved for, is not for the performance of an act expressly enjoined by statute.

It is to deliver a commission; on which subject the acts of Congress are silent. This difference is not considered as affecting the case. It has already been stated that the applicant has, to that commission, a vested legal right, of which the executive cannot deprive him. He has been appointed to an office, from which he is not removable at the will of the executive; and being so appointed, he has a right to the commission which the secretary has received from the president for his use. The act of congress does not indeed order the secretary of the state to send it to him, but it is placed in his hands for the person entitled to it; and cannot be more lawfully withheld by him, than by any other person. . . .

This, then, is a plain case for a mandamus, either to deliver the commission, or a copy of it from the record; and it only remains to be enquired,

Whether it can issue from this court.

The act to establish the judicial courts of the United States authorizes the Supreme Court "to issue writs of mandamus, in cases warranted by the principles and usages of law, to any courts appointed, or persons holding office, under the authority of the United States."

The secretary of state, being a person holding an office under the authority of the United States, is precisely within the letter of the description; and if this court is not authorized to issue a writ of mandamus to such an officer, it must be because the law is unconstitutional, and therefore absolutely incapable of conferring the authority, and assigning the duties which its words purport to confer and assign.

The constitution vests the whole judicial power of the United States in one supreme court, and such inferior courts as congress shall, from time to time, ordain and establish. This power is expressly extended to all cases arising under the laws of the United States; and consequently, in some form, may be exercised over the present case, because the right claimed is given by a law of the United States.

In the distribution of this power it is declared that "the supreme court shall have original jurisdiction in all cases affecting ambassadors, other public ministers and consuls, and those in which a state shall be a party. In all other cases, the supreme court shall have appellate jurisdiction."

It has been insisted, at the bar, that as the original grant of jurisdiction, to the supreme and inferior courts, is general and the clause, assigning original jurisdiction to the supreme court, contains no negative or restrictive words; the power remains to the legislature, to assign original jurisdiction to that court in other cases than those specified in the article which has been recited; provided those cases belong to the judicial power of the United States.

If it had been intended to leave it in the discretion of the legislature to apportion the judicial power between the supreme and inferior courts according to the will of that body, it would certainly have been useless to have proceeded further than to have defined the judicial power, and the tribunals in which it should be vested. The subsequent part of the section is mere surplusage, is entirely without meaning, if such is to be the construction. If congress remains at liberty to give this court appellate jurisdiction, where the constitution has declared its jurisdiction shall be original; and original jurisdiction where the constitution has declared it shall be appellate; the distribution of jurisdiction, made in the constitution, is form without substance.

Affirmative words are often, in their operation, negative of other objects than those affirmed; and in this case, a negative or exclusive sense must be given to them or they have no operation at all.

It cannot be presumed that any clause in the constitution is intended to be without effect, and therefore such a construction is inadmissible, unless the words require it. . . .

When a system organizing fundamentally a judicial system, divides it into one supreme, and so many inferior courts as the legislature may ordain and establish; then enumerates its powers, and proceeds so far to distribute them, as to define the jurisdiction of the supreme court by declaring the cases in which it will take original jurisdiction, and that in others it shall take appellate jurisdiction; the plain import of the words seems to be, that in one class of cases its jurisdiction is original, and not appellate; in the other it is appellate and not original. If any other construction would render the clause inoperative, that is an additional reason for rejecting such other construction, and for adhering to their obvious meaning.

To enable this court then to issue a mandamus, it must be shown to be an exercise of appellate jurisdiction, or to be necessary to enable them to exercise appellate jurisdiction.

It has been stated at the bar that the appellate jurisdiction may be exercised in a variety of forms, and that if it be the will of the legislature that a mandamus should be used for that purpose, that will must be obeyed. This is true, yet the jurisdiction must be appellate, not original.

It is the essential criterion of appellate jurisdiction, that it revises and corrects the procedures in a cause already instituted, and does not create that cause. Although, therefore, a mandamus may be directed to courts, yet to issue such a writ to an officer for the delivery of a paper, is in effect the same as to sustain an original action for that paper, and therefore seems not to belong to appellate but to original jurisdiction. Neither is it necessary in such a case as this, to enable the court to exercise appellate jurisdiction.

The authority, therefore, given to the supreme court, by the act establishing the judicial courts of the United States, to issue writs of mandamus to public officers, appears not to be warranted by the constitution; and it becomes necessary to enquire whether a jurisdiction so conferred, can be exercised.

The question, whether an act, repugnant to the constitution, can become the law of the land, is a question deeply interesting to the United States; but happily, not of an intricacy proportioned to its interest. It seems only necessary to recognize certain principles, supposed to have been long and well established, to decide it.

That the people have an original right to establish, for their future government, such principles as, in their opinion, shall most conduce to their own happiness, is the basis, on which the whole American fabric has been erected. The exercise of this original right is a very great exertion; nor can it, nor ought it be frequently repeated. The principles, therefore, so established, are deemed fundamental. And as the authority, from which they proceed, is supreme, and can seldom act, they are designed to be permanent.

This original and supreme will organizes the government, and assigns, to different departments, their respective powers. It may either stop here; or establish certain limits not to be transcended by those departments.

The government of the United States is of the latter description. The powers of the legislature are defined, and limited; and that those limits may not be mistaken, or forgotten, the constitution is written. To what purpose are powers limited, and to what purpose is that limitation committed to writing, if these limits may, at any time, be passed by those intended to be restrained? The distinction, between a government with limited and unlimited powers, is abolished, if those limits do not confine the persons on whom they are imposed, and if acts prohibited and acts allowed, are of equal obligation. It is a proposition too plain to be contested, that the constitution controls any legislative act repugnant to it; or that the legislature may alter the constitution by an ordinary act.

Between these alternatives there is no middle ground. The constitution is either a superior, paramount law, unchangeable by ordinary means, or it is on a level with ordinary legislative acts, and like other acts, is alterable when the legislature shall please to alter it.

If the former part of the alternative be true, then a legislative act contrary to the constitution is not law: if the latter part be true, then written constitutions are absurd attempts, on the part of the people, to limit a power, in its own nature illimitable.

Certainly all those who have framed written constitutions contemplate them as forming the fundamental and paramount law of the nation, and consequently the theory of every such government must be, that an act of the legislature, repugnant to the constitution, is void.

This theory is essentially attached to a written constitution, and is consequently to be considered, by this court, as one of the fundamental principles of our society. It is not therefore to be lost sight of in the further consideration of this subject.

If an act of the legislature, repugnant to the constitution, is void, does it, notwithstanding its invalidity, bind the courts, and oblige them to give it effect? Or, in other words, though it be not law, does it constitute a rule as operative as if it was a law? This would be to overthrow in fact what was established in theory; and would seem, at first view, an absurdity too gross to be insisted on. It shall, however, receive a more attentive consideration.

It is emphatically the province and duty of the judicial department to say what the law is. Those who apply the rule to particular cases, must of necessity expound and interpret that rule. If two laws conflict with each other, the courts must decide on the operation of each.

So if a law be in opposition to the constitution; if both the law and the constitution apply to a particular case, so that the court must either decide that case comfortably to the law, disregarding the constitution; or conformably to the constitution, disregarding the law; the court must decide which of these conflicting rules governs the case. This is the very essence of judicial duty.

If then the courts are to regard the constitution; and the constitution is superior to any ordinary act of the legislature; the constitution, and not such ordinary act, must govern the case to which they both apply.

Those then that controvert the principle that the constitution is to be considered, in court, as a paramount law, are reduced to the necessity of maintaining that courts must close their eyes on the constitution, and see only the law.

This doctrine would subvert the very foundation of all written constitutions. It would declare that an act, which, according to the principles and theory of our government, is entirely void; is yet, in practice, completely obligatory. It would declare, that the legislature shall do what is expressly forbidden, such act, notwithstanding the express prohibition, is in reality effectual. It would be giving to the legislature a practical and real omnipotence, with the same breath which professes to restrict their powers within narrow limits. It is prescribing limits, and declaring that those limits may be passed at pleasure.

That it thus reduces to nothing what we have deemed the greatest improvement on political institutions—a written constitution—would of itself be sufficient, in America, where written constitutions have been viewed with so much reverence, for rejecting the construction. But the peculiar expressions of the constitution of the United States furnish additional arguments in favor of its rejection.

The judicial power of the United States is extended to all cases arising under the constitution.

Could it be the intention of those who gave this power, to say that, in using it, the constitution should not be looked into? That a case arising under the constitution should be decided without examining the instrument under which it arises?

This is too extravagant to be maintained.

In some cases then, the constitution must be looked into by the judges. And if they can open it at all, what part of it are they forbidden to read, or to obey?

There are many other parts of the constitution which serve to illustrate this subject.

It is declared that "no tax or duty shall be laid on articles exported from any state." Suppose a duty on the export for cotton, of tobacco, or of flour; and a suit instituted to recover it. Ought judgment to be rendered in such a case? Ought the judges to close their eyes on the constitution, and see only the law?

The constitution declares that "no bill of attainder or *ex post facto* law shall be passed."

If, however, such a bill should be passed and a person should be prosecuted under it; must the court condemn to death those victims whom the constitution endeavors to preserve?

"No person," says the constitution, "shall be convicted of treason unless on the testimony of two witnesses to the same overt act, or on confession in open court."

Here the language of the constitution is addressed especially to the courts. It prescribes, directly for them, a rule of evidence not to be departed from. If the legislature should change that rule, and declare *one* witness, or a confession *out* of court, sufficient for conviction, must the constitutional principle yield to the legislative act?

From these, and many other selections which might be made, it is apparent, that the framers of the constitution contemplated that instrument, as a rule for the government of *courts,* as well as of the legislature.

Why otherwise does it direct the judges to take an oath to support it? This oath certainly applies, in an especial manner, to their conduct in their official character. How immoral to impose on them, if they were to be used as the instruments, and the knowing instruments, for violating what they swear to support!

The oath of office, imposed by the legislature, is completely demonstrative of the legislative opinion on this subject. It is in these words, "I do solemnly swear that I will administer justice without respect to persons, and do equal right to the poor and to the rich; and that I will faithfully and impartially discharge all the duties incumbent upon me as according to the best of my abilities and understanding, agreeably to *the constitution,* and the laws of the United States."

Why does a judge swear to discharge his duties agreeably to the constitution of the United States, if that constitution forms no rule for his government? if it is closed upon him, and cannot be inspected by him?

If such be the real state of things, this is worse than solemn mockery. To prescribe, or to take this oath, becomes equally a crime.

It is also entirely unworthy of observation, that in declaring what shall be the *supreme* law of the land, the *constitution* itself is first mentioned; and not the laws of the United States generally, but those only which shall be made in *pursuance* of the constitution, have that rank.

Thus, the particular phraseology of the constitution of the United States confirms and strengthens the principle, supposed to be essential to all written constitutions, that a law repugnant to the constitution is void; and that *courts,* as well as other departments, are bound by that instrument.

POSTSCRIPT

Despite the troublesome circumstances surrounding the origin of judicial review, 200 years of practice have settled the question of whether judges in the United States have the power of judicial review. Today, the more controversial questions are (1) whether constitutional interpretation is a function *exclusively* assigned to judges; and, (2) whether judicial interpretations of the Constitution, especially the Supreme Court's, are more *authoritative* than those of other political institutions, for instance those of Congress or the president. It is arguable that *Marbury v. Madison* gave judges only the right to declare laws and executive actions unconstitutional, not the right to be the sole and preeminent interpreters of the Constitution. As Marshall wrote in *Marbury,* the Constitution was "a rule for the government of courts *as well as* the legislature (emphasis added)," implying that the legislature also interpreted the Constitution and hinting, perhaps, that the Supreme Court's decisions had no special authoritative status. However, Marshall also asserted in *Marbury* that "It is emphatically the province and duty of the judicial department to say what the law is," which seemed to suggest that judges had an authoritative role to play in interpreting the Constitution. Moreover, if Congress could decide when its interpretation of the Constitution was superior to that of the Court, would that not mean, according to Marshall's basic theoretical argument in *Marbury,* that the American attempt to limit legislative power by way of a written constitution had failed? The meaning of *Marbury* is therefore unclear. The best that one can say is that it was ambiguous in regard to the constitutional authoritativeness of Supreme Court decisions.

Throughout American history, presidents have objected to the doctrine that judicial opinions on constitutional questions have any preeminent authority. Thomas Jefferson called the notion that judges were ultimate constitutional arbiters "a very dangerous doctrine indeed, and one which would place us under the despotism of an oligarchy."[14] In 1832 Andrew Jackson expressed the following opinion on the subject of the Supreme Court's authoritativeness:

> The opinion of the judges has no more authority over Congress than the opinion of Congress has over the judges, and on that point the President is independent of both. The authority of the Supreme Court must not, therefore, be permitted to control the Congress or the Executive when acting in their legislative capacities, but to have only such influence as the force of their reasoning may deserve.[15]

More than a century later, in 1937, in a political context that will be explored in the next chapter, Franklin D. Roosevelt said that the nation had reached a point "where we must take action to save the Constitution from the Court and the Court

---

[14]Letter to William C. Jarvis, Sept. 28, 1820, in A. E. Bergh, ed., *The Writings of Thomas Jefferson,* 20 vols. (Washington: Thomas Jefferson Memorial Association, 1904), XV, p. 277.

[15]James Richardson, ed., *Messages and Papers of the Presidents,* 19 vols. (New York: Bureau of National Literature, Inc., 1897), III, p. 1145.

from itself. We must find a way to take an appeal from the Supreme Court to the Constitution itself.”[16]

The Supreme Court indirectly responded to these presidential remarks in *Cooper v. Aaron.* This case dealt with the issue of whether Arkansas officials, on constitutional grounds, could oppose judicial orders to desegregate the public schools of Little Rock. In the opinion of these state officials, *Brown v. Board of Education,* the 1954 Supreme Court case mandating desegregation of public schools, was itself unconstitutional, and they had a right and a duty, they insisted, to oppose judicial orders based on a mistaken interpretation of the Constitution. Seizing upon the relevant language from *Marbury,* the Court claimed that the federal judiciary was the supreme interpreter of the Constitution.

> In 1803, Chief Justice Marshall, speaking for a unanimous Court, referring to the Constitution as “the fundamental and paramount law of the nation,” declared in the notable case of *Marbury v. Madison,* that “It is emphatically the province and duty of the judicial department to say what the law is.” This decision declared the basic principle that the Supreme Court's is supreme in the exposition of the law of the Constitution, and that principle has ever since been respected by the Court and the Country as a permanent and indispensable feature of our constitutional system. It follows that the interpretation of the Fourteenth Amendment enunciated by this Court in the Brown case is the supreme law of the land, and Art. VI of the Constitution makes it of binding effect on the States “any Thing in the Constitution or Laws of any State to the Contrary notwithstanding.” Every state legislator and executive and judicial officer is solemnly committed by oath taken pursuant to Art. VI, cl. 3, “to support this Constitution.”[17]

In *Cooper,* a unanimous decision, every justice signed his name to the opinion, an unusual step that placed the full weight of the Court behind the proposition that the Supreme Court's interpretation of the Constitution was supreme. *Brown v. Board of Education* was authoritative. It was a part of the Constitution, and every government official in the United States was obliged to abide by it.

The Supreme Court's claim in *Cooper* that it is the *ultimate,* if not the *exclusive,* interpreter of the Constitution has received wide support, but it has not gone unchallenged. Most recently, Edwin Meese III, while attorney general of the United States during the Reagan administration, went on record against the doctrine enunciated by the Supreme Court in *Cooper.* On October 21, 1986, in an address at Tulane University, Meese said the following:

> Some thirty years ago, in the midst of great racial turmoil, our highest Court seemed to succumb to . . . temptation. By a flawed reading of our Constitution and *Marbury v. Madison,* and an even more faulty syllogism of legal reasoning, the Court in a 1958 case called *Cooper v. Aaron* appeared to arrive at a conclusion about its own power that would have shocked men like John Marshall and Joseph Story.

---

[16]Samuel I. Rosenman, ed., *Public Papers and Addresses of Franklin D. Roosevelt,* 8 vols. (New York: Macmillan, 1941), vol. 1937, p. 126.

[17]358 U.S. 1, 18 (1958).

In this case, in dictum, the Court characterized one of its constitutional decisions as nothing less than "the supreme law of the land." Obviously constitutional
decisions are binding on the parties to a case; but the implication of the dictum
that everyone should accept constitutional decisions uncritically, that they are
judgments from which there is no appeal, was astonishing. . . . In one fell swoop,
the Court seemed to reduce the Constitution to the status of ordinary constitutional law, and to equate the judge with the lawgiver. Such logic assumes, as
Charles Evans Hughes once quipped, that the Constitution is "what the judges
say it is." The logic of the dictum in *Cooper v. Aaron* was, and is, at war with the
Constitution, at war with the basic principles of democratic government, and at
war with the very meaning of the rule of law. . . .[18]

According to Meese, the Constitution was "the supreme Law of the Land," not
the decisions of the Supreme Court. The decisions were "law," but they were neither equivalent to the Constitution itself nor indisputably valid. Accordingly, because Supreme Court decisions were not "the last words in constitutional construction," the other branches of government also had the responsibility of
interpreting the Constitution, and their interpretations were not necessarily inferior to those of the Court.

Meese's address at Tulane triggered an avalanche of criticism. Newspaper editorial pages overflowed with rebuttals and rejoinders, while scholarly journals reexamined the issue of the Court's authoritativeness. Numerous defenders of the
constitutional authoritativeness of judicial decisions characterized Meese's argument as an invitation to anarchy. What kind of constitutional order do we have if
every public official, not a party to the case, can decide whether to obey a
Supreme Court decision? What kind of rule of law would result? What kind of
democracy? A smaller number of commentators agreed with Meese that the
Court did not have a monopoly on constitutional truth.[19] In any case, the uproar
following Meese's address reveals the nature of the controversy that still sur-
rounds the doctrine of judicial review. Courts may have the right to decide if laws
or executive actions are unconstitutional, but it is still unclear whether citizens
and officials are absolutely obliged to defer to their decisions.

---

[18]Meese's complete speech is printed as "The Law of the Constitution" in the *Tulane Law Review* 61
(1987), pp. 979–90.

[19]For a review of this debate, see the symposium entitled *Perspectives on the Authoritativeness of
Supreme Court Decisions* in the *Tulane Law Review* 61 (1987).

Commerce Power

NLRB v. JONES & LAUGHLIN STEEL CORP.
301 U.S. 1 (1937)

◆

On February 5, 1937, President Franklin Delano Roosevelt proposed to Congress that he and future presidents be allowed to add to the Supreme Court one justice for each sitting justice over the age of seventy who declined to retire.[1] He justified his proposal, which soon came to be called his "court-packing plan," on grounds of utility and politics. With younger justices on it, the rationale went, the Supreme Court would conduct its business more efficiently and interpret the Constitution more flexibly, which Roosevelt thought was necessary if the federal government was going to be able to pull the country out of the Great Depression. The initiative immediately produced a major constitutional crisis involving two fundamental issues of American constitutionalism. First, what can a president do if he disagrees with the Supreme Court's interpretation of the Constitution? Can he, by proposing to "pack" the Court, engage in a thinly disguised form of political intimidation? Second, how is the Supreme Court to interpret the Constitution? Are the justices to assume that the Constitution is an unchanging legal instrument that should be understood according to the intentions of its framers, or is it a "living" entity that the justices must adapt and mold to contemporary needs and political realities? These two fundamental questions are directly implicated in *NLRB v. Jones & Laughlin Steel Corp.*, a decision in which the Court upheld the federal government's power, under the commerce clause, to prevent a manufacturing company from discriminating against its union employees.

The issue of what a president can *do* in response to judicial interpretations of the Constitution is related to the question of the authoritativeness of Supreme Court decisions, a topic briefly discussed in the postscript of Chapter 1. Those who believe that the Court is the ultimate interpreter of the Constitution are

---

[1]The proposal limited the number of justices that a single president could appoint to six.

more likely to have a narrower conception of what a president can do in opposition to a ruling by the Supreme Court than those who deny the Court this status. At a minimum, of course, the president has the right to express his opinion, but can he do more? A brief review of how previous presidents have reacted to specific judicial decisions will help to place FDR's "court-packing plan" in historical context.

In 1807, Thomas Jefferson not only disagreed with a judicial interpretation of the Constitution but also refused to comply fully with a subpoena directing him to appear and to testify at the treason trial of Aaron Burr. John Marshall had issued the subpoena while he was presiding over the trial in the United States Circuit Court of Virginia. Jefferson commented that he did not believe that the court had "a power of *commanding* the executive government to abandon superior duties and attend on them."[2] During the 1830s, Andrew Jackson took exception to the Supreme Court's decision concerning the constitutionality of the controversial national bank. In *McCulloch v. Maryland* (1819),[3] the Court had declared that the federal government had the constitutional authority to create the bank. Nonetheless, in 1832, after Congress had rechartered the bank, Jackson vetoed the bill on constitutional grounds. By exercising his veto power in this fashion, Jackson implicitly endorsed the position that the president could *do* things in opposition to Supreme Court decisions.[4]

Later in the nineteenth century, Abraham Lincoln campaigned for political office by condemning Chief Justice Roger Taney's opinion in *Dred Scott v. Sandford,* the infamous case that invalidated federal attempts to restrict the growth of slavery in the territories. He contended that he could properly oppose the decision "as a political rule," though his opponent, Stephen A. Douglas, insisted that every citizen had a duty to defer to the Supreme Court and claimed that Lincoln was appealing to "mob law." (See Box 2.1.) This exchange between Lincoln and Douglas is interesting for two reasons. First, it pre-dates Lincoln's refusal to honor Taney's decision denying him during the Civil War the right to suspend the writ of habeas corpus without Congressional authority.[5] This particular writ, which is discussed in more detail in the next chapter, is a judicial order compelling any official who has a person in custody to justify before a judge the lawfulness of the detention. Its suspension in the North, of course, led to many military arrests of Southern sympathizers.[6] Second, in this debate, Douglas clearly condemned a tactic that closely resembled FDR's "court-packing" plan. No one, in his judgment, could have any confidence in a court composed of judges "who have been

---

[2]Quoted by Edward S. Corwin, *The President: Office and Powers,* 4th ed. (New York: New York University Press, 1957), pp. 326–27.

[3]4 Wheat. (17 U.S.) 316 (1819).

[4]There is the story that in the same year that Jackson vetoed the bank bill, he said, in reaction to a Supreme Court case concerned with the rights of Indians, "Well, John Marshall has made his decision, now let him enforce it!" The relevant case was *Worcester v. Georgia,* 6 Pet. (31 U.S.) 515 (1832). The historical evidence supporting this story is very thin, and most historians understand it as a legend.

[5]See *Ex Parte Merryman,* 17 F. Cases 144 (1861).

[6]See Mark E. Neely, *The Fate of Liberty* (New York: Oxford University Press, 1991).

┌───┐

BOX 2.1

LINCOLN AND DOUGLAS DEBATE

LINCOLN:
. . . What are the uses of decisions of courts? They have two uses. . . . First—
they decide upon the question before the court. They decide in this case
that Dred Scott is a slave. Nobody resists that. Not only that, but they say to
everybody else, that persons standing just as Dred Scott stands is as he is.
That is, they say that when a question comes up upon another person it will
be so decided again, unless the court decides in another way, unless the
court overrules its decision. Well, we mean to do what we can to have the
court decide the other way. That is one thing we mean to try to do. . . .

DOUGLAS:
. . . Mr. Lincoln intimates that there is another mode by which he can reverse the Dred Scott decision. How is that? Why, he is going to appeal to
the people to elect a President who will appoint judges who will reverse the
Dred Scott decision. . . . [W]hen that Republican President shall have taken
his seat—Mr. Seward, for instance—will he then proceed to appoint judges?
No! he will have to wait until the present judges die before he can do that,
and perhaps his four years would be out before a majority of these judges
found it agreeable to die. . . . But suppose they should die, then how are the
new judges to be appointed? Why, the Republican President is to call up the
candidates and catechize them, and ask them, "How will you decide this
case if I appoint you judge?". . . Suppose you get a Supreme Court composed of such judges, who have been appointed by a partisan President
upon their giving pledges how they would decide a case before it arise, what
confidence would you have in such a court?. . .
    . . . I intend to yield obedience to the highest tribunals in the land in all
cases whether their opinions are in conformity with my views as a lawyer or
not. When we refuse to abide by judicial decisions what protection is there
left for life and property? To whom shall you appeal? To mob law, to partisan caucuses, to town meetings, to revolution? Where is the remedy when
you refuse obedience to the constituted authorities? I will not stop to inquire whether I agree or disagree with all the opinions expressed by Judge
Taney or any other judge. It is enough for me to know that the decision has
been made. It has been made by a tribunal appointed by the Constitution to
make it; it was a point within their jurisdiction, and I am bound by it. . . .

LINCOLN:
    . . . We do not propose that when Dred Scott has been decided to be a
slave by the court, we, as a mob, will decide him to be free. We do not propose that, when any other one, or one thousand, shall be decided by that
court to be slaves, we will in any violent way disturb the rights of property
thus settled; but we nevertheless do oppose that decision as a political rule
which shall be binding on the voter, to vote for nobody who thinks it wrong,

└───┘

which shall be binding on the members of Congress or the President to favor no measure that does not actually concur with the principles of that decision. We do not propose to be bound by it as a political rule in that way. . . .

Source: Paul M. Angle, ed., Created Equal: The Complete Lincoln–Douglas Debates of 1858 (Chicago: University of Chicago Press, 1958), pp. 36, 56–57, 333.

appointed by a partisan President upon their giving pledges how they would decide a case." Is this not exactly what FDR planned to do in 1937?[7]

The question of whether judges should passively interpret an unchanging Constitution according to the literal words of the document and the past intentions of the framers or whether they should actively remake the Constitution according to contemporary political needs and realities has bedeviled American constitutional thought from the founding to the present day. The more traditional outlook, which restricts the judicial role to one of interpretation, perceives the Constitution as an unchanging system of rules that can be altered only by formal amendment. Accordingly, the Constitution today, apart from the amendments, is identical to the one that was ratified in the eighteenth century. One virtue of this point of view is that John Marshall's justification for judicial review in *Marbury* seems to be more compatible with it than with a more activist understanding of the judicial constitutional role. Judges have the power to invalidate laws because they are the "objective mouthpieces" of the "supreme law" ratified by the people. Two centuries of constitutional experience, however, have produced the alternative view that judges do not merely "interpret" the Constitution but rather remake it in the process of constitutional adjudication itself. Accordingly, the Constitution is a "living entity," a set of norms that evolves in accordance with an ever-changing society. Unfortunately, to the degree that this latter model is an accurate reflection of the nature of constitutional adjudication, it seems to call into question the legitimacy of judicial review. How is it that judges have power to declare laws unconstitutional if they remake the Constitution as they interpret it?

The New Deal Era is a good setting in which to consider the relationship between Marshall's justification for judicial review and the character of constitu-

---

[7]Another means by which the Congress and the president can check the Supreme Court is by narrowing its appellate jurisdiction, which is defined by statute. This method was successfully used by the Radical Republicans to keep the Court from reviewing a habeas corpus petition of a Southern newspaper editor held in military custody during Reconstruction. See *Ex Parte McCardle*, 74 U.S. 506 (1869). However, in *United States v. Klein*, 80 U.S. 128 (1872), the Court ruled that Congress cannot take away the Court's jurisdiction if the withdrawal constitutes a legislative attempt to invade the judicial sphere by indirectly deciding a pending case. More recently, commentators have claimed that Congress cannot, by cutting into the Court's appellate jurisdiction, deprive it of its "core" or "essential" functions. For a complete discussion of this complicated topic, see Gerald Gunther, "Congressional Power to Curtail Federal Court Jurisdiction: An Opinionated Guide to the Ongoing Debate," *Stanford Law Review* 36 (1984), pp. 895–922.

tional adjudication. Soon after FDR was elected in 1932, the federal government enacted a comprehensive package of economic legislation designed to lift the country out of the Great Depression, which had begun with the stock market crash of 1929. The main constitutional pillar upon which the New Dealers relied to justify this unprecedented attempt by the federal government to exert control over the economy was Congress's power to regulate interstate commerce (Art. I, Sect. 8). However, in 1935 and 1936, the Supreme Court responded by declaring the bulk of this legislation unconstitutional. In the opinion of the majority of the justices, the interstate commerce clause did not authorize the federal government to regulate local production or manufacturing—an area of economic life that fell within the powers reserved to the states by the Tenth Amendment. The federal government therefore did not have the power to solve the socioeconomic problems of the Great Depression; the Constitution itself stood in the way of what FDR was trying to do. His problem, the justices insisted, was with the Constitution, not with the individual justices. If FDR wanted to rejuvenate the economy through federal action, his only option was to seek an amendment to the Constitution that would give the federal government the power to regulate all forms of production and manufacture.

FDR and his congressional allies interpreted the situation very differently. With the country in a dire crisis, there was no time for an amendment, even if one could be formulated that would be approved—which was not likely—by the necessary two-thirds of each house of Congress and by three-quarters of the states. Moreover, there was no need for an amendment because the problem, according to FDR, was not with the Constitution, but with the people who were interpreting it. The Supreme Court, not the Constitution, needed to be changed. Consequently, after receiving an overwhelming electoral endorsement of the New Deal in the election of 1936, FDR announced his "court-packing plan." Because the number of Supreme Court justices had always been fixed by statute, the lawfulness of FDR's initiative was never in doubt. Nonetheless, even some of FDR's former allies condemned the plan as an implicit attempt to alter the American constitutional system by "packing" the Court with justices who would be receptive to the legitimacy of New Deal legislation. It seemed to be a form of political intimidation: The Court's majority either had to retreat from its constitutional stand against the New Deal or face the real possibility that the Court's stature would be undermined by a series of crass political-judicial appointments.

In the end, one of the justices in the anti–New Deal majority—Owen Roberts—switched sides: "a switch that saved nine." Types of laws that were invalidated on a five-to-four vote in 1935 and 1936 were now upheld by the same measure in 1937. Though FDR continued his fight for the plan after these decisions, congressional support quickly dissipated. The key decision that upheld the federal government's authority to regulate the economy was *National Labor Relations Board v. Jones & Laughlin Steel Corporation.* Students should consider whether the briefs and oral argument support FDR's opinion that the anti–New Deal justices had abused their power of judicial review by interpreting the Constitution too literally and too narrowly. Or do they suggest that these justices had a justifiable interpretation of the Constitution, that it was quite plausible, if not likely, that the framers never meant to give the national government power to regulate local production and manufacture? And what of FDR's attempt at political intimidation? Was it justifiable if the Court was only doing its job of interpreting the "supreme law of the land"? And finally, there is Justice Roberts. What are we to make of a justice who changes his interpretation of the commerce clause in the context of the 1936 election and the court-packing plan? When and in what way, if ever, did he abuse his judicial constitutional role? All of these questions bear directly upon how judges should interpret and understand the Constitution, whether as an unchanging (save by amendment) set of rules inherited from the eighteenth century or as an evolving set of norms that judges have adapted to ever-changing social, economic, and political conditions.

Though the commerce clause had never been used to justify an extensive system of federal control over the economy until the New Deal, it had earlier provided the constitutional basis for separate pieces of federal economic legislation. As early as 1824, in *Gibbons v. Ogden,* Chief Justice John Marshall upheld a federal law that licensed vessels employed in the coastal trade by defining "commerce" in a generous way. Commerce, he said, is "something more" than just the buying and selling of goods; "it is intercourse. It describes the commercial intercourse between nations, and parts of nations, in all its branches, and is regulated by prescribing rules for carrying on that intercourse." Accordingly, Congress does have power to enact laws of navigation because "All America understands, and has uniformly understood, the word 'commerce' to comprehend navigation."[8] However, Marshall continued, Congress did not have power to regulate all commerce, but only "interstate" commerce, only commerce "among the several states."

> It is not intended to say that these words comprehend the commerce which is completely internal, which is carried on between man and man in a state, or between different parts of the same state, and which does not extend to or affect other states. Such a power would be inconvenient, and is certainly unnecessary.[9]

Therefore, according to Marshall, before the federal government could regulate any form of economic activity, it had to be, first, a part of commerce—such as the coastal trade that was regulated by the licensing law considered in *Gibbons*—and, second, it had to "extend," "affect," or "concern" more than one state.

Marshall's insistence that a part of the commercial life of the country was reserved to the states did not mean that valid federal regulations could not be applied within the boundary lines of a particular state. If an aspect of commerce, such as navigation of the coastal trade, "affected" more than one state, then the federal regulations could be applied within the jurisdiction of one of the states. "Commerce among the states cannot stop at the external boundary line of each state," he reasoned, "but may be introduced into the interior."[10]

Late in the nineteenth century, in *United States v. E.C. Knight Company* (1895), the Supreme Court reaffirmed the principle that the interstate commerce

---

[8]*Gibbons v. Ogden,* 22 U.S. 1, 190 (1824).

[9]*Id.* at 194.

[10]*Id.*

clause granted limited authority to the federal government to regulate the commercial life of the country. This case concerned the federal government's attempt, under the Sherman Antitrust Act of 1890, to prevent the American Sugar Refining Company from purchasing four other sugar-refining companies, a purchase that would have given the company control over 98 percent of the sugar refined in the United States. The statute prohibited any attempt or conspiracy "to restrain" or "to monopolize" trade or commerce among the several states. In an opinion written by Chief Justice Melville W. Fuller, the Court held (with one justice dissenting) that the "manufacture" of sugar was beyond the authority of the federal government: "Commerce succeeds to manufacture, and is not a part of it. The power to regulate commerce is the power to prescribe the rule by which commerce shall be governed, and is a power independent of the power to suppress monopoly."[11] Therefore the federal government did not have the authority to prevent monopolies or restraints of trade in manufacturing, even if they did have a large impact upon interstate commerce. "Contracts, combinations, or conspiracies to control domestic enterprise in manufacture, agriculture, mining, production in all its forms, or to raise or lower prices or wages, might unquestionably tend to restrain external as well as domestic trade, but the restraint would be an indirect result, however inevitable and whatever its extent. . . ."[12] Because an intent to monopolize manufacture is not equivalent to an intent "to restrain" or "to monopolize" interstate commerce, monopolies of manufacture are subject to the control of state governments, not the federal government. If it were otherwise, if the federal government could regulate those manufacturing companies that had an "indirect" effect upon interstate commerce, Fuller concluded, "comparatively little of business operations and affairs would be left for state control."[13]

Notwithstanding the *Knight* ruling, two other cases from the pre–New Deal era indicate that the Court recognized the interstate commerce clause as a substantial grant of power. In *Houston E. & W. Texas Ry. Company v. United States* (1914), a decision known as the Shreveport Case, the Court considered whether Congress had the power to regulate the *intrastate* rates of large interstate railroads that were undercutting the rates imposed by the Interstate Commerce Commission upon competing interstate traffic. Though transportation was indisputably commercial in character, the controversy was whether intrastate railroad rates were a part of inter- or intrastate commerce. The federal government would have authority to impose regulations on such traffic only if it fell within the former, not the latter, category. In his majority opinion, Justice Charles E. Hughes admitted that Congress did not have the authority "to regulate the internal commerce of a State" but then argued that it did "possess the power to foster and protect interstate commerce, and to take all measures necessary or appropriate to that end, although intrastate transactions of interstate carriers may thereby be controlled."[14] The federal government could therefore control the intrastate rates

---

[11]*United States v. Knight*, 156 U.S. 1, 12 (1895).

[12]*Id.*

[13]*Id.* at 16.

[14]*Houston E. & W. Texas Ry. Co. v. United States*, 234 U.S. 342, 353 (1914).

of interstate railroads as a means of maintaining "conditions under which interstate commerce may be conducted upon fair terms and without molestation or hindrance."[15] Though this decision, on its face, pertained only to railroads, its significance was indisputable. The Court had recognized that the federal government had the power, if the health of interstate commerce required it, to regulate the internal commerce of a state, at least when the regulated entity also participated in interstate commerce.

In *Stafford v. Wallace* (1922), the Court upheld The Packers and Stockyards Act of 1921, a federal law intended to prevent "unfair, discriminatory, or deceptive practices" by Chicago meatpackers. Against the objection that the law was an unconstitutional attempt to regulate local commercial activities of buying and selling, the Court relied upon the metaphor of a "stream" or "current." If local acts of buying and selling were a part of a "stream of interstate commerce," they were subject to federal control. In the words of Chief Justice William H. Taft, "The stockyards are not a place of rest or final destination. . . . [They] are but a throat through which the current flows, and the transactions which occur therein are only incident to this current from the West to the East, and from one State to another."[16] And because it was "reasonable" to believe that such transactions will "more or less constantly be used in conspiracies against interstate commerce or constitute a direct and undue burden on it," Congress had the power to regulate. "Whatever amounts to more or less constant practice, and threatens to obstruct or unduly to burden the freedom of interstate commerce is within the regulatory power of Congress under the commerce clause, and it is primarily for Congress to consider and decide the fact of the danger and meet it."[17]

In summary, the federal government's power to regulate interstate commerce before the Great Depression can be understood against the background of the four cases discussed here. *Gibbons* established the principle of federal authority if what is regulated is a part of commerce and "affects" more than one state. *Knight* excluded production and manufacture from commerce and thereby from federal control.[18] The last two cases permitted federal control of local commercial activities— intrastate railway rates of interstate railroads and stockyard transactions that were a part of a stream of interstate commerce—if they burdened interstate commerce.

These commerce-clause precedents were not the only potential constitutional obstacles to the development of an extensive system of federal regulation of the economy during the New Deal. During the late nineteenth century, the Supreme Court had formulated a doctrine that soon functioned as an additional barrier to any regulation of the economy, whether by the federal government or by the indi-

---

[15]*Id.* at 351.

[16]*Stafford v. Wallace*, 258 U.S. 495, 515–16 (1922).

[17]*Id.* at 520–21.

[18]*Knight* was reaffirmed in *Hammer v. Dagenhart*, 247 U.S. 251 (1918), a case that invalidated a federal law that excluded from interstate commerce the products of child labor. Even though the law prohibited only the interstate transportation of the products of child labor, not child labor itself, the Court interpreted it as an attempt to regulate local production and manufacture and therefore declared it unconstitutional.

vidual states. The language that the Court used in this effort to provide a constitutional sanction to a *laissez-faire* economy was located within both the Fifth and Fourteenth Amendments: Neither the federal government nor states could deprive a person of life, liberty, or property "without due process of law." At first, the Supreme Court understood this principle of "due process" as a restriction only on what procedures governments had to follow when they deprived a person of life, liberty, or property.[19] But in cases upholding state regulation of rates charged by grain elevators and railroads, the Court said that "unreasonably" low rates would be declared unconstitutional because they deprived the elevators and railroads of property without "due process of law."[20] In this way, "due process" became substantive. A law could be an unconstitutional violation of "due process" not because proper procedures were not followed when the deprivation took place, but because the deprivation itself was an "unreasonable" one.

The Court did not actually invalidate a state law on the ground that it violated due process until *Allgeyer v. Louisiana* (1897).[21] In this case, the issue was not an "unreasonable" deprivation of property but an "unreasonable" deprivation of liberty: the liberty of contract. From *Allgeyer* up until the New Deal crisis, the Court expanded the principle that neither state nor federal governments could interfere with fundamental aspects of contractual liberty. The most prominent elements of contractual freedom protected by the Court in this fashion resided in employer–employee relations, especially in regard to hours, wages, and the right of unions to organize and represent workers—the issue that reappears in *Jones*. In *Lochner v. New York* (1905), the Court invalidated a statute that prohibited bakers from working more than ten hours a day or sixty hours a week.[22] In *Adkins v. Children's Hospital* (1923), the Court overturned a District of Columbia law establishing a minimum wage for women.[23] And in *Coppage v. Kansas* (1915), the Court ruled that a state could not prevent an employer from requiring as a condition of employment that the employee agree not to join a union.[24]

---

[19]For a more extensive discussion of substantive due process, see *Constitutional Debate in Action: Criminal Justice,* Chapter 1.

[20]See *Munn v. Illinois,* 94 U.S. 113 (1877); *Railroad Commission Cases,* 116 U.S. 307 (1886).

[21]165 U.S. 578 (1897).

[22]198 U.S. 45 (1905). In contrast to *Lochner,* the Court upheld a ten-hour maximum for women working in factories and laundries in *Muller v. Oregon,* 208 U.S. 412 (1908). Later the Court upheld a similar law regulating the hours of male factory workers in *Bunting v. Oregon,* 243 U.S. 426 (1917).

[23]261 U.S. 525 (1923).

[24]236 U.S. 1 (1915). The Court had adopted an identical rule in regard to the federal government in *Adair v. United States,* 208 U.S. 161 (1908). However, in 1930 the Court upheld the Railway Labor Act of 1926, which recognized the right of railway workers to bargain collectively and set up a National Mediation Board to mediate disputes. See *Texas & New Orleans Railroad Company v. Brotherhood of Railway and Steamship Clerks,* 281 U.S. 548 (1930). Even though the law addresses labor relations in the national railroad industry, an industry clearly within the federal commercial power, it was an important precedent for the federal government's attempt during the New Deal to regulate labor conditions in the manufacturing sector of the economy. However, in 1935 the Court in *Railroad Retirement Board v. Alton Railroad Co.,* 295 U.S. 330 (1935), overturned a federal law that imposed compulsory retirement and pension plans on all interstate railroads.

These substantive-due-process cases meant that any federal attempt to end the Great Depression by imposing regulations on the economy had two constitutional hurdles to overcome: First, the particular exertion of federal power had to be within the commerce power; second, it could not violate the due process clause. These hurdles confronted FDR even though the need for federal action, as the following passage from William Leuchtenburg's *Franklin D. Roosevelt and the New Deal* suggests, was great and clear.

> By 1932, the unemployed numbered upward of thirteen million. Many lived in the primitive conditions of a preindustrial society stricken by famine. In the coal fields of West Virginia and Kentucky, evicted families shivered in tents in midwinter; children went barefoot. In Los Angeles, people whose gas and electricity had been turned off were reduced to cooking over wood fires in back lots. Visiting nurses in New York found children famished; one episode, reported Lillian Wald, "might have come out of the tales of old Russia." A Philadelphia storekeeper told a reporter of one family he was keeping going on credit: "Eleven children in that house. They've got no shoes, no pants. In the house, no chairs. My god, you go in there, you cry, that's all.[25]

In the spring of 1933, as FDR took office, there was precious little about which one could be cheerful. The collapsed stock market; the rising number of bankruptcies, bank failures, and mortgage foreclosures; and the steep drops in production, employment, and national income created a desperate situation. FDR was determined to act.

In the first few years of his administration, FDR and Congress engaged in bursts of frenzied socioeconomic legislation. Most of these laws, including The National Industrial Recovery Act (NIRA) (1933), the Bituminous Coal Conservation Act (1935), and the National Labor Relations Act (NLRA) (1935), were based on the federal government's power under the interstate commerce clause. The NIRA authorized the president to establish, in any particular industry, "fair codes of competition" that would set prices of commodities, fix the minimum of wages and the maximum of hours, and prohibit unfair labor practices, such as attempts by employers to stop employees from organizing unions. The Coal Act regulated maximum hours and minimum wages in coal mines by taxing those companies that refused to abide by the code. The NLRA reaffirmed the right of employees to form unions and bargain collectively with employers and created a National Labor Relations Board (NLRB) to enforce the provisions of the act in all industries "affecting commerce." The Supreme Court reviewed each of these pieces of legislation: the NIRA in *Schechter Poultry Corp. v. United States* (1935); the Coal Act in *Carter v. Carter Coal Company* (1936); and, after FDR had announced his "court-packing plan," the NLRA in *NLRB v. Jones & Laughlin Steel Corp.* (1937).

Throughout the New Deal crisis, the Court was divided into three voting blocs. On one side, George Sutherland, James C. McReynolds, Willis Van Devan-

---

25William Leuchtenburg, *Franklin D. Roosevelt and the New Deal* (New York: Harper & Row, 1963), pp. 1–2.

ter, and Pierce Butler—"the four horsemen"—resolutely opposed the constitutionality of key legislation that FDR was relying upon to resolve the economic crisis. On the other, Louis D. Brandeis, Benjamin N. Cardozo, and Harlan F. Stone were broadly sympathetic to the New Deal exertions of federal power over the economy. Chief Justice Charles E. Hughes and Justice Owen J. Roberts occupied the crucial middle ground. How they voted often determined whether a law would be upheld or rejected.

For example, in 1934 Roberts and Hughes voted with the three liberal justices in *Home Building & Loan Ass'n v. Blaisdell* (1934) (mortgage moratorium law) and in *Nebbia v. New York* (1934) (milk price regulation).[26] But in *Panama Refining Co. v. Ryan* (1935) (petroleum price regulation), *Railroad Retirement Board v. Alton Railroad Co.* (1935) (compulsory retirement and pension plan), *United States v. Butler* (1936) (farm price regulation), and *Morehead v. New York ex rel. Tipaldo* (1936) (minimum wage law for women),[27] both or either of these two swing votes joined the "four horsemen" to invalidate socioeconomic legislation. If either or both had voted with "the four horsemen," the socioeconomic law failed; if both had voted with the "more liberal" wing of the Court, the law was saved. Rarely did two justices exert so much power over the national scene in a crisis. And because Hughes never voted with the "horsemen" unless Roberts did also, it is arguable that the crucial vote belonged to Roberts.[28] During the New Deal era, if he voted with the *laissez-faire* conservatives, it was either a five-to-four or a six-to-three vote against FDR. If he voted with the liberals, Hughes followed suit, and the law was upheld. It is arguable that no justice has ever had the power—and the responsibility that goes with it—that Justice Roberts had in 1935–37.

In both *Schechter* and *Carter,* the Court invalidated the laws in question because they involved exertions of power beyond what the federal government possessed under the interstate commerce clause.[29] In the first case, the Court unanimously concluded that the federal government did not have the power to punish the Schechter Poultry Corporation, a New York City slaughterhouse, for not abiding by the applicable NIRA code. Even if 96 percent of the chickens came into the municipal market from other states, they were not within a "stream of interstate commerce" because Schechter sold them only to local retailers. The chickens had, as it were, already left "the stream" before they arrived at the slaughterhouse. Nor could it be said that the code's regulations of hours and wages were constitutional. No doubt low wages and long hours might cut costs and ultimately prices, but that result was only "indirect."

---

[26]290 U.S. 398 (1934); 291 U.S. 502 (1934).

[27]293 U.S. 388 (1935); 295 U.S. 330 (1935); 297 U.S. 1 (1936); 298 U.S. 587 (1936).

[28]For a more extensive version of this argument, see Fred Rodell, *Nine Men: A Political History of the Supreme Court, 1790–1955* (New York: Random House, 1955), p. 223.

[29]In *Schechter,* the liberals on the Court—Brandeis, Stone, and Cardozo—voted with the conservatives because the NIRA "improperly" delegated legislative power to the president. As Cardozo put it, "This is delegation run riot." See *Schechter v. United States,* 295 U.S. 495, 553 (1935).

> If the Federal Government may determine the wages and hours of employees in
> the internal commerce of a State, because of their relation to cost and prices and
> their indirect effect upon interstate commerce, it would seem that a similar con-
> trol might be exerted over other elements of cost, also affecting prices, such as
> the number of employees, rents, advertising, methods of doing business, etc.[30]

Chief Justice Hughes's majority opinion continued, "the authority of the Federal
Government may not be pushed to such an extreme" because it would "destroy
the distinction, which the commerce clause itself establishes, between commerce
'among the several States' and the internal concerns of a State."[31] If the federal
government could regulate the wages and hours of a local poultry slaughterhouse
on the basis of the interstate commerce clause, it could regulate every facet of
production and manufacture.

The Court's reasoning in *Carter* (a six-to-three decision, with Hughes and
Roberts in the majority) ran a similar course even though the regulations concerned prices, hours, and wages in coal mining. Coal mining, of course, was an industry that had far more national characteristics than the one considered in
Schechter. Nonetheless, the Court decided that coal mining was not in the "flow
of interstate commerce." "In the Schechter Case, the flow had ceased. Here it had
not begun."[32] Also, the prices, hours, and wages in the coal industry, in the Court's
judgment, did not "directly affect" interstate commerce. "The word 'direct' implies that the activity or condition invoked or blamed shall operate proximately—
not mediately, remotely, or collaterally—to produce the effect." Therefore, it did
not matter that the law regulated factors in the coal industry that had an inevitable
and large "effect" upon interstate commerce. The relevant question to assess the
constitutionality of the law was not "the *extent* of the local activity or condition, or
the *extent* of the effect produced upon interstate commerce." Rather, the crucial
issue was "the *relation* between the activity or condition and the effect."[33] And because wages, prices, and hours in the coal industry did not have a "proximate" effect upon interstate commerce, the Court once again claimed that it had no
choice but to declare the Bituminous Coal Act unconstitutional.

How most of the justices in the majority in *Schechter* and *Carter* understood
the Court's role of interpreting the Constitution can be readily discerned from a
few passages taken from other relevant cases of the period. In *United States v.
Butler* (1936), a decision that overturned the Agricultural Adjustment Act of 1933,
Roberts, the pivotal justice on the Court, said the following:

> It is sometimes said that the court assumes a power to overrule or control the ac-
> tion of the people's representatives. This is a misconception. . . . When an act of
> Congress is appropriately challenged in the courts as not conforming to the con-
> stitutional mandate the judicial branch of the Government has only one duty,—to
> lay the article of the Constitution which is invoked beside the statute which is

---

[30]*Id.* at 549.

[31]*Id.* at 550.

[32]*Carter v. Carter Coal Co.*, 298 U.S. 238, 306 (1936).

[33]*Id.* at 308.

challenged and to decide whether the latter squares with the former. All the
court does, or can do, is to announce its considered judgment upon the question.
The only power it has, if such it may be called, is the power of judgment. This
court neither approves nor condemns any legislative policy.[34]

The Supreme Court, in Roberts's view, did not slowly remake the Constitution.
The Constitution did not evolve at the hands of the judiciary because the judiciary
had no policymaking role whatsoever. As Justice Sutherland said in a 1934 case,
the Constitution "does not mean one thing at one time and an entirely different
thing at another time." Rather, when engaged in constitutional interpretation, the
judge's only purpose should be "to discover the meaning, to ascertain and give effect to the intent, of its framers and the people who adopted it."[35]

Justice Cardozo, in his dissent in *Carter*, expressed the opposing point of
view, in regard both to the Constitution and to the nature of constitutional adjudication. The federal government's power to regulate intrastate transactions that
"directly" affect interstate commerce must be understood as "a matter of degree"
and must "not be read too narrowly." "A survey of the cases shows," he continued,
"that the words have been interpreted with suppleness of adaptation and flexibil-
ity of meaning. *The power is as broad as the need that evokes it* (emphasis
added)."[36] The justices must therefore interpret the Constitution in a flexible way
that permits the legislative branch to solve the socioeconomic problems that it
confronts. A literal reading of the Constitution or one that restricted its meaning
to what the framers intended had to give way to an understanding of constitutional adjudication that looked toward the future and the utility of our society.
"Heed must be taken," he concluded, to ". . . considerations of social benefit or
detriment in marking the division between reason and oppression."[37] The Constitution had to evolve as judges adapted it to the needs and realities of the present
and future.

Although FDR welcomed Cardozo's dissent in *Carter*, he condemned the
majority's view of the commerce power and, by implication, the majority's literal
approach to constitutional adjudication. In a news conference after the Court
handed down *Schechter*, he compared the decision to the infamous Dred Scott
case and insisted that it "relegated" the country to a "horse-and-buggy definition
of interstate commerce."[38] *Carter* and *Morehead v. New York* (1936), a decision
that buttressed the substantive-due-process principle of *Adkins* by declaring New
York's minimum wage law unconstitutional, brought forth from FDR the criticism
that the Court had created "a no-man's land," a place which "no Government—
State or Federal" could enter.[39] The federal government could not enter this "no-
man's land" because it was purportedly beyond its power to regulate interstate

---

[34]*United States v. Butler*, 297 U.S. 1, 62 (1936).

[35]*Home Building & Loan Asso. v. Blaisdell*, 290 U.S. 398, 449, 453 (1934), Sutherland dissenting.

[36]*Carter v. Carter Coal Co.*, 298 U.S. 238, 328 (1936).

[37]*Id.* at 327.

[38]Leuchtenburg, *Roosevelt and the New Deal*, p. 145.

[39]Ibid., p. 231.

Headline 2.1

commerce, whereas the states were barred from entry because any such regulations would purportedly deprive employers and employees of their contractual liberty without due process of law.

His plans for economic recovery frustrated by the Court, FDR bided his time throughout 1935 and 1936, waiting for the right political opportunity. His overwhelming victory at the polls in November 1936, following a campaign in which his Republican opponents defended the Supreme Court, gave him confidence that the people were solidly behind him. Also, a series of sit-in strikes throughout the fall and winter of 1936 reaffirmed the popular perception that the federal government had to do something to curb labor unrest and ameliorate the persistent economic problems that plagued the country. Accordingly, on February 5, 1937, FDR announced his plan to give to the presidency the power to appoint to the Supreme Court, up to a limit of six, a new justice for each one over the age of seventy who declined to retire. (See Headline 2.1.) On March 9, he justified his plan by arguing that the Court had been acting "as a policy-making body" and that it must "resume" its "rightful" task of "building anew on the Constitution 'a system of living law.'" (See Box 2.2.) The Court's proper course, the speech clearly implied, was to "build" upon the "evolving" commerce clause by recognizing Congress's power to solve the current problems of the Great Depression.

Of course, Republicans in Congress and conservative groups around the country immediately attacked the "court-packing plan" and defended what the Supreme Court had done during FDR's first term. What is surprising is that some

FDR JUSTIFIES COURT PLAN

... I want to talk with you very simply about the need for present action in this crisis—the need to meet the unanswered challenge of one-third of a Nation ill-nourished, ill-clad, ill-housed.

Last Thursday I described the American form of Government as a three horse team provided by the Constitution to the American people so that their field might be plowed. The three horses are, of course, the three branches of government—the Congress, the Executive and the Courts. Two of the horses are pulling in unison today; the third is not. Those who have intimated that the President of the United States is trying to drive that team, overlook the simple fact that the President, as Chief Executive, is himself one of the three horses. . . .

The Court . . . has improperly set itself up as a third House of the Congress—a super-legislature, as one of the Justices has called it—reading into the Constitution words and implications which are not there, and which were never intended to be there.

We have, therefore, reached the point as a nation where we must take action to save the Constitution from the Court and the Court from itself. We must find a way to take an appeal from the Supreme Court to the Constitution itself. We want a Supreme Court which will do justice under the Constitution—not over it. In our Courts we want a government of laws and not of men. . . .

When I commenced to review the situation with the problem squarely before me, I came by a process of elimination to the conclusion that . . . [the only solution] was to infuse new blood into all our Courts. We . . . must have Judges who will bring to the Courts a present-day sense of the Constitution—Judges who will retain in the Courts the judicial functions of a court, and reject the legislative powers which the Courts have today assumed. . . .

What is my proposal? It is simply this: whenever a Judge or Justice of any Federal Court has reached the age of seventy and does not avail himself of the opportunity to retire on a pension, a new member shall be appointed by the President then in office, with the approval, as required by the Constitution, of the Senate of the United States.

That plan has two chief purposes. By bringing into the Judicial system a steady and continuing stream of new and younger blood, I hope, first, to make the administration of all Federal justice speedier and, therefore, less costly; secondly, to bring to the decision of social and economic problems younger men who have had personal experience and contact with modern facts and circumstances under which average men have to live and work. This plan will save our national Constitution from hardening of the judicial arteries. . . .

> This plan of mine is no attack on the Court; it seeks to restore the Court to its rightful and historic place in our system of Constitutional Government and to have it resume its high task of building anew on the Constitution "a system of living law.". . .
>
> *Source:* Senate Report No. 711, 75th Cong., 1st Sess., pp. 41–44.

liberal Democrats, former political allies of FDR, also condemned the plan as an illegitimate attempt to "pack" the Court. Realizing that there was a greater chance of defeating the proposal if opposition to it was led by members of the president's own party, the Republicans kept a reasonably low profile throughout the 168 days that the Senate considered the plan. It was Democratic Senator Burton Wheeler of Montana who led the forces marshalled against FDR's proposal. In this fight, his most effective tactic was to convince Chief Justice Hughes to take the unusual step of writing a letter that Wheeler read when he testified before the Senate Judiciary Committee. By establishing that the Court was not behind in its business and that a larger Court would create all sorts of problems, the letter demolished FDR's argument that his bill was justified, at least in part, on the grounds of efficiency. All that remained of FDR's rationale for increasing the size of the Court was that FDR's appointees to the Court would adapt the Constitution to the "needs of the times." However, such a tactic and justification violated, in Wheeler's opinion, the independence of the judiciary. (See Box 2.3.)

After Wheeler testified, the Supreme Court, in an ironic twist, provided the Senate with an additional reason for rejecting FDR's bid to expand the Court. By deciding *NLRB v. Jones & Laughlin* in favor of the government's authority to regulate labor relations in the steel industry under the interstate commerce clause, the Court undermined the political rationale of the plan. *Jones* was argued on February 9, just four days after FDR announced his plan, and was decided on April 12, just a few weeks after Wheeler read the chief justice's letter to the Senate Judiciary Committee. The briefs and oral argument that follow will provide a context in which to evaluate to what degree the legal arguments or the surrounding political atmosphere controlled the result in this case.

The National Labor Relations Board, exercising its powers under the NLRA, had brought an action against the Jones & Laughlin Steel Corporation. The NLRB claimed that the steel company was discriminating against those of its employees who engaged in union activity. In its brief to the Supreme Court, the NLRB highlighted the enormous impact that strikes in the steel industry would have upon interstate commerce and relied heavily upon the Shreveport Case and *Stafford v. Wallace*. These precedents supported the view, the NLRB insisted, that the commerce power enabled the federal government not only to "control" whatever burdened interstate commerce, like a large steel strike, but also to "prevent" the burden from even occurring. It was this "preventive" power that allowed Congress to pass legislation protecting the right of employees to form a union. Moreover, the Court had already upheld federal antitrust actions against certain

BOX 2.3

SENATOR BURTON WHEELER CRITICIZES THE PLAN

. . . I thought it was a reflection upon the Court when it was stated that the Court was behind in its work, and when it was very strongly intimated, if not stated in so many words, that such a condition resulted from the age of the members of the Court. . . .

And I have here now a letter by the Chief Justice of the Supreme Court, Mr. Charles Evans Hughes, dated March 21, 1937, written by him and approved by Mr. Justice Brandeis and Mr. Justice Van Devanter. Let us see what these gentlemen say about it. The letter reads as follows:

> My Dear Senator Wheeler:
>
> . . . The Supreme Court is fully abreast of its work. When we rose on March 15 (for the present recess) we had heard arguments in cases in which certiorari had been granted only 4 weeks before February 15.
>
> During the current term, . . . we have heard argument on the merits in 150 cases . . . and we have 28 cases . . . awaiting argument. We shall be able to hear all these cases, and such others as may come up for argument, before our adjournment for the term. There is no congestion of cases upon our calendar. . . .
>
> On account of the shortness of time I have not been able to consult with the members of the Court generally with respect to the foregoing statement, but I am confident that it is in accord with the views of the justices. I should say, however, that I have been able to consult with Mr. Justice Van Devanter and Mr. Justice Brandeis, and I am at liberty to say that the statement is approved by them.
>
> I have the honor to remain,
>
> Respectfully yours,
>
> CHARLES E. HUGHES
> Chief Justice of the United States

. . . [W]e were led to believe that the reason for passing this bill was that the work of the Supreme Court was in arrears. . . .

Now, mind you, I think that the President of the United States in this matter was guided by the highest motives of patriotism. However, I think it is deplorable that he would be misinformed by his Attorney General in respect of matters about which the Attorney General should know perhaps better than most other men, because he has a duty with regard to the Court. . . .

. . . [And] to say that you want to put six new men on the Supreme Court at this time for the purpose of meeting the needs of the time—well, I just want to talk about the needs of the time for a little bit. . . .

. . . What are the needs of the time? What I think are the needs of the time and what you think are the needs of the time might be entirely different. For example, the Harding administration and the Coolidge administration, with a majority in Congress, thought the needs of the time was one thing. Under this administration they think the needs of the time is another thing. Every time we have a change of administration, are we going to increase the Court to do those things which the particular administration then in power thinks are the needs of the time? That is a dangerous precedent, and it will come back to plague this Senate and the Democratic Party, because if we now increase the Supreme Court by six to meet what we think are the needs of the time, another administration may say: "We are against Mr. Roosevelt and the Democrats and what they consider the needs of the time, and we will undo everything they have put on the statute books, and we will place six men on the Supreme Court to insure that is done.". . .

. . . I think if you put six men upon that Court it is going to seriously affect the integrity of the courts of this country. I think at this particular time one of the worst things that can happen in this country is to bring the courts, and particularly the Supreme Court, into disrepute. I feel very strongly about it. . . .

Source: Hearings on S. 1392, Judiciary Committee, U.S. Senate, 75th Cong., 1st Sess., pp. 487–513.

union strikes and boycotts because of their detrimental effects upon interstate commerce. If the federal government's "control" power was this extensive, the NLRB's brief reasoned, then the Court had already implicitly recognized the federal power to "prevent" strikes by encouraging collective bargaining as a means to preserve the health of interstate commerce.

In contrast, Jones & Laughlin Steel Corporation argued that the NLRA was not a regulation of interstate commerce at all, but rather a disguised labor statute. It was, for this reason, completely invalid because the federal government had no constitutional authority to regulate employee–employer relations in the manufacturing sector of the economy. But even if the NLRA were considered on its own terms, the steel company argued, even if it were viewed as a regulation of interstate commerce, *Carter* and *Schechter* were controlling precedents. The federal government could not regulate labor relations within the steel industry because they had only an "indirect" effect upon interstate commerce. After all, all that the company had done was to dismiss 10 employees (3 of whom were union officers) of the 10,000 employed at their Aliquippa plant. How could such an action trigger federal jurisdiction under the interstate commerce clause? Last, the steel company argued, the law violated substantive due process because it was an "unreasonable" infringement upon the liberty of both the employer and the employees to contract as they saw fit in regard to wages and hours.

The oral argument in *Jones* explored the more practical implications of the extended argumentation found in the briefs. Both sides emphasized that the federal government could enjoin unions whose strikes were directly harming interstate commerce. J. Warren Madden, chairman of the National Labor Relations Board, claimed that if the federal government could enjoin such strikes, then it also had to have the power to prevent strikes by preventing employers from discriminating against union employees. In contrast, Earl F. Reed, laywer for the Jones & Laughlin Steel Corporation, insisted that even if the dismissal of ten employees did result in a strike that harmed interstate commerce, that did not mean that the government had the authority to regulate the company. The union, not the company, was responsible for the strike. If the strike hurt interstate commerce, then the proper remedy was to enjoin the union, not regulate the company—an innocent third party.

Which of these arguments is more persuasive? If the legal justification for the NLRA was that it was a proper measure to prevent strikes that harmed interstate commerce, does it matter that the law itself protected the union's right to strike? Did this particular provision of the NLRA show that the law was, as the steel company argued, a labor statute? And what of the steel company's position? Could the company consistently call upon the federal government to enjoin strikes yet deny it the power to prohibit the sort of discrimination against union employees that caused strikes?

Chief Justice Hughes, who had concurred separately in *Carter,* wrote a majority opinion in *Jones* that differed significantly from his earlier views. In *Carter,* he had said that Congress could not use the commerce clause "as a pretext for the exertion of power to regulate activities and relations within the States which affect interstate commerce only indirectly" and that it was *"not for the Court to amend the Constitution by judicial decision* (emphasis added)."[40] A year later, in *Jones,* after a winter of sit-down strikes, after FDR's unprecedented electoral victory, and after the announcement of the "court-packing plan," Hughes wrote that the question of whether the federal government had the power to enact the NLRA was "necessarily one of degree." It seemed that the distinction between "direct" and "indirect" effects upon interstate commerce, which Hughes had once described as "clear in principle" and as "necessary and well-established,"[41] had lost much of its clarity and status. Why did this change take place? Did the legal arguments in *Jones* induce Hughes to change his mind? Or is it possible or likely that the political climate surrounding *Jones* (see Headline 2.2) had convinced Hughes that the Supreme Court had to adapt the Constitution's commerce clause to the "needs of the times"?[42]

Whether or not Hughes's opinion in *Jones* departed from what he had said in *Carter,* there is no doubt that Justice Roberts changed his opinion concerning the limit of the commerce power during the winter and spring of 1936–37. In *Carter,*

---

[40]*Carter v. Carter Coal Co.,* 298 U.S. 238, 317–18 (1936).

[41]*Schechter v. United States,* 295 U.S. 495, 546 (1935).

[42]A few years earlier, Hughes had written the following: "If by the statement that what the Constitution meant at the time of its adoption it means to-day, it is intended to say that the great clauses of the Constitution must be confined to the interpretation which the framers . . . would have placed upon them, the statement carries its own refutation. It was to guard against such a narrow conception that Chief Justice Marshall uttered the memorable warning—'We must never forget that it is *a constitution* we are expounding'—'a constitution intended to endure for ages to come, and, consequently, to be adapted to the various *crises* of human affairs.'" *Home Building & Loan Asso. v. Blaisdell,* 290 U.S. 398, 443 (1934).

Headline 2.2

Roberts had joined Sutherland's majority opinion, an opinion that decisively rejected the idea that Congress could regulate hours and wages in the coal industry, whereas in *Jones* he joined Hughes's opinion, which supported the federal government's authority to prevent steel companies from discriminating against union employees. Moreover, in *Morehead v. New York* (1936), Roberts upheld a substantive due process objection against a New York minimum wage law, but in *West Coast Hotel v. Parrish* (1937) he joined an opinion affirming the power of states to pass such laws.[43] It is true that Roberts voted in *Parrish* on December 19, 1936, a full month and a half before FDR announced his plan, making it impossible for the plan to have had any effect on Robert's conversion in regard to substantive due process. Nonetheless, it is plausible that the political atmosphere may have had something to do with the somewhat inconsistent way in which Roberts was applying the doctrine of substantive due process during 1936–37.[44]

In any case, whatever might be said as to whether Roberts's understanding of substantive due process changed during the New Deal constitutional crisis, there is no question that his conception of the powers held by the federal government

---

[43]*Morehead v. New York ex rel. Tipaldo*, 298 U.S. 587 (1936); *West Coast Hotel Co. v. Parrish*, 300 U.S. 379 (1937). In an effort to explain the consistency of his decisions, Roberts later said that he voted the way he did in *Morehead* because New York never asked the Court to overrule the earlier precedent.

[44]As reported by Roberts himself, when he voted in favor of the Supreme Court's review of the *Parrish* case, one of the conservatives asked, "What is the matter with Roberts?" See Charles A. Leonard, *A Search for a Judicial Philosophy: Mr. Justice Roberts and the Constitutional Revolution of 1937* (Port Washington, N.Y.: Kennikat Press, 1971), p. 123.

under the commerce clause did undergo a marked transition. In *Carter* (1936), Roberts joined the "four horsemen," whereas in *Jones* he allied himself with the liberal justices on the Court. To what extent FDR's "court-packing plan" had an impact upon Roberts's transition is impossible to say. That it had some kind of an effect, however, is most likely. The controversy raged while the Court considered *Jones,* and in regard to the plan, Roberts later said that "Apart from the tremendous strain and threat to the existing Court, of which I was fully conscious, it is obviously, if ever resorted to, a political device to influence the Court and to pack it so as to be in conformity with the views of the Executive, or the Congress, or both."[45] FDR's attempt to intimidate the Court was therefore at least somewhat effective. It put at least one justice under a "tremendous strain and threat." (See Cartoon 2.1.)

But the plan's effectiveness does not necessarily justify it. Should the president be permitted the use of such "a political device" if his purpose is to "influence" or "pack" the Court? Is it so clear that prior to 1937 "the four horsemen" and Roberts were interpreting the commerce clause so "incorrectly" that such a form of political intimidation was justified? What do you think of Justice McReynold's dissent in *Jones?* Does it not show that legal precedents supported the view that the federal government did not have the power to regulate intrastate production? Perhaps the Court had abused its power when it used substantive due process to prevent the states from engaging in such regulation. However, even if the Court had abused its power in this way, is it still not possible that the "four horsemen" had a plausible interpretation of the federal government's constitutional authority to regulate local production?

On the other hand, even if the "four horsemen" had a plausible interpretation of the Constitution, even if the framers never intended the federal government to be able to do what it did in the New Deal, there remains the fundamental question as to whether the justices should have interpreted the Constitution during the New Deal crisis as an unchanging set of rules inherited from the eighteenth century. Should the justices have interpreted the Constitution in this strict fashion, or, as FDR urged, should they gradually have adapted the "living Constitution" in accordance with contemporary needs and political realities?

Years after the constitutional crisis of 1937, Roberts addressed such themes in a series of lectures that he delivered at Harvard Law School. He said that during the New Deal era the Supreme Court had "surrendered" the role that the Constitution had "intended" it to have. The new principle of American constitutionalism that had arisen during the crisis was *Vox populi, vox Dei:* "the voice of the people is the voice of God." This development was probably "inevitable," Roberts now seemed to think, but also somewhat regrettable. (See Box 2.4.) The country had developed "a unified economy," and, by allowing an expansion of the federal government's commerce power, the Court had perhaps avoided "even more radical changes in our dual structure." Nonetheless, because it had adapted the Constitution to the needs of the Great Depression, the Court could no longer pretend to be only an objective mouthpiece of a written constitution ratified by the people. It

---

[45]"Hearing before a Subcommittee of the Committee on The Judiciary on Senate Joint Resolution 44," January 29, 1954, cited in Leonard, *Search for a Judicial Philosophy,* p. 189.

Cartoon 2.1

was more, but at the same time less. Roberts probably regretted this altered role of the Court, even though he did so much to bring it about by voting the way he did in *Jones*. What are we to make of a justice who, in the highly politically charged atmosphere of 1937, abandoned his traditional understanding of the Constitution and the role of the Supreme Court? Should he be criticized for not fulfilling his responsibilities appropriately? Was it a mistake, but an understandable one given the pressures that were placed upon him? Or is he to be applauded for having finally realized, no matter how reluctantly, the true nature of the U.S. Constitution and the true character of the Supreme Court? In the context of FDR's "court-packing plan," *NLRB v. Jones & Laughlin* focuses attention on these basic questions of American constitutionalism.

BOX 2.4

JUSTICE ROBERTS REFLECTS ON THE NEW DEAL

The continual expansion of federal power with consequent contraction of state powers probably has been inevitable. The founders of the Republic envisaged no such economic and other expansion as the nation has experienced. Looking back, it is difficult to see how the Court could have resisted the popular urge for uniform standards throughout the country—for what in effect was a unified economy. It may be that in a sense the resort of Congress to the taxing power, to the general welfare power, and to the commerce power as means to reach a result never contemplated when the Constitution was adopted, was a subterfuge. An insistence by the Court on holding federal power to what seemed its appropriate orbit when the Constitution was adopted might have resulted in even more radical changes in our dual structure than those which have been gradually accomplished through the extension of the limited jurisdiction conferred on the federal government. . . .

. . . [I]n the light of the pressures, wise or not, for uniform regulation in various fields, the Congress has felt constrained to stretch its granted powers to the utmost and to treat as corollaries of those powers manifestations of police power which tend to reduce the states to administrative districts rather than coordinate sovereigns; and, in the main, the Supreme Court has felt constrained to give full faith and credit to the legislature's declared purpose to exercise, not to transcend, the powers granted it.

❖　　　❖　　　❖

. . . In summary, I think it fair to say that, progressively, the Supreme Court has limited and surrendered the role the Constitution was intended to confer on it. *Vox populi, vox Dei* was not the theory on which the charter was drawn. The sharp division of powers intended has become blurred. Perhaps this was inevitable. Perhaps it is a beneficial development. However that may be, it seems obvious that doctrines announced as corollaries to express grants of power to the Congress have more and more circumscribed the pristine powers of the states, which were intended to be reserved to them by the Constitution, and that resistance to the expansion of those doctrines seems to have weakened as our nation has grown.

Source: Owen J. Roberts, *The Court and the Constitution* (Cambridge, Mass.: Harvard University Press, 1951), pp. 61–63, 95. Reprinted by permission of Harvard University Press.

Bibliography

Aesop, Joseph, and Turner Catledge. *The 168 Days.* New York: Doubleday, Doran & Co., 1938.

Baker, Leonard. *Back to Back: The Duel between FDR and the Supreme Court.* New York: Macmillan, 1967.

Cortner, Richard C. *The Jones & Laughlin Case.* New York: Knopf, 1970.

Epstein, Richard. "The Proper Scope of the Commerce Power," *Virginia Law Review* 73 (1987), pp. 1387–455.

Jackson, Robert. *The Struggle for Judicial Supremacy.* New York: Vintage, 1941.

Leonard, Charles A. *A Search for a Judicial Philosophy: Mr. Justice Roberts and the Constitutional Revolution of 1937.* Port Washington, N.Y.: Kennikat Press, 1971.

Leuchtenburg, William E. "The Origins of Franklin D. Roosevelt's 'Court-Packing' Plan" in *The Supreme Court Review 1966.* Chicago: University of Chicago Press, 1966.

Mason, Alpheus T. *Harlan Fiske Stone: Pillar of the Law.* New York: Viking Press, 1956, Parts IV and V.

BRIEFS

NLRB's Brief

The National Labor Relations Act constitutes an exercise of the power of Congress to protect inter-state commerce from the burden and injury caused by industrial strife. . . .

[1. Effects of past strikes.] The paralyzing effect on interstate commerce of industrial disputes in enterprises similar to that of respondent is a matter of common knowledge. A strike or lockout ordinarily means the complete cessation of business. No materials flow in; no finished products flow out. Effects are immediately felt in other enterprises dependent upon the plant where the dispute occurs for their materials or semi-finished parts. Markets are disrupted; no business commitments can be made. . . .

Industrial strife is of almost daily occurrence. . . . In no year [from 1916 to 1936] has the number of disputes fallen below 650—about two every day—and in some years the number has risen to over 3,500—ten every day. . . .

. . . [D]uring certain periods industrial strife becomes particularly acute. Thus in the four years from 1919 to 1922 there occurred more than 10,000 labor disputes involving more than 8,000,000 employees. Among those which seriously burdened interstate commerce may be noted the strikes of harbor workers in 1919; the strike of 250,000 railway trainmen in August 1919; the general steel strike of 1919 to 1920; the strike of longshoremen in New York in October 1919; the strike of 450,000 bituminous coal miners in November 1919; the marine workers' strike in May 1921; the general strike in the ladies' garment industry in November 1921; the strike of meat packing employees in December 1921; the New

England textile strike which began in January 1922; the widespread strikes in the bituminous and anthracite coal industries in April 1922; the strike in the men's garment industry in New York in June 1922; and the general strike of the railway shopmen beginning in July 1922.

A similar series of major industrial conflicts with equally burdensome effects on interstate commerce occurred in the years 1933 to 1935. Among the strikes of this period which seriously burdened commerce may be noted the maritime workers' strike on the Pacific Coast which began in May 1934 and led to the general strike in San Francisco; the Minneapolis teamsters' strike in May 1934; the national textile strike in September 1934; the strike of enamel workers in Terre Haute, Indiana, in March 1935, which led to a general strike in that city; the strike in the Chevrolet Motor Company at Toledo, Ohio, in April 1935; the Pacific Coast lumber strike in May 1935; and the strike of shipbuilding workers in Camden, New Jersey, in May and August 1935. In addition, major disputes threatening to tie up the steel, automobile, and lumber industries during 1934 and 1935 were prevented only by Federal intervention. . . .

[2. Two types of commerce power.] Federal legislation designed to eliminate or reduce burdens or obstructions to interstate commerce may take either of two forms. First, Congress might enact a statute designed to mitigate the burdens by dealing directly with each particular obstruction as it arose. The Sherman Anti-Trust Act may be referred to as illustrative of this particular type of legislation. Or, second, Congress might have approached the problem by a statute dealing with the *causes* of this burden in anticipation of their probable effect. A statute of the first type will be referred to hereafter as an exercise by Congress of its *"control"* power and a statute of the second type will be referred to hereafter as an exercise by Congress of its *"preventive"* power. Both types of legislation are, of course, merely different means by which Congress may approach the problem of burdens on interstate commerce.

This power of Congress to enact preventive legislation is illustrated by the historical setting of the Packers and Stockyards Act. Many practices prevalent in the stockyards, and in the meat-packing industry in general, had been seriously burdening interstate commerce in both livestock and meat products. In *Swift and Co. v. United States,* some of these practices were effectively punished under the Sherman Act. Congress, not content with action against particular individuals or combinations, then passed the Packers and Stockyards Act, designed to eliminate the causes of the burdens to interstate commerce. This Court, upholding the Act in *Stafford v. Wallace,* stated:

> The language of the law shows that what Congress had in mind primarily was to prevent such conspiracies by supervision of the agencies which would be likely to be employed in it. If Congress could provide for punishment or restraint of such conspiracies after their formation through the Anti-Trust Law as in the *Swift Case,* certainly it may provide regulation to prevent their formation. . . .

The National Labor Relations Act is an example of this preventive legislation, based on the admitted power of Congress to control certain types of industrial disputes when they have occurred. The Act does not deal with injuries to interstate commerce after they have occurred, but seeks to prevent their occurrence by the elimination of certain specified practices which Congress has found lead to such disputes.

Although Congress thus clearly has a power to prevent obstructions to commerce, it is equally clear that the preventive measures must bear a reasonable relation to the end sought to be achieved. The exercise of the preventive power must, in other words, bear a reasonable relation to the elimination of evils which could be subjected to the control power of Congress after they occurred. Congress cannot make the existence of an evil of national concern the excuse for regulating a large measure of affairs of purely local concern.

Nor has it done so in this Act. The Act does not attempt to eliminate causes of strikes in *all* enterprises. The statute, and the mandate addressed to the administrative Board, are specifically directed to the elimination of the practices proscribed by Section 8 only when they are found to be "affecting commerce." This phrase "affecting commerce" is defined in Section 2(7) of the statute as "in commerce, or burdening or obstructing commerce or the free flow of commerce, or having led or tending to lead to a labor dispute burdening or obstructing commerce or the free flow of commerce.". . . In other words, Congress has taken as the ambit of this particular preventive statute the boundaries to which it would be restricted were it exercising to the full its control power. It has not endeavored to exercise its preventive power where it could not have exercised its control power under appropriate legislation. . . .

One further characteristic of preventive legislation should be noted. In eliminating certain practices in situations in which the resulting industrial strife would be likely to come within the control power of Congress, the application of the Act will upon occasion result in the prohibition of activity which, even if allowed to spend its force, would not result in industrial strife which did in fact come within the Federal control power. But, provided that when the practice was indulged in there was a reasonable likelihood that any industrial strife which resulted would be within the control power under appropriate legislation, the Board may apply the preventive measure. To hold otherwise would deprive Congress of any preventive power, since no one can foretell with absolute accuracy what the exact effects of any cause will be. This lack of predictability is particularly true of industrial strife. . . .

The foregoing discussion makes it clear that the question of the validity of a specific application of the present Act depends upon whether industrial strife in the particular enterprise under consideration could, if it occurred, be controlled by the Federal Government, under appropriate legislation. The question of primary importance, therefore, is the extent of the Federal power of control. Since the language of this statute does not go beyond the ambit of this power, whatever it may be determined to be, the statute is clearly constitutional on its face. The only issue is whether it has been constitutionally applied.

[3. Limits of the control power.] This Court has never had occasion to define the full extent to which industrial strife in the manufacturing, producing, or processing divisions of an enterprise engaged extensively in interstate commerce may be subjected to the exercise of the control power of Congress. It has, however, held that certain situations are clearly within the control power, and has further laid down certain general principles on the basis of which it is possible to state three situations in which Congress may exercise its power to control burdens and obstructions on interstate commerce. We shall first briefly state these three situations, and shall then consider each one in detail with particular reference to its application to respondent.

1. It is well settled that an industrial dispute involving an intent to affect interstate commerce is within the control power of Congress.
2. This Court has also recognized that an industrial dispute having the necessary effect of substantially burdening or obstructing commerce is within the control power of Congress.
3. This Court has also recognized that the control power of Congress extends to recurring evils which in their totality may constitute a substantial burden on interstate commerce. . . .

[(1)] It is well settled that an industrial dispute involving an intent to restrain commerce is within the control power of Congress, even though arising out of local activity. Consequently, where the situation in a particular enterprise presents a reasonable likelihood that a dispute, if it occurred, would involve an intent to restrain commerce, then the Board can apply the statute to that enterprise.

The reasonable likelihood of a dispute with the intent to affect commerce might be demonstrated in either of two ways: first, evidence might be presented to the Board that in a particular situation the intent already exists; or second, evidence might be presented to the Board that the situation was comparable to and of the same general type as those situations from which in the past there had evolved controversies with intent to affect commerce, or that in the particular situation confronting the Board such definite intention might reasonably be expected to develop should the strife occur. In the case at bar it is not claimed that there is evidence of the first sort; but there is abundant evidence that the situation is fraught with the risk that after strife developed it would involve the purpose to curtail the movement of goods in commerce. . . .

[After all,] . . . respondent conducts a highly integrated national enterprise operating in some States mines and quarries which are the source of its materials, in other States steel mills and other manufacturing plants, and in still other States wholesale outlets for the distribution of its products. Moreover, it owns and operates certain transportation facilities operating in interstate commerce. In a far-flung, integrated enterprise of this type, controlled by a single employer, industrial strife in any division of the enterprise is peculiarly apt to involve a purpose to promote collective action among employees in other divisions of the enterprise in order to increase the bargaining power of all of the employees as against the common employer. . . .

Thus the evidence in this case warrants the conclusion that there is a reasonable likelihood that industrial strife in respondent's enterprise would if it occurred, involve an intent to affect commerce. This conclusion is particularly justified in all situations where, as here, there is a probability of strife with respect to employees' basic rights to organize and choose representatives for collective bargaining. Such controversies are notoriously bitter and prolonged because of the fundamental issues at stake, tend to involve sympathetic action by organized employees in the same or related industries, and consequently are most likely to result in intentional interferences with sales or shipments in interstates commerce. . . .

[(2)] This Court has recognized that Congress may exercise control over some industrial disputes even where intent cannot be or is not proven. For example, in *United Mine Workers v. Coronado Coal Co.*, a case which arose under the Sherman Act, this Court stated:

> . . . coal mining is not interstate commerce and obstruction of coal mining, though it may prevent coal from going into interstate commerce, is not a restraint of that commerce unless the obstruction to mining is intended to restrain commerce in it *or has necessarily such a direct, material, and substantial effect to restrain it that the intent reasonably must be inferred.*

This language was expressly approved in *Industrial Association v. United States.* The Court there pointed out that the strike in the first *Coronado* case was held not to constitute a conspiracy to restrain interstate commerce "in the absence of proof of an intention to restrain it *or proof of such a direct and substantial effect upon it, that such intention reasonably must be inferred.*". . .

It may be argued that in these cases the Court in referring to such direct and substantial effects upon commerce stated that an *intent* must be inferred. But, this is equivalent to saying that that Act may constitutionally be applied to a situation in which there is no actual specific intent, but only a "necessary effect" on commerce. And it must follow that the power of Congress extends at least as far as the Sherman Act has been enforced—that is, to industrial strife which has only a "necessary effect" on interstate commerce. . . .

. . . [T]hree possible constructions of "necessary effect" may be suggested: (1) industrial strife has the necessary effect of burdening or obstructing interstate commerce when it occurs in an enterprise lying within a well-defined "stream or flow of commerce"; (2) industrial strife is of that type when its effect would be to prevent a substantial proportion of all the commerce in the particular commodity; or (3) industrial strife is of that type when its effect would be to prevent interstate sales or shipments of a substantial volume of goods which would otherwise move in interstate commerce.

We believe that for the purposes of the present case a discussion of the construction of "necessary effect" may be confined to construction (1) [which requires a "stream of commerce]. . . .

Respondent is the fourth largest company in the steel industry. The consolidated assets of respondent and its 19 subsidiaries totaled $181,532,641 as of December 31, 1934. It is "completely integrated," and is engaged directly in the transportation, production, acquisition, sale, and distribution of materials and products. One of its two main plants is located at Aliquippa, Pennsylvania, where normally about 10,000 of respondent's more than 20,000 employees are employed. . . .

It is evident that respondent's transportation facilities and activities are essential to and part of respondent's completely integrated business. Respondent, for the production of steel, is dependent upon three basic materials, iron ore, coke, and limestone, and it maintains its own reserves, mines and quarries at various points in the United States from which it obtains these basic materials. . . .

Some idea of the huge bulk of the raw materials which flow into the Aliquippa works may be gained from the fact that in a representative month, October 1935, the plant received 6,222 full carloads and 237 less than carload lots of materials, 76.5 percent of which originated outside of the State. This average of more than 200 inbound cars per day by railroad is exclusive of the heavy river traffic in coal. Most of these incoming products are used directly without storage. About 97 percent of all the business of the Pittsburgh and Lake Erie Railroad at Aliquippa is dependent upon the continued operation of respondent's plant.

This great bulk of material which flows regularly in interstate commerce to Aliquippa with the aid of respondent's transportation facilities is unloaded by respondent's own employees and equipment, continues its course through respondent's works over respondent's trackage and equipment, and finally moves on to respondent's customers throughout the world with the aid of respondent's transportation facilities, from one or another of respondent's departments in the form of steel in various stages of fabrication. Respondent's product is sold in both semi-finished and finished forms. Each of respondent's departments has its own shipping department to handle materials which are forwarded to customers from that department. Employees are engaged in these various shipping departments to see that orders of customers are carried out and to handle goods which are being placed on cars or barges ready for shipment. Respondent produces steel largely in accordance with orders or specification of customers. . . .

The operations at the Aliquippa works are "a continuous process." They are based largely upon the use of molten pig, "So that when pig iron is made, it has to be processed as quickly as possible." One operation furnishes the material for the next, and at each step it is necessary to move heavy bulky materials with a minimum waste of time. . . .

According to the respondent its "products are sold to its customers throughout the United States and many foreign countries, principally through its own sales offices located in twenty of the larger cities of the country. . . .

From this record it is evident that the Jones and Laughlin Steel Corporation is a nationwide enterprise. It regularly draws its materials in well defined paths of commerce from its properties in various States to its works at Aliquippa. . . . A considerable proportion of respondent's employees are directly engaged in this work of transporting materials to the plant, moving materials within the works, preparing shipments and loading them according to customer specifications, and finally in warehousing and transporting products to customers in respondent's equipment. The extensive ownership by the respondent of the means of transporting this flow of goods to and from its Aliquippa plant is itself conclusive evidence of a regular and definite stream of commerce. . . .

We submit that in the light of these facts, industrial strife in respondent's Aliquippa plant would have the necessary effect of burdening and obstructing interstate commerce even if the limits of the "necessary effect" principle be narrowed as suggested in the first definition suggested above, i.e., industrial strife which occurs in a well-defined stream or flow of commerce. And surely this very limited definition of "necessary effect of burdening or obstructing interstate commerce" is not too broad. . . .

It may be objected, however, that respondent's enterprise cannot be in a "stream or flow of commerce" because respondent engages in manufacturing, the raw materials being held within the plant for a time and then sent out in the form of pig iron or steel. The objection is in direct conflict with the decision of the Court in *Stafford v. Wallace.* . . .

[In this case,] The Court . . . recognized that stoppage for purposes of processing in the packing plant, involving a definite interruption in the physical movement and a very distinct transformation in the nature of the commodity, did not cause a break in the "stream" or "current" of commerce in the constitutional sense.

Moreover, operations in the meat packing plants are as essentially manufacturing as are the operations at Aliquippa. It is common knowledge that meat packing involves a very extensive transformation in the nature of the commodity. . . . Indeed, due to the seasonal character of the supply of raw materials and the stable demand for meat products, with a consequent necessity for much storage, and to the necessary slowness of many of the operations in the meat-packing industry, such as chilling, curing and smoking, the delays or stoppages of the flow of products in that industry are frequently much longer than those in the operations of respondent. . . .

[(3)] This Court has on many occasions enunciated the principle that where Congress, after investigation, directs its legislation to the prevention of certain activities, even though usually only of local concern, which recur with such frequency as to constitute an undue burden on commerce, those activities may be subjected to the control power of Congress.

This principle is most forcibly illustrated by the historical setting of the Packers and Stockyards Act. . . .

. . . That Act regulates the rates of commissions of market agencies and various unfair discriminatory or deceptive practices of such agencies and packers "in commerce." *Stafford v. Wallace* presented the question of the application of the Act, not to the packers, but to the commission men and dealers in the stockyards. . . .

[T]hese dealers and commission men urged that their activities affected interstate commerce only "indirectly," that the Act sought to obliterate the line between the powers of the States and those of Congress, and that if it were sustained, there would be no limit to the scope of the power of Congress under the commerce clause. In rejecting these arguments, the Court pointed out that Congress had found, on the basis of long experience and investigation, that the local acts of commission men and dealers "constitute a direct and undue burden" on interstate commerce which worked an "injurious direct effect." In conclusion the Court said:

> The reasonable fear by Congress that such acts, usually lawful and affecting only
> intra-state commerce when considered alone, will probably and more or less con-
> stantly be used in conspiracies against interstate commerce or constitute a direct

and undue burden on it, expressed in this remedial legislation, serves the same purpose as the intent charged in the Swift indictment to bring acts of similar character into the current of interstate commerce for federal restraint. Whatever amounts to more or less constant practice, and threatens to obstruct or unduly to burden the freedom of interstate commerce is within the regulatory power of Congress under the commerce clause, and it is primarily for Congress to consider and decide the fact of the danger and meet it. . . .

The *Stafford* . . . [case] show[s], therefore, that Congress may legislate with respect to burdens or obstructions to commerce, even where the burdens develop out of local practices, where those practices and burdens are reasonably found constantly to recur. . . .

[Moreover, the] . . . Court has recognized . . . that the finding of Congress of the recurrent nature of the abuses serves the same purpose as the intent charged in the indictments under the Sherman Act. . . .

The Relationship of industrial strife to interstate commerce is even more clearly illustrated by *Texas and New Orleans R. Co. v. Brotherhood of Railway Clerks.* The decision in that case stands clearly for the proposition that at least as far as the railway industry is concerned, the burden upon interstate commerce arising out of industrial strife is sufficiently direct to constitute a valid basis for the exercise of the power of Congress to deal with recurring practices which affect that commerce. We believe that in that respect no distinction can be drawn between railroads or other agencies of interstate transportation and communication and large interstate enterprises such as that of the respondent in the present case.

In the first place, it is obvious that the validity of the Railway Labor Act does not depend on the fact that the employees with whom it is concerned are engaged in interstate commerce. Actually, many of the employees associated in the Brotherhood of Railway Clerks were engaged in purely local activities. That Act is valid because it prevents practices which are likely to and have been considered by Congress to obstruct interstate commerce. It is wholly immaterial whether these burdens find their source in intrastate or interstate activity. Congress clearly may deal with obstructive practices even though they are purely local in origin.

The *Texas* case can be distinguished, then, only upon a showing that industrial strife on the agencies of transportation can reasonably be expected to be more injurious to interstate commerce than industrial strife in an interstate enterprise. We believe that no such showing can be made. A simple illustration will make the point clear. The Pittsburgh and Lake Erie Railroad derives 97 percent of its shipments to and from Aliquippa from respondent. An industrial dispute on that railroad could be dealt with under the commerce power not merely because the employees involved would be employed by an interstate carrier, but because such a dispute would obstruct the shipment of materials and products received and shipped by respondent. Obviously, however, an industrial dispute at respondent's Aliquippa plant would also obstruct the receipt and shipment of respondent's materials and products not only over the Pittsburgh and Lake Erie, but also over every other railroad and every other type of carrier which transports articles to and from respondent's plant. Indeed, it is true that a strike of the employees on the Pittsburgh and Lake Erie might result in only a very slight obstruction to interstate commerce if respondent could arrange to receive its materials and to ship its product by water, motor lines, or other carriers, while a strike among the employees of Jones and Laughlin at Aliquippa would completely stop all interstate commerce into and out of that plant. . . .

[4. *Schechter* and *Carter.*] The distinction between this case and the *Schechter* and *Carter* cases goes to a fundamental distinction in the scope and purpose of the respective statutes involved. The statutes in those two cases regulated basic manufacturing or producing factors—wages and hours—in order to stabilize labor costs throughout a particular industry, or industry generally. Legal justification adduced in support of the regulations was based upon the intricate economic effects of disparate labor costs upon the prices and movement of the product in interstate commerce.

In the *Schechter* case the Government attempted to sustain the validity of the regulation of wages and hours in the business of slaughtering poultry, by showing that wages and hours bore a relation to interstate commerce through a chain of economic causes and effects—the effect upon the price of chickens sold in local commerce which in turn affected the shipment of chickens into New York and other States. . . .

The Bituminous Coal Conservation Act involved in the *Carter* cases was enacted for the purpose of "stabilizing" the bituminous coal mining industry through a regulation of prices and wages by means of a coercive tax. All producers of coal in the United States were to be brought into a Code. This Code set up machinery for the fixing of minimum and maximum prices and the machinery for the determination of minimum wages and maximum hours of employment. . . .

It may be contended, however, that the *Carter* case is directly determinative of the present case because the Act there involved contained a provision for collective bargaining which was among the labor provisions held unconstitutional. However, it is apparent that the [*Carter*] scheme outlined above for the determination of wages and hours by means of collective agreements could not operate without some statutory protection for the right of collective bargaining of the mine workers. Thus the collective bargaining provisions, instead of being directly related to avoiding labor disputes interfering with interstate commerce, were subordinated to the main purpose of stabilization of the industry and were in fact the means through which one of the stabilizing factors—the establishment of uniform wages and hours—was to be effected. . . .

Finally, it should be noted that the National Labor Relations Act as here applied is concerned with activities which occur under circumstances closely related to a flow of commerce, and which directly affect that flow. In the *Schechter* case the flow of goods had ceased; in the *Carter* case the flow had not yet begun. In both cases the Court was careful to restrict its decision to that state of facts, and to distinguish the facts of cases such as *Stafford v. Wallace* and the case at bar. . . .

The argument advanced herein does not carry the implication that the Federal power extends to the fixing of wages on the ground that differences between employers and employees over wages cause industrial strife. Wage regulation might well be thought not reasonably calculated to eliminate the causes of industrial strife, and hence not to bear a reasonable relation to the protection of commerce. Wage fixing would merely transfer the power to determine wages from the private parties to the Government, and differences would still exist over the wages which should be paid in excess of the fixed minimum. True, the number of conflicts might be somewhat reduced, but it seems clear that they would still be numerous. On the other hand protection of the right of employee organization and collective bargaining has been proved by experience to be calculated to eliminate one of the most serious causes of industrial strife. In the railroad industry, for example, the enactment of parallel legislation has virtually eliminated industrial strife. Moreover, this Court has held in the *Texas and New Orleans* case that such legislation is reasonably related to the protection of commerce and does not go beyond what is necessary for that purpose. This statute eliminates entirely the heavy burden on interstate commerce due to industrial strife traceable to the opposition of employer to the recognized right of employees to organize and bargain collectively through representatives of their own choosing. The recognition and protection of that right provide the open door to the reasonable and just settlement of differences with respect to grievances, wages, and other conditions of work, thereby also greatly reducing or mitigating industrial strife over the substantive terms of the employment contract. . . .

Respectfully submitted,

HOMER CUMMINGS,
Attorney General.

JONES & LAUGHLIN STEEL COMPANY'S BRIEF

It is the respondent's position that the National Labor Relations Act is, in reality, a labor statute, and not a true regulation of interstate commerce, from which it should follow that the Act is invalid *in toto.* The petitioner contends, however, that the statute may be saved from the taint of invalidity by attributing to Congress the intent to confine its application to situations which Congress may lawfully regulate under the interstate commerce clause of the Federal Constitution. The respondent's argument will therefore be directed to both issues, maintaining with respect to the first that the Act is unconstitutional *in toto,* and, with respect to the second, that it cannot be lawfully applied to the respondent. . . .

[1. Federalism.] The problem of measuring the constitutional validity of the National Labor Relations Act, in its application to the industrial relations of the respondent, is greatly simplified if the inquiry begins with the Constitution itself and pays true heed to the literal requirements of the document. Much of the dust of controversy which obscures the question of determining the validity of the labor act and similar legislation has been stirred up by arguments and discussions which have lost the true meaning of the constitutional phrase in an effort to remodel our political system on a basis of expediency, by attributing to the central government powers which might be most conveniently exercised from Washington. And as a consequence, the plenary powers of the States, like the Charter on which they rest, are cast aside in an endeavor to reach a theoretically convenient goal. . . .

Arguments of this character, which advocates of a centralized government habitually employ, may have somewhat blurred the line which lies between the reserved powers of the states and the jurisdiction of the Federal government. More than that, they have a spurious persuasiveness, in that they are apt to distract attention from the fundamental phrase of the Constitution to the political issue of national versus local supremacy. So with the petitioner's brief. Deftly it paints the evils of strikes and lockouts and plausibly it argues that Congress *should* be the agency to deal with them, but the conclusive answer is that the Constitution has vested in another sovereignty the power to regulate local employment relations. . . .

The draftsmen of the Constitution foresaw that if economic and political intercourse between the States was to be fostered, and the welfare of the nation protected, it would be necessary to curb the selfish interests of the individual States where they might easily conflict with the interests of the federation as a whole. Therefore, jurisdiction over interstate commerce—a fertile field for controversy among individual States—was granted to the Federal Government. Its jurisdiction involves the power to regulate, restrict and protect interstate commerce, *but it does not include, and was not designed to include, the right to use such jurisdiction as a pretext to interfere with the local sovereignty of the States.* If this one premise is carefully borne in mind, the apparent confusion which sometimes arises as to the limitations on the powers of each of the concurrent governments and which pervades the petitioners' argument is to a large extent removed. . . .

. . . The argument is often made, as in the petitioner's brief, that the nation has come to a new conception of commerce, that business has outgrown the State and has become a matter of national concern, and that our purely internal political, economical and social life is so intimately connected with our national commerce that it has been swallowed up in the latter's importance. On this hypothesis, it is not difficult to argue that the wages of a newsboy, the prices of a grocer and the advertising policies of a local dentist in some degree affect incomes and business. The impact may be slight, but in the end, it may be contended, it either encourages or discourages commerce among the States. . . .

[2. Purpose of the NLRA.] If the principle which we have stressed . . . be accepted, then some pains must be taken to ascertain the true intent and purpose of the National Labor Relations Act. We submit that the legislative history of the statute and its own literal provisions are sufficient to demonstrate conclusively that the Act, although disguised as a regulation of interstate commerce, is in actuality a regulation of labor relationships, a conclusion which the petitioner's brief unwittingly confirms. . . .

The petitioner's brief leans heavily upon the history of Federal regulation of railway labor as an argument for its extension into other fields, but the point proves too much. For one thing, it draws into sharp contrast the inactivity of Congress, until recent times, in other fields of employment relations. What is perhaps more important, it betrays the petitioner's argument as being, in truth, an attack on our Constitutional system rather than a justification of the application of the Labor Act to the present case. If the power of Congress over railroads means that it may sweep all labor relations into its grasp, there is no reason why it should not

be able to subject every business activity to the same exhaustive scheme of regulation which it has imposed upon interstate carriers. Statutory limitations on wages
and hours, compensation laws, safety and fire regulations, and legislative supervision of factory conditions—all would be within the scope of Federal control and
there would be an end to the sovereignty of the separate States. . . .

But what is there in the Act to justify it as a regulation of interstate commerce. Its obvious aim is to organize labor on a national scale. Employers are directed to bargain with national labor unions and to recognize them in given instances as the sole representatives of their employees. The operation of plant
unions is seriously impeded even though they may be, in the long run, far more
conducive to industrial peace and prosperity than national labor organizations.
Strangely enough, while the employer is not permitted to refuse employment to
union members, no matter what he may think of the union's responsibility, he
may, by a contract with an organization, refuse to employ men who are not affiliated with that organization. *Are these regulations of commerce?* If Congress is so
interested in the continuity of interstate commerce, why should it permit an employer to take such a position? Again, the right to strike is expressly conserved by
the Act, and the utmost freedom allowed organizations and employees to violate
their contracts through the use of a strike. *Does this display a Congressional regard for the movement of interstate commerce?* The very function of the Board in
this case is to sit in judgement on the employer's discretion to hire and fire as he
sees fit. Does this show any concern with the plant's efficiency or its ability to
maintain a steady stream of finished products? No one but the blind can be de-
ceived by the attempt to link the statute with the interstate commerce clause. . . .

. . . The possibility of a strike which might cripple the respondent's operations
is urged as a complete justification for the application of the will of Congress, but
no explanation is given of the express legislative sanction of the right to strike or of
the petitioner's avowed policy of encouraging unionization. Yet, which is the more
likely to lead to a break in the continuity of interstate movement—the discharge
of ten employees, which this Act purports to treat as an offense against the
majesty of the Federal government, or a strike which it sanctions?

*On the face of it, it would seem inconceivable that any such legislation would
be the business of the federal government. . . .*

[3. Effect on interstate commerce.] The National Labor Relations Board, in
connection with the instant case, has used the congressional syllogism in "finding"
that the respondent's transactions with its employees "affect" interstate commerce. As we have pointed out, its procedure in reaching this conclusion has been
utterly arbitrary and capricious. The size of the respondent's plant, where the
transactions occurred, its activities elsewhere, and the activities of affiliated corpo-
rations have been probed and the conclusion reached that the respondent's business is an enterprise of some magnitude. The labor history of steel industry, generally, and of other industries, beginning with the turn of the Century, has been
examined and the conclusion reached that strikes and labor disputes are bad for
business. Like Congress, the Board has found itself faced with the task of piling
premise upon premise and hypothesis upon hypothesis to reach the conclusion
that the discharge of a few production employees at the respondent's Aliquippa
Plant has a vital bearing upon the movement of interstate commerce. We submit

that this tortuous line of reasoning does not and cannot save the constitutionality of the Act. *The ultimate fact remains that Congress has enacted a labor law and not a regulation of commerce,* and it does not help to sustain the pretext that there may be an indirect connection between the two. . . .

In the last analysis, the argument of the petitioner impliedly admits the remoteness of the connection between the discharge of ten employees and the movement of interstate commerce, but seeks to justify the application of the statute because of the size and importance of the respondent's operations. So far as the effect on interstate commerce is concerned, there is, in reality, no difference between the respondent's Aliquippa Plant and a neighborhood grocery store; the cause and effect may be larger, but the causal connection is just as remote. In the words of the opinion in *Carter v. Carter Coal Company,*

> the distinction between the direct and indirect effect turns, not upon the magnitude of either the cause or the effect, but entirely upon the manner in which the effect has been brought about.

The very phrase "affecting commerce" contains within itself an admission of indirectness, that here is something which is not in or a part of commerce, but which Congress would, for reasons of expediency, like to regulate. . . .

It is admitted that raw materials are brought from several States to the respondent's plant at Aliquippa. We are equally ready to concede that a large percentage of its manufactured products has found its way to States other than the State of Pennsylvania. But we cannot yield to the proposition that these factors suffice to subject the production activities of the respondent to the regulation of Congress. . . .

. . . [T]he relationship between the employer and his employees is purely a local matter. Although an employee may be employed in indirectly assisting the movement of interstate commerce, his relationship to his employer is not part of commerce. It is a status existing wholly within the State, whose incidents, such as wages, hours of labor and the like are purely domestic in character. It may be true that congressional regulation of the local incidents of employment in cases involving interstate carriers has been sustained, where the Court has found the true object of Congress to be the protection of interstate commerce. But there is no precedent for interference where the real purpose of the regulation is deliberately to interfere in matters which are not the concern of the Federal Government. . . .

[4. The *Carter* case.] The labor provisions of the Bituminous Coal Conservation Act were almost identical with the provisions of the National Labor Relations Act. It, too, was prefaced with a legislative declaration of policy that the right of mine workers to organize and bargain collectively for wages, hours of labor and conditions of employment should be guaranteed in order to prevent constant wage cutting and disparage labor costs detrimental to fair interstate competition and in order to avoid obstructions to interstate commerce that occur in industrial disputes over labor relations at the mine. The Bituminous Coal Conservation Act likewise provided for the creation of a Labor Board to administer the labor provisions of the Code which was imposed by the statute on the producers of coal. . . .

The majority opinion in *Carter v. [Carter] Coal Company* gave careful consideration to these labor provisions and found the conclusion inescapable that labor relations are not in or a part of interstate commerce and therefore cannot be subject to regulation by Congress. In this connection, it was said:

> One who produces or manufactures a commodity, subsequently sold and shipped by him in interstate commerce, whether such sale and shipment were originally intended or not, has engaged in two distinct and separate activities. So far as he produces or manufactures a commodity, his business is purely local. So far as he sells and ships, or contracts to sell and ship, the commodity to customers in another state, he engages in interstate commerce. In respect of the former, he is subject only to regulation by the state; in respect of the latter, to regulation by the federal government. Production is not commerce; but a step in preparation for commerce.
>
> We have seen that the word "commerce" is the equivalent of the phrase "intercourse for the purpose of trade." Plainly, the incidents leading up to and culminating in the mining of coal do not constitute such intercourse. *The employment of men, the fixing of their wages, hours of labor and working conditions, the bargaining in respect of these things—whether carried on separately or collectively—each and all constitute intercourse for the purpose of production, not of trade.* The latter is a thing apart from the relation of employer and employee, which in all producing occupations is purely local in character. Extraction of coal from the mine is the aim and the completed result of local activities. Commerce in the coal mined is not brought into being by force of these activities, but by negotiations, agreements, and circumstances entirely apart from production. Mining brings the subject matter of commerce into existence. Commerce disposes of it. . . .

It could be said in support of the Coal Conservation Act it did seek to regulate other things as well as labor relations and that its labor provisions were merely designed to aid its price-fixing requirements, which, standing alone, might have been valid. The National Labor Relations Act has not even this virtue; it is purely a statutory plan for regulating labor relations. *In the light of the Carter case, can there be any doubt of its invalidity?*

The case of *Texas and New Orleans Railroad Co. v. Brotherhood of Railway and Steamship Clerks* furnishes no precedent for the National Labor Relations Act. This case arose under the Railroad Labor Act of 1926, which set up machinery for the voluntary adjustment and arbitration of labor disputes before boards of adjustment and boards of arbitration. . . .

We submit that the distinction between the present case and that involved in the Texas & New Orleans Railroad Company case is implicit in the opinion of this Court. The transportation of persons and commodities between states is, of course, the very essence of interstate commerce. As a consequence, congressional regulation of rates, transportation facilities, equipment, personnel and related matters has been uniformly sustained. . . .

[5. Stream of commerce is inapplicable.] The decision of the National Labor Relations Board endeavored to find that the respondent's Aliquippa Plant is merely a way station in the transit of commerce, with the thought of justifying the application of the Act to local transactions, because they are merely eddies in the stream of commerce. The facts which we have stated have indicated that the respondent's operations are not merely trifling interruptions of the movement of commerce. Its plant at Aliquippa is extensive in size and represents a very sub-stantial investment in buildings, machinery and equipment. The raw materials which come to the respondent from the State of Pennsylvania and elsewhere are delayed for a long period of time and, after being subjected to the manufacturing processes of the respondent, are changed substantially as to character, utility and value. The finished products which emerge are to a large extent manufactured without reference to pre-existing orders and contracts and are entirely different from the raw materials which enter at the other end. If importation and exporta-tion in interstate commerce do not singly transfer purely local activities into the field of Congressional regulation, it should follow that their combination would not alter the local situation. . . .

Advocates of the legality of the National Labor Relations Act attribute more force to this conception of a stream of commerce than the decisions establishing it warrant. It was useful in conspiracy cases because it obviates the necessity of prov-ing a direct restraint upon an actual train of interstate commerce. In the *Olsen* and *Stafford* cases, it served a somewhat different purpose. Both cases dealt with peculiar situations; they involved focal points, through which the stream of com-merce swept on its way from producer to the ultimate consumer. A stockyard is an institution which assembles live stock from various portions of the country, arranges for its temporary storage and then sends it on its way, after the shift of ownership has been made from the producer to the packer or dealer. The grain exchange which was involved in the *Olsen* case, performs a similar function for grains. Grains are, for the most part, warehoused in transit, where the grain ex-change is located, and the exchange serves as a market place for shifting title and arranging the final destination of the produce. In other words, both stockyards and exchanges are instrumentalities of commerce, in much the same way as the actual carriers of commodities. . . .

It would be impossible to extend the language of the decisions beyond their immediate facts, without entirely obliterating the distinction between that which is interstate commerce and that which is not. From a speculative viewpoint, al-most every business participates, to a limited extent, at least, in the general cur-rent of commerce. This participation is merely magnified in those industries which import and export materials before and after their manufacturing or other operations. But such industries are not instrumentalities of commerce in the same sense as stockyards or grain exchanges and to hold that they are would be to over-emphasize the current of commerce at the expense of local authority. It is, there-fore, reasonable to believe, from a careful consideration of both the *Olsen* and *Stafford* decisions and from a realization of the lengths to which the conception would otherwise be driven, that the doctrine is to be confined to instrumentalities of the broad movement of interstate commerce and not to be tortured into applica-tion to local activities which have merely a remote bearing on interstate trade. . . .

There is another distinguishing factor involved in the cases which we have just seen. Not only are the stockyards and grain exchanges, in practical effect, in-strumentalities of interstate commerce, but in both instances, Congress had en-acted comprehensive regulations to prevent the continuance of constantly recur-ring practices which had and were designed to have direct and immediate effects on interstate commerce. The distinction which we have emphasized throughout comes to the fore again, to set these exceptional decisions apart in their true light. The Court perceived the intimate connection between the local activities involved and the broad movement of interstate commerce and it recognized that the primary object of Congress was to protect the interstate movement of grains and cattle against direct restraints and interferences. But that is no precedent for arguing that this Court should sustain Congressional regulation of remote local activities where the true object of the statute is to regulate such activities and not to assist the movement of commerce. . . .

The constantly recurring evils to which the petitioner refers in its endeavors to draw the present issues into the purview of the Stafford and Olsen cases are not clearly defined in the petitioner's brief. If it is speaking of strikes and lockouts, which actually result in a stoppage of shipments or raw materials, then its argument relates to conditions which are not existent in the present case. If it is speaking of the respondent's relations with the complaining employees, then its argument is equally unconvincing because these are matters traditionally too remote from the stream of commerce to admit of federal intervention, unlike the activities in the Grain Exchange and Stock Yard cases, which were in the very current of commerce, and a part of the instrumentality of commerce which Congress had sought to regulate. The difference between the two situations is as great as the difference between the regulation of safety appliances on interstate carriers, which is obviously a fit subject for Congressional action and the regulation of safety conditions in manufacturing plants, which is not. . . .

[6. An intent to obstruct commerce.] The efforts of the petitioner to fit the present case into the pattern of the conspiracy cases, by fabricating an intent to restrain interstate traffic, are unconvincing. Conceivably, if there were a strike at the respondent's plants or a strike in the Steel Industry generally, the strikers might plan or intend to check the movements of materials to and from the respondent's plant or in the industry as a whole. But clearly, the respondent could not be held responsible for the *voluntary* intervening acts of outside agencies. The possibility of an *intentional* restraint by strangers would, if anything, weaken the connection between the transactions in issue and the movement of commerce rather than strengthen it. The suggestion that the respondent might be charged with an implied intent to destroy or diminish the movement of interstate trade, if a labor dispute should occur, which might lead to a strike, is almost ludicrous. The respondent's sales offices in twenty cities, of which the petitioner makes so much capital in its brief, should provide the answer to this supposition.

In reality, the conspiracy decisions, instead of aiding the petitioner, have thrown it out of court. . . . It is not true, as the petitioner's brief assumes, that if Congress can punish a concerted plan to interrupt or restrain interstate trade, it must therefore have unlimited means to anticipate every situation which *might* develop into a punishable restraint. Would petitioner contend that because the Federal government may move against striking unions for restraining commerce in violation of the Sherman Act, Congress would therefore have the power to prevent a laborer from joining an organization on the theory that he might some day participate in an illicit conspiracy?

There is a definite limitation which inheres in the very language of the commerce clause, and that is, that the "preventive" legislation, as the petitioner terms it, *must be confined to the legitimate regulation of commerce*. Congress can prevent, just as it can punish, direct restraint, but it cannot move in on purely local activities because they might conceivably affect the current of interstate trade. . . .

We have mentioned the implied admission of indirectness in the statuary definition of "affecting commerce," in that it applies not only to practices *burdening* commerce, but also to those which *might* tend to lead to labor disputes which *might* burden the movement of interstate trade. The same indirectness is woven into the fabric of the petitioner's argument, as it was in the *Schechter* case (the term used there was "affecting commerce"), but it is artfully concealed in almost every paragraph of its brief. Again and again the petitioner harkens to the fact that strikes frequently have an adverse effect on the movement of commerce to and from the affected establishment and this hypothetical connection is pleaded as a sufficient justification for the application of the statute to the facts of this case. If this were a proceeding against striking employees under the Anti-Trust Laws, the connection between strikes and stoppages of commerce might be legitimately urged as a reason for inferring an intent to restrain the movement of commerce. But here there is no actual or threatened strike such as the petitioner supposes to exist. Despite the petitioner's efforts to magnify the facts of this case into a national crisis, the controversy remains a simple issue between an employer and ten employees over the propriety of disciplinary acts of the respondent's agents. The fact that the discharges *might* have led to dissatisfaction, which *might* have led to a dispute of more serious consequences, which *might* have resulted in a walk-out, which *might* have led to an interruption or switch in the movement of interstate commerce, does not satisfy the constitutional requirement of a direct and immediate connection. Not only are there several steps in the relation between the issues of this case and the movement of commerce, but each step is built upon the quicksand of doubtful possibility. . . .

[7. Liberty of contract.] . . . State laws regulating hours of labor, working conditions and the payment of wages have been upheld, to protect the physical well-being of employees and to prevent fraud and oppression. But once the Government has gone beyond police measures and deliberately interfered with freedom of contract, to force its temporary economic conceptions upon its citizens, the Court has scrutinized its legislative efforts with the greatest of care. The present statute clearly falls into this category. Its provisions relating to majority rule for purposes of collective bargaining and to unfair labor practices are not designed to protect the property of employers or the well-being of employees, but are rather intended to force a novel economic policy into the relations of employees with each other and with their employers. Therefore, it is proper to consider whether or not they infringe upon the freedom of the parties to such an extent as to render them subject to attack. . . .

The provisions of the Labor Act which are in controversy in the present case present a much greater menace to the employer's freedom of contract than the enactments which were denied validity in the Coppage and Adair cases. In the Adair case the Court had before it a Federal statute prescribing, as a criminal offense, the discharge of an employee because of union activities, while the Kansas statute, which was involved in the Coppage case, merely prohibited employment contracts which required the employee to renounce his membership in a labor organization. The National Labor Relations Act not only prohibits the discharge of employees because of union activities, but it also pretends to give the petitioner authority to require the employer to restore employment. The dangerous implications of such procedure . . . are apparent. The employer may be compelled to continue a relationship which is not of his own seeking and his discretion in hiring and retaining employees is completely overridden. . . .

. . . Courts of equity from time immemorial have refused to compel specific performance of an employment contract as against either the employer or the employee. From the standpoint of the employee, the law has recognized that he should not be forced into a relationship which may be distasteful to him. From the standpoint of the employer, the courts have recognized that the right to judge the capabilities of his employees is absolutely essential to the proper management of a business. A variety of reasons may lead an employer to discharge an employee. It may be a question of efficiency, of application, or discipline. On other occasions the employer may be required to take action to protect the morale of his other employees, to prevent dissatisfaction of other workers, or put an end to suspected theft, sabotage or other undesirable conditions. In such cases, it may be preferable, for obvious reasons of policy, to withhold disclosure of the cause of the discharge. In any case the question of judgement is a delicate one which the law has always seen fit to rest in the personal discretion of the employer. If it is proper for the law to deprive the employer of his right to judgement and to rest the function in a board of this character, and then *to compel* the employer to restore the employee who has been discharged, there is an end to efficient management. . . .

This suggests another dangerous consequence of the Labor Act, which is of peculiar importance in the present case. The decision of the Board argues vehemently that there must have been discrimination, because three of the discharged employees were officers of the union. If union members are a preferred class in "a status equivalent to that of the civil service," it is not surprising that some of the union officers, relying upon their sure tenure of employment and immunity from discipline, should be found among those discharged for insubordination or insolence. If the Act gives union men freedom from discharge, it encourages laziness, violation of rules and inefficiency. . . .

[8. Conclusion.] The bulk of the testimony heard by the petitioner consisted of expert, economic and political opinion which depicted the harmful effects of labor disputes and strikes and extolled the virtues of organization and union contracts. Considering that this phase of the hearing was entirely *ex parte* and that no witnesses appeared to point out the disadvantages of a "closed shop" and its injustice to employees who desire to work without joining any union, it is not surprising that the argument may, at first glance, seem persuasive. The fact is, however, that it is wholly immaterial. . . .

The petitioner is asking that the traditions and precedents of a century be cast aside and the Constitution corrupted for the sake of a temporary expediency. To change *the established meaning* of the Constitution now, by judicial decree, without a proper mandate from the people, would make a mockery of constitutional government.

Respectfully submitted,

EARL F. REED,
Attorney for Respondent.

ORAL ARGUMENT

❖   ❖   ❖

MR. J. WARREN MADDEN [chairman, NLRB]: Suppose . . . the workers involved in this case had said to themselves, "We thought we had three choices. We thought we could either lie down or strike or resort to the law. Now we have found that we have only two choices, and we choose to strike."

. . . [T]he respondent's brief . . . indicates that this would be the respondent's counter to such a strike; it would go into the Federal District Court for the Western District of Pennsylvania and file a bill in equity saying something like this: "A group of men down at our plant have entered into an agreement in restraint of commerce. The consequence is an enormous disruption of the commerce of the Nation. Orders cannot be filled, goods cannot be shipped, mines in Minnesota and Michigan cannot operate, boats on the Lakes are stopped, railroads have nothing to transport and nowhere to unload it if they do transport it. Boats on the Lakes are stopped. Telegraph and telephone messages are coming in all the time from every State in the Union 'Where is the steel that I ordered? It should have been ready for shipment by this time.'" A disruption of commerce which is almost inconceivable.

The petitioner there, or complainant, says, "We are entitled to an injunction against these people. They have no right to enter into an agreement which thus disturbs the commerce of the Nation. Our authority is the language of the Supreme Court in the *Coronado* case. These men are well informed. They must have known when they struck that this would be the effect upon commerce, and therefore the necessary intent will be inferred." Suppose the Court says, "On the authority of the *Coronado* case you seem to be entitled to your injunction, but, by the way, what caused this strike?" "Well," these workers say, and the Labor Board found, that "the strike was caused by a rather small incident. We discharged 10 men because they joined a union." The judge says, "Was that a violation of the National Labor Relations Act?" Counsel says, "It would have been, except that the National Labor Relations Act had no application to the case. The case had nothing to do with interstate commerce."

And we have a situation which it seems to me is quite illogical, that very thing which caused the strike, which caused it immediately, and as a result of which it immediately came about, that thing is held . . . as having no sufficient relation to commerce so that the Federal Government can do anything about it.

*   *   *

... Now, if your Honor please, it seems to me that the flow of commerce which is described in that language and which was the fact in those stockyards cases was a flow of commerce not only through the stockyards but through the meat factories, through the packing plants. The consequence is that the analogy which we draw of the flow of raw materials into and through and flow of finished products out of the steel mills seems to be a logical one.

JUSTICE SUTHERLAND: So far as the cattle are concerned, how far could you go? You say that that is an analogous situation?

MADDEN: That is right.

SUTHERLAND: Taking it back, for instance, to the herder; suppose the herders raising cattle organized a union. Could Congress regulate that?

MADDEN: I should say not, your Honor. I should say that you have with reference to the commerce of the United States a problem somewhat similar—and certainly you have with reference to the extreme concept which this Court has used—you have a problem somewhat similar to that which you have with reference to physical streams of water. The water after it becomes a stream gets a wholly different sort of protection from what it gets when it is surface water or when it is percolating through the ground. At that time it is practically any man's property and it has very little protection from destruction. When it becomes a stream, however, it then comes under the scope of a different set of legal powers.

Now this process of drawing lines between intrastate and interstate activities, it may well be—it is not for us, of course, to cut the pattern for Your Honors—but it may well be that an analogy something like that may be useful in determining the extent to which the National Government can go in the control of the things which affect the commerce of the Nation—how greatly affect, how immediately, how directly, if you will, and so forth.

Now it does seem to me that by your own authority the meat factory is in the stream of commerce. The stream of commerce flows through it. I can imagine no reason why the Government, which has not only the right but the duty to protect that great flow of commerce, cannot protect there as well as it can just before it reaches that point or just after it reaches that point. Indeed, it seems to me that the attempt of the National Government to protect its great streams of commerce is futile if there is somewhere along the stream a point where the hand of the Government is stayed and where stupid State regulation, or lack of regulation, may destroy the whole stream which the Government has so carefully conserved up to that point, and which it is going to pick up again and conserve so carefully beyond that point.

*   *   *

JUSTICE SUTHERLAND: Before you pass to that point, what is the primary effect of a strike in a steel mill? Is it not to simply curtail production?

MR. STANLEY REED [solicitor general]:   Certainly; that is one of the effects.

SUTHERLAND: Isn't that the primary effect, the immediate effect?

REED: Well I should say it was the first effect. I do not mean to split hairs. Of course, that is one of the primary effects of it.

SUTHERLAND: That is the primary effect, to curtail production, and then the curtailment of production in its turn has an effect upon interstate commerce; isn't that true?

REED: As I understand it, no. The strike is not something that is a momentary change of, but instantaneously and at the same time that it stops production stops interstate commerce. It is a single thing that happens, and that stoppage of work stops interstate commerce right at that instant.

SUTHERLAND: It affects interstate commerce just as the cessation of work in a coal mine. The primary effect of that, as suggested in the *Carter* case, was to curtail the production, and then the secondary effect which came from the curtailment of production was the effect upon interstate commerce.

REED: Well, if we were undertaking to defend this act on the ground that Congress had the power to regulate labor conditions as such, I would fully agree with what Your Honor has said, but our contention is that Congress is not undertaking to regulate labor conditions as such; that it is undertaking to protect interstate commerce from situations that develop from these labor conditions, and that the causes which lead to these strikes with intent, and to strikes with the necessary effect, to interfere with interstate commerce are within the regulatory power of Congress.

SUTHERLAND: If by some means you curtail the production of wheat, the immediate effect, of course, is to curtail the production of wheat, and that in its turn has an effect upon interstate commerce. So would you say that Congress could step into the field and regulate the production of wheat under the commerce clause or under some other power?

REED: I am sure that what I would say would not bar Congress on it, but it seems to me that there is a great distinction between whether Congress can regulate production as such and whether Congress can regulate conditions which might interfere with the transportation of agricultural products after produced.

I will say this: That although this act does not apply to agricultural production, probably, if Congress had undertaken to control situations that had for their purpose the stopping of such production, the same rule would apply. Fortunately, we do not have to reach that far in this case.

❊   ❊   ❊

MR. EARL F. REED [attorney for Jones & Laughlin]:   The Government argues that there is the possibility of an intention on the part of the strikers to obstruct interstate commerce. It seems to me that that argument weakens the connection. In the stock-yards cases, in *Swift & Co. v. United States,* the intent to obstruct interstate commerce was clear, proven. The stockyards were regulated on the theory that they might be used as an instrumentality in monopoly. But here the intention that the Government ascribes is an intention on the part of a third party, an intervening agency. They do not claim that in discharging 10 men we had any intention of creating controversy that might obstruct interstate commerce, but the fact of these discharges might lead to dissatisfaction, which might lead to a dispute of more serious consequences, which might result in a walk-out, in which the strikers have an intention to interrupt or change the stream of interstate commerce.

Now, if that reasoning applies, there is not any reason why Congress cannot regulate every activity relating to manufacture. It is just as reasonable to say that, if we do not treat the men properly with respect to workmen's compensation law, if we do not have proper sanitary conditions, or hours of labor, or of everything else, the net result of which may be that there will be a strike, in which there will be an intent on the part of the strikers to obstruct interstate commerce, such an act would apply.

Mr. Madden pointed out that one of the witnesses testified that he was told that he would have to pay his back rent if he joined the union. I don't see any reason why, if this be sound, Congress cannot regulate our rent relations with our employees, because dissatisfaction on the part of the employees who live in our houses may result in a dissatisfaction of some kind that may result in a labor dispute where the intent may be present to interrupt interstate commerce. Now, if we ever get to the place we are having such remote, indirect causes prevail to enable Congress to regulate manufacturing industries, there is no limit to it.

❖   ❖   ❖

Now, in this case the order is made flatly that we reinstate these 10 employees. The Solicitor General says that if they were restored then it would be a hiring at will; that the minute they came back to work they would be working for us at a hiring at will, when they could be discharged for any reason or no reason.

It is difficult for me to see why, if they could have been discharged for no reason, their restoration could be ordered because the Labor Board did not agree with the sufficiency of the reason for which they were discharged.

JUSTICE SUTHERLAND: I did not quite understand the Solicitor General to take that position. I understood that his position was that he could not be discharged because he belonged to a labor union.

REED [attorney for Jones & Laughlin]:   I understood him to say in answer to the Justice's question that it would be a hiring at will, that if they came back their tenure would be at will, and I am assuming that a hiring at will entitles the employer to discharge for any cause or no cause. That much I may be adding myself.

SUTHERLAND: I understood him to make that exception.

REED: I should think that that exception would follow. In other words, I certainly think that if this act is valid it means that when the 10 men come back they cannot be discharged except for a cause which would seem sufficient to the Labor Board. Certainly it does not mean that they could be discharged right away, because the same complaint would be made again.

✿   ✿   ✿

It seems to me that the Government's argument comes down to an economic argument. "It would be a good thing," says Mr. Madden, "If the Federal Government could control the labor relations of industry." But that is not the law, and never has been. He may think the States are handling it "stupidly," as he says. He may think that a centralized government in which the Federal Government controls all of the labor relations of industry is desired. That is not the law and never has been.

For a century this Court has adhered to the simple, literal meaning which Marshall found in the commerce clause, that Congress has power to regulate commerce among the States. It has given assurance to the States when their taxing statutes have arisen that their rights shall be as the Constitution fixes them. The taxing authority or the police power of the States has been protected, and the rights of individuals to maintain their own property have been protected.

What the petitioner is asking is that the traditions and precedents of a century be cast aside and that we change the meaning of the Constitution by a judicial decree and say that things that for a century have not been the business of the Federal Government are now to be subject to regulation, because of the remote possibility that these discharges and things of this kind may obstruct commerce.

THE OPINION

Mr. Chief Justice Hughes delivered the opinion of the Court. . . .

In a proceeding under the National Labor Relations Act of 1935, the National Labor Relations Board found that the respondent, Jones & Laughlin Steel Corporation, had violated the Act by engaging in unfair labor practices affecting commerce. . . . The unfair labor practices charged were that the corporation was discriminating against members of the union with regard to hire and tenure of employment, and was coercing and intimidating its employees in order to interfere with their self-organization. The discriminatory and coercive action alleged was the discharge of certain employees. . . .

The facts as to the nature and scope of the business of the Jones & Laughlin Steel Corporation have been found by the Labor Board and, so far as they are essential to the determination of this controversy, they are not in dispute. The Labor

Board has found: The corporation is organized under the laws of Pennsylvania and has its principal office at Pittsburgh. It is engaged in the business of manufacturing iron and steel in plants situated in Pittsburgh and nearby Aliquippa, Pennsylvania. It manufactures and distributes a widely diversified line of steel and pig iron in the United States. With its subsidiaries—nineteen in number—it is a completely integrated enterprise, owning and operating ore, coal and limestone properties, lake and river transportation facilities and terminal railroads located at its manufacturing plants. It owns or controls mines in Michigan and Minnesota. It operates four ore steamships on the Great Lakes, used in the transportation of ore to its factories. It owns coal mines in Pennsylvania. It operates towboats and steam barges used in carrying coal to its factories. It owns limestone properties in various places in Pennsylvania and West Virginia. It owns the Monongahela connecting railroad which connects the plants of the Pittsburgh works and forms an interconnection with the Pennsylvania, New York Central and Baltimore and Ohio Railroad systems. It owns the Aliquippa and Southern Railroad Company which connects the Aliquippa works with the Pittsburgh and Lake Erie, part of the New York Central system. Much of its product is shipped to its warehouses in Chicago, Detroit, Cincinnati and Memphis—to the last two places by means of its own barges and transportation equipment. In Long Island City, New York, and in New Orleans it operates structural steel fabricating shops in connection with the warehousing of semi-finished materials sent from its works. Through one of its wholly-owned subsidiaries it owns, leases and operates stores, warehouses and yards for the distribution of equipment and supplies for drilling and operating oil and gas mills and for pipe lines, refineries and pumping stations. It has sales offices in twenty cities in the United States and a wholly-owned subsidiary which is devoted exclusively to distributing its product in Canada. Approximately 75 per cent of its product is shipped out of Pennsylvania.

Summarizing these operations, the Labor Board concluded that the works in Pittsburgh and Aliquippa "might be likened to the heart of a self-contained, highly integrated body. They draw in the raw materials from Michigan, Minnesota, West Virginia, Pennsylvania in part through arteries and by means controlled by the respondent; they transform the materials and then pump them out to all parts of the nation through the vast mechanism which the respondent has elaborated.". . .

We think it clear that the National Labor Relations Act may be construed so as to operate within the sphere of constitutional authority. The jurisdiction conferred upon the Board, and invoked in this instance, is found in section 10(a), which provides:

> ". . . The Board is empowered, as hereinafter provided, to prevent any person from engaging in any unfair labor practice . . . affecting commerce."

The critical words of this provision, prescribing the limits of the Board's authority in dealing with the labor practices, are "affecting commerce.". . .

[As defined by the statute,] "The term 'affecting commerce' means in commerce, or burdening or obstructing commerce or the free flow of commerce, or having led or tending to lead to a labor dispute burdening or obstructing commerce or the free flow of commerce.". . .

. . . Whether or not particular action does affect commerce in such a close and intimate fashion as to be subject to Federal control, and hence to lie within the authority conferred upon the Board, is left by the statute to be determined as individual cases arise. We are thus to inquire whether in the instant case the constitutional boundary has been passed. . . .

. . . [I]n its present application, the statute goes no further than to safeguard the right of employees to self-organization and to select representatives of their own choosing for collective bargaining or other mutual protection without restraint or coercion by their employer.

That is a fundamental right. Employees have as clear a right to organize and select their representatives for lawful purposes as the respondent has to organize its business and select its own officers and agents. Discrimination and coercion to prevent the free exercise of the right of employees to self-organization and representation is a proper subject for condemnation by competent legislative authority. Long ago we stated the reason for labor organizations. We said that they were organized out of the necessities of the situation; that a single employee was helpless in dealing with an employer; that he was dependent ordinarily on his daily wage for the maintenance of himself and family; that if the employer refused to pay him the wages that he thought fair, he was nevertheless unable to leave the employ and resist arbitrary and unfair treatment; that union was essential to give laborers opportunity to deal on an equality with their employer. . . . Fully recognizing the legality of collective action on the part of employees in order to safeguard their proper interests, we said that Congress was not required to ignore this right but could safeguard it. Congress could seek to make appropriate collective action of employees an instrument of peace rather than of strife. We said that such collective action would be a mockery if representation were made futile by interference with freedom of choice. Hence the prohibition by Congress of interference with the selection of representatives for the purpose of negotiation and conference between employers and employees, "instead of being an invasion of the constitutional right of either, was based on the recognition of the rights of both.". . .

. . . Respondent says that whatever may be said of employees engaged in interstate commerce, the industrial relations and activities in the manufacturing department of respondent's enterprise are not subject to Federal regulation. The argument rests upon the proposition that manufacturing in itself is not commerce.

[However,] The Government distinguishes these cases. The various parts of respondent's enterprise are described as interdependent and as thus involving a "great movement of iron ore, coal and limestone along well-defined paths to the steel mills, thence through them, and thence in the form of steel products into the consuming centers of the country—a definite and well-understood course of business." It is urged that these activities constitute a "stream" or "flow" of commerce, of which the Aliquippa manufacturing plant is the focal point, and that industrial strife at that point would cripple the entire movement. Reference is made to our decision sustaining the Packers and Stockyards Act. [There] The Court found that the stockyards were but a "throat" through which the current of commerce flowed and the transactions which there occurred could not be separated from that movement. Hence the sales at the stockyards were not regarded as merely local transactions, for while they created "a local change of title" they did not "stop the flow," but merely changed the private interests in the subject of the current. . . .

Respondent contends that the instant case presents material distinctions. Respondent says that the Aliquippa plant is extensive in size and represents a large investment in buildings, machinery and equipment. The raw materials which are brought to the plant are delayed for long periods and, after being subjected to manufacturing processes, "are changed substantially as to character, utility and value.". . .

We do not find it necessary to determine whether these features of defendant's business dispose of the asserted analogy to the "stream of commerce" cases. The instances in which that metaphor has been used are but particular, and not exclusive, illustrations of the protective power which the Government invokes in support of the present Act. The congressional authority to protect interstate commerce from burdens and obstructions is not limited to transactions which can be deemed to be an essential part of a "flow" of interstate or foreign commerce. Burdens and obstructions may be due to injurious action springing from other sources. The fundamental principle is that the power to regulate commerce is the power to enact "all appropriate legislation" for "its protection and advancement"; to adopt measures "to promote its growth and insure its safety"; "to foster, protect, control and restrain." That power is plenary and may be exerted to protect interstate commerce "no matter what the source of the dangers which threaten it." Although activities may be intrastate in character when separately considered, if they have such a close and substantial relation to interstate commerce that their control is essential or appropriate to protect that commerce from burdens and obstructions, Congress cannot be denied the power to exercise that control. Undoubtedly the scope of this power must be considered in the light of our dual system of government and may not be extended so as to embrace effects upon interstate commerce so indirect and remote that to embrace them, in view of our complex society, would effectually obliterate the distinction between what is national and what is local and create a completely centralized government. The question is necessarily one of degree. . . .

The close and intimate effect which brings the subject within the reach of Federal power may be due to activities in relation to productive industry although the industry when separately viewed is local. This has been abundantly illustrated in the application of the Federal Anti-Trust Act. . . .

. . . [T]he Anti-Trust Act has been applied to the conduct of employees engaged in production. The decisions dealing with the question of that application illustrate both the principle and its limitation. Thus in the first Coronado Coal Co. Case, the Court held that mining was not interstate commerce, that the power of Congress did not extend to its regulation as such, and that it had not been shown that the activities there involved—a local strike—brought them within the provisions of the Anti-Trust Act, notwithstanding the broad terms of the statute. . . .

But in the first Coronado Case the Court also said that "if Congress deems certain recurring practices, though not really part of interstate commerce, likely to obstruct, restrain or burden it, it has the power to subject them to national supervision and restraint." And in the second Coronado Coal Co. Case the Court ruled that while the mere reduction in the supply of an article to be shipped in interstate commerce by the illegal or tortious prevention of its manufacture or production is ordinarily an indirect and remote obstruction to that commerce, nevertheless when the "intent of those unlawfully preventing the manufacture or production is shown to be to restrain or control the supply entering and moving in interstate commerce, or the price of it in interstate markets, their action is a direct violation of the Anti-Trust Act." And the existence of that intent may be a necessary inference from proof of the direct and substantial effect produced by the employees' conduct. What was absent from the evidence in the first Coronado Coal Co. Case appeared in the second and the Act was accordingly applied to the mining employees.

It is thus apparent that the fact that the employees here concerned were engaged in production is not determinative. The question remains as to the effect upon interstate commerce of the labor practice involved. . . .

. . . In view of respondent's far-flung activities, it is idle to say that the effect [of a strike] would be indirect or remote. It is obvious that it would be immediate and might be catastrophic. We are asked to shut our eyes to the plainest facts of our national life and to deal with the question of direct and indirect effects in an intellectual vacuum. Because there may be but indirect and remote effects upon interstate commerce in connection with a host of local enterprises throughout the country, it does not follow that other industrial activities do not have such a close and intimate relation to interstate commerce as to make the presence of industrial strife a matter of the most urgent national concern. When industries organize themselves on a national scale, making their relation to interstate commerce the dominant factor in their activities, how can it be maintained that their industrial labor relations constitute a forbidden field into which Congress may not enter when it is necessary to protect interstate commerce from the paralyzing consequences of industrial war? We have often said that interstate commerce itself is a practical conception. It is equally true that interferences with that commerce must be appraised by a judgment that does not ignore actual experience.

Experience has abundantly demonstrated that the recognition of the right of employees to self-organization and to have representatives of their own choosing for the purpose of collective bargaining is often an essential condition of industrial peace. Refusal to confer and negotiate has been one of the most prolific causes of strife. This is such an outstanding fact in the history of labor disturbances that it is a proper subject of judicial notice. . . .

. . . The steel industry is one of the great basic industries of the United States, with ramifying activities affecting interstate commerce at every point. The Government aptly refers to the steel strike of 1919–1920 with its far-reaching consequences. The fact that there appears to have been no major disturbance in that industry in the more recent period did not dispose of the possibilities of future and like dangers to interstate commerce which Congress was entitled to foresee and to exercise its protective power to forestall. It is not necessary again to detail the facts as to respondent's enterprise. Instead of being beyond the pale, we think that it presents in a most striking way the close and intimate relation which a manufacturing industry may have to interstate commerce and we have no doubt that Congress had constitutional authority to safeguard the right of respondent's employees to self-organization and freedom in the choice of representatives for collective bargaining. . . .

Mr. Justice McReynolds delivered the following dissenting opinion . . .

Carter's Case declared—"Whether the effect of a given activity or condition is direct or indirect is not always easy to determine. The word 'direct' implies that the activity or condition invoked or blamed shall operate proximately—not mediately, remotely or collaterally—to produce the effect. It connotes the absence of an efficient intervening agency or condition. And the extent of the effect bears no logical relation to its character. The distinction between a direct and an indirect effect turns, not upon the magnitude of either the cause or the effect, but entirely upon the manner in which the effect has been brought about. If the production by one man of a single ton of coal intended for interstate sale and shipment, and actually so sold and shipped, affects interstate commerce indirectly, the effect does not become direct by multiplying the tonnage, or increasing the number of men employed, or adding to the expense or complexities of the business, or by all combined."

Any effect on interstate commerce by the discharge of employees shown here would be indirect and remote in the highest degree, as consideration of the facts will show. In No. 419 ten men out of ten thousand were discharged: in the other cases only a few. The immediate effect in the factory may be to create discontent among all those employed and a strike may follow, which, in turn, may result in reducing production which ultimately may reduce the volume of goods moving in interstate commerce. By this chain of indirect and progressively remote events we finally reach the evil with which it is said the legislation under consideration undertakes to deal. A more remote and indirect interference with interstate commerce or a more definite invasion of the powers reserved to the states is difficult, if not impossible, to imagine.

The Constitution still recognizes the existence of States with indestructible powers; the Tenth Amendment was supposed to put them beyond controversy.

We are told that Congress may protect the "stream of commerce" and that one who buys raw materials without the state, manufactures it therein, and ships the output to another state is in that stream. Therefore it is said he may be prevented from doing anything which may interfere with its flow.

This, too, goes beyond the constitutional limitations heretofore enforced. If a man raises cattle and regularly delivers them to a carrier for interstate shipment, may Congress prescribe the conditions under which he may employ or discharge helpers on the ranch? The products of a mine pass daily into interstate commerce; many things are brought to it from other states. Are the owners and the miners within the power of Congress in respect of the latter's tenure and discharge? May a mill owner be prohibited from closing his factory or discontinuing his business because so to do would stop the flow of products to and from his plant in interstate commerce? May employees in a factory be restrained from quitting work in a body because this will close the factory and thereby stop the flow of commerce?

May arson of a factory be made a Federal offense whenever this would interfere with such a flow? If the business cannot continue with the existing wage scale, may Congress command a reduction? If the ruling of the Court just announced is adhered to these questions suggest some of the problems certain to arise. . . .

There is no ground on which reasonably to hold that refusal by a manufacturer, whose raw materials come from states other than that of his factory and whose products are regularly carried to other states, to bargain collectively with employees in his manufacturing plant directly affects interstate commerce. In such business, there is not one but two distinct movements or streams in interstate transportation. The first brings in raw material and there ends. Then follows manufacture, a separate and local activity. Upon completion of this, and not before, the second distinct movement or stream in interstate commerce begins and the products go to other states. Such is the common course for small as well as large industries. It is unreasonable and unprecedented to say the commerce clause confers upon Congress power to govern relations between employers and employees in these local activities. In A. L. A. Schechter's Poultry Case we condemned as unauthorized by the commerce clause assertion of federal power in respect of commodities which had come to rest after interstate transportation. And, in Carter's Case, we held Congress lacked powers to regulate labor relations in respect of commodities before interstate commerce has begun.

It is gravely stated that experience teaches that if an employer discourages membership in "any organization of any kind" "in which employees participate, and which exists for the purpose in whole or in part of dealing with employers concerning grievances, labor disputes, wages, rates of pay, hours of employment or conditions of work," discontent may follow and this in turn may lead to a strike, and as the outcome of the strike there may be a block in the stream of interstate commerce. Therefore Congress may inhibit the discharge! Whatever effect any cause of discontent may ultimately have upon commerce is far too indirect to justify Congressional regulation. Almost anything—marriage, birth, death—may in some fashion affect commerce.

That Congress has power by appropriate means, not prohibited by the Constitution, to prevent direct and material interference with the conduct of interstate commerce is settled doctrine. But the interference struck at must be direct and material, not some mere possibility contingent on wholly uncertain events; and there must be no impairment of rights guaranteed. . . .

Section 13 of the Labor Act provides—"Nothing in this Act shall be construed so as to interfere with or impede or diminish in any way the right to strike." And yet it is ruled that to discharge an employee in a factory because he is a member of a labor organization (any kind) may create discontent which may lead to a strike and this may cause a block in the "stream of commerce"; consequently the discharge may be inhibited. Thus the Act exempts from its ambit the very evil which counsel insist may result from discontent caused by a discharge of an association member, but permits coercion of a non-member to join one. . . .

The right to contract is fundamental and includes the privilege of selecting those with whom one is willing to assume contractual relations. This right is unduly abridged by the Act now upheld. A private owner is deprived of power to manage his own property by freely selecting those to whom his manufacturing operations are to be entrusted. We think this cannot lawfully be done in circumstances like those here disclosed. . . .

P O S T S C R I P T

The constitutional crisis of 1937 radically transformed American federalism. Powers traditionally reserved to the states by the Tenth Amendment were now centralized in the hands of the federal government. Important economic policies that had once been made in the various state capitals were now made in Washington, D.C. State autonomy and prestige suffered a corresponding erosion. Though states still played an important role in American life, they no longer occupied the place that they had before 1937. And when the federal government began to regulate the economic activities of the states themselves (for instance, by establishing a minimum wage that states had to pay public employees), the troubling relationship between the commerce power and state autonomy was highlighted in its most dramatic fashion. Was the federal government, a government that purported to be a government of limited and delegated powers, gradually undermining the states that had created it? Was the child slowly strangling its parents? If so, what should be the role of the Constitution and the Supreme Court in these developments? Based upon the Tenth Amendment, should the Court defend the states against federal exertions of the commerce power, or should it refuse to get involved in what is essentially a political, public-policy matter?

After the "court-packing" crisis, FDR and Congress continued "to stretch" the commerce clause. Indeed, within five years of the crisis, the Supreme Court yielded the entire field of socioeconomic regulation to the federal government. *Wickard v. Filburn* was the crucial turning point.[46] Filburn was a small farmer who wanted to grow more wheat than the eleven acres that were allotted to him under the provisions of the Agriculture Adjustment Act of 1938, a law that maintained the price of wheat by limiting its production.[47] Filburn did not want to sell the excess wheat. He wanted to use it to feed himself, his family, and his livestock, plus save some for seed for the following year. Nonetheless, he was fined $117.11. The constitutional question was: Did the federal government, under the commerce clause, have the authority to penalize a farmer for growing wheat that he did not intend to sell on any market?

The Supreme Court upheld this exercise of federal power by denying that the commerce clause could reach only intrastate activities that had a "direct" impact upon interstate commerce. Although this requirement had been acknowledged in Justice Hughes's opinion in *NLRB v. Jones & Laughlin*, Justice Robert Jackson, a former attorney general in FDR's administration, said in *Wickard* that

---

[46]317 U.S. 111 (1942). Another revealing commerce-clause case to consider is *United States v. Darby*, 312 U.S. 100 (1941), which overturned *Hammer v. Dagenhart* (1918), the case that invalidated the federal attempt to exclude products of child labor from interstate commerce.

[47]The act was suspended if one-third of the wheat growers objected to the allotments.

even if appellee's activity be local and though it may not be regarded as commerce, it may still, whatever its nature, be reached by Congress if it exerts a substantial economic effect on interstate commerce, and this irrespective of whether such effect is what might at some earlier time have been defined as "direct" or "indirect."[48]

Moreover, in assessing whether growing wheat for home consumption has a "substantial effect" upon interstate commerce, the government need not only consider the impact that Filburn's actions would have on the market and the price of wheat. "That appellee's own contribution to the demand for wheat may be trivial by itself is not enough to remove him from the scope of federal regulation where, as here, his contribution, taken together with that of many others similarly situated, is far from trivial."[49] If people like Filburn, who grew wheat for home consumption beyond their allotments, would have more than a trivial impact upon the demand for wheat, Jackson concluded, then the federal government had the power to penalize his decision to grow wheat for home consumption beyond his allotment.

Clearly, the scope of federal power had grown measurably between *Jones* and *Wickard.* Jones & Laughlin Steel Corporation was the fourth-largest steel company in the country; Filburn was a small Ohio dairy farmer. Nonetheless, the federal government regulated Filburn's production of wheat, not the state of Ohio.

A couple of decades later, the federal government's commerce power expanded again, but this time the expansion occurred in what seemed to be a noncommercial area. The famous Civil Rights Act of 1964 prohibited racial, ethnic, and religious discrimination in any public accommodation whose operations either "affected" commerce or involved "products" or "services" that moved in commerce. What was unprecedented in this legislation was the use of the *commerce* power to obtain a *moral* objective. It is true that the Supreme Court had upheld earlier efforts by the federal government to bar from interstate commerce certain "sinful" or "impure" commodities: lottery tickets, impure foods, and prostitutes.[50] However, in the Civil Rights Act, the federal government did not exclude anything from interstate commerce. The law had nothing to do with what people could or could not do with commodities that flowed in interstate commerce; instead, the federal government was claiming that it had authority to regulate how people could associate with one another if and when discrimination "affected" commerce or if and when commodities passed through commerce. In this way, the commercial aspects of the law functioned as a rationale for the federal government to regulate an area of life that had traditionally been left to the police power of the states.

The Supreme Court upheld the constitutionality of the Civil Rights Act in two crucial cases: *Heart of Atlanta Motel v. United States* (1964) and *Katzenback v. McClung* (1964).[51] In the Court's view, it did not matter that the law intruded

---

[48]*Wickard v. Filburn,* 317 U.S. 111, 125 (1942).

[49]*Id.* at 127–28.

[50]*Champion v. Ames,* 188 U.S. 321 (1903); *Hipolite Egg Co. v. United States,* 220 U.S. 45 (1911); *Hoke v. United States,* 227 U.S. 308 (1913).

[51]379 U.S. 241 (1964); 379 U.S. 294 (1964).

upon the traditional police power that was the basis for state regulation of health, safety, and morals. As long as there was a "rational basis" for the belief that racial discrimination affected interstate commerce—for instance, by reducing the interstate travel of African-Americans—the Court said that its investigation was "at an end." The federal government could displace state policies in this area by prohibiting racial discrimination in all public accommodations.

Wickard and the cases upholding the Civil Rights Act complement the approach to constitutional adjudication that prevailed in the New Deal constitutional crisis. According to it, the Supreme Court must continuously adapt "the living Constitution" to contemporary needs and political realities. The problem becomes more acute, however, when Congress enacts laws that regulate the economic activities of the states themselves. If the Court should interpret the Constitution according to contemporary needs, what role should it play in this context? Should it defend states from federal exertions of the commerce power that restrict their own internal operations? In earlier decades, the Court did not appear to be too concerned with this issue, perhaps because the extent of federal regulation of state economic activities was at that time negligible. However, by 1968, two justices dissented from a decision that upheld the federal application of the Fair Labor Standards Act to public employees working in state-operated schools and hospitals, a law that forced states to pay minimum wages to certain public employees.[52] These dissents anticipated the emerging doctrine that judges must defend federalism by using the Tenth Amendment to protect state autonomy.

In *National League of Cities v. Usery* (1976), a five-to-four decision, the Court defended state autonomy by invalidating the extension of the Fair Labor Standards Act to all employees of state and local governments.[53] The extension was invalid, according to Justice William Rehnquist's majority opinion, because it regulated "States *qua* States," impermissibly interfered with "integral governmental functions," and "displace[d] the States' abilities to structure employer–employee relationships." Justice William J. Brennan disagreed. In his dissent, he argued that the Tenth Amendment constituted no limitation on the federal government's power to regulate commerce, including the commerce in which states were engaged. States unhappy with federal laws had the ability to turn to the political branches, which "are structured to protect the interests of the States, as well as the Nation as a whole."[54] Judges therefore had no business protecting states from federal economic legislation.

Though a divided Court announced in *National League of Cities v. Usery* that it would protect states from certain exertions of the federal government's commerce power, it has yet to act upon this principle again. In *Equal Employment Opportunities Commission (EEOC) v. Wyoming* (1983), a bare majority of the Court upheld an amendment to the Age Discrimination in Employment Act that

---

[52]*Maryland v. Wirtz*, 392 U.S. 183 (1968).

[53]426 U.S. 833 (1976).

[54]*Id.* at 876. For further argument that the federal government's political branches are designed to ensure adequate state representation, see Jesse Choper, *Judicial Review and the National Political Process* (Chicago: University of Chicago Press, 1980).

extended the law to state employees.[55] In conjunction with *National League of Cities, EEOC* meant that the federal government could not force the states to pay minimum wages to all its employees, but it could bar Wyoming from forcing a game warden to retire at age fifty-five. The question was whether a sensible line could be drawn between these two cases. If the federal government could not regulate the one because it constituted an intrusion upon state autonomy, how could it regulate the other? Was the Court, by implication, making substantive policy decisions by invalidating certain federal regulations of states and upholding others? If the Court wanted to be consistent, did it have to protect states more aggressively from commerce-based federal laws or abandon the field entirely?

In 1982, what appeared to be a rather serious federal intrusion into state autonomy was upheld in another five-to-four decision: *Federal Energy Regulation Commission (FERC) v. Mississippi.*[56] In this case, the Court reviewed the Public Utility Regulatory Policies Act of 1978 (PURPA), a federal law designed to alleviate a nationwide energy crisis. The law required states to follow certain procedures as they considered the adoption of federal "rate designs" and "regulatory standards" for public utilities. By compelling states to "consider" these matters, was the federal government setting the political agendas of the states? By mandating certain procedures, was the federal government defining the internal operations of the states? In his majority opinion, Justice Harry Blackmun, who had voted with the majority in *National League of Cities,* answered these questions negatively. He claimed that the law instituted only a "program of cooperative federalism." Because the federal government had the power to preempt the entire field of public utilities regulation, it could, Blackmun reasoned, let the states remain in the area but require them to do certain things. Such regulations of the states were only conditions for their "continued involvement in a pre-emptible field."

In her dissent, Justice Sandra Day O'Connor objected to Blackmun's assumption that preemption was less of an infringement of state autonomy than a program that permitted their involvement based on terms set by the federal government. First, if Congress preempts a field, the states "may simply devote their energies elsewhere," whereas PURPA "drains the state's inventive energy." Also, such a law "blurs the lines of political accountability" because citizens might hold their local representatives responsible for decisions in fact made in Washington, D.C.[57] O'Connor's conclusion is that PURPA "conscript[s] state utility commissions into the national bureaucratic army. This result is contrary to the principles of *National League of Cities v. Usery,* antithetical to the values of federalism, and inconsistent with our constitutional history."[58] In her view, the Court should have invalidated the law as a violation of the Tenth Amendment.

---

[55]460 U.S. 226 (1983).

[56]*FERC v. Mississippi,* 456 U.S. 742 (1982).

[57]*Id.* at 787.

[58]*Id.* at 775.

A few years later, the still-divided Court reversed itself by overruling *National League of Cities* in *Garcia v. San Antonio Metropolitan Transit Authority* (1985).[59] Justice Blackmun wrote the opinion explaining why a decision he had originally supported, a decision not yet ten years old, had to be abandoned. Recent experience had shown, he argued, that there was no "workable" or "principled" way for the Court to enforce constitutional limitations on Congress's power to regulate the activities of states that affected interstate commerce. "Any rule of state immunity that looks to the 'traditional,' 'integral,' or 'necessary' nature of governmental functions," he explained, "inevitably invites an unelected federal judiciary to make decisions about which state policies it favors and which ones it dislikes."[60] Such judicial policymaking was unacceptable. Rather than making policy under the cover of protecting state autonomy, courts could better support the constitutional value of federalism by refusing to apply any Tenth Amendment objections against commerce-based federal laws. Because the political branches of the federal government were designed by the framers to give states ample opportunity to defend their interests, it was unnecessary for the judiciary to be involved.

The dissents echoed the themes of O'Connor's opinion in *FERC*, reasserted the judicial duty to enforce the Tenth Amendment, and lamented the way in which the Court had overturned such a recent precedent. Indeed, though he declined to "spell out" the "fine points" of his position, William Rehnquist, now Chief Justice, predicted that *Garcia* would suffer the same fate as *National League of Cities*. It would therefore seem that Blackmun's "switch," unlike Roberts's in 1937, had hardly settled anything. It is still unclear which horn of a dilemma the Court should or will take. If it returns to the principle of *National League of Cities*, will the Court not be accepting a policymaking function? Can the Court really pick and choose which commerce-based federal laws intrude upon state sovereignty without making policy? On the other hand, if the Court adheres to *Garcia*, is it not admitting that federal politicians are the only judges of the limits of the commerce power? If so, in what sense can the federal government be a government of limited powers? These questions show once again that the commerce clause and its history are a valuable window into the meaning of American constitutionalism and the role that judges play in it.

---

[59]469 U.S. 528 (1985).

[60]*Id.* at 546.

CHAPTER 3

The War Power

KOREMATSU V. UNITED STATES
323 U.S. 214 (1944)

✦

The most awesome power within the federal government's arsenal is the war power. It, along with the powers granted under the necessary and proper clause, authorizes federal officials to take whatever steps they reasonably believe are necessary to win a war. As a noted commentator put it, "the power to wage war is the power to wage war successfully."[1] One constitutional controversy concerning the war power is the potentially conflicting roles of the Congress and the president in exercising this power. This issue will be briefly addressed in the postscript of this chapter. A different problem arises if the Congress and the president concur in an application of the war power but exercise it in ways that undermine traditional rights and liberties of American citizens. How should the Supreme Court react in such a situation? Is the war power a sufficient justification for the suspension of basic constitutional rights? This sort of question has arisen in every major war effort undertaken by the United States, but its most tragic appearance occurred during World War II. During this life-and-death struggle against fascism, American political and military officials evacuated all U.S. citizens of Japanese descent and all Japanese aliens from the west coast and placed them in internment camps. In *Korematsu v. United States* (1944), a divided Supreme Court affirmed certain aspects of this program. However, although the majority of the justices said that they could not second-guess what military and responsible political officials thought was necessary to wage war successfully, three justices dissented. In their view, the means of winning the war had to be compatible with the ideals of American democracy, and judges had the responsibility of ensuring that the United States did not become a fascist country in its effort to defeat fascism. Which of

---

[1]Charles E. Hughes, "War Powers under the Constitution," *Reports of the American Bar Ass'n* XLII (1917), p. 238.

these contrasting positions is the correct one? This chapter will explore this question concerning the judiciary's role during wartime.

Besides providing an opportunity to consider whether the Supreme Court *ought* to assess the constitutionality of domestic wartime policies, the Japanese internment cases also highlight the more practical question of whether the Court *can* oppose public opinion in the highly charged political atmosphere of total war. The surprise attack on Pearl Harbor, of course, enraged many Americans. Political leaders did little, if anything, to check the rising tide of anti-Japanese sentiment, if only because it was in many ways a military asset. It reconciled the American people to the requirements of a sustained war effort, including the draft, rationing, and wage and price controls. However, given the destruction of the fleet, popular demands for vengeance against the Japanese were not easily satisfied in the days immediately following Pearl Harbor. Public attention gradually centered on the 110,000 Japanese, both citizens and aliens, who resided on the west coast, especially after a presidential commission published its finding on January 25, 1942, that a Japanese espionage ring had been in operation in Hawaii before the Pearl Harbor attack. In such an intense political atmosphere, was it feasible for the Supreme Court to contain the rising tide of racial prejudice against Japanese-Americans and Japanese nationals? Can we reasonably expect judges to stand against predominant public opinion, even if we agree theoretically that it is their duty to do so? Or is it inevitable that politics will determine the degree to which traditional rights and liberties are sacrificed during war?

The normative and practical questions concerning the role of courts in wartime arose in dramatic fashion during the U.S. Civil War. Intent upon preserving the Union, President Abraham Lincoln interpreted his war powers expansively. In 1861, immediately after the attack on Fort Sumter and before Congress met, he appropriated funds, ordered a blockade of Confederate ports, and suspended the writ of habeas corpus (a judicial order requiring any official who has a person in custody to justify before a judge the lawfulness of the detention) in Maryland.[2] Once in session, Congress ratified these actions and, in 1863, enacted a Habeas Corpus Act granting the president broad authority to suspend the writ. Based upon this statute, but also upon his understanding of his own constitutional authority, Lincoln gave his generals the discretion to arrest and try civilians in military courts. In 1863, pursuant to this delegation of power, General Ambrose Burnside arrested former Representative Clement L. Vallandigham, a Democrat

---

[2]The Supreme Court upheld the constitutionally of the blockade by a five-to-four decision in *The Prize Cases,* 67 U.S. 935 (1863), holding that the president did not have to wait for a congressional declaration of war before initiating military action against the Southern insurrection. In the Court's view, Lincoln was "not only authorized but bound to resist force, by force." The Court never reviewed the case involving the suspension of the writ of habeas corpus in Maryland, but Chief Justice Roger B. Taney, sitting alone, declared it unconstitutional in *Ex Parte Merryman,* 17 Fed. Cases 144 (1861). His position was that only Congress could suspend the writ. Lincoln, however, ignored Taney's decision, claiming that the president, as well as Congress, had the power to suspend the writ "when in cases of Rebellion or Invasion the public Safety may require it" (Art. I, Sec. 9). For a full discussion of the constitutionally of Lincoln's actions, see James G. Randall, *Lincoln the President,* 4 vols. (New York: Dodd, Mead, 1945–55); Mark E. Neely, Jr., *The Fate of Liberty: Abraham Lincoln and Civil Liberties* (New York: Oxford University Press, 1991).

from Ohio, and a military commission convicted him of "giving aid and comfort to the Rebels" and sentenced him to imprisonment until the war's end. The case gained such notoriety that Lincoln publicly defended the military's actions in an open letter to Erastus Corning, a New York Democrat who had organized a mass protest of the Vallandigham arrest. (See Box 3.1.) In this letter, Lincoln claimed that he had the authority to order military arrests of individuals who were far from the front lines and who were not charged with any crime. In a reply letter, the Democrats denied this argument, claiming that the suspension of the writ of habeas corpus neither suspended the Bill of Rights nor justified the arrest of anyone who was not charged with a crime. (See Box 3.2.) The exchange is an illuminating discussion of the degree to which traditional rights and liberties restrict the means by which the federal government can make war.

The Supreme Court had no opportunity to express its views on the question of the domestic limits of the war power until the military in Indiana, during the winter and spring of 1864–65, arrested, convicted, and sentenced to death Lambdin P. Milligan, an Indiana Democrat who sympathized with the South. Milligan petitioned the federal courts for a writ of habeas corpus, and the Supreme Court eventually heard the case in *Ex Parte Milligan* (1866).[3] Five of the justices, speaking through Justice David Davis, ruled that Congress could suspend the writ of habeas corpus, but they denied to the federal government the power to conduct military trials of civilians unless there was an invasion and the civilian courts were closed. The majority opinion therefore implied that Congress could authorize Lincoln to suspend the writ far behind military lines. Pursuant to such a statute, "dangerous" civilians could be held indefinitely without any charges or trials. Criminal punishment, however, could not be imposed by military commissions unless civilian courts were inoperative. Of course, for the detainee, the distinction between indefinite detention and a prison sentence was at best an abstract one. However, what the majority's ruling did mean was that, as long as civilian courts were open, the military could not execute those found guilty in military trials.

In his dissenting opinion, Justice Salmon Chase argued that the majority's rule was too restrictive of the war power. Chase (and the three other justices who joined his dissent) agreed with the majority that Congress had not empowered the military to place Milligan on trial. But that did not mean, in his judgment, that Congress could not delegate such powers if it felt that the emergency required such extraordinary procedures. Whether the courts were open or not made no difference. It was up to Congress to decide if the situation warranted giving the military the power to try, punish, and even execute civilians.

Before World War II, *Ex Parte Milligan* was the most important precedent concerning the constitutionality of military detention of civilians during war. And though it denied that the military trials instituted by Lincoln were constitutional, it upheld the lawfulness of the arrests themselves (estimated anywhere from 13,000 to 38,000).[4] Moreover, certain commentators have argued that Lincoln's actions were in fact more authoritative than what the Supreme Court decided.

---

[3]71 U.S. 2 (1866).

[4]See Neely, *The Fate of Liberty*, Chapter 6.

BOX 3.1

Lincoln on War and Civil Liberties

[The suspension of habeas corpus] is allowed by the constitution on purpose that, men may be arrested and held, who can not be proved to be guilty of defined crime; "when, in cases of Rebellion or Invasion the public Safety may require it." This is precisely our present case—a case of Rebellion, wherein the public Safety does require the suspension. Indeed, arrests by process of courts, and arrests in cases of rebellion, do not proceed altogether upon the same basis. The former is directed at the small percentage of ordinary and continuous perpetration of crime; while the latter is directed at sudden and extensive uprisings against the government, which, at most, will succeed or fail, in no great length of time. In the latter case, arrests are made, not so much for what has been done, as for what probably would be done. The latter is more for the preventive, and less for the vindictive, than the former. In such cases the purposes of men are much more easily understood, than in cases of ordinary crime. The man who stands by and says nothing, when the peril of his government is discussed, can not be misunderstood. If not hindered, he is sure to help the enemy. Much more, if he talks ambiguously—talks for his country with "buts" and "ifs" and "ands." . . . [For example, many of the South's military leaders] were all within the power of the [federal] government since [when] the rebellion began, and were nearly as well known to be traitors then as now. Unquestionably if we had seized and held them, the insurgent cause would be much weaker. But no one of them had then committed any crime defined in the law. Everyone of them if arrested would have been discharged on Habeas Corpus, were the writ allowed to operate. In view of these and similar cases, I think the time not unlikely to come when I shall be blamed for having made too few arrests rather than too many.

. . . [Your view is that military arrests] shall not be made "outside of the lines of necessary military occupation, and the scenes of insurrection." Inasmuch, however, as the constitution itself makes no such distinction, I am unable to believe that there is any such constitutional distinction. I concede that the class of arrests complained of, can be constitutional only when, in cases of Rebellion or Invasion, the public Safety may require them; and I insist that in such cases, they are constitutional *wherever* the public safety does require them—as well in places to which they may prevent the rebellion extending, as in those where it may be already prevailing—as well where they may restrain mischievous interference with the raising and supplying of armies, to suppress the rebellion, as where the rebellion may actually be—as well where they may restrain the enticing men out of the army, as where they would prevent mutiny in the army—equally constitutional at all places where they will conduce to the public Safety, as against the dangers of Rebellion or Invasion. . . .

... Long experience has shown that armies can not be maintained unless desertion shall be punished by the severe penalty of death. The case requires, and the law and the constitution, sanction this punishment. Must I shoot a simple-minded soldier boy who deserts, while I must not touch a hair of a wily agitator who induces him to desert? This is none the less injurious when effected by getting a father, or brother, or friend, into a public meeting, and there working upon his feelings, till he is persuaded to write the soldier boy, that he is fighting in a bad cause, for a wicked administration of a contemptible government, too weak to arrest and punish him if he shall desert. I think that in such a case, to silence the agitator, and save the boy, is not only constitutional, but, withal, a great mercy.

... I can no more be persuaded that the government can constitutionally take no strong measure in time of rebellion, because it can be shown that the same could not be lawfully taken in time of peace, than I can be persuaded that a particular drug is not good medicine for a sick man, because it can be shown to not be good food for a well one. Nor am I able to appreciate the danger ... that the American people will, by means of military arrests during the rebellion, lose the right of public discussion, the liberty of speech and the press, the law of evidence, trial by jury, and Habeas corpus, throughout the indefinite peaceful future which I trust lies before them, any more than I am able to believe that a man could contract so strong an appetite for emetics during temporary illness, as to persist in feeding upon them through the remainder of his healthful life.

Source: Letter from A. Lincoln to Erastus Corning, June 12, 1863, reprinted in Roy P. Basler, ed., *Collected Works of Lincoln*, 9 vols. (New Brunswick, N.J.: Rutgers University Press, 1953–55), VI, pp. 264–67.

Edward S. Corwin best summed up this attitude when he said that to suppose that *Milligan* "would be of greater influence in determining presidential procedure in a future great emergency than precedents backed by the monumental reputation of Lincoln would be merely childish."[5] The Court itself had admitted in *Milligan*, a case not decided until after the Civil War was over, that during "the late wicked Rebellion the temper of the times did not allow that calmness in deliberation and discussion so necessary to a correct conclusion."[6] Was this statement an admission that the Court knew that the country could not live with its "correct conclusion" in a real wartime emergency? Again, are there practical limitations of the degree to which the Supreme Court can protect traditional rights and liberties that are infringed upon during the pursuit of victory in war?

---

[5]Cited in Clinton Rossiter, *Constitutional Dictatorship: Crisis Government in the Modern Democracies* (New York: Harcourt, Brace and World, 1963), p. 238.

[6]*Ex Parte Milligan*, 71 U.S. 2, 109 (1866).

BOX 3.2

A Reply to Lincoln

... [Whenever *habeas corpus* is] suspended in time of war, you seem to think that every remedy for a false and unlawful imprisonment is abrogated; and from this postulate you reach, at a single bound, the conclusion that there is no liberty under the Constitution which does not depend on the gracious indulgence of the Executive only. This great heresy once established, and by this mode of induction, there springs at once into existence a brood of crimes or offenses undefined by any rule, and hitherto unknown to the laws of this country; and this is followed by indiscriminate arrests, midnight seizures, military commissions, unheard-of modes of trial and punishment, and all the machinery of terror and despotism. Your language does not permit us to doubt as to your essential meaning, for you tell us, that "arrests are made not so much for what has been done, as for what probably would be done." And again: "The man who stands by and says nothing when the peril of his government is discussed, can not be misunderstood. If not hindered, (of course by arrest,) he is sure to help the enemy, and much more if he talks ambiguously, talks for his country with 'buts' and 'ifs' and 'ands.'" ... Silence itself is punishable according to this extraordinary theory, and still more so the expression of opinions, however loyal, if attended with criticism upon the policy of the Government. We must respectfully refuse our assent to this theory of constitutional law. We think that men may be rightfully silent if they so choose, while clamorous and needy patriots proclaim the praises of those who wield power; and as to the "buts," the "ifs," and the "ands," these are Saxon words, and belong to the vocabulary of freemen. ...

... [W]e can not acquiesce in your dogmas that arrests and imprisonment, without warrant or criminal accusation, in their nature lawless and arbitrary, opposed to the very letter of constitutional guarantees, can become in any sense rightful, by reason of a suspension of the writ of *habeas corpus*. We deny that the suspension of a single and peculiar remedy for such wrongs brings into existence new and unknown classes of offenses, or new causes for depriving men of their liberty. ...

In our deliberate judgement, the Constitution is not open to the new interpretation suggested by your communication now before us. ... The suspension of that remedial process [of the writ of *habeas corpus*] may prevent the enlargement of the accused traitor or conspirator, until he shall be legally tried and convicted or acquitted, but in this we find no justification for arrest and imprisonment without warrant, without cause, without the accusation or suspicion of crime. It seems to us, moreover, too plain for argument that the sacred right of trial by jury, and in courts where the law of the land is the rule of decision, is a right which is never dormant, never suspended, in peaceful and loyal communities and States. ...

This power which you have erected in theory is of vast and illimitable proportions. If we may trust you to exercise it mercifully and leniently, your successor, whether immediate or more remote, may wield it with the energy of Caesar or Napoleon, and with the will of a despot and a tyrant. It is a power without boundary or limit, because it proceeds upon a total suspension of all the constitutional and legal safeguards which protect the rights of the citizen. It is a power not inaptly described in the language of one of your Secretaries. Said Mr. Seward to the British Minister in Washington: "I can touch a bell on my right hand, and order the arrest of a citizen of Ohio. I can touch the bell again, and order the imprisonment of a citizen of New-York, and no power on earth but that of the President can release them. Can the Queen of England, in her dominions do as much?" This is the very language of a perfect despotism, and we learn from you, with profound emotion, that this is no idle boast. It is a despotism unlimited in principle, because the same arbitrary and unrestrained will or discretion which can place men under illegal restraint or banish them, can apply the rack or the thumbscrew, can put to torture or to death. Not thus have the people of this country hitherto understood their Constitution. No argument can commend to their judgment such interpretations of the Great Charter of their liberties. Quick as the lightning's flash, the intuitive sense of freemen perceives the sophistry and rejects the conclusion. . . .

Source: John V. L. Pruyn, *et al.,* "Reply to President's Lincoln's Letter of 12th June, 1863" (Papers from the Society for the Diffusion of Political Knowledge, No. 10), New York, 1863, reprinted in Frank Freidel, ed., *Union Pamphlets of the Civil War, 1861–1865,* 2 vols. (Cambridge, Mass.: Belknap Press of Harvard Univ. Press, 1967), II, pp. 756–62.

Another precedent that deserves mention is *United States v. Curtiss-Wright Export Corporation.* In 1934, Congress authorized the president to prohibit arms sales to two countries—Bolivia and Paraguay—that were fighting each other. President Franklin D. Roosevelt immediately established such an embargo, and Curtiss-Wright was later indicted for conspiracy to sell arms to Bolivia. In his majority opinion upholding FDR's embargo, Justice George Sutherland discussed the "fundamental" differences "between the powers of the federal government in respect to foreign or external affairs and those in respect of domestic or internal affairs." Sutherland argued that the federal government's foreign affairs powers were not merely those enumerated in the Constitution and authorized by the necessary and proper clause. Only the country's domestic powers were to be understood in this fashion because only they were granted to the federal government through the Constitution as ratified by the states. In contrast, "the investment of the federal government with the powers of external sovereignty did not depend upon the affirmative grants of the Constitution. The powers to declare and wage war, to conclude peace, to make treaties, to maintain diplomatic relations with other sovereignties, if they had never been mentioned in the Constitution, would have vested in the federal government as necessary concomitants of nationality."[7] In other words, the federal government had all the "foreign-affairs powers" that inhered in it as a sovereign nation, even if they were not granted to it by the Constitution. Accordingly, in Sutherland's view, the constitutionality of a law affecting individual rights could depend upon whether the law was based upon the federal government's domestic powers or upon its foreign affairs powers, including the war power. Although Sutherland's historical analysis has been criticized,[8] his opinion in *Curtiss-Wright* nonetheless tended to substantiate the conclusion that a law based upon domestic powers could be invalidated, whereas one based upon foreign affairs powers could be upheld, even though the laws in question had an identical impact upon individual rights.

Because the Court was sharply divided in *Milligan,* because Lincoln's actions to some extent have come to overshadow the constitutional significance of this decision, and because the extent of the ruling in *Curtiss-Wright* was unclear and its historical analysis questionable, the constitutional landscape existing at the time the military evacuated and interned the Japanese during World War II was sparse, ambiguous, and of disputable significance. No doubt, in a case of "military necessity," Congress could suspend the writ of habeas corpus, but it was less clear whether military detention required the suspension of the writ, whether the detention could be based upon race and/or ethnicity, and even whether courts should get involved with such questions during war.

Compared with the opaque character of this constitutional background, the facts of what happened to the Japanese are as clear and straightforward as they are tragic. It is now generally agreed that racial prejudice and war fever ("Never again!") had more to do with the treatment of the Japanese during World War II than anything that can be described as "military necessity." A long and sad history of racial prejudice pre-dated the events of World War II. Emigrants from Japan (the Issei) could neither become American citizens nor, for many years, own land in California. Nonetheless, by various tactics, including the transfer of land titles from the Issei to their native-born children who were citizens (the Nisei), the Japanese achieved considerable success in California agriculture. Many whites, including those associated with organizations like the Native Sons and Daughters of the Golden West, envied their success and despised them for it. Pearl Harbor gave such individuals a perfect opportunity to achieve what they had always wanted to do anyway: get the Japanese out of California.

Although no hostile actions were taken against the Japanese on the west coast during the first few weeks following Pearl Harbor, newspaper accounts of a Japanese spy ring and arrests of Japanese aliens who were on a dangerous-aliens list inflated popular fears. Additional reportage about the confiscation of contraband (shortwave radios, cameras, and the like) exacerbated the problem. The Japanese American Citizens' League (JACL), a patriotic organization of Nisei that later

---

[7]299 U.S. 304, 315, 318 (1936).

[8]See Charles A. Lofgren. "*United States v. Curtiss-Wright:* An Historical Reassessment," *Yale Law Journal* 83 (1973), pp. 1–32.

Headline 3.1

played an important role in *Korematsu,* at first took a conciliatory course by informing on "disloyal Issei." This policy, however, did not satisfy the hatemongers. Instead of proving the loyalty of the Nisei, as it was intended, it convinced many Americans that some of the Japanese were dangerously disloyal. By late January 1942, west coast politicians, lobbyists, and the press were demanding the evacuation of the Japanese from the west coast. (See Headline 3.1.)

A select committee of the House of Representatives, known as the Tolan Committee, held hearings on the west coast to consider the issue of evacuation and internment. These hearings are an excellent window into the political atmosphere of the period. They represented the entire spectrum of public debate concerning evacuation of not only the Japanese but also the Germans and Italians. (See Box 3.3.) California's attorney general, Earl Warren—who later became the chief justice of the United States during one of its most progressive and activist periods—testified at these hearings. He was one of the leading proponents of evacuation who had earlier convinced the military that evacuation was necessary.[9] At the hearings, he called upon the military to address the threat posed by disloyal Japanese, arguing that the location of Japanese around strategic points was not always a "coincidence." The testimony of other witnesses shows how many Americans were convinced that the Japanese were somehow different from "ordinary" Americans, not only "culturally" but also "psychically." Others claimed that even the loyal Japanese deserved to be evacuated as a punishment for their "sins."

---

[9]Peter Irons, *Justice at War,* (New York: Oxford University Press, 1983), p. 41.

BOX 3.3

TOLAN COMMITTEE HEARINGS ON JAPANESE INTERNMENT

ATTORNEY GENERAL EARL A. WARREN, OF THE STATE OF CALIFORNIA:

For some time I have been of the opinion that the solution of our alien enemy problem with all of its ramifications, which include the descendants of aliens, is not only a Federal problem but is a military problem. We believe that all of the decisions in that regard must be made by the military command that is charged with the security of this area. I am convinced that the fifth-column activities of our enemy call for the participation of people who are in fact American citizens, and that if we are to deal realistically with the problem we must realize that we will be obliged in time of stress to deal with subversive elements of our own citizenry. . . .

I do not mean to suggest that it should be thought that all of these Japanese who are adjacent to strategic points are knowing parties to some vast conspiracy to destroy our State by sudden and mass sabotage. Undoubtedly, the presence of many of these persons in their present locations is mere coincidence, but it would seem equally beyond doubt that the presence of others is not coincidence. . . .

. . . [I]n any case, it is certainly evident that the Japanese population of California is, as a whole, ideally situated, with reference to points of strategic importance, to carry into execution a tremendous program of sabotage on a mass scale should any considerable number of them be inclined to do so.

MR. VERNE SMITH, CHIEF OF POLICE OF ALAMEDA, CALIFORNIA:

There is, so far as I can ascertain, no particular common meeting ground for the oriental and occidental mind. In other words, as an experienced police officer, I find it practically impossible to obtain information, to obtain true impressions of the Japanese. It is much more difficult, in fact more nearly impossible than it is with the other two classes of aliens [the Germans and Italians].

Therefore, I think it should be treated as a different problem and, to be perfectly blunt about it, I would recommend the internment in the very near future of all male Japanese on the coast here. That is my recommendation. I wish you gentlemen would consider it.

MR. MILLER FREEMAN, PUBLISHER, OF SEATTLE, WASHINGTON:

It is my recommendation that all Japanese, both alien and United States born, be evacuated from the Pacific Coast States, and other defense areas, and kept in the interior under strict control for the duration of the war.

While it may be argued that many American-born Japanese are loyal to the United States there are sufficient numbers who are proven to be assisting Japan's war effort to warrant such action not only in the Nation's interest but for protection of the Japanese themselves.

Two-thirds of the Japanese in this country are now American born, largely of mature years. Those who are genuinely loyal find themselves in their present difficult position through the treacherous attack by Japan on this Nation, and because of their own sins of omission.

Although the American born are strongly organized for proclaimed patriotic purposes, why have they taken no stand against the aggressions of Japan in the Orient over the last 10 years? Why have they not denounced the depredations and enslavement by Japan of the Chinese, the Koreans and other Asiatics?

Why have the loyal American-born Japanese not forced the closing of the hundreds of Japanese-language schools that have been operated continuously right up to December 7 for nearly a half-century in the United States and Hawaii, the sole function of these schools being to train the children up to owe their allegiance to Japan?

Why also have they continued Japanese-language newspapers? Practically all, aliens and American-born alike, read English. Only after the attack by Japan on this country were the Japanese-language newspapers converted into English.

Study of the historical record of Japanese colonization in the United States and its possessions should be made by your committee.... Such study will show that the Japanese Government as a part of its ambitious program of colonization of North and South America, and as a preliminary to conquest, planted its immigrants in the United States by the combined use of fraud, collusion, political and military force, and over the most intense and sustained opposition of the various States of the Pacific coast, and the Territory of Hawaii.

MR. S. W. SPANGLER, *VICE PRESIDENT OF THE SEATTLE FIRST NATIONAL BANK:*
From my own experience and observation, I have found it exceedingly difficult to divine the oriental. By that I mean apparently their mental processes may not be identical with our own.... I would be very loath to think that a vast number of friends of mine who are Japanese ... lack loyalty to the extent of being a dangerous element to the Government. At the same time, I perhaps should confess that I have very scant, and perhaps not sufficient, basis for knowing which is the correct interpretation; that is, whether or not you can rely upon them. In the organization with which I am connected, we have had a Japanese there for, I think 30 years. He is not with us now. I cannot conceive of him being other than reliable. At the same time, I can't divine the character.

GOVERNOR CULBERT L. OLSON OF CALIFORNIA:
... The loyal Japanese people realize also that the average Caucasian can't distinguish between the Japanese. They all look alike. It places them in a most unfortunate disadvantage. I have found a willingness with such loyal Japanese citizens to abide by and voluntarily follow any program of evacuation of all Japanese that may be determined upon.

MR. LOUIS GOLDBLATT, SECRETARY OF THE CALIFORNIA STATE CONGRESS OF INDUSTRIAL ORGANIZATIONS INDUSTRIAL UNION COUNCIL:

We feel, however, that a good deal of this problem has gotten out of hand, Mr. Tolan, inasmuch as both the local and State authorities, instead of becoming bastions of defense, of democracy and justice, joined the wolf pack when the cry came out 'Let's get the yellow menace.'. . .

I am referring here particularly to the attack against the native-born Japanese, an attack which, as far as we can find out, was whipped up. There was a basis for it because there has always been a basis on the Pacific coast for suspicion, racial suspicion, which has been well fostered, well bred, particularly by the Hearst newspapers over a period of 20 to 25 years.

. . . [T]he only people who have shown a semblance of decency and honesty and forthrightness in this whole situation are the second-generation Japanese who, on their own accord, have made the statement . . . that in their opinion the thing they ought to do is get out of here. They are in accord with evacuation now, not in accord in principle but in accord simply because they realize that, perhaps, the only thing they can do now to avoid vigilantism, mob rule, and hysteria, beatings, and riots is to evacuate. Of course, that doesn't speak very well for either our State or local authorities that such a situation was permitted to arise.

. . . [O]nce this policy of making distinctions or determining espionage or sabotage along racial, national lines, has begun there is no end. . . .

CLARENCE RUST, ATTORNEY, OF OAKLAND, CALIFORNIA:

. . . I am utterly in opposition to the adoption of a program of hysteria as a national policy. Our country is strong and virile because its citizenship emerged from the fittest survival of the melting pot. We reject the European and Asiatic doctrine of the attainder of blood. Nor shall any man be discriminated against because of his race, color, or previous condition of servitude.

Japanese, Italians, and Germans are also people. I am profoundly disturbed by the present attempt to heap upon their descendants in this country contempt and hatred. If we are to begin a program which amounts to persecution of sections of our citizenry, because of their race or origin, then Hitlerism has already won America, though the Nazi Army is 4,000 miles away.

MR. MIKE M. MASAOKA, NATIONAL SECRETARY OF THE JAPANESE-AMERICAN CITIZENS LEAGUE:

If, in the judgment of military and Federal authorities, evacuation of Japanese residents from the west coast is a primary step toward assuring the safety of this Nation, we will have no hesitation in complying with the necessities implicit in that judgment. But, if, on the other hand, such evacuation is primarily a measure whose surface urgency cloaks the desires of political or other pressure groups who want us to leave merely from motives of self-interest, we feel that we have every right to protest and to demand equitable judgment on our merits as American citizens.

MICHIO KUNITANI, NISEI DEMOCRATIC CLUB OF OAKLAND, CALIFORNIA:

. . . We come here as Americans, not by virtue of our birth in America, but by the social and cultural forces in America. We come here to be treated as Americans, and we want to live like Americans in America.

As I say, we are Americans, not by the mere technicality of birth, but all these other forces of sports, amusements, schools, churches, which are in our communities and which affect our lives directly.

Some of us are Yankee fans; some of us are Dodger fans; some like to sip beer; some like to go up to the Top of the Mark once in a while; we enjoy Jack Benny; we listen to Beethoven, and even some of us go through the Congressional Record. That is something.

The main idea that our group wanted to present here today was that we didn't want to be treated as a special group of enemy aliens and as descendants of enemy aliens. We want to be treated like Americans, or like other groups, like Italians, Yugoslavs, Finns, or any other group. . . .

CHAUNCEY TRAMUTOLO, AN ATTORNEY REPRESENTING ITALIAN-AMERICANS:

. . . [Joe DiMaggio's father] is not a citizen. Both the father and mother have raised eight children, three which the sports world know as major leaguers. Joe is the outstanding hitter of the entire league, both the American and National, and he has been chosen as the most valuable player in the country. His brother Dominic is with the Boston Red Sox and the other brother, Vincent, is with the Pittsburgh team of the National League.

Now, neither of the DiMaggio seniors, father or mother, are citizens. There are eight children all born here. . . . They are people who are absolutely beyond any question of a doubt as loyal as anybody you can find. . . .

Source: National Defense Migration, H. Report No. 2124, 77th Cong., 2d Sess. (1942), pp. 139–43, 149, 154–55, 204, 255.

For still others, evacuation was a sad necessity. Witnesses from the other side of the political spectrum, of course, condemned the evacuation as blatant racism and a tragic departure from American ideals.

Perhaps the most revealing excerpts were from the Japanese witnesses. Mike M. Masaoka, one of the leaders of the JACL, defended the rights of Japanese-Americans and demanded equitable treatment, but nonetheless he promised that the Japanese would comply with a military judgment that evacuation was necessary. What does this kind of concession say about the political atmosphere of the time? Did the Japanese themselves think that evacuation was inevitable? And what of Michio Kunitani's claim that the Japanese—not because of their place of birth, but because of their attitudes and lifestyles—were just as American as any-

Headline 3.2

one else? The question that he implicitly asked was fundamental. If, as the last excerpt argues, Joe DiMaggio, his brothers and sisters, and his parents were absolutely loyal, why was it so difficult to believe that Japanese Yankee and Dodger
fans were not? What explains the disparate treatment of Italian- and Japanese-
Americans during World War II?

At the center of the political storm reflected in the Tolan hearings, Lieu-
tenant John L. DeWitt, commander of the Western Defense Command (an official military "theatre of operations" that included eight Western states), considered his options. After initially opposing evacuation, in early February he asked
his superiors in Washington for authority to remove the Japanese. To justify his
request, DeWitt pointed to several Japanese submarine attacks on American shipping, to a couple of isolated instances of submarines shelling the coast (see Headline 3.2), and to reports of "signaling" from the coastline, presumably from Japanese agents to the submarines. In a similar vein, there were unsubstantiated
"intercepts" of unauthorized radio transmissions. Based upon these kinds of reports—some true, some imaginary—Dewitt argued that "military necessity" justified evacuation because there was no quick and effective way to separate the loyal
from the disloyal Japanese.

On February 19, President Roosevelt responded by signing Executive Order
9066, which granted military officials the authority to establish military zones
"from which any or all persons may be excluded" by military order. Congress co-
operated by enacting Public Law 503, which imposed criminal sanctions upon
anyone who disobeyed such military orders. These exertions of the federal government's war power gave DeWitt considerable latitude in regard to the "prob-

lem" of Japanese residing on the west coast. Relying upon the executive order and the law, he first imposed a curfew on the Japanese, but soon thereafter, beginning on March 2, he issued a series of evacuation orders requiring the Japanese to leave the west coast. Any possibility of voluntary migration evaporated when the interior states refused to accept the Japanese. Because no one wanted the Japanese, forced evacuation and internment seemingly became the only option. Accordingly, by the end of March, DeWitt issued "freeze orders" prohibiting the Japanese from leaving the areas in which they lived. They had no choice but to wait for the exclusion orders compelling them to report to "assembly centers," from which they were transferred to internment camps known as "relocation centers." All of these orders were enforced by the threat of criminal sanctions.

When FDR issued Executive Order 9066 and Congress enacted Public Law 503, responsible political leaders knew that DeWitt intended to evacuate Japanese-American citizens from the west coast even though the order and the law did not specifically refer to the Japanese. Moreover, as evacuation developed into a policy of internment, both political branches of the federal government acquiesced. The federal government was thereby implicitly claiming that its war power was a sufficient constitutional basis to imprison, without any charges, trials, or individualized hearings, a large group of American citizens defined by their ethnicity. The government could do this, it implied, even though it had neither declared martial law on the west coast nor suspended the writ of habeas corpus.[10]

Presumably, Congress refrained from declaring martial law or suspending the writ because it felt that it was unnecessary to subject all U.S. citizens to arbitrary executive arrest and detention. "Military necessity" required only that the Japanese be subject to such controls. And because Congress had the power to suspend the writ of habeas corpus for all citizens in an emergency, it assumed that it had the authority to take the smaller step of authorizing the evacuation and detention of a group of American citizens, even if the group was an ethnic minority.

Perhaps because of the political atmosphere, very few Japanese fought the constitutionality of their evacuation and confinement: Only one Japanese in ten thousand went to court to fight for his or her rights, and only four cases made their way up to the Supreme Court.[11] The first was *Hirabayashi v. United States* (1943), a case involving a curfew violation and a refusal to obey an evacuation order. The Court acted cautiously. Because the district court had sentenced Hirabayashi to three months' imprisonment for each offense, with the sentences to be served concurrently, the Supreme Court had an opportunity to follow the preferred course of Hugo Black, a justice who usually defended the civil rights and liberties of minorities and individuals: "I want it done on narrowest possible points."[12]

---

[10]The governor of Hawaii, acting under authority granted to him by Hawaii's Organic Act, did declare martial law during World War II.

[11]*Yasui v. United States,* 320 U.S. 115, (1943); *Hirabayashi v. United States,* 320 U.S. 81 (1943); *Korematsu v. United States,* 323 U.S. 214 (1944); *Ex Parte Endo,* 323 U.S. 283 (1944). For the 1/10,000 figure, see Irons, *Justice at War,* p. 76.

[12]Irons, *Justice at War,* p. 231.

In a majority opinion written by Chief Justice Harlan F. Stone, the Court upheld the curfew conviction but declined to address the constitutionality of the
evacuation order. The curfew was within the war power because the federal government had reasonable grounds for believing that it would aid the fight against
sabotage and espionage. "Reasonable grounds" were all that was required, because the Fourteenth Amendment's equal protection clause—the clause of the
Constitution that explicitly prohibited most forms of racial discrimination—restricted only the states, not the federal government. Accordingly, the curfew was
constitutional unless it violated the Fifth Amendment by depriving the Japanese
of life, liberty, or property without "due process of law." But the curfew, Stone
reasoned, did not violate "due process" because the federal government had plausible grounds for its fear that some Japanese would form a "fifth column"—a disloyal group that would aid any Japanese invasion of the West Coast. First, the
Japanese had not assimilated with the white population; second, many Japanese
children went to special language schools that indoctrinated the students with
Japanese nationalistic propaganda or, even worse, returned to Japan for their education (the Kibei); third, a policy of dual citizenship had enabled Japan to maintain its influence over the Japanese-American community. Given these factors,
the military authorities, the president, and Congress could reasonably conclude
that some unspecified number of Japanese, who could not be easily or quickly
identified and separated, were disloyal to the United States. Accordingly, to ensure that the disloyal were confined to their homes at night, the necessity for
prompt action justified imposing a curfew on all persons of Japanese ancestry.

In regard to Hirabayashi's refusal to obey the evacuation order, Stone reasoned that the three-month sentence for the curfew violation would be upheld regardless of what the Court said about evacuation. There was therefore no necessity for the Court to examine the constitutionality of the evacuation itself.
Hirabayashi therefore reveals how the Court can define the constitutional questions that are presented to it. By avoiding the evacuation issue, by focusing instead
on the least objectionable aspect of DeWitt's program, the Court secured a unanimous decision—an important factor in a wartime situation. In addition, the government was quite happy with a decision that left the more controversial constitutional aspects of its program unresolved. Time worked in the government's favor.
The longer it could delay a Supreme Court decision on evacuation or internment,
the more likely it became that events on the front lines would make the whole
question moot.

Apart from these political considerations that inclined the Court to decide
Hirabayashi narrowly, it is arguable that the Court should *always* decide only
those constitutional issues that *must* be decided in any particular case. The unresolved constitutional issues should be left to future decisions in which the Court
would have no choice but to decide them. In this way, the Court determines constitutional law in "small bites." The purported advantage of this slow, incremental
approach to constitutional adjudication is that general doctrines of constitutional
law are tested by experience as they slowly evolve. Wholesale creation of new
rules should be avoided because no judge, no matter how brilliant, can foresee all
the possible situations to which a rule will be applied. Accordingly, judges should
confine their attention to only those issues that must be resolved in order to de-

cide the case before them. They should make constitutional law only in a "retail" fashion.

Of course, in the context of the Japanese internment cases, the people who paid the price for this incremental form of constitutional adjudication were the Japanese. They spent more time behind barbed wire without knowing whether their constitutional rights had been violated or not. Although it may be understandable why the Supreme Court would want to avoid the responsibility for either condemning or endorsing the evacuation and internment of the Japanese, what it did in *Hirabayashi* is nonetheless troubling. Should it have acted differently? Did it have, regardless of the war, an obligation to address all the constitutional issues raised in the case? What about the advantages of the incremental approach to constitutional adjudication?

By upholding the curfew in *Hirabayashi*, the Court legitimated the notion that, during war, judges could and should monitor such policies. This feature of the decision is comforting to those who believe that the war power cannot be a basis for the suspension of the Bill of Rights, at least not unless martial law is justifiably declared. However, the manner by which the Court reviewed the policy is not so reassuring. By describing the grounds for the federal government's curfew policy as "reasonable," the Court did not mean to endorse the curfew as a matter of policy. What the Court thought of the policy itself was purportedly irrelevant to its task of assessing its constitutionality. Where "the conditions call for the exercise of judgment and discretion and for the choice of means by those branches of the Government on which the Constitution has placed the responsibility of war-making, it is not for any court to sit in review of the wisdom of their action or substitute its judgment for theirs."[13] The curfew might be unnecessary or unwise—that was for Congress, the president, and the military to decide—but it was still constitutional because "reasonable grounds" supported it. In this way, the Court relieved itself of responsibility for the curfew policy even though, at the same time, it upheld its constitutionality.

By deciding *Hirabayashi* in this manner, did the Court want to have it both ways? Can the Court say that distinctions "between citizens solely because of their ancestry are by their very nature odious to a free people whose institutions are founded upon the doctrine of equality"[14] and then permit the military to use a racially based curfew without endorsing its wisdom or necessity? At a minimum, *Hirabayashi* shows how ambiguous the Court's role is when it determines the constitutionality of a policy by assessing its "reasonableness." In such instances, is it a court of law or a policymaker second-guessing what the political officials have done? If the latter, should the Court ever second-guess what the military thinks is necessary for victory during war? Does the Court have any competence in this area of policy making?

The Supreme Court decided *Hirabayashi* on June 21, 1943, and did not sit to hear oral argument in *Korematsu* until October 11, 1944. While many Japanese waited in the internment camps during this fifteen-month interval, government

---

[13]*Hirabayashi v. United States,* 320 U.S. 81, 93 (1943).

[14]*Id.* at 100.

lawyers battled with one another because four different governmental entities were involved with the litigation: the Alien Enemy Control Unit (ACU); the solicitor general's office; the War Department; and the War Relocation Authority (WRA), the civilian agency that administered the internment camps. Lawyers affiliated with these distinct governmental institutions had contrasting perspectives on strategy. The result was political infighting and professional misconduct that had a direct impact upon the process of constitutional argumentation in *Korematsu.*

Edward Ennis, director of the ACU, had discovered in April 1943, before the Court decided *Hirabayashi,* that intelligence officers in the Office of Naval Intelligence (ONI), the military agency responsible for investigating the loyalty of Japanese-Americans before the war, had advised that only the Kibei, their parents, and members of Japanese-American military societies (approximately 10,000 people) were potentially disloyal. Accordingly, Ennis asked Charles Fahy, the solicitor general (the official who represents the government before the Supreme Court), whether this information should not be brought to the attention of the Supreme Court. Fahy, however, declined to inform the Court because he knew that such evidence would undermine a central premise of the government's justification for the evacuation.[15] The War Department had claimed that there was not sufficient time to provide individualized hearings for the 110,000 Japanese, but such a procedure would probably have been possible if only 10,000 had required such individualized treatment. The Supreme Court therefore decided *Hirabayashi* without knowing that the military intelligence agency charged with monitoring Japanese disloyalty thought that there were, at most, only 10,000 disloyal Japanese on the west coast at the beginning of U.S. involvement in World War II.

A similar, though more serious, problem arose as the solicitor general prepared the briefs in *Korematsu.* In early 1944, the War Department published DeWitt's *Final Report* on the evacuation of the Japanese from the west coast. In this document, DeWitt claimed that intercepts of unidentified radio transmissions had indicated that Japanese attacks on American shipping off the west coast had been linked to on-shore espionage activity. Ennis and Francis Biddle, the U.S. attorney general, asked the Federal Bureau of Investigation and the Federal Communications Commission (FCC) to comment on DeWitt's allegations. Both of these federal agencies denied having any information supporting DeWitt's claims. Indeed, the FCC said it could provide documentation that it had informed DeWitt before the evacuation had begun that no reports of such radio transmissions had been verified. Ennis therefore wanted a footnote placed in the *Korematsu* brief that would explicitly state that the Justice Department did not accept the espionage claims underlying the War Department's "military necessity" argument for evacuation. In the end, Fahy, subject to political pressure from the War Department, incorporated a footnote that distanced the Justice Department from the *Final Report,* though the footnote did not explicitly criticize the report. (See Brief for the

---

[15]See Irons, *Justice at War,* pp. 202–6.

United States, page 129, note 23).[16] Once again the Justice Department failed to give the Supreme Court specific information that was directly relevant to the constitutionality of the evacuation and detention program.

The general point is that constitutional adjudication is rarely, if ever, merely an academic enterprise of gathering the most relevant legal precedents and marshaling the "best" constitutional arguments. The process of constitutional argumentation, for better or for worse, is itself a political process subject to clashes of personalities, tactics, and institutional policies. Of course, the fear is that such political factors can undermine the integrity of constitutional adjudication, draining it of its legal character and, hence, of its legitimacy. Whether this in fact happened in *Korematsu* is an intriguing and important question.

Ennis, though he signed the Justice Department's brief in *Korematsu*, was not satisfied with Fahy's refusal to inform the Court of the falsehoods contained in DeWitt's *Final Report*. He personally met with Roger Baldwin and other lawyers from the American Civil Liberties Union (ACLU) to help them prepare their side of the *Korematsu* case. It is difficult to believe that he did not advise them, at least generally, of what he had found out about the military's claim of "military necessity."[17] If so, was his conduct justifiable because it aided the ACLU's attack on the fallacious "military necessity" argument? Does it show that the process of constitutional argumentation is a political one that has its self-corrective aspect? Or does Ennis's conduct provide additional evidence that the process, at least when civil liberties are being violated during war, is too political, thereby undermining the Supreme Court's special character?

The political conflicts and manueverings that are recounted here, however, do not make the whole of the *Korematsu* case. The briefs that follow display the substantive constitutional arguments made on behalf of Korematsu, the Justice Department, the ACLU, the JACL, and the Western states of California, Oregon, and Washington. The first two briefs, the main briefs in the case, oppose each other not only in substance but also in style. Korematsu's brief, quite rhetorical in style and self-righteous in tone, was written by Wayne Collins, a young lawyer from San Francisco. Painting the issues of the case in stark, contrasting colors, he condemned the entire program of evacuation and detention as a wholesale violation of the Constitution that, if permitted, would turn the American system of government into a dictatorship no different from Hitler's Nazi Germany. "Military necessity" did not justify the program, Collins argued; even a curfew was completely unnecessary. The entire program, he maintained, was a product of DeWitt's "racism," not one of military necessity. According to Collins, the Supreme Court therefore had made a monumental mistake in *Hirabayashi* that it should correct immediately.

---

[16]For a full account of the conflicts between the government lawyers involved with the internment cases and a more comprehensive discussion of the professional misconduct that occurred, see Irons, *Justice at War*, Chapter 11.

[17]See Irons, *Justice at War*, pp. 302–7.

In contrast, the Justice Department's brief submitted by Solicitor General Charles Fahy was far more legalistic and dispassionate in tone. Rather than the constitutionality of the entire program of evacuation and detention, the brief narrowed the issue before the Court to a specific, more technical question: In time of war, can Congress and the president delegate to a military official the power to exclude a person from a designated military area? Because Korematsu was charged only with staying in an area from which he had been excluded, not with failing to report to an assembly center (even though he had violated this order also), the government argued that detention was not involved with this case—the order to leave an area was "separable" from an order to report to an assembly center. Relying heavily upon this legal doctrine of "separability," the government argued that the war power, as defined and recognized in *Hirabayashi,* was a sufficient constitutional basis for what the government had done. The Court should defer to the military's judgment that the evacuation of the Japanese from the west coast was reasonably related to the war effort and avoid the issue of the constitutionality of detention and internment.

The ACLU, the JACL, and the Western states were not "parties" to the lawsuit initiated by Fred Korematsu against the United States. Nonetheless, the Supreme Court permitted these parties to file *amici curiae* ("friends of the court") briefs because it was quite clear that the case would affect the rights of many more people besides Korematsu. By exploring the wider implications of the Court's decision, such briefs play a valuable role in constitutional adjudication. Also, organizations that finance *amicus curiae* briefs often have greater resources than individual plaintiffs, thereby enabling them to raise the level of constitutional debate. It is arguable that this is what happened in *Korematsu.* Because Roger Baldwin, director of the ACLU, had only contempt for Wayne Collins's abilities and tactics, he instructed his organization's lawyers to develop a careful legal argument showing how detention was inherently involved in *Korematsu.* He feared not only that Collins's aggressive and rhetorical style would antagonize the Court, but also that the government's argument narrowing the issue to one of evacuation would prove victorious unless it was contested in a serious and thoughtful way. Baldwin also thought that the arguments of "military necessity" contained in DeWitt's *Final Report* should be closely scrutinized, not generally condemned. And last, as a tactical matter, it made little sense to condemn *Hirabayashi,* a case that the Court had decided only a year before. Better to show the Court how the facts and issues of *Korematsu* were different from those of *Hirabayashi* than to demand that the Court overturn such a recent precedent.

Were Baldwin's concerns about Collins's brief justified? As an example of constitutional argumentation, was Collins's brief somehow defective? If so, is it possible that a certain style of argumentation is preferred by the Supreme Court? Given the role that the Court plays in our constitutional order, is the preference justifiable or arbitrary?

Rather than contesting the law that the Supreme Court had promulgated in *Hirabayashi,* the 200-page brief submitted by the JACL attacked the factual underpinnings of the federal government's "military necessity" argument. Its length makes it impossible to summarize even briefly all the factual issues that the JACL brought to the Court's attention. The following representative selection tries to rebut the claim that the Japanese were not assimilable and indicts General De-Witt as an American racist. In opposition to the JACL, the brief filed by the three Western states argued that events since the evacuation proved that the military had been right all along. For instance, many Japanese in the internment camps refused to sign a loyalty oath to the United States and instead demanded repatriation to Japan. This clearly indicated their disloyalty to the United States. In the opinion of the Western states, facts such as these clearly justified DeWitt's program of evacuation and internment.

In *Korematsu*, the Court had to decide two basic questions: Did the case involve detention? Did the Court have to defer to the military's finding of "military necessity"? Justice Hugo Black, author of the majority opinion, resolved both of these issues in favor of the federal government. Detention was not a factor in the case because Korematsu had been convicted only of failing to obey an exclusion order. He could have left the area because, in Black's view, the exclusion order had superseded the March 27 "freeze" order forbidding him from leaving San Leandro. Moreover, Black added, if Korematsu had obeyed the exclusion order by reporting to an assembly center, no one could say for sure that he would have been placed in detention in a relocation center.

In regard to whether the Court had to defer to the military's finding of "necessity," Black insisted that the racial basis of the evacuation had to be subjected to "the most rigid scrutiny." Nonetheless, he concluded that he could not "reject as unfounded" the military's judgment that the policy was a "reasonable" precaution. "Real military dangers" had existed, and there had been "evidence of disloyalty of some" of the Japanese. These factors, not racial prejudice, explained why Korematsu had to be evacuated. And the Court "cannot—by availing ourselves of the calm perspective of hindsight—now say that at that time these actions were unjustified."

In their dissents in *Korematsu*, Justice Owen Roberts focused on the argument that detention was not involved in the case, and Justice Frank Murphy ridiculed the claim that the military had ever had sufficient evidence to justify the evacuation of the Japanese. To ignore detention was, Roberts argued, to substitute a "hypothetical case for the case actually before the court," it was "to shut our eyes to reality." In May 1942, Korematsu faced conflicting orders. The March 27 order forbade him from leaving the area; the May 3 order forbade him from staying. His only option was to report to an assembly center and submit to an indefinite period of unconstitutional detention. In this way, the orders functioned as "a cleverly devised trap . . . to lock him up in a concentration camp." Korematsu therefore had to have the right to object to the constitutionality of detention because the military order that he disobeyed was a means to accomplish an unconstitutional result. If the evacuation orders had not been linked to this unconstitutional program of detention, if the program had been one only of excluding the Japanese from the west coast, not interning them, then "the Hirabayashi Case would be authority for sustaining it." But because it was linked to such a program, Roberts concluded, Korematsu had the right to raise constitutional objections to detention.

In contrast, Justice Murphy claimed that even the evacuation of the Japanese minority, apart from detention, was unconstitutional because there was no "military necessity" for it. Judges had the duty of monitoring the "reasonableness" of military orders that affected civilians, and the evacuation order assumed "that *all* persons of Japanese ancestry may have a dangerous tendency to commit sabotage and espionage and to aid our Japanese enemy in other ways." But there was absolutely no warrant for such a proposition. The sociological and racial claims made by the military, according to Murphy, were based on "misinformation, half-truths, and insinuations" of people who were racially prejudiced against the Japanese. Murphy could not accept such a "legalization of racism" because he felt that judges were authorized to review the substantive merits of the military's policies. At least in the absence of martial law, judges were to assess military policy for fear that individuals will be "impoverished of their constitutional rights on a plea of military necessity that has neither substance nor support."

Both Justices Felix Frankfurter and Robert Jackson disagreed with Murphy's proposition that judges could or should second-guess what responsible military and political officials had decided to do during war. "In the very nature of things," Jackson insisted, "military decisions are not susceptible of intelligent judicial appraisal." This was so even though it "would be impracticable and dangerous idealism" to expect the military to "conform to conventional tests of constitutionality." Because the "armed forces must protect a society, not merely its Constitution," defense measures "will not, and often should not, be held within the limits that bind civil authority in peace." Nevertheless, Jackson reasoned, just because a military policy like the evacuation of the Japanese from the west coast is a justifiable one does not mean that it is constitutional. The evacuation was unconstitutional even if valid from a military point of view. Despite its necessity or reasonableness, the Court should not place its constitutional imprimatur upon it because the decision would then lie about "like a loaded weapon ready for the hand of any authority that can bring forward a plausible claim of an urgent need." The Court should declare the policy unconstitutional but not expect the military to respect its decision. According to Jackson, the "chief restraint" upon those exercising the war power is not the Supreme Court but rather "the political judgment of their contemporaries" and "the moral judgments of history."

Frankfurter agreed with Jackson that judges could not review the merits of military policy, but he rejected his argument that judges should nevertheless declare such policies unconstitutional if they violated any part of the Constitution. What Jackson failed to realize, according to Frankfurter, was that the war power gave the federal government additional powers during war, powers that cut into traditional individual rights. Military actions could not "be stigmatized as lawless because like action in times of peace would be lawless." During war, to call such actions "unconstitutional" is "to suffuse a part of the Constitution with an atmosphere of unconstitutionality." Instead, "reasonably expedient military precautions" during war should be considered as constitutional as any reasonable peacetime precautions based upon the commerce power. And judges need not fear that by sanctioning such precedents they undermine the Constitution. The war power is "as much part of the Constitution as provisions looking to a nation at peace."

The five opinions of *Korematsu* constitute an insightful debate on the meaning and significance of the war power's relationship to civil rights and liberties. The substantive arguments contained in them and the briefs balance the political factors lurking in the Japanese internment cases. Both the arguments and the political factors have a bearing upon the central question of this chapter: What could and should the Court have done in *Korematsu?* Did politics or constitutional argumentation, if they can be disentangled, have more of an impact upon what the Court did?

It should be noted that when the Court was considering the arguments in *Korematsu,* the justices knew that FDR and his cabinet were deciding how and when to end the program of Japanese exclusion and detention. By the middle of 1944, everyone agreed that there was no longer—if there ever was—any "military necessity" for the program. However, "insiders" of the administration, perhaps including Justice Frankfurter, knew that FDR wanted to delay the return of the Japanese to the west coast until after the 1944 elections.[18] Presumably, FDR feared than an "early" return would hurt him politically. If so, what is your reaction? Is it disconcerting that political/partisan factors delayed the release of tens of thousands of Japanese, especially given that racial prejudice and war hysteria had so much to do with their detention in the first place?

It is, however, even more troubling that the Supreme Court may have delayed its decisions in *Korematsu* and *Ex Parte Endo.* The Court handed down both of these decisions—one upholding the evacuation, the other denying that an admittedly loyal citizen could be detained[19]—on December, 18, 1944, one day after the military announced the termination of the exclusion and detention program.[20] Such timing tends to substantiate the charge that the Supreme Court gave the Japanese much too little, much too late. Years later, Justice William O. Douglas expressed his regret about what the Court did in the Japanese internment cases yet insisted that people no longer "understood" the military–political context of the time. (See Box 3.4.) Do his recollections suggest that what the Court did in *Korematsu* was regettable but understandable? If so, during war, what can citizens legally and politically expect from the Supreme Court?

During the 1980s, events transpired that alleviated to a small degree the tragedy of the Japanese internment. First, in 1984, a federal district judge vacated the conviction of Fred Korematsu in *Korematsu v. United States.*[21] Then, in 1986, Gordon Hirabayashi's conviction for failing to register for evacuation was similarly vacated, though the judge refused to vacate his curfew-violation conviction.[22] In both cases, the basis for the reversals was governmental misconduct: Executive officials had either withheld relevant information or submitted false information.

---

[18]See Irons, *Justice at War,* pp. 268–77, 320.

[19]The Court never did decide the question of whether the military during war could be authorized, without any suspension of the writ of habeas corpus, to detain citizens of a particular ethnic group whose loyalties were unknown.

[20]For a fuller account, see Irons, *Justice at War,* pp. 344–46.

[21]584 F. Supp. 1406 (N.D.Cal. 1984).

[22]*Hirabayashi v. United States,* 627 F. Supp. 1445 (W.D.Wash. 1986).

BOX 3.4

JUSTICE WILLIAM O. DOUGLAS RECOLLECTS

The war power is a pervasive one. As Hughes once wrote: "The power to wage war is the power to wage war successfully." People are regimented in ways that defy peacetime notions of liberty. Property is controlled and regulated in fashions severe by normal standards. Great restraints are permissible, for the very life of the country is at stake. . . .

The Japanese cases are another illustration of the way in which a state of "war" affects civil rights. Those cases are little understood. They reached the Court in 1943 and 1944, but they arose in 1942 when no one knew where the Japanese army and navy were. . . . [T]he Pentagon advised us on oral argument that the Japanese army could take everything west of the Rockies if they chose to land. Evacuation of the entire population would of course have been permissible by constitutional standards pertaining in time of war. Was it constitutional to evacuate only citizens of Japanese ancestry?. . .

The Pentagon's argument was that if the Japanese army landed in areas thickly populated by Americans of Japanese ancestry, the opportunity for sabotage and confusion would be great. By doffing their uniforms they would be indistinguishable from the other thousands of people of like color and stature. It was not much of an argument, but it swayed a majority of the Court, including myself. . . . Locking up the evacuees after they had been removed had no military justification. I wrote a concurring opinion, which I never published, agreeing to the evacuation but not to evacuation *via* the concentration camps. My Brethren, especially [Hugo] Black and [Felix] Frankfurter, urged me strongly not to publish. "The issue of detention is not here," they said. "And the Court never decides a constitutional issue not present.". . . Technically . . . the question of detention was not presented to us. Yet evacuation via detention camps was before us, and I have always regretted that I bowed to my elders and withdrew my opinion.

. . . Fine American citizens had been robbed of their properties by racists—crimes that might not have happened if the Court had not followed the Pentagon so literally. The evacuation case . . . was ever on my conscience. . . .

. . . [T]he story [is] that the "war power" is a broad, pervasive, concurrent power which gives Congress authority to do things it would never dream of doing in days of peace.

Source: William O. Douglas, *The Court Years: 1939–1975* (New York: Random House, 1980), pp. 279–80.

Finally, in 1988, Congress apologized for the evacuation and internment program and provided reparations. Each living survivor of the program was awarded $20,000 in compensation. Of course, the significance of these efforts at reconciliation pales before the enormity of the constitutional outrage committed against Japanese-Americans during World War II. Their relevance to the basic questions of this chapter are also unclear. Do the vacated convictions, apologies, and awards show that courts should have protected the rights of Japanese more vigorously? In the political atmosphere of war, can courts function in this manner? Or do the events of the 1980s show that courts should defer to what the military and responsible political officials believe is necessary to win a war, letting later generations sort out whether constitutional injustice was done and, if it was, to decide what to do to remedy the wrong?

BIBLIOGRAPHY

Daniels, Roger. *Concentration Camps USA: Japanese Americans and World War II*. New York: Holt, Rinehart & Winston, 1971.

Dembitz, Nanette. "Racial Discrimination and the Military Judgment," *Columbia Law Review* 45 (1945), pp. 175–239.

Fairman, Charles. "The Law of Martial Rule and the National Emergency," *Harvard Law Review* 55 (1942), pp. 1253–302.

Grodzins, Morton. *Americans Betrayed: Politics and the Japanese Evacuation*. Chicago: University of Chicago Press, 1949.

Irons, Peter. *Justice at War*. New York: Oxford University Press, 1983.

Rossiter, Clinton. *The Supreme Court and the Commander in Chief*. Ithaca, N.Y.: Cornell University Press, 1951.

Rostow, Eugene. "The Japanese-American Cases—A Disaster," *Yale Law Journal* 54 (1945), pp. 489–533.

tenBroek, Jacobus, et al., *Prejudice, War and the Constitution*. Berkeley: University of California Press, 1954.

BRIEFS

BRIEF FOR FRED KOREMATSU

[1. The war power.] . . . It were a novel concept that the Chief Executive, either in his civil capacity as President or in his military capacity as Commander in Chief might treat civilians as being subject to his rule without Constitutional or Congressional authority. It were novel, indeed, were the existence of a state of war which vests in him the disposition of the military power would vest in him unlimited power and control over civilian activities and properties and enable him to delegate these powers either expressly or impliedly to his subordinates. No such power is conferred upon him for such would amount to an outright suspension of the Constitution. No such power has been conferred upon him by Congress for such would amount to a delegation of power not lodged in Congress and, in effect, would constitute an abandonment of its constitutional duties and automatically elevate the Commander in Chief to the position of dictator and his military commanders to federal chieftains. If the Commander in Chief had any such power over civilians there would be nothing to prevent him from commanding all voters to vote for him at the coming election and, in the event of disobedience to his command, to imprison the disobedient in concentration camps or have them shot in manner following the Nazis. The only method of prevention of such occurrences would be the constitutional power to impeach him which could be circumvented by like treatment or by ordering them enrolled in the military forces. We hope America never reaches such a state. In neither capacity is the President the "ruler" of the American people. What he is not permitted to do no military commander may do with impunity. The sufferings of 1775–1781 were a hollow mockery were our Courts to allow military power to override civilian right upon the pretext offered by an obscure military commander that a spurious military necessity called for a suspension or destruction of all the constitutional rights and liberties of a segment of our citizenry upon an ancestral origin basis.

. . . Citizens outside a theater of war are not triable by military tribunals. Protection against espionage and sabotage in civilian ranks is [therefore] not a military function. If a military commander may usurp these functions he might as well take over the general police functions of the civil authorities and arrest and try civilians for vagrancy and other civil offenses. If a military commander, with or without presidential or congressional consent, can take over these duties and do these things with impunity we may as well acknowledge that our government has ceased to be a republic under a constitutional form and admit that even the pretense no longer is apparent and that what we have is a dictatorship distinct from the European and Asiatic types only in the hollow form that is held up to public gaze. Is war power to be regarded as a shallow excuse to hide the fact of dictatorship? Are Congress, the Courts and the Nation so impotent they are to be deemed parts of the tail to a military commander's kite either in war or in peace. . . .

The statute, Public Law No. 503, was applied as the enforcement machinery for Civilian Exclusion Order No. 34, the military proclamations and orders which were designed and scheduled to banish the appellant and similarly situated citizens from the Pacific Coast and to imprison them in concentration camps. The purpose to which the statute, proclamations and orders was put, insofar as they affected the appellant and other American citizens, was unlawful from its inception. The consequent curtailment of the appellant's liberties and the deprivation of his rights of national and state citizenship are irreparable. As applied to the citizen appellant the statute and the military proclamations and orders to which it gave effect are unconstitutional and void upon the following grounds:

1. For delegating to military commanders, Courts and juries the legislative power to determine what are military areas and what acts or omissions therein on the part of the appellant shall be deemed criminal in nature and punishable, in violation of Section 1 of Article 1 of the Constitution.

2. For delegating unlimited judicial power to a military commander to function in lieu of Courts by enabling him to hold in the recesses of his own mind a mock trial of the citizen appellant and the other citizens of like stock in an area free from martial rule and to condemn them to deportation and imprisonment on mere suspicion or heresay or simply because he harbors prejudice against them because of their Japanese ancestry, in violation of Section 1 of Article III of the Constitution.

3. As constituting a bill of attainder forbidden by Section 9, clause 3 of Article I of the Constitution in that it aided, enabled, and encouraged the military commander to banish him not for the commission of a crime but solely by reason of his type of ancestry.

4. As aiding the military commander to seize his person without legal process and without probable cause in violation of the unreasonable search and seizure clause of the 4th Amendment.

5. As depriving him of the following, among other inalienable rights of national and state citizenship in violation of the due process clause of the 5th Amendment. The "right so vital in maintenance of democratic institutions." The right of a citizen "to live and work where he will." The right "to establish a home." The right to "freedom of movement."

6. As depriving him of his right to work and to the fruits of his labor without due process of law in violation of the 5th Amendment. These are property rights. Inasmuch as General DeWitt's orders assert that the deprivation of these property rights was necessitated for a public purpose the deprivation constituted a taking of private property for public purposes without just compensation in violation of the 5th Amendment. . . .

7. In denying him the equal protection of the laws which is implicit in the due process clause of the 5th Amendment. Due process of law forbids racial discrimination. Although the equal protection clause does not appear in the 5th the legal significance of the due process clause in the 5th and 14th Amendments are identical. The utter inequality which has been practiced herein would seem to violate the due process clause of the 5th Amendment for due process is synonymous with "law of the land" which in America cannot mean one law for one citizen and another for another citizen. The guaranty of due process of law in the 5th Amendment was not originally designed to decrease but to expand the rights of a citizen.

8. As holding the appellant to answer for an infamous crime, the nature of which is unknown, in violation of the provisions of the 5th Amendment. Banishment is a type of infamous punishment forbidden by the 5th Amendment.

9. As subjecting him to deportation and internment without charging him with crime and without informing him of the nature and cause of any accusation against him and without affording him a fair trial on the question of the necessity and right to banish and intern him, in violation of the 6th Amendment. The denial of such a fair trial also violates the due process clause of the 5th Amendment. In issuing and enforcing his penal *lettres de cachet* against the appellant and similarly wronged citizens the General prejudged him and them in the secret recesses of his own mind and condemned them to deportation. Even if he is a self-appointed military tribunal no such power is lodged in him by the Constitution or by statute.

10. As inflicting upon him the cruel and unusual punishment of banishment and internment in the absence of crime upon his part and without an accusation of wrongdoing being brought against him, in violation of the 8th Amendment.

11. As imposing upon him in an internment camp a condition of slavery and involuntary servitude, imposed not for crime but solely by reason of his type of ancestry, which is forbidden by the 13th Amendment. In the W.R.A. [War Relocation Authority] camps the internees have been put to work assigned by the au-

thorities in charge at peon wages. As an unskilled person the appellant was scheduled to receive not more than $12 per month for devoting 8 hours per day to such labor.

12. As working a corruption of blood and forfeiture upon him, without trial, upon the theory of the constructive treason of his remote ancestors which is forbidden by Section 2, clause 2 of Article III of the Constitution.

[If the military's program of evacuation and detention does not violate these constitutional guarantees,] . . . it is time we stopped teaching our children that the Constitution has any significance and that the Bill of Rights is a charter of our rights and liberties. We should tell them instead that arbitrary power is lodged in each Administration that captures or falls heir to the reins of government. If this terrible imprisonment program is valid we should call a Constitutional Convention to write another Constitution which will tell us the harsh truth.

[2. DeWitt and racism.] There was no substantial basis for a belief upon General DeWitt's part that any threat of espionage or sabotage to our military resources from the appellant or any of these evacuated citizens was real or imminent or that he or they presented any clear and present danger to national security. . . .

The General prejudged these people *in masse* and sought their banishment from the Pacific Coast. That his whole brutal evacuation program was the result of his personal prejudice against them and not in anywise based upon any facts whatsoever that would form a rational basis for this program. . . .

. . . We find what he offers in lieu of reasons in his *"Final Report"* on the Japanese evacuation from the West Coast first made public on January 19, 1944, two years after the evacuation was completed. His strange silence for this period is explainable on no grounds except prejudice against these deportees. The document asserts his military excesses are to be ascribed to his astuteness and sagacity, products of reason. His report demonstrates them to have been born of bias and war hysteria, products of emotion. What he offers therein does not permit an honest conclusion that his revolting program was based upon an exercise of sound discretion and mature judgement. It proves the prattle of military necessity was medicine he wished the public to swallow, proscribed for a non-existent disease. The public hypnosis that followed his punitive orders was caused by fear of invoking military wrath. The silence of the victims was caused by fear that military reprisals might be taken against them. The program was inspired by prejudice, the fierce tyranny of prejudice of the military commander and nothing else. We were intellectually dishonest were we to deny the fact.

Oppression is not excused by presuming the General acted in good faith. Such would be tantamount to presuming that the oppressed were guilty of conduct justifying arbitrary military action against them, that is, that they were guilty of criminal acts which necessitated the use of military force. It is never "good faith" that is justification. Good faith has caused the extermination of too many millions of innocents during the past 6000 years. It is usually an excuse offered to save the reputation of evil doers. Thousands of good citizens have been impoverished and thousands of innocent lives have been ruined by General DeWitt. His recklessness is not equivalent to good faith. There may be a few who smirk over the irreparable injuries suffered by these people but those who do never have understood and never will understand that this Republic stands for equality in the treatment of its citizens. . . .

. . . His conclusion that the distribution of these people on the Pacific Coast "appeared to manifest something more than coincidence" was a specter of his own creation. His qualified conclusion that these people were ideally situated to embark upon a tremendous program of sabotage "should any considerable number of them have been inclined to do so" is a hypothesis based entirely upon prejudice and base suspicion. It is an escape from fact and reality. . . .

. . . Can it be said that his own statements as to what inspired him to order this banishment in anywise suggest he was activated by proper motives or that it was based upon an exercise of sound discretion and mature judgement? . . . His suspicions are purely imaginative. We do not hesitate to state that never did a Nazi official in Germany draw more unjust conclusions than General DeWitt who would punish these people not for harboring dangerous thoughts but for thoughts he would impute to them or project into their minds. . . . An unorganized minority is always the object of oppression. In Germany it was the Jews. Here it is Americans whose ancestors were Japanese subjects. . . .

He has the temerity to declare these people were traitors to this nation. Why doesn't he tell this to the 100th Infantry Battalion—to the 442nd Combat Team—to the wounded—to those American youths of Japanese ancestry who have died that America might survive? All America and our Allies are grateful to these youthful warriors except, apparently, General DeWitt and a scattered few others whose prejudice blinds what reason they possess. . . .

We are not willing to trust all of our traditional constitutional rights to any military commander. We are not willing to vest in General DeWitt the right to determine who shall and who shall not enjoy the privileges and immunities of national citizenship. He is not infallible. A military man may be an authority on military matters but when he invades the domain of civil right he is usually in a maze. The American public does not worship at the shrine of any man. The banishment program was the product of the outright personal prejudice of General DeWitt against these people probably mixed with vague suspicion he entertained of them based upon gross hearsay. . . .

[3. *Hirabayashi*.] In the *Hirabayashi* opinion this Court concluded that there was "support for the view that social, economic, and political conditions" prevailing since the Japanese came to this country "have intensified their solidarity" and, in a measure, have "prevented their assimilation as an integral part of the white population." The aliens are ineligible to citizenship. This has prevented them from assimilation into our political activities but not from our social and economic life. The citizens are native born and participate in our political activities. Very few of the foreign born long would have remained aliens had we made them eligible to citizenship. None have been so eager as these for citizenship. . . .

This Court also assumed that there was relatively little social intercourse between these people and the white population and that the restriction of privileges and opportunities afforded persons of Japanese extraction "have been sources of irritation and may well have tended to increase their isolation and in many instances their attachments to Japan and its institutions." The Court erred in its assumption. These citizens have been reared in our communities, have attended the same public schools, have frequented the same places of amusement and have enjoyed the same entertainments. They have engaged in the same employments, businesses, and professions. The aliens have enjoyed substantially the same privileges. The sources of irritation to which the Court refers were of an historical nature existing until the turn of the century; the isolation ceased at that time. The conclusion of a possible attachment to Japan and its institutions is not borne out by facts. The aliens came here in the first instance to avoid the social, economic, and political conditions they experienced in Japan. Our European ancestors settled here for like reasons. Neither they nor we should be ashamed of the poverty or misfortune of our ancestors. . . .

This Court's conclusion in the *Hirabayashi* case that the "association of influential Japanese residents with Japanese consulates has been deemed a ready means for the dissemination of propaganda and for the maintenance of the influence of the Japanese Government with the Japanese population in this country" does not seem to be warranted. . . . [Such propaganda] was ineffective—the loyalty of the American-born youth in this war demonstrates that quite conclusively. This country has been flooded for a good many years with Communist, Nazi, and Fascist propaganda from consulates, foreign organizations and domestic organizations but it can be said that although the American public has been inoculated the vaccination has not taken. Propaganda addressed to youths of Japanese ancestry has not influenced them against this country. We are unable to discover any reliable evidence that propaganda from Japanese sources was designed or had the effect to turn these people against this nation.

The sending of children to Japanese language schools after regular school hours is just as harmless as sending children to supplementary schools to learn any of the European tongues. Some suspicion has been aroused over the existence of these schools. The ignorant always slander and would suppress what they do not comprehend. This Court stated in the *Hirabayashi* opinion that "some of these schools are generally believed to be sources of Japanese nationalistic propaganda, cultivating allegiance to Japan." Suspicion on the part of persons wholly unfamiliar with the purposes of these schools affords no basis to characterize them as subversive. There is no evidence whatever that any of these schools spread Japanese propaganda or in anywise endeavored to indoctrinate the pupils with noxious ideas. These schools originally were set up to teach Christianity and to Americanize children. . . .

[4. Conclusion.] Between December 7, 1941, and the time each civilian exclusion order was issued General DeWitt had ample opportunity to arrange for the Army or civil authorities to examine into the loyalty of each person he intended to evacuate. He desired no such examinations. He would brook no opposition to his plan. He was bent upon mass banishment and imprisonment. His then unexpressed accusation that they or some among them might have had a predisposition to the commission of acts of espionage or sabotage and that their removal was a public security measure is spun of sheer mist. A military commander who cannot or will not endeavor to distinguish between a loyal citizen and a hostile alien lacks perception as well as judgement. It is a poor gardener who doesn't perceive the difference between a native plant and an alien weed. General DeWitt uprooted the whole garden. . . .

It is not unlikely that General DeWitt entertained the opinion that the courts would sustain his action despite the fact that he long failed to divulge his reasons for this imprisonment program. This must have been based upon a notion that the courts in time of war conceive of themselves primarily as warriors and only secondarily as guardians of the civil liberties of citizens. Apparently he did not realize that our courts function as the sole barrier between democracy and tyranny. They constitute the bridge which links us to a republican tomorrow or to a totalitarian tomorrow.

Who is this DeWitt to say who is and who is not an American and who shall and who shall not enjoy the rights of citizenship? Did he think he was a "leader" called to summon these, our people, to a Munich or Berchtesgaden? Did he think he was our chamberlain and yet forget he was the sworn servant of these citizens? While he was toying with the notion of a military dictatorship over them and trifling with its dangerous paraphernalia did he think he was acting the part of our savior? A messianic delusion is a dangerous thing in a military mind. Napoleon had it and brought Europe to ruin. Mussolini had it and brought Italy to ruin. Hitler has it and has brought Germany to ruin.

General DeWitt let Terror out to plague these citizens but closed the lid on the Pandora box and left Hope to smother. It is your duty to raise the lid and revive Hope for these, our people, who have suffered at the hands of one of our servants. Do this speedily as the law commands you. History will not forget your opinion herein. . . .

Respectfully submitted,

WAYNE M. COLLINS

BRIEF FOR THE UNITED STATES[23]

[1. *Hirabayashi.*] . . . This Court ruled in the *Hirabayashi* case that the joint war power of the President and the Congress is sufficiently broad to cover a measure which there is "any substantial basis" to conclude is "a protective measure necessary to meet the threat of sabotage and espionage which would substantially affect the war effort and which might reasonably be expected to aid a threatened enemy invasion." We submit that there was a substantial basis for concluding that the Exclusion Order, equally with the curfew which was sustained in the *Hirabayashi* case, was such a necessary protective measure.

The pertinent circumstances were in large part the same as those which rendered appropriate the imposition of the curfew. The initiation of the exclusion

---

[23]The footnote by which the Justice Department distanced itself from DeWitt's *Final Report,* located on page 11 of the brief, reads, in part, as follows: "The Final Report of General DeWitt . . . is relied on in this brief for statistics and other details concerning the actual evacuation and the events that took place subsequent thereto. We have specifically recited in this brief the facts relating to the justification for the evacuation, of which we ask the Court to take judicial notice, and we rely upon the *Final Report* only to the extent that it relates to such facts."

program by the promulgation of the first Civilian Exclusion Order occurred on the same date as the curfew proclamation, and the violation by the petitioner herein occurred during the same month as Hirabayashi's violation. With respect to the conditions then prevailing this Court has said

> ... That reasonably prudent men charged with the responsibility of our national defense had ample ground for concluding that they must face the danger of invasion, take measures against it, and in making the choice of measures consider our internal situation, cannot be doubted

❖   ❖   ❖

> ... The German invasion of the Western European countries had given ample warning to the world of the menace of the "fifth column." Espionage by persons in sympathy with the Japanese Government had been found to have been particularly effective in the surprise attack on Pearl Harbor. At a time of threatened Japanese attack upon this country, the nature of our inhabitants' attachments to the Japanese enemy was consequently a matter of grave concern.

❖   ❖   ❖

> ... Whatever views we may entertain regarding the loyalty to this country of the citizens of Japanese ancestry, we cannot reject as unfounded the judgement of the military authorities and of Congress that there were disloyal members of that population, whose number and strength could not be precisely and quickly ascertained. We cannot say that the war-making branches of the Government did not have ground for believing that in a critical hour such persons could not readily be isolated and separately dealt with, and constituted a menace to the national defense and safety, which demanded that prompt and adequate measures be taken to guard against it.

The concurring Justices indicated no difference of view with respect to these justifications for the curfew.

The appropriateness of the exclusion rests on the additional fact that the danger to be apprehended from any disloyal members of the population of Japanese ancestry would remain great if such persons should continue to reside on the West Coast. It is obvious that the opportunity for espionage and sabotage, as well as the aid to be derived therefrom by the enemy, would be greatest in the region most exposed to the striking power of Japan. The curfew was a method which dealt only partially with the danger, while the exclusion removed the danger during all hours and without resort to the impossible task of individual surveillance. A group of over 110,000 persons was involved, in which the number and identity of the possible disloyal members were not known. Prevention of acts of espionage and sabotage through surveillance obviously was fraught with extreme difficulty, if not wholly impossible.

On the basis of pertinent data a judgement to resort to exclusion was made by those responsible for military and protective measures. Differences of opinion as to the correctness of that judgement cannot take from it the substantial basis upon which it rested.

In the court below petitioner argues, as he does here, that his exclusion was nevertheless a violation of the due process clause of the Fifth Amendment. His argument appears to be based partially upon the proposition that, aside from the racial discrimination involved in the exclusion measure, it is an unreasonable method of preventing espionage or sabotage to exclude from a substantial portion of the country any large group of residents because of apprehension that a minority of them might engage in disloyal acts. It is true that prohibition of residence of a group of persons in an area in which they have established homes, relationships, employment, and business enterprises is a more stringent deprivation to the persons affected than the curfew involved in the *Hirabayashi* case, or than the establishment of fire lines during fire and the confinement of people to their homes during an air raid alarm, which this Court cited in sustaining the curfew. Nevertheless, in view of the overwhelming importance of securing the country against invasion and the undoubted assistance which could be rendered to an invading enemy by persons within the community, the exclusion of loyal persons along with the disloyal is not an unreasonable infringement of liberty or a denial of due process where, as here, there were strong grounds to believe that the identity of the disloyal persons could not be readily ascertained and that invasion was threatened. It is to be noted that there is no implication in either the majority or the concurring opinion in the *Hirabayashi* case that the exclusion orders might be a violation of due process.

[2. War power.] Measures coming within the war power do not violate the Fifth Amendment, whether or not they could be sustained in normal times, although that Amendment must be considered in determining the validity of a particular exercise of the war power under the circumstances which evoke it. As is true with respect to other governmental powers the limitations imposed by due process upon the war power mark the boundaries of the power itself. To call in question the exclusion program under the Fifth Amendment is, therefore, to challenge in another way the sufficiency of the war power to support the action taken by the President and Congress and by the military authorities.

This Court has made clear the great scope of the war power and that the limitations imposed by due process of law permit the exercise of a correspondingly wide discretion.

> . . . the Congress and the President exert the war power of the nation, and they have wide discretion as to the means to be employed successfully to carry on. . . . The measures here challenged are supported by a strong presumption of validity. . . . As applied . . . the statute and executive orders were not so clearly unreasonable and arbitrary as to require them to be held repugnant to the due process clause of the Fifth Amendment.

In the *Selective Draft Law Cases*, the Court, although it did not refer specifically to the Fifth Amendment, denied the limiting effect of several other Constitutional provisions with respect to the power of Congress to require military service, with all its sacrifices on the part of individuals who are drafted.

As was said in the *Hirabayashi* case, if an order "was an appropriate exercise of the war power its validity is not impaired because it has restricted the citizen's liberty." The Fifth Amendment protects the individual from arbitrary deprivations in war as in peace; but it does not invalidate measures, however extreme, which respond reasonably to the necessities of war.

The fact that the exclusion measure adopted was directed only against persons of one race does not invalidate it under the circumstances surrounding its adoption. Persons of Japanese ancestry were not marked out for separate treatment because of their race but because other considerations made the ethnic factor relevant. As this Court noted in the *Hirabayashi* case:

> The fact alone that attack on our shores was threatened by Japan rather than another enemy power set these citizens apart from others who have no particular associations with Japan.
> . . . We cannot close our eyes to the fact, demonstrated by experience, that in time of war residents having ethnic afflictions with an invading enemy may be a greater source of danger than those of a different ancestry.

Certainly the proportion of persons who might render aid to the enemy in the event of a Japanese invasion was reasonably thought to be greater in the West Coast population of Japanese ancestry than in the West Coast population as a whole or in groups of other ancestries living in that area at the time the Exclusion Order was issued. . . .

[3. Relevance of detention.] . . . In challenging his allegedly threatened "internment" and "imprisonment," petitioner contends in effect that the exclusion feature of the order, even though in itself valid, was so coupled with other measures to accomplish the exclusion as to force him, if he should obey the order, to incur detriments which could not lawfully be imposed upon him.

The Government does not dispute that petitioner, had he obeyed all of the provisions of the order and the accompanying Instructions, would have found himself for a period of time, the length of which is not that ascertainable, in a place of detention. It does not follow that this detention, which did not become actual, is an issue in the present case. It was solely and specifically petitioner's unlawful presence in the area which was charged in the information. His defense at the trial was no broader than this charge and no evidence was introduced by the Government to meet wider issues. The majority at least of the Circuit Court of Appeals considered the question to be simply the validity of petitioner's exclusion from the defined area. Petitioner was not accused or convicted of eluding detention or of not reporting for evacuation; he was solely charged with remaining where he had no lawful right to be. His desire was to stay there. The only relevant question is whether the provision of the order which forbade his presence is valid. Had he submitted to evacuation, petitioner could have brought other proceedings to challenge his detention. . . .

Petitioner's contention in striking at the [detention] provisions of the order . . . is in substance that it was impossible to charge a violation of the order based upon his remaining in the area. He contends in effect that he could not be accused of remaining in the area without also involving other, allegedly invalid parts of the order and Instructions and that, even though the exclusion was valid, yet he and all others in similar circumstances could remain, because as means of accomplishing the exclusion the order laid out a course which would have involved detention in an Assembly Center.

It seems clear that petitioner should not now be permitted to seek indirectly to nullify the vital military measure of exclusion of persons of Japanese ancestry from the West Coast area because of the claimed invalidity of accompanying features of the exclusion program. The exclusion was a measure taken under the urgency of military necessity, based upon a threat of invasion, at a critical point in the war. It would be a misapplication of the doctrine of inseparability, scarcely consistent with the national security or welfare, to hold that this measure may now be attacked, and not because of its own invalidity but because of the alleged unconstitutionality of the means adopted to effectuate it, when violation of these means is not charged. . . .

. . . We have contended that none of the detention of evacuees which has been involved in the exclusion program is properly in issue in this case; for the issue framed by the information does not embrace it, no evidence relating to it was introduced at the trial, and more appropriate proceedings have at all times been available whereby petitioner could have challenged the detention, had he wished to do so. Even if this contention is wrong and petitioner should be held to be entitled to call in question the detention which attended the removal of the evacuees and compelled their residence in Assembly Centers pending more permanent provisions for them, he cannot seek to avoid his conviction by attacking a still later phase of the exclusion program which had not developed at the time of his violation and to which he might not have been subjected.

Petitioner could not have known at the time he disregarded Civilian Exclusion Order No. 43 by failing to report for evacuation on May 9, 1942, that detention in a Relocation Center, of indefinite duration might follow detention in an Assembly Center if he should comply; nor is it certain that in his case it would have. On May 30, 1942, the date of the offense which is charged in the information, Civilian Restrictive Order No. 1 of May 19, 1942, which required persons of Japanese ancestry residing in Relocation Centers to remain there, gave notice that detention outside an Assembly Center was possible. Not until May 26, 1942, however, were any evacuees actually transferred from Assembly to Relocation Centers; and none of those from the Tanforan Center, to which petitioner would almost certainly have been taken, were moved until September of that year. . . .

In view of this history, it cannot be asserted upon any realistic basis that petitioner's violation could have been motivated by a desire to avoid detention other than that in an Assembly Center or that any other detention need in fact have occurred in his case had he obeyed the Exclusion Order. The relocation phase of the exclusion program, including the detention of evacuees in Relocation Centers, is a separate aspect of the whole program, which was not present in a definite sense in the situation that confronted petitioner at the time of his violation. If detention in a Relocation Center had later come to apply to him, he could, of course, have brought habeas corpus to challenge its continuance. . . .

The detention in Assembly Centers, consequently, was a means of accomplishing the evacuation and of mitigating the harmful consequences of the exclusion which was ordered for the purpose of preventing espionage and sabotage on the West Coast. Hence the detention was a collateral measure closely related to the exclusion and, as such, came within the purpose as well as the literal terms of Executive Order No. 9066. If Congress understood that the Executive Order, which it ratified, authorized measures to deal with the consequences of the evacuation which was envisaged, these measures came also within the Act of March 21, 1942. It is not to be doubted that Congress conferred upon the military authorities in exercising their powers the authority to execute them with reasonable regard to the conditions that might be precipitated by the measures they were directed to take. . . .

[4. Justification for detention implicit in evacuation.] Petitioner did not seek to show, by evidence or otherwise, that detention in Assembly Centers as a method of accomplishing the evacuation was not reasonably appropriate to the basic purpose of exclusion. The alternative which his position seems to suggest is that the evacuation, although compulsory and to be accomplished quickly, should not have been accompanied by any restraint; that the thousands of families and individuals who were involved should have been required to leave their homes in the restricted areas with such assistance as they might voluntarily accept. The result might have been a great mass movement of the persons affected, by all possible means of transportation, or without transportation, entailing great hardship and confusion, and with continued if not increased danger of espionage and sabotage which it was the purpose of the whole program to avert. The result, further, might have been the arrival of many individuals in communities unreceptive to them and without provision for them. It could not have been known when or where they would arrive and under what conditions.

The Assembly Center was reasonably calculated at least to mitigate these hardships and also to avoid the dangers which lay behind the decision to require evacuation. The constitutional validity of the restraint of liberty entailed by the Assembly Center must be judged in relation to the reasonableness of the basic purpose and the means available for its execution. The question involves the validity of a particular method adopted for carrying out an exclusion which was itself justified by factors of common knowledge.

Petitioner, in challenging the method used, labors under a heavy burden, particularly when, in the posture which the case has assumed, a decision in accordance with his contention would strike down not only the method adopted but also, in practical effect, the exclusion itself. For if petitioner was wrongfully convicted because detention in an Assembly Center would have resulted from full obedience to the order, and if he could not validly be convicted, as he was, of violating only that feature of the order which prohibited his remaining in the area, then the exclusion, as ordered, was unenforceable by legal means.

Petitioner has not borne the burden which rested upon him. The indications of hostility to evacuees, which lay at the basis of the decision to impose detention, have not been negatived. The belief of the military authorities in the danger of violence has not been shown to have been unreasonable. The existence of that belief is undisputed. The Final Report of General DeWitt states that "widespread hostility" had developed "in almost every state and every community. It was literally unsafe for Japanese migrants." The report refers to "one example among many" of actual threats against evacuees. These are said to have numbered "several thousand."

The judgement of the military authorities is confirmed by that of the Tolan Committee. Reporting on May 13, that Committee stated:

Voluntary settlement outside of prohibited and restricted areas has been complicated, if not made impossible for an indefinite period, by the resentment of communities to, what appeared to them, an influx of people so potentially dangerous to our national security as to require their removal from strategic military areas. The statement was repeated again and again, by communities outside the military areas, "We don't want these people in our State. If they are not good enough for California, they are not good enough for us."

In addition, the need of providing adequately for evacuees during the difficult period of physical transfer to new locations and of readjustment to new conditions argued for controlled migration. Undoubtedly the Government bore a heavy responsibility to the people whom it was uprooting from their homes and accustomed means of livelihood—a responsibility which it was justified in taking strong measures to meet, even at the cost of temporarily restraining the liberty of the evacuees. The needs of the evacuees confronting the military authorities and the appropriateness of the measures adopted to meet these needs, like the danger of violence, were affirmed by the Tolan Committee in the following language:

> While apparent respect for the rights of citizens prompted an early disposition to permit voluntary relocation outside prohibited areas, the seemingly insurmountable obstacles to such a program has led to an emphasis on Federal responsibility for resettlement. Only under a Federal program, providing for financial assistance, protection to person and property and an opportunity to engage in productive work, did it appear possible to minimize injustice.

It may properly be urged, in addition, that the primary purpose of the evacuation, namely the prevention of espionage and sabotage, would have suffered as a result of confusion, disorder, and resentment flowing from an uncontrolled migration of 100,000 persons. As this Court recognized in *Hirabayashi v. United States,* there was reason to believe that a disloyal minority existed among the evacuees. Its size and the identity of its member were not known. To force this group suddenly into the interior upon its own resources might well have been to shift the locale of the danger of espionage and sabotage without eliminating it. Although the same danger might have been present to some degree had the self-arranged migration, which preceded the enforced evacuation, been more successful than it was, the danger would certainly have been at its maximum if an uncontrolled mass evacuation had been ordered.

[5. Conclusion.] The detention of persons, whether citizens or aliens, in the interest of the public safety or their own welfare or both, apart from punishment for commission of offenses, is a measure not infrequently adopted by government. The arrest and detention of persons suspected of crime but presumed to be innocent, with release dependent upon ability to furnish bail, are of daily occurrence, with resulting hardships to blameless victims perhaps comparable in a year's time in the United States to the mental and spiritual sufferings of the Japanese evacuees. The detention of jurors, and of material witnesses whose disappearance is feared, is a related phenomenon. Even apart from the emergency of war, but during a proclaimed state of "insurrection," the detention of individuals by executive action in the interest of order, the courts being open to afford a remedy to persons seeking to challenge their detention, has been sustained by this Court.

The effect of a war in empowering the Government to impose restraints which might be invalid in normal times has often been noted. And the war power extends to measures for dealing with the consequences of war in the social and economic order as well as to measures designed to aid in carrying force to the enemy. Both as a means of forestalling possible espionage or sabotage and as a method of meeting conditions precipitated by the exclusion of persons of Japanese ancestry from the West Coast, therefore, the controlled evacuation and the detention which it entailed were a valid exercise of the war power.

In essence, the military judgement that was required in determining upon a program for the evacuation was one with regard to tendencies and probabilities as evidenced by attitudes, opinions, and slight experience, rather than a conclusion based upon objectively ascertainable facts. "There was neither pattern nor precedent for an undertaking of this magnitude and character," at least [not] in this country. Impairment of personal liberty resulted from the decision that was made. It cannot be said, however, even with the benefit of hindsight, that the decision was clearly unreasonable under the circumstances. That being so, it came within the purview of the war power exercised to accomplish the exclusion and did not violate due process of law. To the extent that the consequential detention in an Assembly Center can be questioned in this case, the conclusion should be that the impairment of liberty which was entailed resulted from the use of measures responsibly and reasonably calculated to further a validly inaugurated program based on military necessity.

CHARLES FAHY
Solicitor General

ACLU *AMICUS CURIAE* BRIEF

[1. Separability.] . . . The United States . . . attempts to sustain the conviction of petitioner by seeking to persuade this Court that the issue before it is solely one of the validity of the evacuation of persons of Japanese ancestry from certain areas on the Pacific Coast. We believe, with petitioner, that this evacuation was without adequate military justification, and in itself was a deprivation of his constitutional rights. But we also believe, and will seek to demonstrate below, that the true issue here is more serious even than that. The true issue posed by this case is whether or not a citizen of the United States may, because he is of Japanese ancestry, be confined in barbed wire stockades euphemistically termed Assembly Centers or Relocation Centers—actually concentration camps. Because petitioner refused to submit to such treatment, he has been adjudged guilty of a crime. The [American Civil Liberties] Union believes that such a judgment must not be allowed to stand. . . .

When Public Proclamation No. 1 was issued, petitioner made no move to leave his home. He remained in San Leandro, as he unquestionably had every right to do. Indeed, he was actually given no warning by that proclamation that he would ever have to move, since it was not addressed to any specific group, but simply served notice that exclusion would later be ordered of "such persons or classes of persons as the situation might require." Petitioner, as a loyal American citizen (as he admittedly is) certainly need not have assumed that he would be affected. On and after March 24, 1942, he became subject to, and presumably obeyed, the curfew regulations contained in Public Proclamation No. 3. *Before he was ever told, however, that he would have to leave his home, he was forbidden by Public Proclamation No. 4 to leave the Pacific Coast.* He had never a choice between ignoring or obeying a warning to leave voluntarily. From March 27 onward, petitioner was helpless to avoid the consequences of his Japanese ancestry without violating the terms of some order.

His situation materially worsened on May 3, 1942. On that date, by the terms of Civilian Exclusion Order No. 34, he was ordered to report to the Civilian Control Station on May 4 or 5, 1942. By the contemporaneous mandatory Instructions, he was, in the meantime, forbidden to leave the territory covered by Civilian Exclusion Order No. 34, and at the same time he was also forbidden to remain in that territory after May 8, 1942. At this point he rebelled. He did not report, nor did he leave San Leandro. He was still there when arrested on May 30.

But for the fact that the Government makes an argument to the contrary, we should feel that we were attacking a straw man in arguing that petitioner cannot stand convicted unless he could legally be required to submit to internment. The Government cannot, and does not, deny that petitioner had but two choices—to violate the Order and mandatory Instructions, or to submit to internment for an indeterminate period of time. And they were not remote choices, nor were they in any degree hypothetical. They were immediate and inevitable.

Yet after making that admission, the Government's argument proceeds just as it would in a case in which the defendant had a third choice—to leave the area and avoid *either* internment or violation of the Order. Had that choice existed, we would have quite a different case. Had that choice existed, the Government could argue, at least, that for a defendant who stayed on when he should have gone away, *exclusion* would be the sole issue. But *this is not that case.* Petitioner had no such choice. His choice was either to violate the Order and Instructions or to accept imprisonment. By every rational principle, he must now be able to question the validity of that imprisonment, and to go free of the stigma of criminal conviction if that imprisonment was illegal or unconstitutional.

Actually, we do not overstate the case when we say that in reality there was never any *exclusion* planned at all, and that *internment* was from the beginning the actual objective. We need only bear in mind a few facts. First, persons of Japanese ancestry (except for 257 in Zone 1 in late March, 1942) never had any choice except to submit to internment. Second, when they were interned, they were not necessarily *evacuated;* four of the ten Relocation Centers were *within* the prescribed area, and the persons sent there have actually never been evacuated. Third, the Government now states in its brief that it would have been equally contrary to the program if persons of Japanese ancestry had simply been shifted to the interior, i.e., evacuated with nothing more. Therefore, the Government argues that imprisonment of the evacuees was essential. Could there be better proof than this that the real program, the heart of the whole plan, was *internment.* . . .

. . . [T]he salient fact is that this is not an ordinary separability case. It does not raise the question involved in the cases cited by the Government. There the issue is simply whether the statute is such that the portion of it directly involved can stand alone, even if other parts may later be found invalid. If it can, it is "separable," and the validity . . . of the other parts can be ignored. . . . But here the Government is trying to separate an *inevitable, immediate consequence.* The Government's brief admits that internment was the only way to avoid a violation of the Order, and at the same time argues that it is a "separable" feature. Unless words have lost their ordinary meaning, nothing could have been more *inseparable* than immediate internment.

The Government furnishes its own *reductio ad absurdum.* The brief seems to say that had petitioner violated the Order and Instructions in *another* way—by fleeing—he could then have challenged the validity of the detention provisions. That is simply nonsense. Detention is no more and no less separable from remaining in Zone 34 than from fleeing it.

Loss of liberty, even temporary, is not to be treated lightly. Confinement in a barbed wire stockade under military guard is, or should be, held in horror by us all. Concentration camps, where citizens are sent without warning, without trial, without even individual charges of guilt of anything but ethnic characteristics, should—must—remain the objects of destruction by our armies, not the objects of condonation by our prosecutors and our courts. And they are condoned here, glossed over, minimized. The Government's brief suggests that petitioner submit to loss of liberty and then litigate by *habeas corpus.* It should be unnecessary to assume a worse punishment and ask if the answer would be the same, but perhaps in no other way can the issue be made as vivid as it must be. Does the Government urge that American citizens should have submitted to the Orders and Instructions had they contemplated not only barbed wire concentration camps, but chains, hard labor, bread and water, and the whipping post? Does the loss of liberty become less "separable" if it is thus implemented? Does petitioner, who valued his liberty enough to believe that he could not be thus required to submit to loss of it, lose his standing to challenge the Order only because the plan could have been worse? Unless the answer is "No," we have lost a large segment of a precious heritage of freedom. . . .

Finally, the Government urges . . . the petitioner's internment should be split up, and that even if the Assembly Center portion of it be held inseparable, the Relocation Center portion be nevertheless held separable and beyond the scope of proper review in this case. That is hairsplitting with a vengeance. Assembly Centers and Relocation Centers were at all times considered as inseparable concomitants of the internment program. Assembly Centers were admittedly temporary; they served as preliminary concentration camps, in the literal meaning of that term. . . . Indeed, if more proof be needed that the Assembly Centers and the Relocation Centers are in truth inseparable components of the program, it is supplied by the fact that two Assembly Centers—Manzanar and Colorado River— later became Relocation Centers. At Manzanar, the persons who had been "assembled" there were transferred to a Relocation Center by the simple process of transforming their prison from an "Assembly Center" to a "Relocation Center." In addition, many "evacuees" never went to Assembly Centers at all; they were transported directly to a Relocation Center.

[2. Military necessity.] General DeWitt does try to show military necessity by reference to reported illegal radio signals which could not be located, lights on the shore, and the like. The government's brief states, however: "We have specifically recited in this brief the facts relating to the justification for the evacuation, of which we ask the court to take judicial notice, and we rely upon the Final (De-Witt) Report only to the extent that it relates to such facts." This singular repudiation of General DeWitt's testimony on the military necessities, which obviously could be required only by the existence of reliable conflicting information from other sources, is made even more remarkable by comparison of the Government's brief and Chapter II of the DeWitt Report. The brief contains no reference, for example, to illicit radio signals, signal lights visible from the Coast, or to the significance attached by the Report to hidden caches of contraband, location of Japanese settlements near defense installations, fascistic or militaristic pro-Japanese organizations and Emperor-worshiping programs, and Japanese language schools. Moreover, in several respects the recital in the DeWitt Report is wholly inconsistent with other facts of public knowledge. It is well known, of course, that radio detection equipment is unbelievably accurate; a "fix" can be obtained which will locate a radio transmitter not only in a specific house, but in a specific room. Secondly, the fact that no person of Japanese ancestry has been arraigned for any sabotage or espionage since December 7, 1941, certainly suggests, in view of the unquestionable efficiency of the F.B.I., that no such acts were committed by such persons. Nor can it be said to be wholly without significance that in four of the five cases in which, during this war, trial courts have taken testimony on alleged military necessity for action against civilians (by direct testimony of military authorities), the asserted military necessity has been found not to exist in fact. . . .

But what is in the DeWitt Report and not in the Government's brief is scarcely less significant than what is not in the DeWitt Report. . . . [N]owhere in a volume obviously designed as an apologia for the greatest compulsory mass migration in our history is there a line, a word, about the reports of other security officers. General DeWitt does not tell us whether he consulted either the Director of the Federal Bureau of Investigation or the Director of the Office of Naval Intelligence. Before the enormously drastic, difficult and expensive step of mass evacuation was recommended, one would suppose that General DeWitt would have sought information from these other sources as to whether their investigation of the persons of Japanese ancestry on the Pacific Coast indicated that the population *as a whole* was so dangerous that it must be wholly evacuated, and whether they could assist in some less drastic solution. If the Office of Naval Intelligence and the Director of the Federal Bureau of Investigation recommended complete evacuation, undoubtedly that would have been mentioned in the DeWitt Report. It prints much of the correspondence and memoranda that were exchanged during this period. Since no recommendations from either the O.N.I. [Office of Naval Intelligence] or the F.B.I. are referred to, one can only assume either that they were not sought or that they were opposed to mass evacuation. In either case, the inference becomes overwhelmingly strong that what was involved was not military security but race prejudice and hysteria generated in late January and February, 1942, by a small but vocal group on the Pacific Coast. . . .

How else can one explain the difference between the treatment of citizens of Japanese parentage on the Pacific Coast and in Hawaii. Hawaii was more gravely threatened than the Coast, and it was plainly more important to guard in the Islands against subversive persons. Yet there were no mass evacuations or internments of persons of Japanese ancestry in Hawaii, notwithstanding the fact that there were more of them there, concentrated around our greatest naval base, than there were in the whole of the Pacific coastal strip.

Finally, apart from the fact that the DeWitt Report is thus a wholly untrustworthy recitation, the fact is apparent that even its own statements make no showing of the necessity for complete evacuation of all persons of Japanese ancestry from a huge area. A military necessity for some action does not support a military necessity for *any* measure, no matter how drastic. How can military necessity require the evacuation of over a hundred thousand persons from the Pacific Coast and only a handful from Hawaii?

[3. *Hirabayashi.*] We should emphasize that we are not now seeking to review the action of the Court in the *Hirabayashi* case. There, the Court was forced to speculate upon the military needs, since no statement of them had yet been made. Now we have in the DeWitt Report a complete explanation, apologia, and it is wholly proper that former speculative conclusions should be reexamined in the light of the facts.

But if there is every reason to believe that there was no military necessity for *evacuation,* there is no doubt at all that there was no military necessity for the subsequent *imprisonment* of the evacuees. We take General DeWitt's word for it, for he states:

> Essentially, military necessity required only that the Japanese population be removed from the coastal area and dispersed in the interior, where the danger of action in concert during any attempted enemy raids along the coast, or in advance thereof as preparation for a full scale attack, would be eliminated.

The *only* justification for imprisonment of American citizens is stated to be the unwillingness of other states and communities to accept them, and the consequent fear of resulting disturbances in the interior states.

We believe that even this reason is magnified out of all proportion to reality. But we need not explore that. The significant fact is that this Court is asked to sanction the act of imprisoning American Citizens without charges, without trial, without conviction, without any safeguards whatever, *because it is asserted that it is sociologically desirable.* And at the risk of tiresome repetition, we should point out again that even this reason carries no shadow of justification for more than a plan of voluntary refuge for evacuees; *internment* was wholly unnecessary. If this can be permitted under the Constitution, much of Germany's anti-Semitic program can be duplicated in this country with no violation of constitutional rights.

And this internment has not been temporary. Both the exclusion and the internment of persons of Japanese ancestry have continued for over two years. Persons of unquestioned loyalty, who have been through the most intensive investigation and found not wanting in any respect, still remain confined by machine guns to their camps. When a program is continued practically unchanged beyond the

need which is alleged to have brought it into existence, the most compelling inference is that the alleged basis is not the true basis at all. The true basis, as we have
said above, was hysteria, race prejudice, and a vocal minority which high-pres-
sured a military need for the security measures found adequate elsewhere—as in
Hawaii—into a mass uprooting and internment of tens of thousands of innocent
persons. . . .

Respectfully submitted,

AMERICAN CIVIL LIBERTIES UNION,
Amicus Curiae.

JACL *AMICUS CURIAE* BRIEF

[1. Japanese assimilation.] . . . Since Americans of Japanese ancestry have been
treated differently from all other citizens, those who favor this discriminatory
treatment and those who uphold it are logically forced to assert or to assume that
these young people are in fact different from all other elements of our population.
And since variations of race or physical type are not legitimate grounds for discriminatory treatment under our Constitution, they must argue that the differences are social or cultural as well as biological. The racists and divisionists among
us do not hesitate to use this argument. They are eager to convince the country
that those who are physically distinct from the majority are also separate in customs and mentality, and therefore should be barred from coming to our shores or
eliminated if they are already here. But it is a dark day for liberty when this doctrine of vast social and psychological gulfs between groups in our population becomes dignified and implemented by favorable mention in the decisions of this
Court. Persecution has become so common in our day and the rationalizations for
persecutions so specious that the grounds on the basis of which discrimination
against any group of citizens is urged should be weighted on the most sensitive
scales of justice that free men can devise. If this Court upholds discriminatory
treatment of certain citizens on the basis of "ethnic affiliations" with an enemy of
our country, its thrice solemn responsibility is to ascertain that so serious a contention is actually true and is not asserted merely because it is the only legally sup-
portable assumption that will excuse what was done in haste and folly.

The credo of democracy is that men of all races, colors and faiths can be
molded to common ideals and a common national devotion by the institutions
which they inherit and share. The alacrity with which a General, some politicians
and some Judges are ready, in spite of a rich store of reassuring evidence, to abandon this conception for the assumption that our young people are motivated, not
by the social dynamics and values of America, not by her schools, churches, and
athletic fields, but by considerations of race or dim parental memories of a distant
land, is grim and disillusioning indeed.

Every argument for evacuation expresses or implies the conviction that
Americans of Japanese ancestry are not assimilated into American life and therefore could not be expected to be as loyal and devoted as other elements of the
population. Those who advance these arguments ordinarily know very little about

culture, about assimilation, or about Americans of Japanese ancestry. They always confuse the concept of "intermingling" with the concept of "assimilation." The Negroes of Harlem participate in American culture. Certainly they have no knowledge of the African tribal life of their remote ancestors. They listen to, dance to, and create American music. They eat American-type foods. They speak English. In all important aspects of behavior they conform closely to common American standards. Yet they dwell by themselves in a special section of the city. In the same way, because of property restrictions, persons of Japanese ancestry often lived together in certain sections of West Coast cities. But this is no more reason than it is in the case of the Negro to assume that they were not there conforming to genuine American habits of thought and action. After all they were attending the same kind of American schools, they were listening to the same radio programs, they were singing the same popular tunes, and were using the same slang as were boys and girls who lived elsewhere. The 100th battalion and the 442nd battalion are formed almost entirely of Americans of Japanese ancestry. But this does not prevent them from facing America's enemies, wearing American uniforms, using American weapons and tactics, fighting America's fight and shedding American blood. The unrestricted intermingling of races and peoples may be an ideal in itself, but it is by no means necessary for assimilation. We protest against the narrow and superficial assumption which we find in every statement of General DeWitt and every brief of the Government on this subject, namely, that because people of Japanese ancestry lived together, they must have been carrying on mysterious and un-American customs of oriental origin.

In extenuation of his orders General DeWitt has called the persons whom he banished, most of them American citizens, "a large, unassimilated, tightly knit racial group, bound to an enemy nation by strong ties of race, culture, custom, and religion." This theme he repeats over and over. . . . But what do those who are somewhat more qualified by training and contacts to speak on the subject have to say?. . .

As long ago as 1928, Dr. Robert E. Park, chairman of the Department of Sociology of the University of Chicago, directed a large-scale study of resident Orientals which was called "Survey of Race Relations of the Pacific Coast." A number of publications resulted, and the large body of materials which were gathered were placed in a depository of the Survey at Stanford University. The undertaking was ambitious and extensive, being supported by a $55,000 budget. Scholars and leading citizens of the West Coast as well as from other parts of the country participated in the research. Dr. Park and his associates, to sum up their findings as far as assimilation is concerned, determined that the American of Japanese ancestry "born in America and educated in our western schools is culturally an Occidental, even though he be racially an Oriental, and this is true to an extent that no one who has investigated the matter disinterestedly and at first hand is ever likely to imagine."

In 1929 a substantial grant was made to Stanford University by the Carnegie Corporation, for study of Americans of Japanese ancestry on the West Coast. The work was carried out under the direction of Professor E. K. Strong and resulted in the appearance of four volumes, the first published in 1933. A large staff of trained workers co-operated to gather and analyze the materials. Every device known to social science was employed. The general conclusion, to use Professor Strong's own words, was that:

> The word "assimilation" has two meanings—interbreeding and comprehension of political and social conditions. In the latter sense, the young Japanese are more readily assimilated than people of several European races. . . .

Through the years there have been a number of other studies and investigations by impartial and competent students and they all support the findings of Strong and Park.

In all the loose talk about "lack of assimilation" and "close-knit racial groups" there is no hint that the trained investigators who have pursued the subject for years were even consulted. The Tolan Committee called politicians and sheriffs before it to testify concerning questions of assimilation and acculturation. The men who had made a life study of these questions, Professors Strong, Bell and Farnsworth of Stanford and Professor Bogardus of the University of Southern California, among others, were never consulted or approached. We talk a great deal about the irrationality and anti-intellectualism of the Nazis and Fascists, of their appeal to violent prejudice and emotion instead of to knowledge. The Nazi pattern was never better exemplified than in this particular crisis. With good reason has Professor Freeman written:

> When the final history of the Japanese evacuation is written, it will almost certainly appear that decisions were made on misinformation, assumptions, prejudices, half-truths, when excellent scientifically accurate material was available.

There is little need to deal at length with the argument that Americans of Japanese ancestry would have turned upon the country of their birth because of past discrimination and treatment. The argument itself is a twisted and peculiar one, implying that the cure for injustice is more injustice. It gives to racists a powerful weapon to use at some future time against any minority which has experienced local prejudice—against Negroes, Jews, Catholics, Mexicans and Orientals other than Japanese. If this conception is accepted by the Courts, no minority group can ever "be above suspicion." The facts we have reviewed dispose of this argument as far as Americans of Japanese ancestry are concerned. As we have shown, these citizens were making rapid and remarkable progress in educational, artistic, scientific and economic endeavors. They had reason to be proud of their achievements and they were proud of their achievements. If they had their enemies among Caucasians they also had many kind and powerful friends. To the question of whether they would aid an enemy for *any* reason, history has given an unequivocal answer. The reaction of those of Japanese ancestry in Hawaii when the attack came and the services which have since been rendered to the country's cause in all theaters of war by Americans of Japanese ancestry is the complete rejoinder to this unworthy rationalization.

We ask this Court to review the evidence we have submitted with particular care, because in the *Hirabayashi* case it accepted much too easily the assumptions and broad charges that we have gone to some trouble to answer here. The opinion of the Court in the *Hirabayashi* decision refers to conditions which "have in a large measure prevented their assimilation as an integral part of the white population." It accepts without question the assertion that "there has been relatively little social intercourse between them and the white population." It speaks of their "isolation" and, most disturbing of all, it justifies the imposition of a curfew by reference to "ethnic affiliations with an invading enemy." We contend that whatever affiliation citizens of Japanese ancestry may have with the Pacific enemy is of a general biological nature. We contend that the ethnic affiliations of these people are solidly with America. To assert otherwise is to ignore the rich store of evidence that scholarship and history have heaped high for us, and is to imply the Nazi doctrine that race and physical type determine loyalty and "ethnic affiliations.". . .

[2. General DeWitt.] Why then did General DeWitt, in spite of what he knew or could easily have learned, act upon the advice of racists and mean-spirited economic rivals?. . .

We contend that General DeWitt accepted the views of racists instead of principles of democracy because he is himself a confessed racist. This is no discovery of ours and it requires no extended argument on our part to prove this. General DeWitt has gone to unusual lengths to make perfectly clear his unalterable hostility, *on racial grounds,* to all persons of Japanese ancestry, regardless of citizenship and regardless of evidences of loyalty. . . .

It was a different voice from that of the military realities to which General DeWitt harkened. His impetus to action is found in his statement:

> . . . In the war in which we are now engaged racial affinities are not severed by migration.
>
> The Japanese race is an enemy race and while many second and third generation Japanese born on United States soil, possessed of United States citizenship, have become "Americanized," the racial strains are undiluted. . . .

On April 13, 1943, in testifying before a House Naval Affairs Committee in San Francisco, General DeWitt amplified his stand. This time he said:

> A Jap's a Jap. It makes no difference whether he is an American citizen or not. I don't want any of them. We got them out. They were a dangerous element. The West Coast is too vital and too vulnerable to take any chances. They are a dangerous element, whether loyal or not. It makes no difference whether he is an American citizen. Theoretically, he is still a Japanese and you can't change him. You can't change him by giving him a piece of paper. . . .

Only one other man has, to our knowledge, used the same figure of speech in complaining that citizenship in his country was not at that time based upon considerations of race. This is Adolph Hitler, who wrote in *Mein Kampf:*

> Today the right of citizenship is acquired, as above mentioned, primarily by birth within the boundaries of a state. Race or membership in the nation plays no part whatever. A negro who used to live in the German protectorates, and now has a residence in Germany, thus brings a "German citizen" into the world if he has a child. In this same way any Jewish or Polish, African or Asiatic child can be declared a German citizen without more ado. . . . This conjuring trick is accomplished by a State President. What Heaven could not attempt, one of these

Theophratsus Paracelsuses does in the turn of a hand. One scratch of the pen and a Mongolian ragamuffin is suddenly turned into a real "German."

. . .

In his concurring opinion in the *Hirabayashi* case, Mr. Justice Douglas wrote: "We must credit the military with as much good faith . . . as we would any other public official acting pursuant to his duties." We do not doubt the good faith of General DeWitt. We do not doubt the good faith and burning fanaticism of Adolph Hitler in his belief that the Jews of Germany must be removed and eliminated, and that no act of theirs could attest of their worth. But we do question the outlook upon which the faith of these men is based. The faith of men who said "A Jap's a Jap" is not the faith of the men who wrote: "Loyalty is a matter of mind and of heart not of race. That indeed is the history of America. Moreover, guilt is personal under our constitutional system." It is not the faith of the Court which proclaimed, "Distinctions between citizens solely because of their ancestry are by their very nature odious to a free people whose institutions are founded upon the doctrine of equality." It is not the faith of the man who asserted, "Distinctions based on color and ancestry are utterly inconsistent with our traditions and ideals." We can only ask that in the decision now before them the members of this Court will keep that high faith which is the finest tradition of our land. . . .

Respectfully submitted,

SABURO KIDO,
Japanese American Citizens' League.

WESTERN STATES' *AMICUS CURIAE* BRIEF

The prospect that there were a substantial number [of Japanese on the West Coast] who were disloyal but unidentified or whose potential loyalty required careful checking is now materializing.

Among those evacuated, 6096 persons of Japanese ancestry of the age of 18 and over, born in the United States, have thus far requested expatriation to Japan. . . . The number of applications has increased each month in the last six months.

This loyalty question was asked of male citizens of Japanese ancestry, 17 years of age and older, in War Relocation Centers:

Will you swear unqualified allegiance to the United States of America and faithfully defend the United States from any or all attacks by foreign or domestic forces and foreswear any form of allegiance or obedience to the Japanese emperor, or any other foreign government, power or organization?

Out of 19,104 questionnaires checked, 4850 [Japanese] American citizens or 25.4% answered in the negative. 9.7% of the female citizens of Japanese ancestry, 17 years of age and older, whose questionnaires were checked, also answered this question in the negative.

It has now been discovered that many thousands of Japanese, resident in the United States, had a financial stake in Japan through the purchase of "Fixed Yen Deposits" and other moneys on deposit in Japanese banks.

On the other hand it is likewise becoming evident that there are a large number of American-Japanese among those evacuated who were and are loyal to the United States. In time of war, however, a citizen, as member of a particular group of citizens—the military age group, for example—may be called upon to make many a sacrifice of those things of liberty and property normally safeguarded by our Constitution. He may be required even to make the supreme sacrifice in his country's cause. If then, a citizen such as the appellant here, happens to be a member of a group of persons, among whom there are unidentified persons who are potentially disloyal, can it be said in view of the grave danger that his constitutional rights were improperly curtailed when he was required to move, as a member of the group, from sensitive military areas if that was a reasonable way to insure the removal of those other members of the group who might weaken our defense against invasion or interfere with the successful prosecution of the war by the commission of espionage and sabotage?

In time of war, evacuation has been held to be a reasonable method of removing potentially dangerous persons from critical military areas. The Canadian Government also found it necessary to order the removal of all persons of the Japanese race from a specified area along the Pacific Coast. . . .

A realistic consideration of the facts pertaining to the evacuation cannot avoid noting the charges made by appellant and others that the removal of alien and citizen Japanese from the Pacific Coast military areas was the result of pressure from "anti-Japanese" groups opposed to the Japanese for racial and economic reasons, who secured the removal under the cloak of a war measure. There is no evidence that such pressure motivated the military decision. Because of the very fact that social and economic problems have existed in California, Oregon, and Washington, with reference to persons of Japanese ancestry, it is important that this court state that the action was taken as a matter of military necessity to safeguard national security from enemy action, both from without and from within. . . .

ROBERT KENNY,
Attorney General of the State of California,

GEORGE NEUNER,
Attorney General of the State of Oregon,

SMITH TROY,
Attorney General of the State of Washington.

THE OPINION

Mr. Justice Black delivered the opinion of the Court. . . .

The petitioner, an American citizen of Japanese descent, was convicted in a Federal district court for remaining in San Leandro, California, a "Military Area," contrary to Civilian Exclusion Order No. 34 of the Commanding General of the

Western Command, U.S. Army, which directed that after May 9, 1942, all persons of Japanese ancestry should be excluded from that area. No question was raised as to petitioner's loyalty to the United States. The Circuit Court of Appeals affirmed, and the importance of the constitutional question involved caused us to grant certiorari.

It should be noted to begin with, that all legal restrictions which curtail the civil rights of a single racial group are immediately suspect. That is not to say that all such restrictions are unconstitutional. It is to say that courts must subject them to the most rigid scrutiny. Pressing public necessity may sometimes justify the existence of such restrictions; racial antagonism never can. . . .

In the light of the principles we announced in the *Hirabayashi Case,* we are unable to conclude that it was beyond the war power of Congress and the Executive to exclude those of Japanese ancestry from the West Coast war area at the time they did. True, exclusion from the area in which one's home is located is a far greater deprivation than constant confinement to the home from 8 p.m. to 6 a.m. Nothing short of apprehension by the proper military authorities of the gravest imminent danger to the public safety can constitutionally justify either. But exclusion from a threatened area, no less than curfew, has a definite and close relationship to the prevention of espionage and sabotage. The military authorities, charged with the primary responsibility of defending our shores, concluded that curfew provided inadequate protection and ordered exclusion. They did so, as pointed out in our Hirabayashi opinion, in accordance with congressional authority to the military to say who should, and who should not, remain in the threatened areas. . . .

Like curfew, exclusion of those of Japanese origin was deemed necessary because of the presence of an unascertainable number of disloyal members of the group, most of whom we have no doubt were loyal to this country. It was because we could not reject the finding of the military authorities that it was impossible to bring about an immediate segregation of the disloyal from the loyal that we sustained the validity of the curfew order as applying to the whole group. In the instant case, temporary exclusion of the entire group was rested by the military on the same ground. The judgement that exclusion of the whole group was for the same reason a military imperative answers the contention that the exclusion was in the nature of group punishment based on antagonism to those of Japanese origin. That there were members of the group who retained loyalties to Japan has been confirmed by investigations made subsequent to the exclusion. Approximately five thousand American citizens of Japanese ancestry refused to swear unqualified allegiance to the United States and to renounce allegiance to the Japanese Emperor, and several thousand evacuees requested repatriation to Japan.

We uphold the exclusion order as of the time it was made and when the petitioner violated it. In doing so, we are not unmindful of the hardships imposed by it upon a large group of American citizens. But hardships are part of war, and war is an aggregation of hardships. All citizens alike, both in and out of uniform, feel the impact of war in greater or lesser measure. Citizenship has its responsibilities as well as its privileges, and in time of war the burden is always heavier. Compulsory exclusion of large groups of citizens from their homes, except under circumstances of direst emergency and peril, is inconsistent with our basic governmental institutions. But when under conditions of modern warfare our shores are threatened by hostile forces, the power to protect must be commensurate with the threatened danger. . . .

It does appear, however, that on May 9, the effective date of the exclusion order, the military authorities had already determined that the evacuation should be effected by assembling together and placing under guard all those of Japanese ancestry, at central points, designated as "assembly centers," in order "to insure the orderly evacuation and resettlement of Japanese voluntarily migrating from military area No. 1 to restrict and regulate such migration." And on May 19, 1942, eleven days before the time petitioner was charged with unlawfully remaining in the area, Civilian Restrictive Order No. 1 provided for detention of those of Japanese ancestry in assembly or relocation centers. It is now argued that the validity of the exclusion order cannot be considered apart from the orders requiring him, after departure from the area, to report and to remain in an assembly or relocation center. The contention is that we must treat these separate orders as one and inseparable; that, for this reason, if detention in the assembly or relocation center would have illegally deprived the petitioner of his liberty, the exclusion order and his conviction under it cannot stand.

We are thus being asked to pass at this time upon the whole subsequent detention program in both assembly and relocation centers, although the only issues framed at the trial related to petitioner's remaining in the prohibited area in violation of the exclusion order. Had petitioner here left the prohibited area and gone to an assembly center we cannot say either as a matter of fact or law that his presence in that center would have resulted in his detention in a relocation center. Some who did report to the assembly center were not sent to relocation centers, but were released upon condition that they remain outside the prohibited zone until the military orders were modified or lifted. This illustrates that they pose different problems and may be governed by different principles. The lawfulness of one does not necessarily determine the lawfulness of the others. This is made clear when we analyze the requirements of the separate provisions of the separate orders. These separate requirements were that those of Japanese ancestry (1) depart from the area; (2) report to and temporarily remain in an assembly center; (3) go under military control to a relocation center there to remain for an indeterminate period until released conditionally or unconditionally by the military authorities. Each of these requirements, it will be noted, imposed distinct duties in connection with the separate steps in a complete evacuation program. Had Congress directly incorporated into one Act the language of these separate orders, and provided sanctions for their violations, disobedience of any one would have constituted a separate offense. There is no reason why violations of these orders, insofar as they were promulgated pursuant to congressional enactment, should not be treated as separate offenses. . . .

. . . It is sufficient here for us to pass upon the order which petitioner violated. To do more would be to go beyond the issues raised, and to decide momentous questions not contained within the framework of the pleadings or the evidence in this case. It will be time enough to decide the serious constitutional issues which petitioner seeks to raise when an assembly or relocation center is applied or is certain to be applied to him, and we have its terms before us.

Some of the members of the Court are of the view that evacuation and detention in an Assembly Center were inseparable. After May 3, 1942, the date of Exclusion Order No. 34, Korematsu was under compulsion to leave the area not as he would choose but via an Assembly Center. The Assembly Center was conceived as a part of the machinery for group evacuation. The power to exclude includes the power to do it by force if necessary. And any forcible measure must necessarily entail some degree of detention or restraint whatever method of removal is selected. But whichever view is taken, it results in holding that the order under which petitioner was convicted was valid.

It is said that we are dealing here with the case of imprisonment of a citizen in a concentration camp solely because of his ancestry, without evidence or inquiry concerning his loyalty and good disposition towards the United States. Our task would be simple, our duty clear, were this a case involving the imprisonment of a loyal citizen in a concentration camp because of racial prejudice. Regardless of the true nature of the assembly and relocation centers—and we deem it unjustifiable to call them concentration camps with all the ugly connotations that term implies—we are dealing specifically with nothing but an exclusion order. To cast this case into outlines of racial prejudice, without reference to the real military dangers which were presented, merely confuses the issue. Korematsu was not excluded from the Military Area because of hostility to him or his race. He was excluded because we are at war with the Japanese Empire, because the properly constituted military authorities feared an invasion of our West Coast and felt constrained to take proper security measures, because they decided that the military urgency of the situation demanded that all citizens of Japanese ancestry be segregated from the West Coast temporarily and finally, because Congress, reposing its confidence in this time of war in our military leaders—as inevitably it must—determined that they should have the power to do just this. There was evidence of disloyalty on the part of some, the military authorities considered that the need for action was great and the time was short. We cannot—by availing ourselves of the calm perspective of hindsight—now say that at that time these actions were unjustified.

Mr. Justice Frankfurter, concurring . . .

The provisions of the Constitution which confer on the Congress and the President powers to enable this country to wage war are as much part of the Constitution as provisions looking to a nation at peace. And we have had recent occasion to quote approvingly the statement of former Chief Justice Hughes that the war power of the Government is "the power to wage war successfully." Therefore, the validity of action under the war power must be judged wholly in the context of war. That action is not to be stigmatized as lawless because like action in times of peace would be lawless. To talk about a military order that expresses an allowable judgement of war needs by those entrusted with the duty of conducting war as "an unconstitutional order" is to suffuse a part of the Constitution with an atmosphere of unconstitutionality. The respective spheres of action of military authorities and of judges are of course very different. But within their sphere, military authorities are no more outside the bounds of obedience to the Constitution than are judges within theirs. "The war power of the United States, like its other powers . . . is subject to applicable constitutional limitations." To recognize that military orders are "reasonably expedient military precautions" in time of war and yet to deny them constitutional legitimacy makes of the Constitution an instrument for dialectic subtleties not reasonably to be attributed to the hard-headed Framers, of whom a majority had had actual participation in war. If a military order such as that under review does not transcend the means appropriate for conducting war, such action by the military is as constitutional as would be any authorized action by the Interstate Commerce Commission within the limits of the constitutional power to regulate commerce. And being an exercise of the war power explicitly granted by the Constitution for safe-guarding the national life by prosecuting war effectively, I find nothing in the Constitution which denies to Congress the power to enforce such a valid military order by making its violation an offense triable in the civil courts. . . .

Mr. Justice Roberts . . .

I dissent, because I think the indisputable facts exhibit a clear violation of Constitutional rights.

This is not a case of keeping people off the streets at night as was *Hirabayashi v. United States,* nor a case of temporary exclusion of a citizen from an area for his own safety or that of the community, nor a case of offering him an opportunity to go temporarily out of an area where his presence might cause danger to himself or to his fellows. On the contrary, it is the case of convicting a citizen as a punishment for not submitting to imprisonment in a concentration camp, based on his ancestry, and solely because of his ancestry, without evidence or inquiry concerning his loyalty and good disposition towards the United States. If this be a correct statement of the facts disclosed by this record, and facts of which we take judicial notice, I need hardly labor the conclusion that constitutional rights have been violated. . . .

The predicament in which the petitioner thus found himself was this: He was forbidden, by Military Order, to leave the zone in which he lived; he was forbidden, by Military Order, after a date fixed, to be found within that zone unless he were in an Assembly Center located in that zone. General DeWitt's report to the Secretary of War concerning the program of evacuation and relocation of Japanese makes it entirely clear, if it were necessary to refer to that document—and in the light of the above recitation, I think it is not—that an Assembly Center was a euphemism for a prison. No person within such a center was permitted to leave except by Military Order.

In the dilemma that he dare not remain in his home, or voluntarily leave the area, without incurring criminal penalties, and that the only way he could avoid punishment was to go to an Assembly Center and submit himself to military imprisonment, the petitioner did nothing. . . .

The Government has argued this case as if the only order outstanding at the time the petitioner was arrested and informed against was Exclusion Order No. 34 ordering him to leave the area in which he resided, which was the basis of the information against him. That argument has evidently been effective. The opinion refers to the Hirabayashi Case, to show that this court has sustained the validity of a curfew order in an emergency. The argument then is that exclusion from a given area of danger, while somewhat more sweeping than a curfew regulation, is of the same nature—a temporary expedient made necessary by a sudden emergency. This, I think, is a substitution of an hypothetical case for the case actually before the court. I might agree with the court's disposition of the hypothetical case. The liberty of every American citizen freely to come and go must frequently, in face of sudden danger, be temporarily limited or suspended. The civil authorities must often resort to the expedient of excluding citizens temporarily from a locality. The drawing of fire lines in the case of conflagration, the removal of persons from the area where a pestilence has broken out, are familiar examples. If the exclusion worked by Exclusion Order No. 34 were of that nature the Hirabayashi Case would be authority for sustaining it. But the facts above recited, and those set forth in *Ex parte Endo,* show that the exclusion was but a part of an overall plan for forcible detention. This case cannot, therefore, be decided on any such narrow ground as the possible validity of a Temporary Exclusion Order under which the residents of an area are given an opportunity to leave and go elsewhere in their native land outside the boundaries of a military area. To make the case turn on any such assumption is to shut our eyes to reality. . . .

. . . The two conflicting orders, one which commanded him to stay and the other which commanded him to go, were nothing but a cleverly devised trap to accomplish the real purpose of the military authority, which was to lock him up in a concentration camp. The only course by which the petitioner could avoid arrest and prosecution was to go to that camp according to instructions to be given him when he reported at a Civil Control Center. We know that is the fact. Why should we set up a figmentary and artificial situation instead of addressing ourselves to the actualities of the case?. . .

Again it is a new doctrine of constitutional law that one indicted for disobedience to an unconstitutional statute may not defend on the ground of the invalidity of the statute but must obey it though he knows it is no law and, after he has suffered the disgrace of conviction and lost his liberty by sentence, then, and not before, seek, from within prison walls, to test the validity of the law. . . .

Mr. Justice Murphy, dissenting . . .

This exclusion of "all persons of Japanese ancestry, both alien and non-alien," from the Pacific Coast area on a plea of military necessity in the absence of martial law ought not to be approved. Such exclusion goes over "the very brink of constitutional power" and falls into the ugly abyss of racism.

In dealing with matters relating to the prosecution and progress of a war, we must accord great respect and consideration to the judgements of the military authorities who are on the scene and who have full knowledge of the military facts. The scope of their discretion must, as a matter of necessity and common sense, be wide. And their judgements ought not to be overruled lightly by those whose training and duties ill-equip them to deal intelligently with matters so vital to the physical security of the nation.

At the same time, however, it is essential that there be definite limits to military discretion, especially where martial law has not been declared. Individuals must not be left impoverished of their constitutional rights on a plea of military necessity that has neither substance nor support. Thus, like other claims conflicting with the asserted constitutional rights of the individual, the military claim must subject itself to the judicial process of having its reasonableness determined and its conflicts with other interests reconciled. . . .

The judicial test of whether the Government, on a plea of military necessity, can validly deprive an individual of any of his constitutional rights is whether the deprivation is reasonably related to a public danger that is so "immediate, imminent, and impending" as not to admit of delay and not to permit the intervention of ordinary constitutional processes to alleviate the danger. Civilian Exclusion Order No. 34, banishing from a prescribed area of the Pacific Coast "all persons of Japanese ancestry, both alien and non-alien," clearly does not meet that test. Being an obvious racial discrimination, the order deprives all those within its scope of the equal protection of the laws as guaranteed by the Fifth Amendment. It further deprives these individuals of their constitutional rights to live and work where they will, to establish a home where they choose and to move about freely. In excommunicating them without benefit of hearings, this order also deprives them of all their constitutional rights to procedural due process. Yet no reasonable relation to an "immediate, imminent, and impending" public danger is evident to support this racial restriction which is one of the most sweeping and complete deprivations of constitutional rights in the history of this nation in the absence of martial law. . . .

Justification for the exclusion is sought, instead, mainly upon questionable racial and sociological grounds not ordinarily within the realm of expert military judgement, supplemented by certain semi-military conclusions drawn from an unwarranted use of circumstantial evidence. Individuals of Japanese ancestry are condemned because they are said to be "a large, unassimilated, tightly knit racial group, bound to an enemy nation by strong ties of race, culture, and religion." They are claimed to be given to "emperor worshipping ceremonies" and to "dual citizenship." Japanese language schools and allegedly pro-Japanese organizations are cited as evidence of possible group disloyalty, together with facts as to certain persons being educated and residing at length in Japan. . . .

The main reasons relied upon by those responsible for the forced evacuation, therefore, do not prove a reasonable relation between the group characteristics of Japanese Americans and the dangers of invasion, sabotage and espionage. The reasons appear instead to be largely an accumulation of much of the misinformation, half-truths and insinuations that for years have been directed against Japanese Americans by people with racial and economic prejudices—the same people who have been among the foremost advocates of the evacuation. A military judgement based upon such racial and sociological considerations is not entitled to the great weight ordinarily given the judgements based upon strictly military considerations. Especially is this so when every charge relative to race, religion, culture, geographical location, and legal and economic status has been substantially discredited by independent studies made by experts in these matters.

The military necessity which is essential to the validity of the evacuation order thus resolves itself into a few intimations that certain individuals actively aided the enemy, from which it is inferred that the entire group of Japanese Americans could not be trusted to be or remain loyal to the United States. No one denies, of course, that there were some disloyal persons of Japanese descent on the Pacific Coast who did all in their power to aid their ancestral land. Similar disloyal activities have been engaged in by many persons of German, Italian and even more pioneer stock in our country. But to infer that examples of individual disloyalty prove group disloyalty and justify discriminatory action against the entire group is to deny that under our system of law individual guilt is the sole basis for deprivation of rights. Moreover, this inference, which is at the very heart of the evacuation orders, has been used in support of the abhorrent and despicable treatment of minority groups by the dictatorial tyrannies which this nation is now pledged to destroy. To give constitutional sanction to that inference in this case, however well-intentioned may have been the military command on the Pacific Coast, is to adopt one of the cruelest of the rationales used by our enemies to destroy the dignity of the individual and to encourage and open the door to discriminatory actions against other minority groups in the passions of tomorrow. . . .

I dissent, therefore, from this legalization of racism. Racial discrimination in any form and in any degree has no justifiable part whatever in our democratic way of life. It is unattractive in any setting but it is utterly revolting among a free people who have embraced the principles set forth in the Constitution of the United States. All residents of this nation are kin in some way by blood or culture to a foreign land. Yet they are of the new and distinct civilization of the United States. They must accordingly be treated at all times as the heirs of the American experiment and as entitled to all the rights and freedoms guaranteed by the Constitution.

Mr. Justice Jackson, dissenting . . .

It would be impracticable and dangerous idealism to expect or insist that each specific military command in an area of probable operations will conform to conventional tests of constitutionality. When an area is so beset that it must be put under military control at all, the paramount consideration is that its measures be successful, rather than legal. The armed services must protect a society, not merely its Constitution. The very essence of the military job is to marshal physical force, to remove every obstacle to its effectiveness, to give it every strategic advantage. Defense measures will not, and often should not, be held within the limits that bind civil authority in peace. No court can require such a commander in such circumstances to act as a reasonable man; he may be unreasonably cautious and exacting. Perhaps he should be. But a commander in temporarily focusing the life of a community on defense is carrying out a military program: he is not making law in the sense the courts know the term. He issues orders, and they may have a certain authority as military commands, although they may be very bad as constitutional law.

But if we cannot confine military expedients by the Constitution, neither would I distort the Constitution to approve all that the military may deem expedient. That is what the Court appears to be doing, whether consciously or not. I cannot say, from any evidence before me, that the orders of General DeWitt were not reasonably expedient military precautions, nor could I say that they were. But even if they were permissible military procedures, I deny that it follows that they are constitutional. If, as the Court holds, it does follow, then we may as well say that any military order will be constitutional and have done with it. . . .

Much is said of the danger to liberty from the Army program for deporting and detaining these citizens of Japanese extraction. But a judicial construction of the due process clause that will sustain this order is a far more subtle blow to liberty than the promulgation of the order itself. A military order, however unconstitutional, is not apt to last longer than the military emergency. Even during that period a succeeding commander may revoke it all. But once a judicial opinion rationalizes such an order to show that it conforms to the Constitution, or rather rationalizes the Constitution to show that the Constitution sanctions such an order, the Court for all time has validated the principle of racial discrimination in criminal procedure and of transplanting American citizens. The principle then lies about like a loaded weapon ready for the hand of any authority that can bring forward a plausible claim of an urgent need. Every repetition imbeds that principle more deeply in our law and thinking and expands it to new purposes. All who observe the work of courts are familiar with what Judge [Benjamin N.] Cardozo [a former justice of the Supreme Court who had earlier been a judge on the New York Court of Appeals] described as "the tendency of a principle to expand itself to the limit of its logic." A military commander may overstep the bounds of constitutionality, and it's an incident. But if we review and approve, that passing incident becomes the doctrine of the Constitution. There it has a generative power of its own, and all that it creates will be in its own image. Nothing better illustrates this danger than does the Court's opinion in this case.

It argues that we are bound to uphold the conviction of Korematsu because we upheld one in *Hirabayashi v. United States,* when we sustained these orders in so far as they applied a curfew requirement to a citizen of Japanese ancestry. . . .

. . . [I]n spite of our limiting words we did validate a discrimination on the basis of ancestry for mild and temporary deprivation of liberty. Now the principle of racial discrimination is pushed from support of mild measures to very harsh ones, and from temporary deprivations to indeterminate ones. And the precedent which it is said requires us to do so is *Hirabayashi.* The Court is now saying that in *Hirabayashi* we did decide the very things we there said we were not deciding. Because we said that these citizens could be made to stay in their homes during the hours of dark, it is said we must require them to leave home entirely; and if that, we are told they may also be taken into custody for deportation; and if that, it is argued they may also be held for some undetermined time in detention camps. How far the principle of this case would be extended before plausible reasons would play out, I do not know.

I should hold that a civil court cannot be made to enforce an order which violates constitutional limitations even if it is a reasonable exercise of military authority. The courts can exercise only the judicial power, can apply only law, and must abide by the Constitution, or they cease to be civil courts and become instruments of military policy. . . .

POSTSCRIPT

Since World War II, the United States has sent its armed forces into battle many times. Some of these engagements were minor in character, others were wars. None, however, was of the character of the second world war. These were not "total wars" requiring deep, painful sacrifices of most or all Americans. Not one of these operations or "limited wars," for example, necessitated any substantial violation of traditional American rights and liberties, at least not to the degree present in the Japanese internment program. However, the "limited American wars" of the second half of the twentieth century, from Korea to the Persian Gulf, have raised their own distinctive set of constitutional questions. These "limited" wars have often been "divided" ones, with a substantial number of American citizens opposing the war effort or the military operation in question. Opponents of any particular commitment of American forces coalesce around Congress, the institution that is not running the day-to-day military operations of the engagement, to contest the constitutional authority of the president to make war without congressional approval. In this way, the constitutional issue is joined. Does the president or Congress have ultimate control over the American military? The president, relying upon the "Commander in Chief" clause (Art. II, Sect. 2), claims that he has the power to decide if, when, and where American military forces are to be sent, while Congress points to its powers to "declare war" and to "raise and support Armies" (Art. I, Sect. 8) to substantiate its position that Congress must, at a minimum, have a veto over any executive decision to make war.

Though the question of the respective war powers of the president and Congress has become more salient in the post–World War II era, it is in fact an old constitutional debate. At the Philadelphia Convention, an early draft of the Constitution gave Congress the power to "make war." However, the language was changed to "declare war" because the framers realized that the president had to be able to resist sudden attacks.[24] It will be recalled that the Supreme Court endorsed this argument during the Civil War when it ruled in the *Prize Cases* that President Lincoln had the authority to blockade Southern ports without a congressional declaration of war.[25]

After the new Constitution was ratified, the debate continued among certain of the founding fathers. Did the Constitution ultimately assign the power to make

---

[24]For a comprehensive discussion of the framers' views on the war power, see W. Taylor Reveley III, *War Powers of the President and Congress* (Charlottesville: University Press of Virginia, 1981), Chapters 3–5.

[25]See p. 100, note 2.

war to the president or to the Congress? Alexander Hamilton sided in favor of a wide conception of presidential war powers. In 1793, he said the following:

> It deserves to be remarked, that as the participation of the Senate in the making of treaties, and the power of the Legislature to declare war, are exceptions out of the general "executive power" vested in the President, they are to be construed strictly, and ought to be extended no further than is essential to their execution.[26]

The tenor of Hamilton's remark suggested that, in his view, the president could employ troops as he felt necessary, even if the likelihood of armed conflict was high. James Madison disagreed—it was up to Congress to decide if war was justified.

> The power to declare war . . . including the power of judging the causes of war, is fully and exclusively vested in the Legislature, that the executive has no right in any case, to decide the question whether there is, or is not cause for declaring war.[27]

The debate concerning war powers is therefore an old and venerable one. No general consensus has existed beyond the general assumption that the president has the constitutional authority and duty to defend the country.

However, the scope of the president's constitutional authority to "defend" the United States is less clear in practice than in theory because the distinction between offense and defense is a very slippery one. At times, the best defense is a good offense: a preemptive attack. And what exactly can the president defend without congressional approval: only the United States itself? what of American territories? American troops stationed abroad? American citizens living or traveling abroad? American interests? In a symbolic way, these questions suggest how, over the past 200 years, the president's defensive duties and his powers as "commander in chief" have given him, in practice, an ever larger share of the offensive power to "make war."[28] Only Congress can "declare war," but the president's power to wage war without congressional approval has been firmly demonstrated throughout the twentieth century.

Partly because the Constitution's language concerning war powers is so vague, it is widely believed that the Supreme Court should not attempt to delineate the respective war powers of the Congress and the president by the ordinary means of constitutional litigation. The issue is thought to be a "political question" that is not suitable for judicial resolution.[29] For example, in *Mora v. McNamara*

---

[26]Quoted in Robert F. Turner, "The Powers of the Purse," Howard E. Shuman and Walter R. Thomas, eds., *The Constitution and National Security* (Washington: National Defense University Press, 1990), p. 76.

[27]Quoted in Robert S. Wood, "And the Imperial Republic," in Shuman and Thomas, eds., *The Constitution and National Security*, p. 100.

[28]For the history of war power developments, see Reveley, *War Powers*, Chapters 6–7; Thomas Eagleton, *War and Presidential Power* (New York: Liveright, 1974), Part I.

[29]Despite judicial reluctance to address the war powers issue, the Court ruled as early as 1800 that the president can legitimately make war without a congressional declaration of war. See *Bas v. Tingy*, 4 U.S. 36 (1800); *Talbot v. Seeman*, 5 U.S. 1 (1801).

(1967), a group of draftees sought a declaratory judgment that the Vietnam War was "illegal." The lower federal courts dismissed their suit, and the Supreme Court, by denying certiorari and refusing to hear the case, declined to address the constitutionality of this particularly controversial undeclared war.

However, Justices Potter Stewart and William O. Douglas dissented from the denial of certiorari. They both felt that the Court should "squarely face" the constitutional problems presented by this wartime litigation. According to Stewart, the issues were the following: (1) Was the military action in Vietnam a "war" within the meaning of the Constitution? (2) If it was a "war," could the president order draftees to participate in the conflict if Congress had not "declared" the war? (3) Does the United States have any treaty obligations that would have a bearing on the president's power to send troops to Vietnam? (4) Of what importance was the August 10, 1964, Joint Congressional Resolution (the "Gulf of Tonkin Resolution") that gave President Lyndon B. Johnson sweeping powers over military operations in southeast Asia?[30] According to Stewart, the Supreme Court had a responsibility to address these questions.

What do you think? Do you think that the Court should address these kinds of questions? Are they similar to other constitutional issues, or are they more "political" in character? In what way are they more "political"? What kind of expertise is required to resolve such questions? What about the rights of the draftees? Does a citizen drafted into the armed forces have a right to refuse to participate in an undeclared war? Can such an individual appeal to the Supreme Court? Does the Court have an obligation to hear such a case?

In whatever way these questions are answered, the Court itself has exercised a great deal of restraint in the area of war powers. It has said very little concerning the constitutional requirements of a lawful war, and it has refused, in any way, to define in any detail the offensive, as opposed to the defensive, war powers of the president. However, in *United States v. Curtiss-Wright Export Corporation*, the same case in which the Court had concluded that the federal government's "foreign affairs powers" were more expansive than its "domestic affairs powers," the Court endorsed a broad conception of presidential power in the area of international relations. Speaking through Justice George Sutherland, it said:

> Not only, as we have shown, is the Federal power over external affairs in origin and essential character different from that over internal affairs, but participation in the exercise of the power is significantly limited. In this vast external realm, with its important, complicated, delicate and manifold problems, the President alone has the power to speak or listen as a representative of the nation. He *makes* treaties with the advice and consent of the Senate; but he alone negotiates. Into the field of negotiation the Senate cannot intrude; and Congress itself is power-less to invade it. . . .
>
> It is important to bear in mind that we are here dealing not alone with an authority vested in the President by an exertion of legislative power, but with such an authority plus the very delicate, plenary and exclusive power of the President

---

[30]389 U.S. 934, 934–35 (1967). See also *Massachusetts v. Laird,* 400 U.S. 866 (1970); *Sarnoff v. Schultz,* 409 U.S. 929 (1972).

as the sole organ of the federal government in the field of international relations—a power which does not require as a basis for its exercise an act of Congress, but which, of course, like every other governmental power, must be exercised in subordination to the applicable provisions of the Constitution."[31]

Though this passage is *obiter dicta* (language from an opinion that is not necessary for the Court's ruling), it has been widely cited as authority for the conclusion that the president has broad constitutional authority to initiate military action. Therefore, although the Court has avoided making any specific ruling as to the offensive war powers of the president and the Congress, some of its language has sanctioned the degree to which historical events have determined that the president does have wide authority to initiate military action.

Because the Court has avoided making any specific ruling on war powers, the issue of which branch of government ultimately controls the offensive use of the armed forces has often been determined by political factors, with public opinion usually having a decisive impact in regard to any particular exertion of military power. If the American people are behind the president's military initiatives, Congress either supports his policies or acquiesces. For instance, in 1964, after two American destroyers were purportedly attacked without provocation in the Gulf of Tonkin, Congress, reflecting the public's anger, passed the Gulf of Tonkin resolution, which gave President Johnson almost unlimited authority to fight North Vietnam. However, after the war lost its luster, as the number of casualties mounted with little or no visible gains in the field, the American people grew tired of the war, and Congress reacted accordingly. In 1973, using its power over appropriations, Congress prohibited the expenditure of any funds for military activities in Indochina, including Vietnam, Laos, and Cambodia. President Richard M. Nixon vetoed the cutoff, but he soon had no choice but to compromise by agreeing to seek congressional authorization for any further military action in Indochina.

In the same year that Congress cut off all funds for military operations in southeast Asia, it also changed the terms of the war powers debate by passing the War Powers Resolution. Enacted over Nixon's veto, it set up guidelines that limited the degree to which the president could engage in offensive military operations without active congressional support. First, in its "Purpose and Policy" section, the resolution said that the president could introduce American forces into combat "only pursuant to (1) a declaration of war, (2) specific statutory authorization, or (3) a national emergency created by attack upon the United States, its territories or possessions, or its armed forces." The president was therefore not authorized to send troops on his own initiative to protect either "American interests" or even the lives of Americans who were not in the military.[32] Second, it required the president to "consult" with Congress "in every possible instance" both before

---

[31]*United States v. Curtiss-Wright Export Corp.*, 299 U.S. 304, 319–20 (1936).

[32]The operative force of these restrictions, however, has been questioned because they are contained in the "Purpose and Policy" section of the Resolution, a section that may have little or no operative effect.

and after introducing troops into military action. Third, within forty-eight hours of sending troops into a hostile situation the president had to submit to Congress a "report" that would explain and justify the operation. Fourth, within sixty days of sending the troops (with the possibility of a thirty-day extension), the president had to withdraw them unless the Congress declared war or specifically approved the commitment of American troops. Last, the president had to withdraw the troops immediately if Congress so directed by a concurrent (two-house) resolution.[33]

Since the passage of the War Powers Resolution, every sitting president save for President Bill Clinton has condemned it as a violation of the executive's war power. Moreover, many recent presidents have violated its literal provisions. For instance, in 1975 President Gerald Ford ordered the armed forces to evacuate Americans and South Vietnamese from Saigon, and, in 1980, President Jimmy Carter initiated an unsuccessful military attempt to rescue hostages held in Iran. Of course, these operations were quick, non-aggressive rescue missions of American citizens. It is therefore debatable whether the War Powers Resolution was ever intended to cover such operations, and, if it was, whether such an operation would then be an unconstitutional exertion of executive power.

Is the War Powers Resolution constitutional in regard to such rescue missions? One of its provisions says that it is applicable whenever armed forces are introduced "into hostilities, or into situations where imminent involvement in hostilities is clearly indicated by the circumstances." If so, must the president "consult" with and "report" to Congress whenever he places American military personnel at risk in an attempt to rescue Americans who are, in his judgment, endangered in a foreign country? Or, do the executive's war powers allow the president "to make war" for the purpose of saving Americans abroad, if the operation is quick and not overly aggressive? Can the same logic be used for an attempt to save American allies or clients? At what point, if ever, must the president consult Congress if his basic purpose is humanitarian rather than bellicose? If you think that Congress must be consulted before such dangerous "rescue attempts," how is security for the operation to be maintained? Can the mission remain a secret if 535 members of Congress have to be consulted beforehand? If not, should the president be required to consult with some members of Congress? With whom? Party leaders? Relevant congressional committees? Congressional committee chairpersons?

---

[33]This particular provision of the War Powers Resolution is constitutionally suspect because it is analogous to a "legislative veto." Such a veto exists when a statute authorizes a committee of Congress, a house of Congress, or both houses of Congress to veto any particular exertion of a power that Congress has delegated to the executive branch or to an executive agency. In a case dealing with immigration, the Supreme Court ruled that legislative vetoes were unconstitutional. See *INS v. Chadha,* 462 U.S. 919 (1983). It is arguable, however, that *Chadha* is not applicable to the War Powers Resolution because no statutory delegation of power is involved. On this interpretation, Congress can veto any offensive American military operation because, as the War Powers Resolution makes clear, Congress has never delegated to the executive branch its ultimate authority over whether the United States should go to war.

Of course, recent presidents have engaged in military operations that have not, in any meaningful sense, been humanitarian rescue operations. President Ronald Reagan, for instance, used force to achieve his foreign policy goals in regard to Central America, Lebanon, Libya, and Grenada.[34] The degree of congressional participation in these various military operations depended upon the political context and the type of operation. In regard to the bombing raid on Libya, which was meant to punish Colonel Muammar el-Qadafi for his sponsorship of terrorism, Congress had a negligible role to play. President Reagan claimed that security considerations prevented any consultation with Congress before the attack, and the attack was over before most members of Congress knew about it. In contrast, when he deployed troops in Lebanon, Reagan worked with Congress and within the provisions of the War Powers Resolution. He did so reluctantly, insisting that the resolution was unconstitutional, but he could not ignore those in Congress who feared that since Reagan's objectives in Lebanon were ill-defined, they would entangle the United States in another Vietnam. The resolution therefore was somewhat effective in certain cases during the 1980s. When Reagan engaged in a controversial military policy that had possible long-term costly implications, he grudgingly respected the spirit of the resolution by seeking the support of Congress soon after troops were committed. Whether Reagan would have acted in this fashion if public opinion was decisively behind his policy is an open question.

In the main, the two military operations ordered by President George Bush support, with some qualifications, the foregoing conclusions. Bush did not seek congressional approval of the 1989 invasion of Panama or invoke the provisions of the War Powers Resolution. However, Operation Just Cause, as it was called, was quick, like the invasion of Grenada, and not too costly: Only 23 Americans were killed, including three civilians. Also, the operation was quite popular among the American people because they despised Panama's leader, General Manuel Noriega. In the public mind, Noriega's earlier anti-American activities and rhetoric, his reported links to Colombian drug dealers, and his reputation as an abuser of human rights helped to alleviate concern about whether Bush was acting beyond his constitutional authority by sending American forces into battle without congressional authorization. Congress may have the power "to declare war," but the American people hated Noriega more than they cared about the meaning or efficacy of this particular constitutional provision. They were not about to let a constitutional scruple ruin their satisfaction at seeing Noriega locked up in an American jail.

Such political factors were also quite evident throughout Operation Desert Storm, though the politics and the operation were vastly different from Just Cause. When Saddam Hussein's Iraqi forces invaded Kuwait, Bush proclaimed that the invasion would "not stand." He kept his promise, but it was not one he

---

[34]President Reagan justified the Grenada invasion as an attempt to rescue American medical students, but events following the invasion suggest that humanitarianism was not his only motive for sending troops. After overthrowing the pro-Cuban government, American forces took complete control of the island and installed a regime that was, besides being more popular with the inhabitants of Grenada, more sympathetic to American interests.

could fulfill alone. The cooperation of both the Security Council of the United Nations and the Congress of the United States were important to the success of Bush's efforts to expel Iraq from Kuwait. On November 29, 1990, after it became clear that economic sanctions would not induce Hussein to leave Kuwait, the Security Council authorized "all necessary means" to achieve this goal, including the use of military force after January 15, 1991. Bush argued that the UN resolution gave him all the authority he needed to initiate an offensive war against Iraq. He therefore refused to call Congress into special session during late November and December, claiming at a news conference that he could not "consult with 535 strong-willed individuals." He added: "Nor does my responsibility under the Constitution compel me to do that."[35]

It is revealing that during December the Democratic leadership of Congress also declined to reconvene the legislature. While Bush continued a military buildup in Saudi Arabia and the Persian Gulf, members of Congress stood on the sidelines, watching events unfold and trying to gauge the trend of public opinion. Clearly, the American people were worried. Some were afraid that a war against the Iraqis, a people supposedly hardened by a preceding eight-year war against Iran, would be a long, drawn-out, and costly affair. And was it necessary? Many thought that the economic sanctions were not being given a chance to work. On the other hand, a substantial segment of the American people quickly came to see Hussein as a brutal aggressor who was on the verge of developing nuclear weapons. They thought that it would be better to smash him now, rather than to wait until he became a more formidable opponent.

In sum, the American people were sharply divided about the merits of an offensive war against Iraq. Congress, when it officially convened in January 1991, reflected these deep divisions in the public mind. On January 12, just three days before the UN deadline permitting the use of force against Iraq, both the Senate and the House passed resolutions authorizing the use of force against Hussein, but the support for these measures was thin and tentative. In the Senate, the margin of victory was fifty-two to forty-seven, while the House Democratic leadership brought forward another resolution (besides the one authorizing force) urging the administration to remain on the defensive and give the economic sanctions additional time to work.[36] Congress therefore gave Bush a "green light"; after January 12 there was no constitutional doubt that Bush could legally initiate hostilities if he chose to do so, but it refused to back his war plans wholeheartedly. The results, of course, are well known. On January 15, an extensive American bombing campaign began against Iraq. A ground invasion followed on January 24. The war that many Americans feared never came to pass. The ground fighting was over 100 hours after it started, ending on January 28.

Because Congress specifically authorized Desert Storm, it was clearly a lawful war within the provisions of the War Powers Resolution. The more difficult question is whether constitutional norms concerning who had the ultimate legal control of the armed forces had much of a bearing on what happened. Certainly the

---

[35]Robert A. Strong *Decisions and Dilemmas: Case Studies in Presidential Foreign Policy Making* (Englewood Cliffs, N.J.: Prentice-Hall, 1992), p. 228.

[36]Ibid., pp. 228–29.

courts did nothing to apply the Constitution to the events of the day. In November 1990, fifty-four members of Congress attempted to stop Bush from attacking Iraq without congressional approval by filing suit in the U.S. District Court for the District of Columbia. However, on December 13, District Judge Harold H. Greene ruled that no court could order the executive not to make war unless a majority of Congress brought suit. The case was therefore dismissed for lack of "ripeness."[37]

In the end, politics dictated whether the United States should go to war against Iraq. And, in such a political contest, the president has many advantages over Congress. Having immediate control over troops, he has the initiative while Congress has to react to what he does. He sends troops and presents Congress with a *fait accompli*. Of course, it is conceivable that in such a situation, even though the president would be using his considerable access to the media to shape and influence the public debate, Congress might still oppose the operation. But the burden is on Congress to stop the drift of events. If public opinion is behind the president, Congress can function only as a rubber stamp, even if the military operation has the potential of drawing the United States into a costly and ill-advised adventure. Conversely, in the unlikely case that public opinion is decidedly against the operation, Congress will have a meaningful role to play only if the president foolishly perseveres in his politically disastrous decision to commit American troops. It seems that Congress has little to do in regard to the war power as long as the American people are either decidedly in favor of or opposed to the military operation in question.

In contrast, if the American public is divided in regard to a particular exertion of presidential war power, as it was in the Gulf War, Congress could have a crucial impact on the decision as to whether the nation should go to war. However, if a large portion of the American people support the president's policy, it would take a great deal of political courage for members of Congress to vote to withdraw troops. In such a situation, most politicians would want to avoid the label of having "let down" the men and women in uniform. It would be so much easier for Congress to do what the House of Representatives did before the Gulf War: authorize the attack, but advise against it. This option is less politically risky than either supporting or opposing the war.

Accordingly, if it is likely that individual members of congress will seek political cover if public opinion is sharply divided about a certain military operation, is the Congress institutionally capable of exercising the war power it legally shares with the president? On the other hand, if only the president is capable of making the ultimate decision as to whether to go to war or not, is this the way a constitutional democracy should operate? Should one person have such power? And what of the Supreme Court? Does it have a justifiable role to play in defining who has what share of the power to make offensive war? How would its role bear upon the political realities that now seem to have such a decisive impact upon the question of who ultimately controls the armed forces of the United States?

---

[37]See *Dellums v. Bush*, 752 F Supp 1141 (1990).

Presidential Emergency Powers

YOUNGSTOWN SHEET & TUBE CO. V. SAWYER
343 U.S. 579 (1952)

✦

The preceding two chapters dealt with two powers of the federal government, the commerce power and the war power, and their relationship to the powers of states and the rights of individuals. This chapter and the one that follows one will address certain powers of the three branches of the federal government: the Congress, the presidency, and the judiciary. Based on the principle of separation of powers, the U.S. Constitution divides the national government into these three branches, with each branch, in the main, exercising a different type of political power: legislative, executive, or judicial. However, because the Constitution separates power so that political institutions can check and balance one another, the branches are not always autonomous within their distinct areas. At crucial junctures, powers are shared between the branches: For example, the president has the legislative power to veto legislation, and Congress has the judicial power of impeachment. The federal government is, therefore, a complicated system of separate yet shared powers, a system that provides ample opportunity for disagreement and conflict, especially between Congress and the president.[1] Often these conflicts are settled politically, with public opinion having a large impact upon the result. At times, however, such disputes find their way into court, and judges have to decide whether Congress or the president has the power in question. This is a particularly difficult judicial responsibility if only because relevant legal

---

[1]See Louis Fischer, *The Politics of Shared Power: Congress and the Executive* (Washington: Congressional Quarterly Press, 1981).

precedents in the area of separation of powers are few and far between. *Youngstown Sheet & Tube Co. v. Sawyer* is therefore an interesting case. It provides an excellent opportunity to consider how judges should interpret the Constitution as they go about the sensitive task of delineating the respective spheres of Congress and the president.

The ultimate constitutional question addressed in *Youngstown* is whether President Harry Truman, in an emergency, could order his secretary of commerce, Charles Sawyer, to seize and take control of the steel industry without any statutory authorization by Congress. Is such a seizure of private property a legislative act requiring Congress's approval, or does the president have the "inherent power" to do whatever is necessary in an emergency?

This ultimate constitutional question presented by *Youngstown,* however, was entangled with a nonconstitutional issue that significantly complicated the case. In this litigation, the steel companies were asking the courts for an *injunction* against Sawyer.[2] An injunction is a court order compelling or restraining the performance of some action by an individual or government official. A request for an injunction is a very different proceeding from an ordinary civil suit for damages in which a plaintiff demands compensation for a harm that he or she has suffered. Instead of compensating a harm done, an injunction prevents an *irreparable* harm from occurring or continuing. Accordingly, injunctions are granted only if the person harmed has *no other adequate remedy at law.* An additional requirement is that the *balance of equities* must favor the injunction. This means that an injunction must cause more good than harm. It will not be granted for A's benefit, even if A is suffering an irreparable injury, if it will cause a greater harm to the general public. A judge must "balance the equities" to decide if the irreparable harm is great enough to outweigh any general harm that the injunction itself might cause.

The rules governing injunctive relief made *Youngstown* a very difficult case. Even if Truman was acting illegally, even if he was acting beyond his constitutional powers, it was arguable that the steel companies' request for an injunction should have been denied because they had not shown that they were suffering "irreparable injury" or that the "balance of equities" favored their request. On the other hand, it was arguable that the unlawfulness of Truman's action was the decisive factor in the "balance of equities" that justified injunctive relief. Such entanglements of nonconstitutional issues with constitutional ones are not rare occurrences in constitutional adjudication, and they have a direct bearing upon one's view of the role of the judiciary. In cases in which constitutional and nonconstitutional issues are entangled, should a judge "passively" avoid the constitutional issue by deciding the case on the nonconstitutional ground, or should the judge "actively" confront the constitutional issue as a precondition for deciding the nonconstitutional one? *Youngstown* is an excellent opportunity to consider this basic question because during this litigation, at the district court level, one judge

---

[2]The companies asked for an injunction against Sawyer, even though Truman had ordered the seizure, because they doubted that the courts could issue an injunction against a sitting president. The question of whether a president is ever amenable to a court order is explicitly addressed in *United States v. Nixon,* the case that is discussed in the next chapter. In the *Youngstown* litigation, the assumption was that the president could not be enjoined, but that his subordinates, such as Sawyer, were amenable to court orders.

followed a "passive" approach whereas another pursued a more "active" one. Comparing how these two judges functioned in the *Youngstown* litigation will therefore enable students to deepen their understanding of the role of the judiciary.

The events leading up to Truman's seizure of the steel plants began in 1951. The contract between the steel companies and the United Steelworkers of the World expired on December 31, 1951, and the union planned to strike if its demands were not met. The companies and the union had been negotiating, but with no success. To prevent the strike, Truman could have invoked the Labor Management Relations Act of 1947 (the Taft–Hartley Act). This law empowered the president to seek an injunction against a strike by a union for eighty days but did not authorize any seizures of private property during labor disputes. (For a more comprehensive description of the procedures of the Taft–Hartley Act, see the steel companies' brief.) However, instead of invoking Taft–Hartley, Truman referred the dispute on December 22 to the Wage Stabilization Board, an entity established by the Defense Production Act of 1950. Its function was to control inflation during the Korean War by keeping wages under control, just as its counterpart, the Office of Price Stabilization, was to keep prices, including the price of steel, in check.

In response to Truman's actions, the union suspended its strike while the wage board considered the dispute. The board's recommendations, submitted to Truman on March 20, 1952, were acceptable to the union, but the steel companies rejected them, especially the suggested wage increases, unless the government would approve a corresponding hike in the price of steel. The union then called for a strike on April 9. In a late-night radio announcement on April 8 (see Box 4.1), Truman explained to the American people why, in the context of the Korean War, a large increase in the price of steel and a strike in the steel industry were both unacceptable. Given his constitutional responsibilities to defend the nation and control inflation, he claimed that he had no choice but to order his secretary of commerce to take possession of the steel plants as of 12:01 A.M. April 9.

The following morning, the steel companies were in federal district court, asking for an injunction against Sawyer. The case first came before Judge Alexander Holtzoff and then, later in the month, before Judge David Pine. A comparison of how these two district court judges responded to the issues involved in *Youngstown* is a good way to appreciate how a judge's understanding of his role can have a large impact upon the way he decides a case in which nonconstitutional issues are entangled with great constitutional questions. On April 9, Holtzoff refused the request for an injunction because he thought that the requirements for an injunction had not been met, but on April 29 Pine granted the request because he thought that the constitutional issue had a bearing on whether the requirements had been satisfied. Of course, during the twenty-day interim, the government had initiated changes in the operations of the steel plants. These changes not only gave the steel companies an opportunity to return to court but also may have changed the legal situation, entitling the steel companies now to seek an injunction. Nevertheless, the contrasting decisions of Holtzoff and Pine were also the result, to some degree, of the two judges' different perceptions and evaluations of the basic judicial role.

BOX 4.1

PRESIDENT TRUMAN JUSTIFIES SEIZURE

My fellow Americans:

Tonight, our country faces a grave danger. We are faced by the possibility that at midnight tonight the steel industry will be shut down. This must not happen.

Steel is our key industry. It is vital to our defense effort. It is vital to peace.

We do not have a stockpile of the kinds of steel we need for defense. Steel is flowing directly to the plants that make it into defense production.

If steel production stops, we will have to stop making the shells and bombs that are going directly to our soldiers at the front in Korea. If steel production stops, we will have to cut down and delay the atomic energy program. If steel production stops, it won't be long before we have to stop making engines for the Air Force planes. . . .

I have no doubt that if our defense program fails, the danger of war, the possibility of hostile attack, grows much greater.

I would not be faithful to my responsibilities as President if I did not use every effort to keep this from happening.

With American troops facing the enemy on the field of battle, I would not be living up to my oath of office if I failed to do whatever is required to provide them with the weapons and the ammunitions they need for their survival. . . .

. . . [Therefore,] I am directing the Secretary of Commerce to take possession of the steel mills, and to keep them operating. . . .

I want you to understand clearly why these measures are necessary, and how this situation in the steel industry came about. . . .

There are plenty of other industries that would like to have big price increases. Our price control officials meet every day with industries that want to raise their prices. For months they have been turning down most of these requests, because most of the companies have had profits big enough to absorb cost increases and still leave a fair return. . . .

All these industries have taken "no" for an answer, and they have gone home and kept right on producing. That's what any law abiding person does when he is told what he'd like to do is against the rules.

But not the steel companies. Not the steel companies. The steel industry doesn't want to come down and make its case, and abide by the decision like everybody else. The steel industry wants something special, something nobody else can get. . . .

It is perfectly clear, from the facts I have cited, that the present danger to our stabilization program comes from the steel companies' insistence on a big jump in steel prices.

The plain fact of the matter is that the steel companies are recklessly forcing a shutdown of the steel mills. They are trying to get special preferred treatment, not available to any other industry. And they are apparently willing to stop steel production to get it.

As President of the United States it is my plain duty to keep this from happening. And that is the reason for the measures I have taken tonight. . . .

Source: The Public Papers of the Presidents of the United States, 1952–53 (Washington: Government Printing Office, 1966), pp. 246–49.

On the morning of the 9th, before Judge Holtzoff, John Wilson, representing Youngstown Sheet & Tube Company, outlined why the seizure caused an "irreparable injury" to the owners. He referred to the possibility that the government would raise wages and require every employee to belong to the union. Judge Holtzoff responded,

> Of course, I can't consider that. You are trying to prognosticate the future, what the Government might do at some future time. The mere fact that the Government might do something, which you say would be illegal if it did it, is no reason, in itself, for granting an injunction at this time.[3]

In other words, a judge cannot issue an injunction based on *fear* of what the government might do—such fear does not represent an irreparable injury. Rather, the steel companies must show that the seizure alone constituted an "irreparable injury" and that the "balance of equities" favored their request for an injunction on the existing set of facts, not on speculation as to what might happen. As the following passage from his opinion indicates, Judge Holtzoff did not think that the steel companies had satisfied these requirements for injunctive relief.

> Another circumstance that must be considered is whether the plaintiffs will sustain irreparable damage if a temporary restraining order [a temporary injunction] were denied. The Court heard counsel at length on this point, *because that is a matter that seemed to the Court to be of vital importance.* The situation, as it presents itself at this stage, is that the president of each company, and his managerial staff, remain in control and are named as operating agents for the United States. They have not been dispossessed or displaced. They are still in possession and will continue to conduct the company's operations.
>
> True, plaintiffs fear that other drastic steps may be taken which would displace the management or which would supersede its control over labor relations. It seems to the Court that these possibilities *are not sufficient to constitute a showing of irreparable damage.* If these possibilities arise, applications for restraining orders, if they are proper and well-founded, may be renewed and considered.

---

[3]Transcript of the Proceedings before Judge Holtzoff, included in U.S. Congress, House, *The Steel Seizure Case,* H.R. Doc. No. 534, 82d Cong., 2d Sess. (1952), Part I, p. 225.

On the other hand, to issue a restraining order against Mr. Sawyer, and in effect nullify an order of the President of the United States, promulgated by him to meet a nation-wide emergency problem, is something that the Court should not do, unless there is some very vital reason for the Court stepping in.

The Court feels that the *balance of the equities is in favor of the defendant* [the government], so far as the present application is concerned. This conclusion is fortified by the concessions of Government counsel, to the effect that, in any event, the plaintiffs have an adequate remedy in suits for damages. Government counsel concede that if, as they say it is, the seizure is lawful and a legal taking of property, a suit for just compensation will lie in the Court of Claims against the United States.

On the other hand, Government counsel further concede that if the seizure is illegal, an action for damages lies against the United States under the Federal Tort Claims Act. The Court is of the opinion that such actions would lie. . . .[4] (Emphases added.)

In sum, according to Holtzoff, because no irreparable damage had been shown and because the balance of equities favored the government, the steel companies' request for an injunction had to be denied. Because the case could be disposed of on nonconstitutional grounds, he declined to consider the constitutional issue of presidential emergency power.

While Judge Holtzoff embodies the ideal of a "passive" judiciary, one unwilling to get involved in a constitutional crisis unless there was no other option, Judge Pine represents the exact opposite. The steel companies, on April 24, were requesting a temporary injunction not against the seizure itself (the issue litigated before Judge Holtzofff), but against any government attempt to raise wages or change the conditions of employment in the steel industry. Pine's "activist" attitude, his desire to get to the issue of the legality of the seizure itself, is clearly expressed in the following exchange between himself and Wilson.

MR. WILSON: . . . [If] we may have time of Your Honor to consider the ultimate legal question, we certainly want that opportunity to convince you that the action of the President is illegal . . .

JUDGE PINE: If you should convince me of that, you wouldn't want me to perpetuate the illegality, would you?

WILSON: I never look a gift horse in the face, Your Honor.

PINE: I am not speaking facetiously.

WILSON: I am not either.

PINE: I think it is an inconsistent position you are taking.

WILSON: For us not to want ultimate relief?

PINE: Yes; I think because unless you ask for it [ultimate relief from seizure] you admit the legality [of the seizure].

---

[4]*Youngstown Sheet & Tube Co. v. Sawyer*, 103 F. Supp. 978, 981 (D.D.C. 1952). Holtzoff's opinion is also located in *The Steel Seizure Case*, pp. 263–66.

WILSON: We ask for it and of course we argue the act [of seizure] is illegal, but whether a Judge on an application for temporary restraining order [against a wage increase] will give the time and have the opportunity to give the time to resolve the ultimate question is a matter which occurred to me. . . .

But of course if Your Honor is going to have the patience to listen to the ultimate legal question, we are ready to argue it.

PINE: I have the patience. . . .[5]

Judge Pine, in effect, refused to confine himself to the question of whether the government should be enjoined from changing wages and other conditions of employment. To the surprise and the delight of the steel companies' lawyers, he expressed his intention to address the ultimate merits of Truman's seizure of the steel industry.

In his decision on the merits, Judge Pine ruled that the seizure was illegal. He therefore issued a preliminary injunction that did not merely order the government not to raise the wages of the steel workers. Instead, he ordered Sawyer to return the steel companies to their rightful owners. To justify his order, Pine not only noted that the steel companies' injuries were "irreparable" but also explained his understanding of the relationship between the illegal character of Truman's actions and the "balance of equities."

> . . . As to the necessity for weighing the respective injuries and balancing the equities, I am not sure that this conventional requirement for the issuance of a preliminary injunction is applicable to the case where the Court comes to a fixed conclusion, as I do, that defendant's acts are illegal.[6]

But assuming that he had to "balance the equities," Pine weighed the injury to the steel companies against the likelihood of a crippling steel strike and concluded that the injunction should issue because the union might not strike, or if it did, the Taft–Hartley Act could be invoked or Congress could legislate "immediately and appropriately to protect the nation from this threatened disaster." Moreover, Pine continued, even if the strike had "awful results," it

> would be less injurious to the public than the injury which would flow from a *timorous* judicial recognition that there is some basis for this claim to unlimited and unrestrained Executive power, which would be implicit in a failure to grant the injunction. Such recognition would undermine public confidence in the very edifice of government as it is known under the Constitution.[7] (Emphasis added.)

Pine therefore believed that the constitutional issue of the legality of Truman's actions was either a sufficient reason to dispense with one of the requirements of an

---

[5]Transcript of the Proceedings before Judge Pine, included in *The Steel Seizure Case*, Part I, pp. 315–16.

[6]*Youngstown Sheet & Tube Co. v. Sawyer*, 103 F. Supp. 569, 576 (D.D.C. 1952), included in *The Steel Seizure Case*, p. 74.

[7]*Id.* at 577; *The Steel Seizure Case*, p. 75.

injunction or a decisive factor in the "balance of equities." In either case, the constitutional issue of the legality of Truman's actions was crucial. In Pine's view, a judge should not ignore it, even if the requested relief was an injunction.

The contrast between the two judges is evident. Holtzoff had a conception of the judicial role that has been described best by Justice Louis B. Brandeis.

> The Court will not pass upon a constitutional question although properly presented by the record, if there is also present some other ground upon which the case may be disposed of. This rule has found most varied application. Thus, if a case can be decided on either of two grounds, one involving a constitutional question, the other a question of statutory construction or general law, the Court will decide only the latter.[8]

Following Brandeis's understanding of the judiciary's constitutional role, Holtzoff avoided the constitutional issue of the lawfulness of Truman's seizure by deciding the case on the nonconstitutional ground of the legal requirements for an injunction. In contrast, Judge Pine followed the spirit of the following passage from Chief Justice John Marshall:

> It is most true that this Court will not take jurisdiction if it should not: but it is equally true that it must take jurisdiction if it should. The judiciary cannot, as the legislature may, avoid a measure because it approaches the confines of the constitution. We cannot pass it by because it is doubtful. With whatever doubts, with whatever difficulties, a case may be attended, we must decide it, if it be brought before us.[9]

True to the tenor of Marshall's understanding of the role of the judiciary, Pine insisted that the constitutional question had to be resolved if the nonconstitutional one was to be decided correctly. The issue separating Holtzoff and Pine is therefore a controversial one. The government's brief in *Youngstown* chided Judge Pine for his "loose" interpretation of the rules governing injunctive relief, but the steel companies' brief endorsed his reasoning and conclusions as clear and self-evident. In your view, which of these opposing views describes the constitutional responsibilities of the American judiciary? Which side has the better understanding of the judiciary's role in the area of separation of powers?[10]

Whether Holtzoff or Pine had the better approach to the judiciary's constitutional role, the issue of the legal requirements for an injunction lost some of its significance as the case came before the Supreme Court.[11] Once Pine had ruled on the constitutional merits of Truman's actions, the American public expected

---

[8]*Ashwander v. TVA*, 297 U.S. 288, 347 (1936).

[9]*Cohens v. Virginia*, 6 Wheat. (19 U.S.) 264, 404 (1821).

[10]For a full discussion of whether courts should avoid constitutional issues by deciding cases on nonconstitutional grounds, see Gerald Gunther, "The Subtle Vices of the 'Passive Virtues,'" *Columbia Law Review* 64 (1964), pp. 1–25.

[11]The case skipped the Court of Appeals. Both the government and the steel companies applied to the Supreme Court for certiorari before judgment in the Court of Appeals—a rarely invoked procedure. On May 3, the Supreme Court, by a vote of seven to two, granted the petition for certiorari and honored the government's request to "stay" (suspend the enforcement of) Pine's injunction. However, the Court added to the stay a condition that prohibited, while the Supreme Court was considering the case, the government from raising the wages in the steel industry or changing the working conditions.

the Supreme Court to deliver a decisive answer to the substantive question of the legality of the seizure. A number of factors contributed to the transformation of *Youngstown* into a cause célébrè. First, on the evening of April 9, one day after Truman's nationwide speech, Clarence Randall, the president of Inland Steel, responded to the president's charges by characterizing the seizure as a political payoff for labor's help in Truman's presidential victory in 1948. It had not, he insisted, "the slightest shadow of legal right." In his view, the seizure was obviously illegal because the Constitution "was adopted by our forefathers to prevent tyranny, not to create it." (See Box 4.2.) Furthermore, the steel companies ran full-page ads in newspapers across the country condemning the seizure, including one that quoted from relevant newspaper editorials. (See Box 4.3.) Later in the month, Assistant Attorney General Holmes Baldridge, the lawyer who argued the government's position in the proceedings before Judge Pine, raised the intensity of the debate by claiming that the president's emergency powers were "unlimited" and unreviewable by courts. Attorneys for the steel companies happily included Baldridge's remarks in their brief to the Supreme Court (see Brief for the Steel Companies, page 182), claiming that they indicated the extreme character of the government's position.

Truman tried to distance himself from Baldridge's claims, but headlines around the country had already had their impact. (For instance, the *Washington Post*'s headline on April 25 read "U.S. Argues President Is Above Courts.") More newspaper editorials appeared, vehemently attacking the "dictatorial" character of the government's argument. Truman later condemned the public relations campaign waged by the steel companies and the kind of "editorial intervention" that occurred in the case. (See Box 4.4.) At a minimum, the public uproar that ensued made it politically difficult for the Supreme Court to avoid the issue of the seizure's constitutionality. Once Judge Pine addressed the constitutional merits of the seizure, once he let the constitutional cat out of the bag, it was nearly impossible to coax it back in. After his decision, the focus of the case therefore shifted from the requirements of injunctive relief to the constitutionality of Truman's actions.[12] Accordingly, do you think Truman was right that the steel companies' public relations campaign had an unjustifiable impact on the litigation? Should the Supreme Court be subject to such influences? How could they be controlled?

In the briefs to the Supreme Court, the arguments revolved around four key issues. First, did a real emergency exist? Second, if one did exist, did the president have to act in accordance with the Labor Management Relations Act of 1947 (the Taft–Hartley Act), a law that did not give the president authority to seize private property in labor disputes? Third, if the president was not obliged to apply the relevant provisions of Taft–Hartley, did he have the constitutional power to seize private property in an emergency? Fourth, if the president did not have the constitutional power, did the steel companies deserve an injunction? The steel companies' brief concentrated more on the second and third questions, arguing that Taft–Hartley Act was controlling in the circumstances and that the president had no constitutional authority to seize. In contrast, the government's brief dwelled on the considerations that made the situation an emergency and the various constitu-

---

[12]For a review of the role that public opinion played in *Youngstown*, see William Rehnquist, "Constitutional Law and Public Opinion," *Suffolk University Law Review* 20 (Winter 1986), pp. 751–69.

BOX 4.2

CLARENCE RANDALL REPLIES TO TRUMAN

I have a deep sense of responsibility as I face this vast audience on the air. I am here to make answer on behalf of the steel industry to charges flung over these microphones last night by the man who then stood where I stand now. I am a plain citizen. He was the President of the United States.

Happily we still live in a country where a private citizen may look a President in the eye and tell him he was wrong, but actually it is not the President of the United States to whom I make answer.

It is Harry S. Truman, the man, who last night so far transgressed his oath of office, so far abused the power which is temporarily his, that he must now stand and take it.

I shall not let my deep respect for the office which he holds stop me from denouncing his shocking distortions of fact. Nor shall I permit the honor of his title to blind the American people from the enormity of what he has done.

He has seized the steel plants of the nation, the private property of one million people, most of whom now hear the sound of my voice. This he has done without the slightest shadow of legal right. No law passed by the Congress gave him this power. He knows this and speaks of general authority conferred upon him by the Constitution.

But I say, my friends, that the Constitution was adopted by our forefathers to prevent tyranny, not to create it. When he asked the Congress for power to seize private property they said no. They gave him instead the Taft–Hartley Act which he now spurns and the power which they denied him he now has seized.

For whom has he done this? Let no American be misled. This evil deed, without precedent in American history, discharges a political debt to the C.I.O. [Committee for Industrial Organization]. Phil Murray [president of the United Steelworkers of America] now gives Harry S. Truman a receipt marked "paid in full.". . .

And heartsick as many Americans were last night at what their President said, they were pained also at what he did not say. He was purporting to tell the facts, yet he withheld from the public one significant fact. He made no mention of the closed shop. He dealt with money but omitted principle. . . .

Has liberty sunk so low in Harry Truman's scale of values that he no longer thinks it worth mentioning? Or should he in all candor have taken the opportunity last night, talking as he was to every fireside in America, to make clear whether or not he had seized the steel plants in order to compel workers to join a union against their will?. . .

This is America at the crossroads. To the housewife this means that the whole giddy spiral of inflation starts again. To freedom-loving people it means the closed shop and compulsory unionism. To the business man it is the threat of nationalization. A sad chapter has been written in American history, which must be erased.

Source: From a radio and television broadcast by Clarence Randall, April 9, 1952. Excerpts from text used with permission of Mary Randall Gilkey.

BOX 4.3

THE NEW YORK TIMES, TUESDAY, APRIL 15, 1952

How the Nation's Press Views the

Government's Seizure of Steel

The government's illegal seizure of the steel mills has stirred the greatest Constitutional issue since the "Court Packing Plan" of 1937.

Newspapers throughout the United States have commented vigorously on this issue. Following are typical excerpts from their editorial comment:

Mark this day and date on your calendar.

It is the day on which, without the formality of an election, the government of the United States ceased to be a government by and for the people and came into the open frankly and nakedly as a labor dictatorship. *The Indianapolis (Ind.) News*

A stop must be put to Executive assertion and exercise of powers not clearly belonging to it or else our whole Constitutional system is doomed to destruction. *Detroit (Mich.) Free Press*

If the President gets away with what amounts to virtual confiscation of the steel industry, no other business in the United States is safe from the socialistic planners. *Topeka (Kan.) Daily Capital*

President Truman has precipitated a constitutional and political crisis that reaches well beyond the immediate strife and dangers of inflation. His seizure of the steel industry raises constitutional issues as fundamental as the Roosevelt court-packing plan of 1937. *The Christian Science Monitor, Boston, Mass.*

President Truman stood before the American people Tuesday night and proclaimed himself a dictator, as far as the nation's steel industry is concerned. *The Plain Dealer, Cleveland, Ohio*

Last night (Harry Truman) put the government into the steel business without authority of Congress, or the people, ignoring the law adopted by Congress for dealing with this kind of emergency. *Chicago Daily News*

President Truman's seizure of the steel industry will probably go down in history as one of the most high-handed acts committed by an American President. *The Washington (D. C.) Post*

The President has demonstrated a willingness to place the vast, war-inflated powers of government on the side of a great labor union in its demand for higher wages and the union shop. He has done this without going through intermediary steps, such as invoking the Taft-Hartley law's cooling-off period. *Newark (N. J.) Star Ledger*

Mr. Truman should not be allowed dictatorially to by-pass legislation in force and make his own law. The precedent he is attempting to establish would allow the President to take over any property, institution or concern as he desired. *The Boston Herald*

In our view the President has chosen untrustworthy weapons in his proclaimed defense of the national welfare, and has tried to arrogate to himself authority that is not his to assume. *San Francisco Chronicle*

The President has authored a new principle in American law; the Chief Executive may in time of peace and without any specific authority seize the property of any party that disagrees with the Government's "recommendation" in an industrial dispute. *Pittsburgh Post-Gazette*

The President is behaving like a dictator, ignoring the lawful procedures set up by the Congress for government intervention in strikes. If he gets away with this, there's no telling what might be the next step in confiscation of private property and infringement of personal liberties. *The Cleveland News*

To get to the Nazi-Fascist character of Truman's act:

He sprung this seizure after bypassing the Taft-Hartley law, under which the strike could have been legally delayed for 80 days while the unions and companies bargained. He attempted to justify the grab under a vaguely asserted constitutional power to protect the national welfare. *Daily News, New York, N. Y.*

STEEL COMPANIES IN THE WAGE CASE

Rm. 5401, 350 Fifth Ave., N. Y. 1, N. Y.

BOX 4.4

Truman's Later Reflections on Seizure

. . . It seems to me that there have been few instances in history where the press was more sensational or partisan than in its handling of the steel seizure. What was more disturbing was what amounted to editorial intervention by the press of America in a case pending before the Supreme Court of the United States. News stories and editorials decrying seizure and inflaming public opinion were prejudging and deciding the case at the very time the Court itself was hearing arguments for both sides. The steel companies bought full-page advertisements and ran them in newspapers throughout the country to denounce the President of the United States. Large sums of money were spent to influence public opinion against the government.

For the government, I took the position that, once the case had reached the courts, it was not proper for me to express an opinion. I have always believed that the way our newspapers sometimes comment on matters pending in the courts is an unethical attempt to influence a judge in deciding a case. Certainly in the steel case every effort made was to spread a slanted view of the situation and to color the atmosphere. The public relations experts for the companies skillfully shifted public attention from the price demands of the industry to the supposedly abnormal and unprecedented act of the President.

A little reading of history would have shown that there was nothing unusual about this action—that strike-threatened plants had been seized before by the government, even before the nation was engaged in any shooting conflict. But these matters received no mention or, if they were mentioned, were glossed over quickly, as if they had no meaning for the present.

I would, of course, never conceal the fact that the Supreme Court's decision, announced on June 2, was a deep disappointment to me. I think Chief Justice Vinson's dissenting opinion hit the nail right on the head, and I am sure that someday his view will come to be recognized as the correct one. . . .

Whatever the six justices of the Supreme Court meant by their differing opinions about the constitutional powers of the President, he must always act in a national emergency. It is not very realistic for the justices to say that comprehensive powers shall be available to the President only when a war has been declared or when the country has been invaded. We live in an age when hostilities begin without the polite exchanges of diplomatic notes. There are no longer sharp distinctions between combatants and noncombatants, between military targets and the sanctuary of civilian areas. Nor can we separate the economic facts from the problems of defense and security.

In this day and age the defense of the nation means more than building an army, navy, and air force. It is a job for the entire resources of the nation. The President, who is Commander in Chief and who represents the interest of all the people, must be able to act at all times to meet any sudden threat to the nation's security. A wise President will always work with Congress, but when Congress fails to act or is unable to act in a crisis, the President, under the Constitution, must use his powers to safeguard the nation.

Source: Harry S. Truman, *Memoirs,* 2 vols. (Garden City, N.Y.: Doubleday, 1956), II, pp. 475–78. Reprinted with permission of Margaret Truman Daniel.

tional sources of the president's emergency power to seize private property. In such an emergency, Taft–Hartley was a statutory option for the president, but it was not his only option. Because it was not mandatory, the president could seize private property based upon his inherent emergency powers.

Oral argument in *Youngstown* took place on May 12 and 13. Recognizing the importance of the issues involved, the Supreme Court took the highly unusual step of granting five hours for oral argument, two-and-a-half for each side. The steel companies were privileged to be represented by John W. Davis, the 1924 Democratic presidential nominee and a former solicitor general of the United States. He had successfully appeared before the Supreme Court many times in a long and illustrious career. Indeed, his career was so long, varied, and illustrious that Chief Justice Fred Vinson, in his dissenting opinion in *Youngstown*, took the opportunity to note that Davis had once argued, as solicitor general, that the president did have inherent emergency power—a position that seemed to contradict what he was saying in the steel seizure case (see Vinson's dissent). Nonetheless, Davis's argument for the steel companies, which took about eighty-five minutes, was a masterful performance with few interruptions by the justices.

In contrast, Philip Perlman, solicitor general of the United States and acting attorney general, confronted a series of skeptical and even hostile questions by the justices. They wanted to know whether the president would still have inherent power to seize property if Congress explicitly prohibited such seizures. If he would not, they queried, in what sense did the president have the constitutional right to seize—a right that presumably Congress could not take away? And what was the relevance of the war power, given that the president had called the Korean War a "police action"? Perlman also had an interesting exchange with Justice Robert Jackson, who had been a proponent of presidential emergency powers while he was attorney general under President Franklin D. Roosevelt. Perlman wanted to use what Jackson had written to justify Truman's actions, but Jackson did not want the steel seizure laid at his "door." He insisted that the circumstances of Roosevelt's seizures were different from those of the steel case, but Justice Felix Frankfurter remarked that Jackson was not "His Honor" when he defended Roosevelt's actions, suggesting that Jackson's view of emergency powers, not the circumstances, had perhaps changed. It is interesting to speculate as to which of these possibilities is the more likely one, especially given that Vinson's dissent endorsed the view of Attorney General Jackson.

Headline 4.1

Why did the justices react so negatively to Perlman's arguments? Was Perlman somehow at fault in his delivery, or did his substantive arguments provoke the justices? Which explanation is more credible? In reading the excerpts, do you discern any tactical mistakes made by Perlman? If he made any, what were they, and how would you have avoided them? Did Perlman take offense at a remark made by Justice Frankfurter? Was his reaction justifiable? Was it wise? Do you think such incidents have an impact upon the results of constitutional adjudication?

The Supreme Court, in a six-to-three decision, upheld Judge Pine's injunction against Sawyer and the president. Banner headlines announced Truman's defeat. (See Headline 4.1.) Justice Hugo Black wrote for the majority, but each of the other five Justice in the majority also wrote separately to explain their exact positions on the crucial question of presidential emergency power. Therefore, including Chief Justice Fred Vinson's dissenting opinion, there were seven opinions delivered in the case. *Youngstown* did not therefore result in a decisive ruling. It did not settle once and for all the question of what a president can do in an emergency without statutory authority. All the justices seemed to agree that if Congress prohibited the seizure of private property, then the president could not seize in an emergency. Beyond this simple rule, however, consensus on the Court disappeared. Two of the justices, Black and William O. Douglas, concluded that the president alone could not do anything "legislative" in an emergency. If an emergency called for a solution that normally required legislation, then Congress had to pass a law. The president could not implement a legislative policy based upon his emergency powers. The three dissenting justices, on the other hand, thought that Truman did have the power to seize private property because no statute forbade seizure. The other four justices, whose votes determined the result in *Youngstown*, were in the middle. Their position, in general, was that the Taft–Hartley Act was controlling in the circumstances of *Youngstown*. In the view of these four "middle" justices, the crucial fact was that Congress had considered, while enacting Taft–Hartley, giving the president emergency powers to seize private property during labor disputes, but had declined to do so.

Because the ruling in *Youngstown* was not a clearly decisive one, much of its significance derives from how certain of the justices interpreted the Constitution to define the relevant but ambiguous standards governing presidential emergency powers. Justice Black's majority opinion suggests one approach. Its basic premise is that presidential power to seize private property, if it exists, "must be found in some provision of the Constitution."[13] The government relied upon three different provisions of Article II: "The executive Power shall be vested in a president . . . "; that "he shall take Care that the Laws be faithfully executed"; and that he "shall be Commander in Chief of the Army and Navy of the United States." In Black's opinion, none of these provisions, either explicitly or implicitly, granted a right to seize private property. The commander-in-chief clause, primarily relevant to actions taken in a "theatre of war," gave the president no power to seize private property in domestic labor disputes. Resolving labor disputes and maintaining economic production was "a job for the Nation's lawmakers, not for its military authorities." And the fact that the president was to "take care that the Laws be faithfully executed" refuted the notion that he could, in emergencies, function as a legislator. The executive power was "vested" in the president, but that power was confined to enforcing the laws, not making them.

The strength of Black's argument resides in its simplicity and in its consistency with bedrock principles of American constitutionalism. The written Constitution is the "supreme law of the land," and it divides political power into what appear to be three sharply separated branches: the legislative, the executive, and the judicial. The initial question is, therefore, What do the relevant words of the Constitution *mean?* In a difficult case like *Youngstown*, the judge must also ask whether any of the constitutional provisions *logically implies* the power under dispute. This *analytical* exercise, of course, is dependent on the earlier assessment of the meaning of relevant constitutional language, including the basic categories of legislation, execution, and adjudication. Black's basic message, therefore, is that judges should interpret the Constitution in the spirit of a written constitution, focusing upon the literal words and their logical implications.

The strengths of Black's approach directly correspond to its weaknesses. In a note to the majority opinion that he joined in *Youngstown*, Justice Frankfurter explained why he had to write a concurring opinion: "the considerations relevant to

---

[13]The following quotations are from the opinions delivered in *Youngstown*. Those that are not footnoted appear in the excerpts from the opinions included below.

the legal enforcement of the principle of separation of powers seem to me more complicated and flexible than may appear from what Mr. Justice Black has written."[14] They were more "complicated," according to Frankfurter, because the branches and powers established by the Constitution were "partly interacting, not wholly disjointed." Quoting from Justice Oliver Wendell Holmes, Frankfurter argued that the legislative and executive grants of power did not "establish and divide fields of black and white." A disputed power could be a "gray" one, meaning that a judge could not decide which branch had the power by "an abstract analysis." In this kind of case, a different approach was necessary.

Moreover, Frankfurter continued, if the Constitution was confined to the written words and their logical implications, it would be "inflexible." It would not be able to adapt to the inevitable crises that each generation of Americans must face. An "inflexible" approach ignores the fact that the American Constitution is not just a written document but "a framework of government" that has grown and evolved over time. Accordingly, "Deeply embedded traditional ways of conducting government cannot supplant the Constitution or legislation, but they give meaning to the words of a text or supply them." In this way, history and precedent are windows into the Constitution's meaning. Constitutional adjudication does not depend primarily upon a dictionary, as Black's method seems to suggest, but rather upon legal and constitutional history. "It is an inadmissibly narrow conception of American constitutional law to confine it to the words of the Constitution and to disregard the gloss which life has written upon them." In the gray areas of constitutional law, judges are to divide and distribute power among the three branches of the federal government according to historical experience, not logic.

Frankfurter's approach meant that "a systematic, unbroken, executive practice, long pursued to the knowledge of the Congress and never before questioned . . . may be treated as a gloss on 'executive Power' vested in the president. . . ." However, in *Youngstown,* after searching the historical record, Frankfurter could not find "a systematic, unbroken, executive practice" of settling labor disputes by seizures of private property. He could find only three instances of seizure in circumstances comparable to those in *Youngstown*—not enough, in his judgment, to constitute a "gloss" on presidential power. For this reason, though his approach was very different, he came to the same result as did Justice Black—Truman had acted unconstitutionally. Truman did not have the right to seize the steel mills, not because such seizures were logically "legislative" in character, not because the president was logically confined to "executive" functions, but because American history had not added this particular "gloss" to the president's powers.

Justice Robert Jackson also rejected Black's approach to the Constitution, calling it a "doctrinaire textualism," but he also could not accept Frankfurter's historical methodology for interpreting the Constitution in the area of separation of powers. The past, in his opinion, especially the legal past with its "narrow," "doctrinal" focus, was far too unclear to offer guidance to judges who were delineating the respective legal powers of Congress and the president.

---

[14]*Youngstown Sheet & Tube Co. v. Sawyer,* 342 U.S. 579, 589 (1952).

Just what our forefathers did envision, or would have envisioned had they fore-seen modern conditions, must be divined from materials almost as enigmatic as the dreams Joseph was called upon to interpret for Pharaoh. A century and a half of partisan debate and scholarly speculation yields no net result but only supplies more or less apt quotations from respected sources on each side of any question. They largely cancel each other.

Jackson's alternative was to examine the "practical advantages" of any distribution of political power. By this phrase, he did not mean that a judge should decide in favor of those presidential exertions of power that he liked and against those that he disliked. Rather a judge's attention should be directed at the "enduring conse-quences" that his decision will have on "the balanced power structure of our Re-public." The judge therefore should take the long-range point of view, but it is a view of the future, not of the past.

With this perspective, Jackson divided presidential actions into three differ-ent categories: those that Congress approved of, those that it was silent about, and those that it prohibited. Presidential power falls to its lowest ebb when it is in this third category of actions that conflict with congressional will. However, Jackson insisted, a statute denying presidential power is not necessarily valid. Congress cannot take away the enumerated powers of the president—for example, the com-mander-in-chief power or the power to faithfully execute the laws. And Jackson willingly gave to the president's enumerated powers "the scope and elasticity af-forded by what seem to be *reasonable, practical implications*" (emphasis added). Nevertheless, Truman's seizure of the steel mills was deemed unconstitutional be-cause the "practical implications" did not justify reading the president's enumer-ated powers to be this extensive. Such a presidential power of seizure would have a detrimental impact upon the future of our "balanced power structure."

Based upon the same kind of reasoning, Jackson denied the existence of any "inherent" or "emergency" powers not enumerated in Article II. The contempo-rary experience of European governments in the twentieth century, especially Germany's, "suggests that emergency powers are consistent with free government only when their control is lodged elsewhere than in the Executive who exercises them." It was also relevant, in Jackson's view, to note the large expansion of presi-dential *political* power that has occurred since the eighteenth century. His "real" powers have expanded enormously even if his legal "paper" powers have re-mained the same. Given these developments, it would be unwise for a judge to recognize a presidential right to seize private property. Hence, according to Jack-son, the judge's job of constitutional interpretation was one of practical statesman-ship. By taking into account all the relevant facts, not just those of history and precedent, the judge must try to maintain a meaningful balance of power between the legislature and the executive, thereby preserving freedom and the rule of law.

To better understand these three approaches to constitutional adjudication, Chief Justice Vinson's dissenting opinion is useful for two reasons. First, it proves that two judges can pursue the same approach but come to different conclusions; second, because Vinson's dissenting opinion reflects two methods of interpreting the Constitution, it shows that these methods are not mutually exclusive: A judge can use two methods at the same time.

Vinson relied upon both Frankfurter's and Jackson's approaches to constitutional adjudication, but his substantive conclusion was different from theirs. In his view, if there was no statute prohibiting seizure, the president could, in an emergency, temporarily seize private property until Congress had an opportunity to decide what should be done. Vinson justified this conclusion on the grounds of both historical precedent and good sense. We need, he insisted, "only look to history and time-honored principles of constitutional law—principles that have been applied consistently by all branches of the government throughout our history." Agreeing with Frankfurter that historical practice was an important factor in deciding cases that distributed power among the branches, Vinson argued that history had confirmed a presidential emergency power of seizure. In an emergency, as long as no statute was violated, the president could do whatever he thought was necessary to preserve the status quo for Congress.

Vinson, however, was not merely making an historical argument. He artfully blended history with Justice Jackson's emphasis upon practical wisdom. "In passing upon the question of presidential powers in this case, we must first consider the context in which those powers were exercised." We "should be mindful that these are extraordinary times" and be open to the possibility that extraordinary executive powers may be necessary. Under a "messenger-boy concept" of the presidency, in which the president can take no action other than reporting the emergency to Congress, there is no assurance that "Congress will have something left to act upon." Accordingly, if history had not added a "gloss" to the president's emergency powers, the Constitution would have to be updated. This is possible because the Constitution is "a living document adaptable to new situations." However, Vinson concluded, no such adaptation is necessary in the case of presidential emergency powers. Not only has history recognized such powers, but the founders themselves saw the need for an active and independent executive. It was Alexander Hamilton who wrote, "Energy in the Executive is a leading character in the definition of good government." History and good sense therefore converge. According to Vinson, "[t]he Framers knew, as we should know in these times of peril, that there is real danger in Executive weakness."

Youngstown Sheet & Tube Co. v. Sawyer provides students with an excellent opportunity to consider not only the substantive constitutional rule concerning presidential emergency powers, but also the different methods of interpreting the Constitution in the difficult area of separation of powers represented by justices Black, Frankfurter, and Jackson. When the Supreme Court must decide which branches have what powers, authoritative judicial precedents are neither numerous nor clear. How, therefore, should the Court proceed? Should the literal words of the Constitution be decisive? the gloss of history? practical implications? Truman himself remained convinced that every president must have the power to take action in an emergency. (See Box 4.4.) What is your view? Of course, in *Youngstown,* the problem of interpretation was complicated by the fact that the constitutional issue was entangled with nonconstitutional questions. How does this entanglement affect your evaluation of what the Court did in *Youngstown?* The steel seizure litigation allows students to consider these dilemmas in a context in which judges disagreed sharply about their constitutional responsibilities in the area of separation of powers and about the proper way to interpret the Constitution.

When the Court's decision came down on June 2, 1952, the steel union immediately went out on strike and all steel production ceased. On July 20, steel shortages forced the nation's largest shell-making plant to shut down. Four days later a settlement was reached. The union got the basic wage increase it was looking for, but the government approved a $5.20 hike in the price of a ton of steel. Did Congress's price stabilization program pay the price of the Court's refusal to support presidential emergency powers? Was the trade-off worth the price?

BIBLIOGRAPHY

Banks, Robert F. "Steel, Sawyer, and the Executive Power," *University of Pittsburgh Law Review* 14 (1953), pp. 467–537.

Corwin, Edward S. "The Steel Seizure Case: A Judicial Brick Without Straw," *Columbia Law Review* 53 (1953), pp. 53–66.

Freund, Paul. "Foreword: The Year of the Steel Seizure Case," *Harvard Law Review* 66 (1952), pp. 89–97.

Kemper, Paul. "The Steel Seizure Case: Congress, the President, and the Supreme Court," *Michigan Law Review* (1952), pp. 141–82.

Marcus, Maeva. *Truman and the Steel Seizure Case.* New York: Columbia University Press, 1977.

Richberg, Donald. "The Steel Seizure Case," *Virginia Law Review* 38 (1952), pp. 713–27.

BRIEFS

BRIEF FOR THE STEEL COMPANIES

[1. Taft–Hartley Act.] The Labor Management Relations Act of 1947 created careful procedures for avoiding disastrous consequences to the nation's economy while encouraging mutually satisfactory reconciliation of conflicting interests. By Section 206 of that Act, the President is authorized to appoint a Board of Inquiry when a threatened or actual strike or lockout, affecting an entire industry or a substantial part of it, would imperil the national health or safety. Section 207 empowers that Board to conduct hearings to ascertain the facts of the dispute. After receiving the Board's report the President is authorized by Section 208 to direct the Attorney General to seek an injunction against the strike or lockout. While the injunction is in effect, the Federal Mediation and Conciliation Service, created by Section 202, is to assist the parties to the labor dispute in their efforts to adjust the settlement of their differences. After 60 days, if the dispute remains unsettled, the Board of Inquiry appointed by the President is to report the current position of the parties, the efforts made for settlement, and a statement of the employer's last offer of settlement. This report is to be made available to the public *and is to be followed, within 15 days, by a secret ballot of the employees to ascertain whether they wish to accept this last offer of settlement.* When the results of this ballot are certified to the Attorney General, or if a settlement has been reached by the parties, the Attorney General must then move the court to discharge its injunction. After the injunction is discharged, *the President is required to submit to Congress his report,* including the findings of the Board of Inquiry, *with his recommendations for appropriate action.* There is, of course, nothing to prevent him from reporting to Congress, and asking additional legislation, at any earlier date.

Accordingly, Congress left no procedural void in its program for protecting the national interest when imperiled by a threatened strike. It did not leave for the Executive the determination of the course of action to be followed when the procedures detailed in the Act are exhausted without the dispute having been settled.

The inescapable intent of Congress was that, if the dispute was not resolved during the 80-day period in which the injunction was in effect, the President should present the situation to Congress for necessary legislation. The Senate Report states that if the dispute is not terminated during the 80-day period, "the bill provides for the President's laying the matter before Congress for whatever legislation seems necessary to preserve the health and safety of the Nation in the crisis.". . .

. . . [Indeed,] Congress expressed its will against the procedure adopted by Mr. Sawyer. *A proposed amendment which would have provided for governmental seizure in the event of emergency was specifically rejected* by an overwhelming vote. . . .

It was asserted in the District Court, and it may be asserted here, that the President is not required by law to set in motion in any given case the procedure prescribed by the Labor Management Relations Act. But it does not follow that by failing to use the procedure provided by Congress the Executive can thereby create for itself a right to invoke unwarranted emergency procedures altogether contrary both to the Constitution and to the plain intent of Congress. . . .

[2. Presidential emergency power.] . . . [T]he asserted right to seize and exercise control over the steel industry—including the right to supplant the steel companies in collective bargaining and to change terms of employment—rests solely upon a claimed prerogative or "inherent power" of the President as Chief Executive and as Commander in Chief of the armed forces. These purported rights are claimed to inure to the Executive simply by virtue of his office. Under Mr. Sawyer's position the President may exercise virtually unlimited powers in any field where he chooses to say that an emergency exists. For, in his counsel's view, the executive declaration of emergency is non-reviewable and, once the emergency is proclaimed, the Executive action is beyond the control of the Courts.

This position was thus stated by Mr. Sawyer's counsel in the argument before Judge Pine:

JUDGE PINE: So you contend the Executive has unlimited power in time of an emergency?

MR. BALDRIDGE: He has the power to take such action as is necessary to meet the emergency.

PINE: If the emergency is great, it is unlimited, is it?

BALDRIDGE: I suppose if you carry it to its logical conclusion, that is true. But I do want to point out that there are two limitations on the Executive power. One is the ballot box and the other is impeachment.

PINE: Then, as I understand it, you claim that in time of emergency the Executive has this great power.

BALDRIDGE: That is correct.

PINE: And the Executive determines the emergencies and the Courts cannot even review whether it is an emergency.

BALDRIDGE: That is correct.

❖   ❖   ❖

JUDGE PINE: So, when the sovereign people adopted the Constitution, it enumerated the powers set up in the Constitution but limited the powers of Congress and limited powers of the judiciary, but it did not limit the powers of the executive.

Is that what you say?

MR. BALDRIDGE: That is the way we read Article II of the Constitution. . . .

This concept of unbridled and unchecked executive power is presented in its most extreme posture by the action here challenged. . . . In essential analysis, this is an attempt, without any vestige of statutory authority and solely on the assertion of inherent executive power, to appropriate plaintiffs' funds for payment of wages in whatever amounts Mr. Sawyer may choose to establish. . . .

The present claim of the Executive to an inherent right to do whatever he considers necessary for what he views as the common good—without consulting the legislature and without any authority under law—is not a new claim. It is precisely that which was made more than three centuries ago by James I of England when he claimed for himself the right to make law by proclamation and asserted that it was treason to maintain that the King was under the law. It is precisely the claim for which Charles I lost his life and James II his throne. Most importantly, it is precisely the claim for which George III lost his American colonies. In short, it was the continued effort of the English Crown to exercise unfettered prerogative that culminated in the War of Independence and the establishment of the United States under the form of government provided in the Constitution. . . .

The controversies between the Crown and Parliament came to a head under Charles I in the celebrated *Case of Ship Money (The King v. John Hampden)*. . . . What is particularly interesting about that case in the present connection is that the Crown lawyers based their claims squarely upon the claims of "national emergency," "common defense," and "inherent powers of the Commander in chief."

After proclamations had been made reciting that although England was then at peace there were wars raging on the continent of Europe, that the seas were unsafe, and that England was in danger of losing control of the sea and of invasion, the King required various counties forthwith to provide ships for the common defense. One citizen (John Hampden) resisted. His case was heard in the Exchequer Chamber before all twelve judges of the three common-law courts.

The Solicitor General and Attorney General, appearing for the Crown, put their arguments squarely on the inherent emergency powers of the King as

Commander in Chief, and argued that in time of emergency even Magna Carta and statutes must give way to those "inherent powers."

A majority of the judges accepted the King's views. Mr. Justice Crawley, in words surprisingly similar to the contentions advanced on behalf of Mr. Sawyer in the case at bar, said:

> It doth appear by this record, that the whole kingdom is in danger, both by sea and land, of ruin and destruction, dishonor and oppression, and that the danger is present, imminent and instant, and greater than the king can, without the aid of his subjects, well resist: Whether must the King resort to Parliament? No. We see the danger is instant and admits of no delay.

In the same vein, other judges asserted that any statute which attempted to bind the King's prerogative as Commander in Chief was invalid, that Parliament moved too slowly in emergencies and that the King was the sole judge of the necessity.

A minority of judges, headed by Coke, voted against the King. But the aftermath was interesting. In 1640 Mr. Justice Crawley (author of the statement above quoted) and some of his colleagues who had voted for the King were impeached for having

> . . . traitorously and wickedly endeavored to subvert the fundamental laws and established government of the realm of England: and instead thereof, to introduce an arbitrary and tyrannical government against law. . . .

The judgement in the *Ship Money* case itself was directed by Parliament to be canceled as being

> . . . against the laws of the realm, the subject's right of property, and contrary to former resolutions in Parliament and to the Petition of Right.

In the reign of James II the controversy broke out afresh. The King claimed the power in cases of urgent necessity to dispense with the laws. Finally, when he pushed the matter too far by indicting for seditious libel those who opposed his views, there was a reaction; and in the *Case of the Seven Bishops* Mr. Justice Powell declared that the claimed royal prerogative "amounts to an abrogation and utter repeal of all the laws" and that:

> If this be once allowed of, there will need no parliament; all the legislature will be in the king, which is a thing worth considering.

The culmination was the exile of James II and the passage under his successors of the English Bill of Rights, from which many of the provisions of our own Bill of Rights are taken. That document specifically limited the powers of the Crown in the following respects:

1. That the pretended power of suspending of laws, or the execution of laws, by regal authority, without consent of parliament, is illegal.

2. That the pretended power of dispensing with laws, or the execution of laws by regal authority, as it hath been assumed and exercised of late, is illegal.

Thus, by the start of the 18th century, the English people, after a long and bloody struggle, finally established that the Crown was under the law. It was clear that the seizure of property by the Crown without authority of Parliament was illegal.

In the decades preceding the War of Independence the American colonists were faced with their own struggle against actions of George III and his ministers. Throughout the struggle, the colonists constantly appealed to their fundamental rights as Englishmen under Magna Charta and the English Bill of Rights. In cataloging the grievances of the colonists against the King, the Declaration of Independence states that he "has kept among us, in times of peace, standing Armies without the consent of our legislature" and "has affected to render the military independent of and superior to, the Civil Power." Various attempts of British generals at the beginning of the Revolution to enforce martial rule were denounced by the legislatures of various colonies as tyrannical and despotic.

It was against this background that the Founding Fathers drafted our Constitution. The constitutional debates, as reported in Madison's Journal, reveal with graphic clarity that the delegates had firmly in mind the recent excesses of the English Crown against the colonies and the long and costly struggle that had been waged by the people of England and of other European countries, such as Holland, before the royal power had been circumscribed and placed under the law. It was in this framework that the delegates—all men who knew at first hand the evil resulting from the unfettered exercise of the royal prerogative, and many of them lawyers deeply read in the constitutional history of the mother country—drafted our own Constitution. It is against this real fear of uncontrolled executive action that the provisions of the Constitution must be considered.

As is well known, the framers of the Constitution believed firmly that in a tripartite form of government lay one of the surest safeguards of the people's liberties. They took especial care, therefore, to prevent any concentration of executive and legislative powers in the same hands.

Article I sec. 1 of the Constitution unequivocally vests in Congress alone all legislative powers granted. . . .

The office of the Presidency is covered in Article II. It opens with a provision that "The executive Power shall be vested in a President of the United States of America" and proceeds to define that power. The responsibilities assigned to the President, in keeping with the division of powers basic to the tripartite system of government, are intrinsically executive and administrative. The provisions of the Article upon which Mr. Sawyer apparently relies as authority for his actions, in addition to the clause just quoted, are these:

> Section 2. The President shall be Commander in Chief of the Army and Navy of the United States and of the Militia of the several States, when called into the actual Service of the United States:. . .
> Section 3. . . . he [the president] shall take care that the Laws be faithfully executed. . . .

The duty to execute the laws is by its terms an executive function—to implement and administer the laws enacted by Congress. It is equally clear, as a matter of both history and settled judicial interpretation, that the President's military power as Commander in Chief is limited to a command or executive function—the direction of the armed forces. The President's military functions do not encompass any power to legislate on war or related questions. . . .

The limits on the power of the President as Commander in Chief have been clearly delineated by this Court. It has long been settled that under this authority, which is strictly military in character, the President has the power to control civilian activity only where the emergency is so imminent and the threat of military danger to the nation so pressing that the slightest delay would lead to disaster; and even then his action is subject to court review. . . .

This stringent requirement for the exercise of military power over civilian activity and civilian property was re-emphasized in *United States v. Russell*, where this Court again made it apparent that extreme public danger, making recourse to normal governmental process impossible, must be established. There the Court said:

> Extraordinary and unforeseen occasions arise, however, beyond all doubt, in cases of extreme necessity in time of war or of immediate and impending public danger, in which private property may be impressed into public service, or may be seized and appropriated to the public use, or may even be destroyed without the consent of the owner. . . . Where such an extraordinary and unforeseen emergency occurs in the public service in time of war no doubt is entertained that the power of the government is ample to supply for the moment the public wants in that way to the extent of the immediate public exigency, but the public danger must be immediate, imminent, and impending, and the emergency in the public service must be extreme and imperative, and such as will not admit of delay or a resort to any other sources of supply, and the circumstances must be such as imperatively require the exercise of that extreme power in respect to the particular property so impressed, appropriated, or destroyed. Exigencies of the kind do arise in time of war or impending public danger, but it is the emergency, as was said by a great magistrate, that gives the right, and it is clear that the emergency must be shown to exist before the taking can be justified.

Moreover the power as Commander in Chief, being strictly military in character, is designed for exercise only within the theater of war. Indicative of the proper scope of the power is the sustaining by the courts of such action as destruction, by military commanders in the field, of railroad bridges during a war and the seizure, when confronted with armed rebellion, of neutral vessels running a blockade. The nationwide properties of the steel industry situated throughout the continental United States and seized indiscriminately, regardless of what proportion or type of products were designed for military use, certainly cannot be characterized as being within a theater of military operations.

Although the Presidential power as Commander in Chief justifies the taking or destruction of property when the stringent requirements for its exercise are present, it does not encompass the function of eminent domain. When, as in the present situation, there is no foundation for interference with private property under the President's military power, any taking of property must be made under the congressional power of eminent domain. Taking of property for public use is a power of the legislature; the right of the executive department to take property by eminent domain must be based on Congressional authorization. "The taking of private property by an officer of the United States for public use, without being authorized, expressly or by necessary implication, to do so by some act of Congress, is not the act of the government.". . .

In January, 1951, the President, in his message on the State of the Union, placed major emphasis on the threat of aggression and the need to present a strong national defense. The Korean hostilities have continued for close to two years. It is clear beyond argument that the present controversy does not present a situation of a sudden emergency.

The affidavits submitted in opposition to the applications for injunctive relief are themselves the most eloquent testimony that the present controversy can, by no stretch of the imagination, be said to involve the sudden and imminent threat of military disaster which justifies the exercise of presidential power as Commander in Chief. Those affidavits clearly reveal that what is involved here is a problem of more than two years' standing. The problem of securing necessary steel for military equipment, for the production of civilian vehicles and other transport facilities, for Atomic Energy Commission construction programs and for petroleum industry expansion is a broad and continuing question within the province of Congress. . . .

Patently, these continuing problems, which have been in existence for periods ranging from a minimum of several months to a number of years, present no basis for any sudden exercise of the military power of the President as Commander in Chief. Any contention that Mr. Sawyer's seizure and other action can be based on the President's military power is based on a completely indefensible perversion of that authority as provided in the Constitution and delineated by the courts. . . .

Despite the fact that the memorandum filed on behalf of Mr. Sawyer in the District Court, and his petition for certiorari here, pay lip service to the requirement that the President's power must be found somewhere in the Constitution, the argument below proceeded specifically, and the argument here proceeds by necessary implication, upon the nebulous theory of a "broad residuum of powers" in the President and of his "aggregate" of powers.

In essential analysis, this theory boils down to a claim that executive action which is not authorized under any specific provision of the Constitution or any law of the United States, and is indeed inconsistent with every specific existing statute, somehow achieves validity when all provisions of the Constitution and statutes are considered together.

We respectfully submit that the Executive Order and action purportedly taken thereunder, being without authority under any constitutional or statutory provision, cannot be validated by the application of labels such as "broad residuum" or "aggregate" of powers.

Closely related to the foregoing contention is the suggestion that the Executive Order and Mr. Sawyer's action are justified by various instances in which

Presidents in the past have apparently acted without constitutional or legislative authority. For example, the memorandum in the District Court lists 12 properties seized by President Roosevelt prior to the passage of the War Labor Disputes Act under his purported powers as President. For a variety of reasons, the lawfulness of none of these seizures was ever put to judicial test. . . .

Past executive acts of doubtful validity can furnish no support for sustaining the Executive Order and defendant's past and threatened actions. As a recent commentator observed:

> Acts based on this law of necessity and assumed probability of excuse or of subsequent ratification do not pretend to be supported by constitutional authority, and are, of course, of no value as precedents establishing the existence of constitutional power.

There could be no more dangerous principle—nor one more foreign to the Constitution—than a rule that past illegality can through some legerdemain serve as authority to legalize present illegality. . . .

[3. Seizure violates due process.] . . . [E]ven if it were to be assumed that the executive could under some circumstances authorize action of the kind here challenged, despite the utter lack of statutory basis, the seizure and other action necessarily contravene the due process clause.

The argument advanced on behalf of Mr. Sawyer ignores the guaranty of the Fifth Amendment that no person shall be deprived of property without due process of law. The seizure of property by Executive fiat, leaving the plaintiffs literally at the mercy of Mr. Sawyer's discretion, is completely incompatible with that requirement, which, as this Court has said, embraces the "fundamental principles of liberty and justice which lie at the base of all our civil and political institutions.". . .

Negation of the sweep of executive power which is here claimed for Mr. Sawyer's actions would not result in a sterile construction of the Constitution or leave the Government powerless to deal with emergencies within the framework of the Constitution. It is true that the Constitution is a dynamic and continuously operative charter of government which is capable of meeting the varying demands of our society; but it does not follow from that that the executive action here challenged must be recognized as valid. The executive is not the only branch of the government which is concerned in the matter. As the District Court stated, in pointing out the role of Congress:

> . . . our procedures under the Constitution can stand the stress and strains of an emergency today as they have in the past, and are adequate to meet the test of emergency and crisis.

The idea of a strong and unreviewable executive power, easily available to deal with real or imagined emergencies as deemed expedient, has a deceptive simplicity and certainty which should not lull us, as it has other nations, into forgetting that it is alien to our fundamental concept of a government of laws and not of men, or blind us to the fact that the Constitution created a government of limited powers, consisting of those powers expressly granted and those reasonably to be implied therefrom, all other powers being reserved to the people or to the States by the Ninth and Tenth Amendments. . . .

[4. Requirements for injunctive relief.] There is a far reaching controversy between the plaintiffs and the Union in connection with the formulation of a new and comprehensive collective bargaining agreement. Over 100 issues are in dispute between the parties. Extensive as were the recommendations of the Wage Stabilization Board, even they did not deal with all the issues. It is a basic principle of labor negotiations that all outstanding issues be resolved together. In the present case outstanding unresolved issues of vital concern to management include those having a direct effect upon the efficiency of operation.

Whatever may be the order which Mr. Sawyer is even now prepared to issue—whether it be full Wage Stabilization Board recommendations, or something less—the result will be to create a new and higher floor for the Union in its continued and future negotiations with the plaintiffs. The Union has already made that abundantly clear to this Court in its *amicus* brief filed in connection with the petitions for certiorari. There the Union said that, "when the mills are restored to their [the plaintiffs'] possession they will have the right and it will again be their duty to bargain with the Union concerning *the then current* wages and working conditions."

As a practical matter, once new terms and conditions are prescribed, it would be impossible to turn back the clock and ever to negotiate from the respective positions of the parties as they are now. Government-imposed terms and conditions always have their consequences beyond the period of government seizure. . . .

Consequently, Mr. Sawyer's threatened action would be injurious to plaintiffs not only in the immediate dollars and cents damage consequent upon increased wages but also in the weakening of the plaintiffs' bargaining position today with respect to all the unresolved issues in the labor dispute with the Union and—of equal or even greater importance—in the weakening of the plaintiffs' bargaining position at all times in the future with respect to any and all issues which will be faced at the end of the seizure period and thereafter. . . .

No adequate money damages, of course, could be recovered from Mr. Sawyer personally, even for that portion of the injuries which might be measured in money. His individual wealth could not approach the amount of damage which this industry will suffer.

There remains only the question whether money damages would be recoverable against the United States, as Mr. Sawyer's counsel has suggested. It is plain that they would not. . . .

The argument in support of such a remedy necessarily assumes that the seizure was lawful. Indeed Mr. Sawyer's counsel expressly so conceded before Judge Pine. If the seizure was unlawful, as we insist, Mr. Sawyer's actions was not a "taking" by the United States for which just compensation is recoverable. . . .

[5. Conclusion.] Whether the position be baldly stated as in the District Court—or an effort made superficially to present it in less extreme form—the conclusion remains inescapable that counsel for Mr. Sawyer rely on a doctrine of Executive immunity from constitutional limitations and judicial restraints. They seek to justify a seizure, clearly without any vestige of support in the Constitution, on the ground that because an emergency has been declared by the Executive any action thereunder is sacrosanct. This doctrine is presented in its most extreme form in the present case where the "emergency" has been created by the device of ignoring the detailed statutory machinery specifically designed by the Congress for use in precisely the situation here presented. If the present Executive can seize properties and appropriate funds to force an increase in wages, a clear precedent will be established by which some future Executive can by similar arbitrary action force a decrease in wages or compel workers to labor for whatever hours and under whatever conditions he may choose to impose. It is not the rights of these plaintiffs alone which are at stake here. Our system of government has no place for any such concept of arbitrary power which, if once established, must be fatal to our liberties. . . .

Respectfully submitted,

JOHN W. DAVIS,
Counsel for United States Steel Company.

BRIEF FOR THE GOVERNMENT

[1. The emergency.] The absolute necessity for continuous steel production which led to the President's seizure of the steel plants on April 8 arises from the fact that the military security of the United States and other countries is endangered by the aggressions of the Soviet Union and its satellite states.

Within a few years after World War II, the Soviet Union had succeeded in annexing Lithuania, Latvia, and Estonia, and in establishing in Poland, Rumania, Hungary, Bulgaria, and Czechoslovakia regimes which completely subordinated the interests of those countries to the interests of the Soviet Union. Similar threats to the independence of Greece and Turkey were averted only through American military and economic aid extended pursuant to the Greek and Turkish Assistance Act of May 22, 1947. . . .

The Soviet Union has maintained since World War II ground forces much larger than those presently available to the United States and the countries joined with it in mutual security arrangements. In addition, the Soviet Union has maintained the largest air force in the world. In general, the Soviet Union has consistently devoted a much larger portion of its industrial production to military items than has any other country. In the years immediately following World War II, it was widely believed that the United States' exclusive possession of atomic weapons constituted a powerful deterrent to Soviet aggression. However, in 1949, the Soviet Union produced an atomic explosion.

With the sudden and unprovoked attack of North Korean Communist forces upon the Republic of Korea on June 25, 1950, the United Nations, including the United States, were confronted with naked armed aggression. . . .

As a result of these events, and pursuant to the decisions of the Security Council, the United States and other members of the United Nations, under command of General MacArthur and later General Ridgway, have engaged in nearly two years of military operations to preserve the independence of the Republic of Korea. This task was greatly increased by the large-scale intervention of Chinese Communist forces in November 1950. In addition, the Communist forces in Korea have been and are being steadily supplied by the Soviet Union with such items as military aircraft, tanks, guns, and radar. . . .

In brief, a world still suffering from the devastation of World War II is confronted by an aggressive Soviet Union commanding massive armaments. The attack upon Korea has demonstrated the willingness of the Soviet Union and its satellites to employ military force for conquest. The United States and the other free nations of the world have resolved that the only hope of deterring aggression and thereby avoiding subjugation or, at the best, a great war, is to place themselves in a military posture which will make military adventures too dangerous. They have also resolved to repel any aggression which may be attempted. The United States is therefore carrying on an unprecedented program to rearm itself and to assist other countries to rearm for these purposes. More than ever before, we are the arsenal of the free world. More immediately, we must continue to produce and deliver military supplies to the United Nations forces in Korea who have been fighting Soviet aggression for two years, and to the NATO forces in Europe who must maintain a constant state of readiness against political aggression.

In this context of military necessity, the President found that any interruption in the production of steel would endanger the security of the United States, its armed forces abroad, and its allies. The Nation's critical need for such continuous production is set forth in uncontradicted affidavits filed with the district court. . . .

. . . It is true that the President and other executive officers might possibly have insured continued production of steel otherwise than by seizing the steel mills. Specifically, if they had granted the substantial increase in maximum ceiling prices for steel which plaintiffs were interested in securing, the plaintiffs and the union might have reached an agreement that would have prevented a strike. . . .

. . . [But] the President determined that to grant the substantial price increase desired by the plaintiffs would scuttle the Nation's stabilization program. Taking into consideration both his obligations to insure military security of the United States and its armed forces by maintaining steel production, and his obligation to carry out the national stabilization policy expressed in the Defense Production Act, he determined that he could effectuate both of these basic national policies only by seizing and operating the steel mills. Given conditions under which a cessation of steel production will endanger immediately the military security of the Nation, its armed forces and its allies, we believe the President's power under the Constitution to avert such danger by seizing and operating the steel mills is not lost merely because production might possibly have been maintained by acquiescing in price increases which in his judgement would endanger the national economy. . . .

[2. Requirements for injunctive relief.] Under the fundamental rules governing equitable jurisdiction, plaintiffs are entitled to injunctive relief only if they can show either that legal relief is not available to them or that such legal remedy, although available, would be inadequate. We believe that plaintiffs' recourse to injunctive relief is barred because they have an effective remedy in the Court of

Claims. . . . It has, of course, been settled in a long line of cases, beginning with *United States v. Great Falls Mfg. Co.*, that where the United States takes property for public use a right to compensation is enforceable in the Court of Claims. . . .

Plaintiffs' argument is that this remedy is not available to them unless Secretary Sawyer's acts are supported by statutory or constitutional authority; hence, that the preliminary question whether plaintiffs have an adequate remedy at law hinges on the very merits of the case. We submit, on the contrary, that plaintiffs have a remedy in the Court of Claims, and that therefore the Court need not reach any of the constitutional questions in order to decide that an injunction may not issue.

In such a practical matter as the granting or withholding of an injunction, the formal concession of government counsel, repeated in three courts, that suit may be brought and that no defense of lack of jurisdiction can or will be raised, should be sufficient. . . .

Apart from the availability of an adequate remedy at law, plaintiffs have failed to establish a threat of such irreparable injury to themselves as could outweigh the evident irreparable injury to the public interest which would flow from the granting of an injunction. Plaintiffs' obligation in this respect is twofold. They must first make a clear showing of irreparable injury and, second, any such injury must be balanced against the injury to the public. . . .

Plaintiffs have made no such clear showing. Their general allegations as to interference with their power of management, etc., by the seizure are, on the facts alleged and on every reasonable probability, speculative in the extreme. . . . The gravamen of their complaints is that the defendant threatens to impose new wages and conditions of employment. But the assertion that such threatened action exposes them to irreparable injury disregards several highly pertinent considerations.

a. Plaintiffs ignore the fact that the *status quo* which existed at the time the President acted was that the union had called a strike and workers had started to leave the plants. The President's action thus conferred a great benefit on plaintiffs, by averting a strike which would have caused them enormous damages. Plaintiffs' position apparently is that they may ignore the benefit conferred upon them by the President's action while obtaining relief in respect of any damages assertedly flowing from that action. . . . They would like to have the benefits of a guaranty against strikes without having to pay any price, in terms of increased wages and changes in working conditions, for the achievement of those benefits. But, we do not see how, in good conscience, they can do so. . . .

b. Plaintiffs' asserted injuries from the granting of a wage increase and other changes in conditions of employment are grossly overstated. They ignore, for example, the fact that some increase in wages and change in working conditions were almost inevitable. This was the first occasion since 1947 for a thorough review and revision of the collective bargaining agreement. Moreover, the fact that the Wage Stabilization Board had recommended substantial changes, which it described as in the nature of a "catch-up," designed to equate the position of steel workers with workers in comparable industries, made it practically certain that the union would never enter into an agreement calling for no change. . . .

c. Finally, plaintiffs ignore the effect of any price increase which might be allowed. That such a price increase would compensate, in part or in whole, for any wage increase was clearly recognized in the complaints of United States Steel Co. . . .

We do not mean to suggest that this Court need pass on the present controversy between the plaintiffs and the Office of Price Stabilization. But the fact that plaintiffs would have been willing to agree to wage increases such as those which they now complain are threatened to be imposed on them, provided only a substantial price increase were allowed, certainly sheds light on their claims that imposition of those terms would result in enormous and irreparable injury. . . .

Assuming, however, that plaintiffs' showing, by itself, is sufficient to establish irreparable injury to them, that showing must be balanced against the showing of injury to the public from the granting of an injunction. The rule is well settled that "an injunction is not a remedy which issues as of course." Particularly where great public interests are involved, it is established that "Courts of equity may, and frequently do, go much farther both to give and withhold relief in furtherance of the public interest than they are accustomed to go when only private interests are involved.". . .

The injury to the public interest from any return to the *status quo* which existed on the night of April 8, 1952, would be enormous and irreparable, affecting our national safety, our discharge of international commitments, and the lives of our soldiers. Unlike the allegations of petitioners' affidavits, many of which we are prepared to controvert, the showing of damage to the public interest from any stoppage of production is not, and cannot be, controverted. The district judge erroneously rejected that showing. He doubted whether he should balance the equities at all. Moreover, in attempting to do so, he assumed, contrary to fact, that the *status quo* which he sought to preserve did not include any likelihood of a strike. In fact, not only was a strike imminent on April 8, but one began on April 30, 1952, fifteen minutes after Judge Pine's order. Whether that strike was justified or not is aside from the point; any realistic appraisal of the situation should have recognized its likelihood.

In essence, moreover, the judge rested his idea of balancing equities on a prejudging of the merits. He felt that the enormous damage from a cessation of production "would be less injurious to the public than the injury that would flow from a timorous judicial recognition that there is some basis" for the defendant's contentions in this case as he misconceived them. We submit the proper procedure is the other way; the balancing of equities must be before determination of the merits, and where public action is sought to be enjoined, the normal presumption of constitutionality of the act of a coordinate branch of Government should lead the courts, on preliminary injunction, to assume at least a substantial likelihood that the public officer will prevail on the merits, and to consider seriously the damage to the public interest that would result on the assumption that he acted constitutionally. . . .

[3. Presidential emergency power.] . . . Whatever view might be taken, broad or narrow, as to the scope of the President's function under any particular clause of Article II of the Constitution, we think it clear that the complex and completely integrated nature of the situation in which the emergency arose brought into play all of his powers.

Each part of the Constitution, as well as the charter as a whole, must be given living and flexible meaning so that it can be ever adapted to vastly differing occasions in the course and development of our national life. "It is no answer . . . to insist that what the provision of the Constitution meant to the vision of that day it must mean to the vision of our time. If by the statement that what the Constitution meant at the time of its adoption it means today, it is intended to say that the great clauses of the Constitution must be confined to the interpretation which the framers, with the conditions and outlook of their time, would have placed upon them, the statement carries its own refutation. It was to guard against such a narrow conception that Chief Justice Marshall uttered the memorable warning—'We must never forget that it is *a constitution* we are expounding'—'a constitution intended to endure for ages to come, and consequently, to be adapted to the various *crises* of human affairs.' When we are dealing with the words of the Constitution, said this Court in *Missouri v. Holland,* 'we must realize that they have called into life a being the development of which could not have been foreseen completely by the most gifted of its begetters. . . . The case before us must be considered in the light of our whole experience and not merely in that of what was said a hundred years ago.'"

Thus, even if the validity of the President's action in these cases had to be resolved exclusively in terms of any one of the granting clauses of Article II, as plaintiffs appear to insist, we submit that each clause is sufficiently broadly drawn and wide in purpose to support emergency executive action.

Section 1 of Article II provides that "the executive Power shall be vested in a President of the United States of America." In our view, this clause constitutes a grant of all the executive powers of which the Government is capable. Remembering that we do not have a parliamentary form of Government but rather a tripartite system which contemplates a vigorous executive, it seems plain that Clause 1 of Article II cannot be read as a mere restricted definition which would leave the Chief executive without ready power to deal with emergencies. Here, as in connection with each aspect of the President's constitutional powers, a specific and compelling frame of record is provided by the nature of the grave crisis with which the country was faced in the event of a production stoppage in the steel industry.

Again, Section 2 of Article II provides that "the President shall be Commander in Chief of the Army and Navy of the United States. . . ." Powers stemming from the President's position as Commander-in-Chief, specifically invoked in Executive Order 10340, are also clearly available as the basis for the challenged action in these cases. The place of steel at the very heart of our defense and combat activities, and those of our allies, is forcefully demonstrated by the material described above. Included in any consideration of the relationship between steel production and the President's position as Commander in Chief must be a genuine recognition of his affirmative power in connection with the safety and effectiveness of American troops in Korea. . . . Perhaps the most forceful illustration of the scope of Presidential power in this connection is the fact that American troops in Korea, whose safety and effectiveness are so directly involved here, were sent to the field by an exercise of the President's constitutional powers.

In addition to the general grant of executive power in Section 1 and the powers thus clearly stemming from the Commander in Chief clause, the President is under the duty imposed on him by Section 3 of Article 2 to "take Care that the Laws be faithfully executed." The broad scope of Section 3 has been delineated by this Court and is also available to justify the action taken by the President in these cases as a necessarily implied part of his express obligation to carry out our national policy to deter and repel aggression.

But the validity of the President's action on April 8 is not to be determined, either as a matter of common sense construction or as a matter of historic judicial method, by reference to one specific clause. On the contrary, from the beginning of the Republic, it has been recognized that Presidential power to act on a particular occasion may derive from more than one of the grants contained in Article II. . . .

It is thus plain that, in the light of the circumstances which confronted the President on April 8, there could be no justification for a requirement that his action be seen as confined to any one of the provisions set forth in Article II. On the contrary, this power to act must be taken as having sprung from all the available clauses. Rigid concepts, comparable to notions of common law pleading, which would require either the President or the Congress to specify particular powers as the basis for necessary and valid action, at their peril, should be taken as of no more value in resolving the living problems present in these cases than is the discredited technique of constitutional adjudication, based on "immutable" principles, which was employed by the court below. . . .

The real question here, therefore, is whether seizure was a means available to the President, in the exercise of his constitutional powers, to meet the pressing emergency which faced the nation. On this issue, ample support is to be found in executive and legislative precedent for the President's action. Moreover, there is direct judicial recognition of executive seizure as a means of meeting emergency situations.

1. *Executive construction.*—During the Revolution and the War of 1812 there were numerous instances of taking of property for the benefit of the armed services by military officers. While the exact nature of these takings is seldom clear from the available records, most of them appear to have been based entirely on executive authority. The records show that during the Revolution, the buildings of Rhode Island College, as well as other buildings throughout the country, were taken over for use as hospitals and barracks. Other instances were the taking of wagons, horses, and slaves required for public service. During the War of 1812 the property of traders at Chicago was taken to prevent its falling to the enemy, rope walks at Baltimore were destroyed for the same purposes, a house was taken to hold military stores and was later blown up to prevent those stores falling to the enemy, and, in Louisiana, General Jackson freely took plantations, fencing, and supplies as the emergency dictated. By the close of the War of 1812, it was firmly established that property could be taken in wartime emergencies as an exercise of independent executive power.

More pertinent parallels in history are found during the administrations of Presidents Lincoln, Wilson, and Franklin D. Roosevelt.

The first discovered instance of a taking by order of the President himself, as distinguished from a taking by a subordinate military official, occurred in the first year of the Civil War. On April 27, 1861, Secretary of War Cameron, at the direction of the President, issued a declaration taking over the railroads and telegraph lines between Washington and Annapolis.

Confronted with secession, President Lincoln exercised greater executive power than had been exercised by any previous President. His most dramatic act of executive taking was his Emancipation Proclamation of January 1, 1863, an action resting exclusively on his constitutional powers as Commander in Chief. . . .

Following the precedent set by President Lincoln, Wilson, too, exercised his constitutional powers to seize the property of the Smith & Wesson Company on August 31, 1918. In describing that action in a letter to striking workmen of the Remington Arms Company in Bridgeport, Connecticut, Wilson stated:

> The Smith & Wesson Company, of Springfield, Mass., engaged in government work, has refused to accept the mediation of the National War Labor Board and has flaunted [sic] its rules of decision approved by Presidential Proclamation. With my consent the War Department has taken over the plant and business of the Company to secure continuity in production and to prevent industrial disturbance.
>
>   It is of the highest importance to secure compliance with reasonable rules and procedure for the settlement of industrial disputes. Having exercised a drastic remedy with recalcitrant employers, it is my duty to use means equally well adapted to the end with lawless and faithless employees.

In addition to his actual seizure of Smith & Wesson and his threat of a similar measure as a sanction against the employees of the Remington Arms Company, Wilson also seriously contemplated the seizure of the Colorado coal mines in 1914 because of a strike there. No seizure was effected, however.

The most recent and extensive exercise of the executive power to seize property without statutory authority occurred during the administration of Franklin D. Roosevelt. On twelve occasions prior to the enactment of the War Labor Disputes Act of June 25, 1943, which authorized the seizure of plants, President Roosevelt issued Executive Orders taking possession of various companies when it appeared that a work stoppage would seriously impede operations. The first seizure occurred as much as six months prior to Pearl Harbor, and a total of three plants were seized before our entry into the War. . . .

2. *Legislative construction.*—As noted above, the first discovered instance of a Presidential taking was Lincoln's seizure, through his Secretary of War, of the railroad and telegraph lines between Washington and Annapolis in 1861. In January 1862, legislation was enacted which confirmed the Presidential power to take over any railroad or telegraph line in the United States and provided penalties for interference with their operation by the Government. Throughout the debates on the proposed legislation, virtually every Senator and Representative who addressed himself to the subject either assumed or declared that the President had the inherent constitutional power to take railroads and telegraph lines if he thought it necessary in the exercise of his war powers. The supporters of the bill

advocated its passage as a declaration of existing law and as a means of providing a rigorous system of penalties.

Thus, the sponsor of the bill in the Senate, Senator Wade, stated, "Mr. President, this bill confers no additional power upon the Government, as I understand it, beyond what they possess now. It attempts to regulate the power which they undoubtedly have; for they may seize upon private property anywhere, and subject it to the public use by virtue of the Constitution." And the sponsor of the bill in the House, Representative Blair, similarly stated that the bill "does not confer on the Secretary of War any new or any dangerous powers. The Government has now all the powers conferred by this bill; and the simple object of the bill is to regulate, limit, and restrain the exercise of those powers.". . . .

The legislative history of the War Labor Disputes Act of June 25, 1943, is strikingly similar. . . .

As with the Civil War Congress, discussed above, it was again generally recognized in consideration of the bill that the President already had full constitutional power to take the actions contemplated by the Act. Again, some Congressmen voted against the bill on the ground that it was unnecessary but others thought legislative action desirable to remove any possible doubt. Representative May, Chairman of the House Military Affairs Committee, to which the bill was referred, said

> . . . We hear it said the President already has power to do this. I think he has, and I think he exercised it wisely when he took over the plant in Inglewood, Calif. . . .

On the other hand, Representative Dirksen contended that the bill was unnecessary:

> Secondly, let me submit to you that the Commander in Chief who can occupy Iceland with the troops of the United States and advise Congress of this action 6 days later does not need any legislation to occupy a plant in the United States of America. He has done it once and he can do it again. Surely no proponent of the pending bill will arise to confess that what the President did before in California was or is illegal.

. . . The congressional debate reveals no purpose to impugn the President's constitutional power, but rather, indicates to the contrary. . . .

3. *Judicial precedent.*—Even were there no direct judicial authorities, we believe that these historical precedents would be sufficient support for the President's action here. As Mr. Justice Holmes has cogently observed, "a page of history is worth a volume of logic." Contrary to plaintiffs' assertions that these precedents prove a usage but do not establish its validity, "even constitutional power, when the text is doubtful, may be established by usage." "Both officers, law-makers and citizens naturally adjust themselves to any long-continued action of the Executive Department—on the presumption that unauthorized acts would not have been allowed to be so often repeated as to crystallize into a regular practice. That presumption is not reasoning in a circle but the basis of a wise and quieting rule that in determining the meaning of a statute or the existence of a power, weight shall be given to the usage itself—even when the validity of the practice is the subject of investigation."

In any event, direct judicial recognition of the executive power to seize property to avert a crisis in time of war or national emergency is not lacking. As this Court said in *United States v Russell:*

> . . . in cases of extreme necessity in time of war or of immediate public danger, . . . private property may be impressed into the public service, or may be seized and appropriated to the public use, or may even be destroyed without the consent of the owner. Unquestionably such extreme cases may arise, as where the property taken is imperatively necessary in time of war to construct defenses for the preservation of a military post at the moment of an impending attack by the enemy, or for food or medicine for a sick and famishing army utterly destitute and without other means of such supplies, or to transport troops, munitions of war, or clothing to reinforce or supply an army in a distant field, where the necessity for such reinforcement or supplies is extreme and imperative, to enable those in command of the post to maintain their position or to repel an impending attack, provided it appears that other means of transportation could not be obtained, and that the transport impressed for the purpose were imperatively required for such immediate use. Where such an extraordinary and unforeseen emergency occurs in the public service in time of war no doubt is entertained that the power of government is ample to supply for the moment the public wants in that way to the extent of the immediate public exigency, but the public danger must be immediate, imminent, and impending, and the emergency in the public service must be extreme and imperative, and such as will not admit of delay or a resort to any other source of supply, and the circumstances must be such as imperatively require the exercise of that extreme power in respect to the particular property so impressed, appropriated, or destroyed. . . .

The *Russell* case, if it stood alone, would, we submit, sustain the President's action here. This Court squarely held there that in time of "immediate and impending public danger . . . private property may be impressed into the public service. . . ."

. . . In the present case, we submit, there was no less clear an implication of power to seize the steel companies from an array of statutes and treaties which commit the Nation by law to a program of self-preservation which could not fail to suffer from a loss of steel production. As Attorney General Jackson said of a situation substantially identical with the one presented here:

> The Constitution lays upon the president the duty "to take care that the laws be faithfully executed." Among the laws which he is required to find means to execute are those which direct him to equip an enlarged army, to provide for a strengthened navy, to protect Government property, to protect those who are engaged in carrying out the business of the Government, and to carry out the provisions of the Lend-Lease Act. For faithful execution of such laws the President has back of him not only each general law-enforcement power conferred by the various acts of Congress but the aggregate of all such laws plus that wide discretion as to method vested in him by the Constitution for the purpose of executing the laws.
>
> The Constitution also places on the President the responsibility and vests in him the powers of Commander in Chief of the Army and of the Navy. These weapons for the protection of the continued existence of the Nation are placed in his sole command and the implication is clear that he should not allow them to

become paralyzed by failure to obtain supplies for which Congress has appropriated the money and which it has directed the President to obtain.

It bears emphasis that, in the period of over a month since the Presidential action the steel companies attack, Congress has done nothing to repudiate or countermand that action. The President has made clear his readiness to accept and execute any Congressional revision of his judgement as to the necessary and appropriate means of dealing with the emergency in the steel industry. In the absence of such revision, we believe that the authority the President has invoked under the Constitution and laws is clearly valid. . . .

[4. Taft–Hartley Act.] Even considered by itself, the Labor Management Relations Act was plainly not intended to be either an exclusive or a mandatory means of dealing with labor disputes threatening a national emergency. Thus Section 206 of that Act provides that when in the President's opinion a threatened or actual strike or lockout . . . will, if permitted to occur or continue, imperil the national health or safety, he *may* appoint a board of inquiry into the issues involved in the dispute and to make a written report to him within such time as he shall prescribe." Similarly, section 208 provides that upon "receiving a report from a board of inquiry the President *may* direct the Attorney General" to seek an injunction. The legislative history of these provisions, revealing an express rejection of proposals which would have made the board-of-inquiry and injunction procedures mandatory, makes it clear beyond doubt that the decision as to when or whether such measures were to be invoked was committed to the President's discretion. . . .

[5. Conclusion.] One of the great problems of the age is whether the democracies can find sufficient vigor and energy to respond promptly and decisively to the crises of our time. The century and a half since the drafting of the Constitution has witnessed an extraordinary growth in the magnitude, complexity, and interrelationship of the nation's problems. There has been an enormous increase in the tempo at which events occur, and decisions must be made. And above all there is the necessity with which the democracies are faced, if they are to maintain their very existence, to meet and overcome the challenge of dictatorship whether on the field of battle or in the market places of the world, where goods and ideas are traded.

We believe that these problems, like other problems which have arisen in the past, can be met within the framework of our Constitution. But they can be met only by regarding the Constitution as a "continuously operative charter of government," which is capable now as in the past of adapting itself to the needs of new circumstances without sacrificing the basic principles of democracy and liberty. This Court has recently emphasized that "it is of the highest importance that the fundamental purposes of the Constitution be kept in mind and given effect" and that "in time of crisis nothing could be more tragic and less expressive of the intent of the people than so to construe their Constitution that by its own terms it would substantially hinder rather than help them in defending their national safety." As was said by Chief Justice Hughes, "We have a fighting Constitution" which "marches" with events. "There are constantly new applications of unchanged powers, and it is ascertained that in novel and complex situations, the old grants contained, in their general words and true significance, needed and adequate authority." "Equally in war and peace" the particular provisions of the Constitution "must be read with the realistic purposes of the entire instrument fully in mind."

The present case does not require this Court to "fix the outermost line." As we have sought to show, the issue before this Court is whether, in dealing with an immediate crisis gravely threatening the continuance of the production of perhaps the most essential commodity of our present civilization, the President could take temporary action, of a type not prohibited by either the Constitution or the statutes, to avert the imminent threat, while recognizing fully the power of Congress by appropriate legislation to undo what he has done or to prescribe further or different steps. We believe that the solution does not require the pressing of juristic principles to "abstract extremes," but only a realistic consideration of the "necessities of the situation.". . .

Respectfully submitted,

PHILIP B. PERLMAN,
Acting Attorney General and Solicitor General.

ORAL ARGUMENT [15]

MR. DAVIS: I think that from this review of Congressional action three things clearly emerge:

The first is that Congress fully understands the nature and scope of the power to seize private property for Government purposes;

Second: It recognizes [that] the right of the Executive to exercise this power is drawn entirely from Legislative sources, and;

Third: That the power should be granted, if at all, sparingly, for specific reasons and for limited purposes and with appropriate safeguards. . . .

Now, we do not contend that the President is under mandatory authority to utilize the Taft–Hartley law. He may or he may not resort to that machinery for settlement, but the fact of its existence points up a claim we make here that, having that weapon at hand, any effort on his part to forge a new and a different weapon only aggravates the claim of usurpation which we are compelled to make. . . .

There is no—according to our contention and the Defendants's admission, there is no statutory framework into which this seizure can possibly be fit. What then? What then?

There is one other source of Executive power and that, of course, is in the Constitution itself. My friends, my learned friends, are not very specific when

---

[15]Excerpted from Philip Kurland and Gerhard Casper, eds., *Landmark Briefs and Arguments of the Supreme Court of the United States: Constitutional Law* (Arlington, Va.: University Publications of America, 1975), Vol. 48, pp. 877–995.

they undertake to deduce their power or the power of the Executive from Constitutional sources. They speak of the Executive enjoying all the Executive power of which the Government is capable. I would agree, but they intimate that, perhaps lurking in some of the clauses of Section 2 of the Constitution, there are powers from which this action may be deduced. . . .

Now, having vested the Executive power in . . . [a president], the framers of the Constitution went on with a carefully catalogued tabulation of the scope which that Executive power embraced and said just what it might occupy. There are ten categories so enumerated and I think there is but one, at most two, which the President of his own volition may occupy or exercise subject to no check from either one of the other branches of the Government— only two and perhaps only one; I am not sure. . . .

[The one unrestricted power] . . . is the power to pardon. This may be another, although I am not sure; it may be. However, I will cite it. From this is deduced the power of the President to recognize or refuse to recognize foreign ambassadors and ministers, and whether he can, against his will, be constrained by the Legislative branch to recognize the foreign representative of other governments whom he refuses to recognize—it may be that that power to receive ambassadors, like the power to extend pardon, is unrestricted and cannot be restrained.

Then there is this: ". . . he shall take care that the laws be faithfully executed." That is his great administrative duty. It is an executive duty imposed on him and it is to take care of laws, and the only laws that he can take care that they be faithfully executed are the laws enacted by the Legislative branch of the Government, in whom all lawmaking power is vested. I do not concede that under the power to "take care that the laws be faithfully executed" he may, by his own *ipse dictum,* proclaim a law, and then proceed to execute it in accordance with his own proclamation. . . .

Now, it is out of that category of power that the learned Solicitor General proposes to draw a power that is attempted to be exercised by the President in this instance. It is supposed that out of that category of power there is a sum which makes the whole . . . [greater than] the aggregate of all its parts.

It is true that the Constitution shall be the law to rule and regulate all alike, and it provides for crises such as occur in time of war, and it is the only source of any branch of the Government available for the drawing of power under our theory. And I am not helped by the statement made by my friend in his brief that the only power here springs from that one clause. I think I must notice a paragraph in this brief which I am not willing to leave without comment. . . . :

> Rigid concepts, comparable to notions of common law pleadings, which would require either the President or the Congress to specify particular powers as the basis for necessary and valid action, at their peril, should be taken as of no more value in resolving the living problems present in these cases than is the discredited technique of constitutional interpretation, based on "immutable" principles, which was employed by the court below. . . .

Well, if the Court please, is it or is it not an immutable principle that our Government—and that under our system of government—it is one of limited and granted powers? Is it or is it not an immutable principle that powers of government are distributed in a tripartite type of division of legislation, execution and judgment? Is it or is it not an immutable principle that ours is a Government of laws and not of men? Is it or is it not an immutable principle that, under the Fifth Amendment, private property, life, and liberty—and while there is a descending importance there, life first, liberty next and property—are all alike protected from seizure without due process of law?

Now, you cannot, my friends, you cannot dispose of these immutable principles by saying anything like that. You cannot dispose of these principles merely by a seizure of this kind. . . .

❖   ❖   ❖

It is contended further that the President is the sole judge of the emergency, and that claim, Your Honors, has not been abandoned. It is contended that the President also is the sole judge of the remedy and as to his selection of the remedy and the determination of the emergency; and it is contended that that is uncontrolled and uncontrollable, and that if the remedy the Congress provides failed, then the protection clause of the Fifth Amendment would control; but that does not place any barrier in his path.

Now, what is the difference between conditions like that and conditions phrased in the language employed by counsel for the Defendant in the Court of Appeals? It is a mere gloss upon words and comes out the same, and is the same thing. It is a reassertion of the kingly prerogatives which have been the foundation of every struggle against sovereignty that has existed in Anglo-Saxon history.

Think of the struggle during the reign of King George; Runnymeade; Bishop; the Prize cases; the Bill of Rights; the indictment of George III; and the Declaration of Independence. What are they? What are they all but the demonstrable, uncontrollable resistance of the so-called kingly prerogative? . . .

❖   ❖   ❖

There is one more thing that I wish to say in my opening. The controversy here between the management of these companies and the employees of these companies is highly regrettable. The interruption, if any there has been or will be, in the production of steel, a vital article of commerce, is necessarily most unfortunate. But it is as certain as the rising of tomorrow's sun that all of that, which has thus far happened, is a mere transient incident. The day will come beyond peradventure when these furnaces will glow as now, when the mills will turn as they turn now, and sooner or later, when a line of contented workmen will pass the window and receive the wages they are justly entitled to.

I say "sooner or later." One may think it will be sooner without Government intervention. One may think it may be later if the Government does not intervene. But these views are the mere casual ideas of a wholly uninstructed bystander and are not under consideration here. But all of that will some day be history. All of those incidental will be gone, but our country will not perish and there will be the determination of the extent of the power of the Chief Executive of this country, the limitation of that power by the legislature, and the duty of the courts to hold that balance even. All that will be as lasting as the life of the Republic itself, and, knowing by history how power grows by what it feeds upon, you can but insist that those who occupy offices under the Government, no matter how lofty or personal, are still servants of the public and are servants exercising their duties under the power given them by the Congress and only under that power.

It is not necessary for me to go back, as Brother Tuttle did in his brief, to remind ourselves of Washington's Farewell Address and his admonition. I think of another sentence which I believe to be as pregnant as any ever written or penned in our history, the words that Jefferson wrote in the Kentucky Resolution, which in a sentence sums up the entire theory of American Constitutional Government:

> In questions of power let no more be said of confidence in man, but bind him down from mischief by the chains of the Constitution.

MR. CHIEF JUSTICE VINSON: Mr. Solicitor General?

MR. PERLMAN: . . . Your Honors have just listened to an eloquent argument that is designed to turn the minds of this Court away from the facts in this case, away from the reasons which prompted the President of the United States to take the action that he did. Very little, if anything, was said to this Court about the conditions in the world today, about the struggle in which this Nation is engaged. And, Your Honors, practically nothing at all was said about the necessity, the vital necessity, to keep the plants owned by the Plaintiffs here in operation without interruption of any kind. And it is argued here that Your Honors should practically ignore that situation and pass on some constitutional interpretation of the powers that the President exercised, powers which have been exercised by presidents, maybe in times of peace and maybe in times of war, but without any regard to the situation in which the whole Nation finds itself today. . . .

Now it is interesting to point out that the President took over the steel industry on April 9th, or on the night of April 8, 1952. It is interesting to note that, on the morning of April 9th, the President sent a message to the Congress telling them of what he had done. He invited the immediate passage of legislation by the Congress of the United States, so that his action not only would be ratified by any legislation that the Congress passed, but if Congress did not agree with his action, they could reject it and propose some other method by which to solve the problem that faces the American people. . . .

MR. JUSTICE REED: How could they reject this?

PERLMAN: They could reject this, if Your Honor please, by passing an Act rejecting it and enacting other legislation.

REED: Passing a resolution to do what?

PERLMAN: Passing a resolution or terminating the action the President had taken.

MR. JUSTICE JACKSON: If the President has independent authority to do it under the Constitution, how could Congress do that? Don't you refute your own argument?

PERLMAN: The answer to that is that the President told Congress that he would abide by any action it had taken. That is not at issue, though. He said to them that he had done a certain thing officially. He gave to Congress an opportunity to do otherwise and said that he would abide by the action of Congress. But first of all, he told Congress how he had measured up to the emergency of the country, and he would put into action any course that Congress chose to take.

    Whether he has the Constitutional authority to ignore that action is not an issue here, because he took the position that he was justified, and rightfully, in doing what he did do, but nevertheless, he would abide by what Congress finally did—and Congress has done nothing. . . .

VINSON: Do I understand that you concede any power exists in the Congress to effect any course that would affect the Presidential action?

PERLMAN: No, sir, I do not concede the power. But I say that that is not in issue here because the President in a message to Congress said to Congress that he would abide by what Congress did.

VINSON: Voluntarily withdraw his action, or turn the properties back? Is that what you mean? Anything that the Congress desired he would follow voluntarily?

PERLMAN: That is right. He made that crystal-clear in his message of April 2nd.

MR. JUSTICE FRANKFURTER: That assumes that even though he had inherent power and Congress acquiesces, it does not limit the inherent power. Suppose it to be admitted that he had the inherent power. . . . Are you suggesting that because Congress did not act there is any legal significance to be drawn? Congress does not act; is that to be taken to mean that what has been affirmatively done by him indicates that he has been given that power, you say, because Congress did not do anything?

PERLMAN: Yes.

FRANKFURTER: From that, then, what meaning do you draw? Assume that the President is unlimited in his powers: What is the significance of the fact that Congress did not do anything? . . .

PERLMAN: I think it can be inferred from their failure to act that they were content to let the Presidential action stand.

FRANKFURTER: We have a very wide range of opinions of the Court to the effect that non-action is not to be so regarded.

PERLMAN: Under these circumstances, in the teeth of the two messages asking Congress to accept responsibility, telling Congress that he would abide by anything that Congress passed, then I think if Congress did not suggest anything different from what the President had done, it can be inferred that Congress was quite satisfied with the situation.

FRANKFURTER: What does that mean legally? All you can say is that they were satisfied to let this stand. That is all, isn't it?

PERLMAN: Yes, that is all. But I will come to an argument here that usage and custom has a bearing on the solution of this problem.

FRANKFURTER: That is a different question. I was listening to you with a great deal of interest, to what you were saying, and I shall listen to you with a great deal of interest when you argue the question of usage. But that is a very different theme.

PERLMAN: That would be an illustration.

FRANKFURTER: Well, all right.

❖   ❖   ❖

MR. JUSTICE FRANKFURTER: . . . In the *Myers* case there was a good deal of "tall talk," and in the *Humphreys* case the unanimous Court said that these principles were disproven.

MR. PERLMAN: The Court there—Mr. Justice Jackson pointed out in his book, "Struggle for Judicial Supremacy"———

FRANKFURTER: I point out what the Court said.

MR. JUSTICE JACKSON: Justice Frankfurter did not read the book.

PERLMAN: I suppose I should take advantage of this opportunity to recommend it to him.

FRANKFURTER: Doctor Johnson said, you know, you can give a person knowledge, but not understanding.

PERLMAN: If that is meant for me, it is a dirty dig.

FRANKFURTER: It is meant for me. . . .

❖   ❖   ❖

MR. PERLMAN: . . . Your Honors will find that ever since the Revolutionary days there have been wartime executive acts in seizing private property. There has been a lot of indignation expressed over the action of the President of the United States as if, constitutionally, the Chief Executive of this nation had undertaken an act that no one could have foreseen or heard of before. This is not the fact.

As we go back in history and watch and see what the Chief Executives have done, Your Honors cannot help but know that from the very beginning Article II of the Constitution has been construed at least by the Executives themselves as vesting in them that authority to meet emergencies that is necessary to be exercised where there is not other provision for meeting the emergencies, no other way in which the emergencies may be met, except by prompt action and except by prompt action by the Executive. . . .

. . . The first seizure made by President Franklin D. Roosevelt, during his Administration, was that of the plants of the North American Aviation Company. That was seized on June 9, 1941, and that was before, six months before, Pearl Harbor. There was no war at the time and there was no statutory authority for that seizure. . . .

MR. JUSTICE JACKSON: Are you not taking a good deal for granted when you take that as a precedent here? Looking back at the matter, if I remember rightly, North American was under direct contract with the United States, and they were subject to control, to that extent, by the United States.

PERLMAN: I think they were.

JACKSON: The Government owned the materials, the goods, and had control of the plants, and the whole thing, in a measure, was in the hands of the Government. There is no Government property here.

PERLMAN: No, there is no property here.

JACKSON: The strike in that case was on an entirely different basis. Here we have a collective bargaining contract that was in force, and this is what I take to be a legitimate labor dispute over wages and other terms and conditions of employment. If you will examine the report of what transpired at that time, that was in essence a strike against the Government, and the President did not sign that proclamation until there were men outside the plant who were not admitted, and there were Communists even, and they were not admitted to the plant, and there was a statement that authorized the seizure of the plant on the basis that they did not comply with the obligatory orders. All they looked at there may have been the question whether it was a breach of voluntary contract.

The other distinction in that case, when compared with this, is that the owners all did acquiesce in the seizure, and there was never a contest of it, as far as I recall. They welcomed it, and went through with it to the end.

I do not believe that unless you amend those points you can make that stand as a precedent for this. I looked it up because I wondered how much of this was laid at my door.

PERLMAN: Your Honor, we lay a lot of it at your door.

JACKSON: Perhaps rightly.

PERLMAN: I think the statement—

JACKSON: I claimed everything, of course, like every other Attorney General does. It was a custom that did not leave the Department of Justice when I did.

PERLMAN: Let's see what you did do, though. A part of your statement that we set out in our brief where we mention the case does not . . . mention the Communists. I do not think it mentioned the ownership by the Government of any part of the material there or any part of the plant. But the principle you laid down we think is good. All the principles that you laid down in that regard we think are good and are applicable here, and this is what you said. Let me read it [See Brief for the Government, pages 198-199]. . . .

JACKSON: I agree, so far, but you stop [quoting from my statement] a little early. The statement continues: "The situation of North American plants more nearly resembles insurrection . . . " and goes on further.

PERLMAN: That is right, Your Honor, but the part we have reproduced in our brief we think correctly explains the Constitutional powers of the president in the absence of any statutory provisions, and what Your Honor said with respect to the seizure of North American Aviation by the President more clearly states the Constitutional power vested in him. I think you will find that to be so, Your Honor.

MR. JUSTICE FRANKFURTER: He was not "Your Honor" when he said that.

PERLMAN: I beg your pardon.

FRANKFURTER: I say that Justice Jackson was not "His Honor" when he said that.

PERLMAN: Yes, that is so. Well, he is "His Honor" now, and I refer to him as such.

❖   ❖   ❖

MR. JUSTICE FRANKFURTER: . . . [The steel companies] have tried this whole controversy as if it were a normal case, a case in which there would be the normal exercise of authority and power. But that is not this case. This is an extraordinary case and it calls for the exercise of the authority that the Chief Executive has exercised in order to avert a national catastrophe.

Here we have the Secretary of Defense, the head of the Army, Navy, and Air Force, in affidavits saying that the very existence of the whole United States is threatened, and that the only manner in which the Chief Executive of this nation can assure the continued production of steel, necessary for the whole war effort—and we are at war, and while some of the cases cited yesterday were treated lightly because they were cases of [government] taking [possession of property] in time of war, nevertheless this is wartime.

MR. JUSTICE JACKSON: Has not Congress categorically disclaimed this as war, but denominates it rather as a police action? It looks like war to me, but Congress has specifically disclaimed this as war. I do not know what you invite us to do. Can we say it is a war when the President says, "No, it is not"?

MR. PERLMAN: You can say without fear of contradiction————

JACKSON: It looks like war; people know it.

PERLMAN: You can say without contradiction to anyone that we are under war conditions, and whether it may be a police action, nevertheless we are engaged with every other nation in an effort to repel aggression overseas.

JACKSON: You are raising different questions now than when you were dealing with counsel.

FRANKFURTER: I thought you did this yesterday when answering Justice Douglas. Yesterday, when Justice Douglas asked you if you were relying on the War Powers Act, you answered, "No"—you answered his questions quite categorically. You cannot say that you are not in a war on one hand and on the other say that the President is exercising war powers when he is not. I thought that was gone into quite definitely and you answered Justice Douglas categorically.

PERLMAN: No, Your Honor, the order issued by the President, the Executive Order which authorized the seizure, expressly states that he was taking that step under his authority as Commander-in-Chief of the Army and Navy.

FRANKFURTER: But he has said that in the most peaceful era of our country that there ever was.

PERLMAN: We are, unfortunately————

MR. CHIEF JUSTICE VINSON: You had seizures prior to Pearl Harbor that looked toward preparedness for eventualities that did come.
    Your time has expired.

PERLMAN: Thank you.

THE OPINION

Mr. Justice Black delivered the opinion of the Court. . . .

The President's power, if any, to issue the order must stem from an act of Congress or from the Constitution itself. There is no statute that expressly authorizes the President to take possession of property as he did here. Nor is there any act of Congress to which our attention has been directed from which such a power can fairly be implied. . . .

It is clear that if the President had authority to issue the order he did, it must be found in some provision of the Constitution. And it is not claimed that express constitutional language grants this power to the President. The contention is that presidential power should be implied from the aggregate of his powers under the Constitution. Particular reliance is placed on provisions in Article II which say that "The executive Power shall be vested in a President . . . "; that "he shall take Care that the Laws be faithfully executed"; and that he "shall be Commander in Chief of the Army and Navy of the United States."

The order cannot properly be sustained as an exercise of the President's military power as Commander in Chief of the Armed Forces. The Government attempts to do so by citing a number of cases upholding broad powers in military commanders engaged in day-to-day fighting in a theater of war. Such cases need not concern us here. Even though "theater of war" be an expanding concept, we cannot with faithfulness to our constitutional system hold that the Commander in Chief of the Armed Forces has the ultimate power as such to take possession of private property in order to keep labor disputes from stopping production. This is a job for the Nation's lawmakers, not for its military authorities.

Nor can the seizure order be sustained because of the several constitutional provisions that grant executive power to the President. In the framework of our Constitution, the President's power to see that the laws are faithfully executed refutes the idea that he is to be a lawmaker. The Constitution limits his functions in the lawmaking process to the recommending of laws he thinks wise and the vetoing of laws he thinks bad. And the Constitution is neither silent nor equivocal about who shall make laws which the President is to execute. The first section of the first article says that "All legislative Powers herein granted shall be vested in a Congress of the United States. . . ." After granting many powers to the Congress, Article I goes on to provide that Congress may "make all Laws which shall be necessary and proper for carrying into Execution the foregoing Powers, and all other Powers vested by this Constitution in the Government of the United States, or in any Department or Officer thereof."

The President's order does not direct that a congressional policy be executed in a manner prescribed by Congress—it directs that a presidential policy be executed in a manner prescribed by the President. The preamble of the order itself, like that of many statutes, sets out reasons why the President believes certain policies should be adopted, proclaims these policies as rules of conduct to be followed, and again, like a statute, authorizes a government official to promulgate additional rules and regulations consistent with the policy proclaimed and needed to carry that policy into execution. The power of Congress to adopt such public policies as those proclaimed by the order is beyond question. It can authorize the taking of private property for public use. It can make laws regulating the relationships between employers and employees, prescribing rules designed to settle labor disputes, and fixing wages and working conditions in certain fields of our economy. The Constitution does not subject this lawmaking power of Congress to presidential military supervision or control. . . .

The Founders of this Nation entrusted the lawmaking power to the Congress alone in both good and bad times. It would do no good to recall historical events, the fears of power and the hopes for freedom that lay behind their choice. Such a review would but confirm our holding that this seizure cannot stand. . . .

Mr. Justice Frankfurter, concurring. . .

Before the cares of the White House were his own, President Harding is reported to have said that government after all is a very simple thing. He must have said that, if he said it, as a fleeting inhabitant of fairyland. The opposite is the truth. A constitutional democracy like ours is perhaps the most difficult of man's social arrangements to manage successfully. Our scheme of society is more dependent than any other form of government on knowledge and wisdom and self-discipline for the achievement of its aims. For our democracy implies the reign of reason on the most extensive scale. The Founders of this Nation were not imbued with the modern cynicism that the only thing that history teaches is that it teaches nothing. They acted on the conviction that the experience of man sheds a good deal of light on his nature. It sheds a good deal of light not merely on the need for effective power, if a society is to be at once cohesive and civilized, but also on the need for limitations on the power of governors over the governed. . . .

The question before the Court comes in this setting. Congress has frequently—at least 16 times since 1916—specifically provided for executive seizure of production, transportation, communications, or storage facilities. . . . The power to seize has uniformly been given only for a limited period or for a defined emergency, or has been repealed after a short period. Its exercise has been restricted to particular circumstances such as "time of war or when war is imminent," the needs of "public safety" or of "national security or defense," or "urgent and impending need." The period of governmental operation has been limited, as, for instance, to "sixty days after the restoration of productive efficiency." . . .

Congress in 1947 was again called upon to consider whether governmental seizure should be used to avoid serious industrial shutdowns. Congress decided against conferring such power generally and in advance, without special Congressional enactment to meet each particular need. Under the urgency of telephone and coal strikes in the winter of 1946, Congress addressed itself to the problems raised by "national emergency" strikes and lockouts. The termination of wartime seizure powers on December 31, 1946, brought these matters to the attention of Congress with vivid impact. A proposal that the President be given powers to seize plants to avert a shutdown where the "health or safety" of the Nation was endangered was thoroughly canvassed by Congress and rejected. . . .

It is one thing to draw an intention of Congress from general language and to say that Congress would have explicitly written what is inferred, where Congress has not addressed itself to a specific situation. It is quite impossible, however, when Congress did specifically address itself to a problem, as Congress did to that of seizure, to find secreted in the interstices of [the Taft–Hartley] legislation the very grant of power which Congress consciously withheld. To find authority so explicitly withheld is not merely to disregard in a particular instance the clear will of Congress. It is to disrespect the whole legislative process and the constitutional division of authority between President and Congress. . . .

To be sure, the content of the three authorities of government is not to be derived from an abstract analysis. The areas are partly interacting, not wholly disjointed. The Constitution is a framework for government. Therefore the way the framework has consistently operated fairly establishes that it has operated according to its true nature. Deeply embedded traditional ways of conducting government cannot supplant the Constitution or legislation, but they give meaning to the words of a text or supply them. It is an inadmissibly narrow conception of American constitutional law to confine it to the words of the Constitution and to disregard the gloss which life has written upon them. In short, a systematic, unbroken, executive practice, long pursued to the knowledge of the Congress and never before questioned, engaged in by Presidents who have also sworn to uphold the Constitution, making as it were such exercise of power part of the structure of our government, may be treated as a gloss on "executive Power" vested in the President by section 1 of Article II.

Such was the case of *United States v. Midwest Oil Co.* The contrast between the circumstances of that case and this one helps to draw a clear line between authority not explicitly conferred yet authorized to be exercised by the President and the denial of such authority. In both instances it was the concern of Congress under express constitutional grant to make rules and regulations for the problems with which the President dealt. In the one case he was dealing with the protection of property belonging to the United States; in the other with the enforcement of the Commerce Clause and with raising and supporting armies and maintaining the Navy. In the *Midwest Oil* case, lands which Congress had opened for entry were, over a period of 80 years and in 252 instances, and by Presidents learned and unlearned in the law, temporarily withdrawn from entry so as to enable Congress to deal with such withdrawals. No remotely comparable practice can be vouched for executive seizure of property at a time when this country was not at war, in the only constitutional way in which it can be at war. It would pursue the irrelevant to reopen the controversy over the constitutionality of some acts of Lincoln during the Civil War. Suffice it to say that he seized railroads in territory where armed hostilities had already interrupted the movement of troops to the beleaguered Capital, and his order was ratified by the Congress.

The only other instances of seizures are those during the periods of the first and second World Wars. In his eleven seizures of industrial facilities, President Wilson acted, or at least purported to act, under authority granted by Congress. Thus his seizures cannot be adduced as interpretations by a President of his own powers in the absence of statute.

Down to the World War II period, then, the record is barren of instances comparable to the one before us. Of twelve seizures by President Roosevelt prior to the enactment of the War Labor Disputes Act in June, 1943, three were sanctioned by existing law, and six others were effected after Congress, on December 8, 1941, had declared the existence of a state of war. In this case, reliance on the powers that flow from declared war has been commendably disclaimed by the Solicitor General. Thus, the list of executive assertions of the power of seizure in circumstances comparable to the present reduces to three in the six month period from June to December of 1941. We need not split hairs in comparing those actions to the one before us, though much might be said by way of differentiation. Without passing on their validity, as we are not called upon to do, it suffices to say that these three isolated instances do not add up, either in number, scope, duration, or contemporaneous legal justification, to the kind of executive construction of the Constitution revealed in the *Midwest Oil* case. Nor do they come to us sanctioned by long-continued acquiescence of Congress giving decisive weight to a construction by the Executive of its powers.

A scheme of government like ours no doubt at times feels the lack of power to act with complete, all-embracing, swiftly moving authority. No doubt a government with distributed authority, subject to be challenged in the courts of law, at least long enough to consider and adjudicate the challenge, labors under restrictions from which other governments are free. It has not been our tradition to envy such governments. In any event our government was designed to have such restrictions. The price was deemed not too high in view of the safeguards which these restrictions afford. I know no more impressive words on this subject than those of Mr. Justice Brandeis:

> The doctrine of the separation of powers was adopted by the Convention of 1787, not to promote efficiency but to preclude the exercise of arbitrary power. The purpose was, not to avoid friction, but, by means of the inevitable friction incident to the distribution of the governmental powers among three departments, to save the people from autocracy. . . .

Mr. Justice Jackson, concurring. . .

That comprehensive and undefined presidential powers hold both practical advantages and grave dangers for the country will impress anyone who has served as legal advisor to a President in a time of transition and public anxiety. While an interval of detached reflection may temper teachings of that experience, they probably are a more realistic influence on my views than the conventional materials of judicial decision which seem unduly to accentuate doctrine and legal fiction. But as we approach the question of presidential power, we half overcome mental hazards by recognizing them. The opinions of judges, no less than executives and publicists, often suffer the infirmity of confusing the issue of a power's validity with the cause it is invoked to promote, of confounding the permanent executive office with its temporary occupant. The tendency is strong to emphasize transient results upon policies—such as wages or stabilization—and lose sight of enduring consequences upon the balanced power structure of our Republic.

A judge, like an executive advisor, may be surprised at the poverty of really useful and unambiguous authority applicable to concrete problems of executive power as they actually present themselves. Just what our forefathers did envision, or would have envisioned had they foreseen modern conditions, must be divined from materials almost as enigmatic as the dreams Joseph was called upon to interpret for Pharaoh. A century and a half of partisan debate and scholarly speculation yields no net result but only supplies more or less apt quotations from respected sources on each side of any question. They largely cancel each other. And court decisions are indecisive because of the judicial practice of dealing with the largest questions in the most narrow way.

The actual art of governing under our Constitution does not and cannot conform to judicial definitions of the power of any of its branches based on isolated clauses or even single Articles torn from context. While the Constitution diffuses power the better to secure liberty, it also contemplates that practice will integrate the dispersed powers into a workable government. It enjoins upon its branches separateness but interdependence, autonomy but reciprocity. Presidential powers are not fixed but fluctuate, depending upon their disjunction or conjunction with those of Congress. We may well begin by a somewhat over-simplified grouping of practical situations in which a President may doubt, or others may challenge, his powers, and by distinguishing roughly the legal consequences of this factor of relativity.

1. When the President acts pursuant to an express or implied authorization of Congress, his authority is at its maximum, for it includes all that he possesses in his own right plus all that Congress can delegate. . . .

2. When the President acts in absence of either congressional grant or denial of authority, he can only rely upon his own independent powers, but there is a zone of twilight in which he and Congress may have concurrent authority, or in which its distribution is uncertain. . . .

3. When the President takes measures incompatible with the expressed or implied will of congress, his power is at its lowest ebb, for then he can rely only upon his own constitutional powers minus any constitutional powers of Congress over the matter. Courts can sustain exclusive presidential control in such a case only by disabling the Congress from acting upon the subject. Presidential claim to a power at once so conclusive and preclusive must be scrutinized with caution, for what is at stake is the equilibrium established by our constitutional system.

Into which of these classifications does this executive seizure of the steel industry fit? It is eliminated from the first by admission, for it is conceded that no congressional authorization exists for this seizure. . . .

Can it then be defended under flexible tests available to the second category? It seems clearly eliminated from that class because Congress has not left seizure of private property an open field but has covered it by three statutory policies [including Taft–Hartley] inconsistent with this seizure. . . .

This leaves the current seizure to be justified only by the severe tests under the third grouping, where it can be supported only by any remainder of executive power after subtraction of such powers as Congress may have over the subject. In short, we can sustain the President only by holding that seizure of such strike-bound industries is within his domain and beyond control by Congress. Thus, this Court's first review of such seizures occurs under circumstances which leave presidential power most vulnerable to attack and in the least favorable of possible constitutional postures.

I did not suppose, and I am not persuaded, that history leaves it open to question, at least in the courts, that the executive branch, like the Federal Government as a whole, possesses only delegated powers. The purpose of the Constitution was not only to grant power, but to keep it from getting out of hand. However, because the President does not enjoy unmentioned powers does not mean that the mentioned ones should be narrowed by a niggardly construction. Some clauses could be made almost unworkable, as well as immutable, by refusal to indulge some latitude of interpretation for changing times. I have heretofore, and do now, give to the enumerated powers the scope and elasticity afforded by what seem to be reasonable, practical implications instead of the rigidity dictated by a doctrinaire textualism.

The Solicitor General seeks the power of seizure in three clauses of the Executive Article, the first reading, "The executive Power shall be vested in a President of the United States of America." Lest I be thought to exaggerate, I quote the interpretation which his brief puts upon it: "In our view, this clause constitutes a grant of all the executive powers of which the Government is capable." If that be true, it is difficult to see why the forefathers bothered to add several specific items, including some trifling ones.

The example of such unlimited executive power that must have most impressed the forefathers was the prerogative exercised by George III, and the description of its evils in the Declaration of Independence leads me to doubt that they were creating their new Executive in his image. Continental European examples were no more appealing. And if we seek instruction from our own times, we can match it only from the executive powers in those governments we disparagingly describe as totalitarian. I cannot accept the view that this clause is a grant in bulk of all conceivable executive power but regard it as an allocation to the presidential office of generic powers thereafter stated.

The clause on which the Government next relies is that "The President shall be Commander in Chief of the Army and Navy of the United States. . . ." These cryptic words have given rise to some of the most persistent controversies in our constitutional history. Of course, they imply something more than an empty title. But just what authority goes with the name has plagued presidential advisors who would not waive or narrow it by nonassertion yet cannot say where it begins or ends. It undoubtedly puts the Nation's armed forces under presidential command. Hence, this loose appellation is sometimes advanced as support for any presidential action, internal or external, involving use of force, the idea being that it vests power to do anything, anywhere, that can be done with an army or navy.

That seems to be the logic of an argument tendered at our bar—that the President having, on his own responsibility, sent American troops abroad derives from that act "affirmative power" to seize the means of producing a supply of steel for them. To quote, "Perhaps the most forceful illustration of the scope of Presidential power in this connection is the fact that American troops in Korea, whose safety and effectiveness are so directly involved here, were sent to the field by an exercise of the President's constitutional powers." Thus, it is said, he has invested himself with "war powers."

I cannot foresee all that it might entail if the court should endorse this argument. Nothing in our Constitution is plainer than that declaration of a war is entrusted only to Congress. Of course, a state of war may in fact exist without a formal declaration. But no doctrine that the Court could promulgate would seem to me more sinister and alarming than that a President whose conduct of foreign affairs is so largely uncontrolled, and often even is unknown, can vastly enlarge his mastery over the internal affairs of the country by his own commitment of the Nation's armed forces to some foreign venture. . . .

We should not use this occasion to circumscribe, much less to contract, the lawful role of the President as Commander in Chief. I should indulge the widest latitude of interpretation to sustain his exclusive function to command the instruments of national force, at least when turned against the outside world for the security of our society. But, when it is turned inward, not because of rebellion but because of a lawful economic struggle between industry and labor, it should have no such indulgence. His command power is not such an absolute as might be implied from that office in a militaristic system but is subject to limitations consistent with a constitutional Republic whose law and policy-making branch is a representative Congress. . . .

The third clause in which the Solicitor General finds seizure powers is that "he shall take Care that the Laws be faithfully executed. . . ." That authority must be matched against words of the Fifth Amendment that "No person shall be . . . deprived of life, liberty or property, without due process of law. . . ." One gives a governmental authority that reaches so far as there is law, the other gives a private right that authority shall go no farther. These signify about all there is of the principle that ours is a government of laws, not of men, and that we submit ourselves to rulers only if under rules.

The Solicitor General lastly grounds support of the seizure upon nebulous inherent powers never expressly granted but said to have accrued to the office from the customs and claims of preceding administrations. The plea is for a resulting power to deal with a crisis or an emergency according to the necessities of the case, the unarticulated assumption being that necessity knows no law.

Loose and irresponsible use of adjectives colors all nonlegal and much legal discussion of presidential powers. "Inherent" powers, "implied" powers, "incidental" powers, "plenary" powers, "war" powers, and "emergency" powers are used, often interchangeably and without fixed or ascertainable meanings.

The vagueness and generality of the clauses that set forth presidential powers afford a plausible basis for pressures within and without an administration for presidential action beyond that supported by those whose responsibility it is to defend his actions in court. The claim of inherent and unrestricted presidential powers has long been a persuasive dialectical weapon in political controversy. While it is not surprising that counsel should grasp support from such unadjudicated claims of power, a judge cannot accept self-serving press statements of the attorney for one of the interested parties as authority in answering a constitutional question, even if the advocate was himself. But prudence has counseled that actual reliance on such nebulous claims stop short of provoking a judicial test. . . .

The appeal, however, that we declare the existence of inherent powers *ex necessitate* to meet an emergency asks us to do what many think would be wise, although it is something the forefathers omitted. They knew what emergencies were, knew the pressures they engender for authoritative action, knew, too, how they afford a ready pretext for usurpation. We may also suspect that they suspected that emergency powers would tend to kindle emergencies. Aside from suspension of the privilege of the writ of habeas corpus in time of rebellion or invasion, when the public safety may require it, they made no express provision for the exercise of extraordinary authority because of a crisis. I do not think we rightfully may so amend their work, and, if we could, I am not convinced it would be wise to do so, although many modern nations have forthrightly recognized that war and economic crises may upset the normal balance between liberty and authority. Their experience with emergency powers may not be irrelevant to the argument here that we should say that the Executive, of his own volition, can invest himself with undefined emergency powers. . . .

This contemporary foreign experience may be inconclusive as to the wisdom of lodging emergency powers somewhere in a modern government. But it suggests that emergency powers are consistent with free government only when their control is lodged elsewhere than in the Executive who exercises them. That is the safeguard that would be nullified by our adoption of the "inherent powers" formula. Nothing in my experience convinces me that such risks are warranted by any real necessity, although such powers would, of course, be an executive convenience. . . .

In view of the ease, expedition and safety with which Congress can grant and has granted large emergency powers, certainly ample to embrace this crisis, I am quite unimpressed with the argument that we should affirm possession of them without statute. Such power either has no beginning or it has no end. If it exists, it need submit to no legal restraint. I am not alarmed that it would plunge us straightway into dictatorship, but it is at least a step in that wrong direction.

As to whether there is imperative necessity for such powers, it is relevant to note the gap that exists between the President's paper powers and his real powers. The Constitution does not disclose the measure of the actual controls wielded by the modern presidential office. That instrument must be understood as an Eighteenth-Century sketch of a government hoped for, not as a blueprint of the Government that is. Vast accretions of federal power, eroded from that reserved by the States, have magnified the scope of presidential activity. Subtle shifts take place in the centers of real power that do not show on the face of the Constitution.

Executive power has the advantage of concentration in a single head in whose choice the whole Nation has a part, making him the focus of public hopes and expectations. In drama, magnitude and finality his decisions so far overshadow any others that almost alone he fills the public eye and ear. No other personality in public life can begin to compete with him in access to the public mind through modern methods of communications. By his prestige as head of state and his influence upon public opinion he exerts a leverage upon those who are supposed to check and balance his power which often cancels their effectiveness.

Moreover, rise of the party system has made a significant extraconstitutional supplement to real executive power. No appraisal of his necessities is realistic which overlooks that he heads a political system as well as a legal system. Party loyalties and interests, sometimes more binding than law, extend his effective control into branches of government other than his own and he often may win, as a political leader, what he cannot command under the Constitution. Indeed, Woodrow Wilson, commenting on the President as leader both of his party and of the Nation, observed, "If he rightly interpret the national thought and boldly insist upon it, he is irresistible. . . . His office is anything he has the sagacity and force to make it." I cannot be brought to believe that this country will suffer if the Court refuses further to aggrandize the presidential office, already so potent and so relatively immune from judicial review, at the expense of Congress.

But I have no illusion that any decision by this Court can keep power in the hands of Congress if it is not wise and timely in meeting its problems. A crisis that challenges the President equally, or perhaps primarily, challenges Congress. If not good law, there was worldly wisdom in the maxim attributed to Napoleon that "The tools belong to the man who can use them." We may say that power to legislate for emergencies belongs in the hands of Congress, but only Congress itself can prevent power from slipping through its fingers. . . .

Mr. Chief Justice Vinson, dissenting. . .

In passing upon the question of presidential powers in this case, we must first consider the context in which those powers were exercised.

Those who suggest that this is a case involving extraordinary powers should be mindful that these are extraordinary times. A world not yet recovered from the devastation of World War II has been forced to face the threat of another and more terrifying global conflict. . . .

One is not here called upon even to consider the possibility of executive seizure of a farm, a corner grocery store or even a single industrial plant. Such considerations arise only when one ignores the central fact of this case—that the Nation's entire basic steel production would have shut down completely if there had been no Government seizure. Even ignoring for the moment whatever confidential information the President may possess as "the Nation's organ for foreign affairs," the uncontroverted affidavits in this record amply support the finding that "a work stoppage would immediately jeopardize and imperil our national defense.". . .

Accordingly, if the President has any power under the Constitution to meet a critical situation in the absence of express statutory authorization, there is no basis whatever for criticizing the exercise of such power in this case. . . .

The whole of the "executive Power" is vested in the President. Before entering office, the President swears that he "will faithfully execute the Office of President of the United States, and will to the best of [his] Ability, preserve, protect, and defend the Constitution of the United States."

This comprehensive grant of the executive power to a single person was bestowed soon after the country had thrown the yoke of monarchy. Only by instilling initiative and vigor in all of the three departments of Government, declared Madison, could tyranny in any form be avoided. Hamilton added: "Energy in the Executive is a leading character in the definition of good government. It is essential to the protection of the community against foreign attacks; it is not less essential to the steady administration of the laws; to the protection of property against those irregular and high-handed combinations which sometimes interrupt the ordinary course of justice; to the security of liberty against the enterprises and assaults of ambition, of faction, and of anarchy." It is thus apparent that the Presidency was deliberately fashioned as an office of power and independence. Of course, the Framers created no autocrat capable of arrogating any power unto himself at any time. But neither did they create an automaton impotent to exercise the powers of Government at a time when the survival of the Republic itself may be at stake.

In passing upon the grave constitutional question presented in this case, we must never forget, as Chief Justice Marshall admonished, that the Constitution is "intended to endure for ages to come, and, consequently, to be adapted to the various *crises* of human affairs," and that "[i]ts means are adequate to its ends." Cases do arise presenting questions which could not have been foreseen by the Framers. In such cases, the Constitution has been treated as a living document adaptable to new situations. But we are not called upon today to expand the Constitution to meet a new situation. For, in this case, we need only look to history and time-honored principles of constitutional law—principles that have been applied consistently by all branches of the Government throughout our history. It is those who assert the invalidity of the Executive Order who seek to amend the Constitution in this case.

. . . In *United States v. Midwest Oil Co.* the President's action was sustained as consistent with executive practice throughout our history. An excellent brief was filed in the case by the Solicitor General, Mr. John W. Davis, together with Assistant Attorney General Knaebel, later Reporter for this Court. In this brief, the situation confronting President Taft was described as "an emergency; there was no time to wait for the action of Congress." The brief then discusses the powers of the President under the Constitution in such a case:

> Ours is a self-sufficient Government within its sphere. "Its means are adequate to its ends," and it is rational to assume that its active forces will be found equal in most things to the emergencies that confront it. While perfect flexibility is not to be expected in a Government of divided powers, and while division of power is one of the principle features of the Constitution, it is the plain duty of those who are called upon to draw the dividing lines to ascertain the essential, recognize the practical, and avoid a slavish formalism which can only serve to ossify the Government and reduce its efficiency without any compensating good. The function of making laws is peculiar to Congress, and the Executive can not exercise that function to any degree. But this is not to say that all of the *subjects* concerning which laws might be made are perforce removed from the possibility of executive influence. The executive may act upon things and upon men in many relations which have not, though they might have, been actually regulated by Congress. In other words, just as there are fields which are peculiar to Congress and fields which are peculiar to the Executive, so there are fields which are common to both, in the sense that the Executive may move within them until they shall have been occupied by legislative action. These are not the fields of legislative prerogative, but fields within which the lawmaking power may enter and dominate whenever it chooses. This situation results from the fact that the President is the active agent, not of Congress, but of the Nation. As such he performs the duties which the Constitution lays upon him immediately, and as such, also, he executes the laws and regulations adopted by Congress. He is the agent of the people of the United States, deriving all his powers from them and responsible directly to them. In no sense is he the agent of Congress. He obeys and executes the laws of Congress, not because Congress is enthroned in authority over him, but because the Constitution directs him to do so. . . .

This brief is valuable not alone because of the caliber of its authors but because it lays bare in succinct reasoning the basis of the executive practice which this Court approved in the *Midwest Oil* case. . . .

Some six months before Pearl Harbor, a dispute at a single aviation plant in Inglewood, California, interrupted a segment of the production of military aircraft. In spite of the comparative insignificance of this work stoppage to total defense production as contrasted with the complete paralysis now threatened by a shutdown of the entire basic steel industry, and even though our armed forces were not then engaged in combat, President Roosevelt ordered the seizure of the plant "pursuant to the powers vested in [him] by the Constitution of the United States, as President of the United States of America and Commander in Chief of the Army and Navy of the United States." The Attorney General (Jackson) vigorously proclaimed that the President had the moral duty to keep this Nation's defense effort a "going concern." His ringing moral justification was coupled with a legal justification equally well stated:

> The Presidential proclamation rests upon the aggregate of the Presidential powers derived from the Constitution itself and from statutes enacted by the Congress.
>
> The Constitution lays upon the President the duty "to take care that the laws be faithfully executed." Among the laws which he is required to find means to execute are those which direct him to equip an enlarged army, to provide for a strengthened navy, to protect Government property, to protect those who are engaged in carrying out the business of the Government, and to carry out the provisions of the Lend-Lease Act. For the faithful execution of such laws the President has back of him not only each general law-enforcement power conferred by the various acts of Congress but the aggregate of all such laws plus that wide discretion as to method vested in him by the Constitution for the purpose of executing the laws.
>
> The Constitution also places on the President the responsibility and vests in him the powers of Commander in Chief of the Army and of the Navy. These weapons for the protection of the continued existence of the Nation are placed in his sole command and the implication is clear that he should not allow them to become paralyzed by failure to obtain supplies for which Congress has appropriated the money and which it has directed the President to obtain.

At this time, Senator Connally proposed amending the Selective Training and Service Act to authorize the President to seize any plant where an interruption of production would unduly impede the defense effort. Proponents of the measure in no way implied that the legislation would add to the powers already possessed by the President and the amendment was opposed as unnecessary since the President already had the power. . . .

This is but a cursory summary of executive leadership. But it amply demonstrates that Presidents have taken prompt action to enforce the laws and protect the country whether or not Congress happened to provide in advance for the particular method of execution. At the minimum, the executive actions reviewed herein sustain the action of the President in this case. And many of the cited examples of Presidential practice go far beyond the extent of power necessary to sustain the President's order to seize the steel mills. The fact that temporary executive seizures of industrial plants to meet an emergency have not been directly tested in this Court furnishes not the slightest suggestion that such actions have been illegal. Rather, the fact that Congress and the courts have consistently recognized and given their support to such executive action indicates that such a power of seizure has been accepted throughout our history.

History bears out the genius of the Founding Fathers, who created a Government subject to law but not left subject to inertia when vigor and initiative are required. . . .

The President reported to Congress the morning after the seizure that he acted because a work stoppage in steel production would immediately imperil the safety of the Nation by preventing execution of the legislative programs for procurement of military equipment. And, while a shutdown could be averted by granting the price concessions requested by plaintiffs, granting such concessions would disrupt the price stabilization program also enacted by Congress. Rather than fail to execute either legislative program, the President acted to execute both. . . .

Whatever the extent of Presidential power on more tranquil occasions, and whatever the right of the President to execute legislative programs as he sees fit without reporting the mode of execution to Congress, the single Presidential purpose disclosed on this record is to faithfully execute the laws by acting in an emergency to maintain the status quo, thereby preventing collapse of the legislative programs until Congress could act. The President's action served the same purposes as a judicial stay entered to maintain the status quo in order to preserve the jurisdiction of a court. In his Message to Congress immediately following the seizure, the President explained the necessity of his action in executing the military procurement and anti-inflation legislative programs and expressed his desire to cooperate with any legislative proposals approving, regulating, or rejecting the seizure of the steel mills. Consequently, there is no evidence whatever of any Presidential purpose to defy Congress or act in a way inconsistent with the legislative will.

In *United States v. Midwest Oil Co.*, this Court approved executive action where, as here, the President acted to preserve an important matter until Congress could act—even though his action in that case was contrary to an express statute. In this case, there is no statute prohibiting the action taken by the President in a matter not merely important but threatening the very safety of the Nation. Executive inaction in such a situation, courting national disaster, is foreign to the concept of energy and initiative in the Executive as created by the Founding Fathers. The Constitution was itself "adopted in a period of grave emergency. . . . While emergency does not create power, emergency may furnish the occasion for the exercise of power." The Framers knew, as we should know in these times of peril, that there is real danger in Executive weakness. There is no cause to fear Executive tyranny so long as the laws of Congress are being faithfully executed. Certainly there is no basis for fear of dictatorship when the Executive acts, as he did in this case, only to save the situation until Congress could act. . . .

The broad executive power granted by Article II to an officer on duty 365 days a year cannot, it is said, be invoked to avert disaster. Instead, the President must confine himself to sending a message to Congress recommending action. Under this messenger-boy concept of the Office, the President cannot even act to preserve legislative programs from destruction so that Congress will have something left to act upon. There is no judicial finding that the executive action was unwarranted because there was in fact no basis for the President's finding of the existence of an emergency for, under this view, the gravity of the emergency and the immediacy of the threatened disaster are considered irrelevant as a matter of law.

Seizure of plaintiffs' property is not a pleasant undertaking. Similarly unpleasant to a free country are the draft which disrupts the home and military procurement which causes economic dislocation and compels adoption of price controls, wage stabilization and allocation of materials. The President informed Congress that even a temporary Government operation of plaintiffs' properties was "thoroughly distasteful" to him, but was necessary to prevent immediate paralysis of the mobilization program. Presidents have been in the past, and any man worthy of the Office should be in the future, free to take at least interim action necessary to execute legislative programs essential to survival of the Nation. A sturdy judiciary should not be swayed by the unpleasantness or unpopularity of necessary executive action, but must independently determine for itself whether the President was acting, as required by the Constitution, to "take Care that the Laws be faithfully executed."

... No basis for claims of arbitrary action, unlimited powers or dictatorial usurpation of congressional power appears from the facts of this case. On the contrary, judicial, legislative, and executive precedents throughout our history demonstrate that in this case the President acted in full conformity with his duties under the Constitution.

POSTSCRIPT

Subsequent to the Supreme Court decision in *Youngstowm*, the more prominent exertions of presidential emergency power have not involved seizures of private property. Instead, freedom of the press has been at the center of the controversy concerning what a president can do in an emergency. Can a president, without any statutory authorization, prevent the publication of material that arguably undermines national security? The First Amendment of the Constitution says that "Congress shall make no law ... abridging the freedom of speech, or of the press. ..." Does this prohibition mean that the president can never "restrain" a publisher from publishing what is damaging to national security? Because such a "restraint" prevents material from being published, it is a kind of infringement of free speech— called a "prior restraint"— that has generally been considered unconstitutional. Imposing criminal or civil liability on publishers for what they have already published is one thing; preventing them from publishing what they want to publish is something else, something more serious, something that conflicts with the core meaning of freedom of the press.

American judges have been very hostile to prior restraints because the very purpose of the free-press clause, they have insisted, was to prevent any system of governmental licensing for the press. Such a system, which operated in England in the seventeenth century, would constitute explicit censorship of the press in direct violation of the First Amendment. In *Near v. Minnesota* (1931), Chief Justice

Charles E. Hughes said the following: "In determining the extent of the constitutional protection, it has been generally, if not universally, considered that it is the chief purpose of the guaranty to prevent previous restraints upon publication. The struggle in England, directed against the legislative power of the licenser, resulted in renunciation of the censorship of the press."[16] However, in this very case, Hughes carved out a potential exception to the broad rule against prior restraints.

> The objection has also been made that the principle as to immunity from previous restraint is stated too broadly, if every such restraint is deemed to be prohibited. That is undoubtedly true; the protection even as to previous restraint is not absolutely unlimited. . . . No one would question but that a government might prevent actual obstruction to its recruiting service or the publication of the sailing dates of transports or the number and location of troops.[17]

Hughes therefore thought that the government could impose prior restraints upon the press in certain kinds of national security emergencies. But he was quite vague on specifics. Did a state of war have to exist? Did the war have to be "declared" by Congress? Could the president restrain the press without statutory authorization?

These are the kinds of questions that arose in the 1970s after the Supreme Court had rejected presidential emergency powers in *Youngstown*. In *New York Times Co. v. United States* (1971),[18] more popularly known as the "Pentagon Papers Case," the Nixon administration sought to enjoin the *New York Times* and the *Washington Post* from publishing a top-secret study of the history of American involvement in Vietnam. The classified study was written for the Department of Defense by the Rand Corporation, but Daniel Ellsberg, one of its authors, gave copies of it to the newspapers. Could the newspapers publish these "Pentagon Papers" despite the government's contention that such publication would harm national security? Did it make any difference that in 1971 the United States was in an "undeclared" war against Vietnam, just as in 1952, when Truman ordered the seizure of the steel mills, the country was involved in a "police action" in Korea?

Of course, important differences existed between *Youngstown* and the "Pentagon Papers Case." First, as noted earlier, the cases concerned different constitutional freedoms and rights. Second, though injunctions were involved in both cases, the burden of proof had shifted. In *Youngstown,* because the steel companies were requesting an injunction, they had to prove, among other things, that they were suffering an "irreparable injury." In *New York Times Co. v. United States,* the government was the party seeking an injunction, and therefore it had to satisfy the requirements for injunctive relief. Therefore, in *Youngstown,* the steel companies could have lost their case on the merits or because they did not satisfy the legal requirements for an injunction. In the "Pentagon Papers Case," because the newspapers were not seeking an injunction, they were in a better position than the steel companies because they could lose their case only if the Supreme Court decided the constitutional issue against them.

---

[16]283 U.S. 697, 723 (1931).

[17]*Id.* at 715–16.

[18]403 U.S. 713 (1971).

In general, the result of the case was very similar to the one in *Youngstown:* a six-to-three decision against the government, but the majority could agree only on a brief *per curiam* opinion. All the justices wrote separately, including those in dissent. The result was that many of the basic questions of the case were not clearly resolved. Justices Hugo Black and William O. Douglas claimed that prior restraints were never permissible, whereas Justice William Brennan maintained that a restraint was justifiable only in a very clear case of averting immediate disaster. He provided two possible examples: during wartime, if the publication would endanger the transport of troops; or in peacetime, if the publication "would set in motion nuclear holocaust."[19] The government had offered no such proof, and therefore the temporary injunctions against the newspapers were unconstitutional.

Justices Byron White, Potter Stewart, and Thurgood Marshall, like Justices Felix Frankfurter and Robert Jackson in *Youngstown,* emphasized that Congress, through various statutes, had authorized the criminal prosecution of only those who stole or misused various types of classified information. Because Congress had considered in 1917 giving the president broad powers to prevent the publication of information detrimental to national security but had declined to do so, the president was acting without, or perhaps even against, congressional will. Given these circumstances, the three justices concluded that no prior restraint of the press was constitutionally permissible.

In contrast, Chief Justice Warren Burger and Justices John M. Harlan and Harry Blackmun dissented, insisting that the government should have been given more time to substantiate its claim that publication would harm national security. The case—which began with the publication by the *New York Times* of certain of "the papers" on June 13, 1971, and ended with the Supreme Court decision on June 30—was rushed through the courts, with the result, according to Burger, Harlan, and Blackmun, that the president's power to conduct foreign affairs and to protect the national interest was not given the respect it deserved.

In contrast to the "Pentagon Papers Case," in *United States v. Progressive, Inc.* (1979),[20] the government was able to convince a federal district judge to impose a prior restraint upon a magazine that intended to publish an article written by Howard Morland entitled "The H-Bomb Secret: How We Got It, Why We're Telling It." The publisher and the author claimed that no injunction should be granted because the country was not at war and because all the information in the article was nonclassified. The government countered that national security—specifically the nation's policy against nuclear proliferation—justified censorship of information in the public domain if it produced, "when drawn together, synthesized and collated," an "immediate direct and irreparable harm to the interests of the United States."[21]

The district court, siding with the government, explained that the "Pentagon Papers Case" was different in three ways: (1) the Pentagon Papers contained only

---

[19]*Id.* at 726.

[20]467 F. Supp. 990 (1979).

[21]*Id.* at 991.

history, whereas Morland's article included technical information that was potentially dangerous; (2) in the earlier case, the government had not shown any real harm to the United States, whereas the danger of nuclear proliferation was obvious in *Progressive;* (3) the publishing of the H-bomb article violated a statute—the Atomic Energy Act—which authorized the use of injunctions, whereas no such statute was applicable to the Pentagon Papers case. The significance of this third point, however, was unclear because the district judge also said he would have issued the injunction without statutory authorization because "of the existence of the likelihood of direct, immediate and irreparable injury to our nation and its people."[22] Even though the article was not a do-it-yourself guide to building an H-bomb, the danger that it would increase nuclear proliferation was so serious that it justified "the first instance of prior restraint against a publication in this fashion in the history of this country. . . ."[23] The basic underlying premise of the district court's reasoning was that "one cannot enjoy freedom of speech, freedom to worship or freedom of the press unless one first enjoys the freedom to live."[24] Stopping nuclear proliferation justified a prior restraint on the press because it protected our right to life.

The ruling in *Progressive* was appealed, but the issue never made it to the Supreme Court. Other magazines, not subject to the district court's injunction, began publishing the substance of Morland's article, a development that made further proceedings pointless. The result is that the American government has never successfully placed a prior restraint upon the press on the basis of the national security exception established in *Near v. Minnesota.* The Supreme Court invalidated the injunction in the Pentagon Papers case, while third parties circumvented the one issued in *Progressive.*[25] Perhaps in some future set of circumstances, the government will in a national security emergency successfully impose a prior restraint on the press. If some publication of tomorrow posed an immediate and catastrophic risk to national security and the government sought a prior restraint, it is simply not clear what the Supreme Court would decide, even if no statutory authorization existed. The legal precedents governing presidential emergency power are neither decisive nor clear. Therefore, as in the case of *Youngstown,* perhaps the more important consideration is how the Supreme Court should go about deciding the issue. Is Justice Black's literal approach to constitutional adjudication the proper way to determine the scope of presidential

---

[22]*Id.* at 1000.

[23]*Id.* at 996.

[24]*Id.* at 995.

[25]The English government's attempt to enjoin the publication of Peter Wright's autobiography, *Spycatcher* (New York: Dell, 1988), experienced a fate similar to the American government's attempt to enjoin Morland's article. Despite an injunction against English publishers, the book, an exposé of the British Secret Service, was first published in the United States, followed by publication in Canada, Australia, New Zealand, and Europe. Its substance soon "leaked" into England, proving that in the contemporary world, there are so many publishers and so many jurisdictions that it is extremely difficult, not as a legal matter but as a practical one, to stop a publication from seeing the light of day. And once one publisher in one jurisdiction publishes, the value of any injunction against other publishers in other jurisdictions is seriously eroded.

emergency powers, including the question of whether the president can ever impose prior restraints upon the press on the ground of national security? What of Justice Frankfurter's historical orientation? of Justice Jackson's perspective of practical statesmanship? None of these different viewpoints can definitively establish the substantive constitutional rule, whether in regard to the legitimacy of prior restraints or of seizures of private property, but they do focus our attention on the relevant questions.

CHAPTER 5

Executive Privilege

UNITED STATES V. NIXON
418 U.S. 683 (1974)

✦

The Watergate constitutional crisis began on June 17, 1972, when five men engaged in illegal political surveillance of the offices of the Democratic National Committee were arrested for burglary. It ended more than two years later, on August 9, 1974, when Richard Nixon became the first person ever to resign from the office of president of the United States. Many individuals and institutions played prominent roles in the evolution and resolution of this constitutional drama. Bob Woodward and Carl Bernstein, investigative reporters for the *Washington Post;* North Carolina's Sam Ervin, chairman of the Senate Watergate Committee; Archibald Cox and Leon Jaworski, Special Watergate Prosecutors; Judge John J. Sirica, federal district court judge in Washington, D.C.; and finally, New Jersey's Peter Rodino, chairman of the House Judiciary Committee, all made vital contributions. But if one had to point to a single event that sealed Nixon's fate, it would most probably be the Supreme Court's July 24, 1974, decision in *United States v. Nixon.* This unanimous opinion forced Nixon, despite his claim of executive privilege, to turn over to the Special Prosecutor certain subpoenaed tapes of presidential conversations that allegedly concerned the coverup of the Watergate burglary. Although the House Judiciary Committee had already voted in favor of impeachment in late July, Nixon took a fateful step when he released to the public tapes that the Supreme Court had ordered him to hand over to the Special Prosecutor. Once the public became familiar with one of these tapes—the tape of June 23, 1972— Nixon had little choice. Deciding that it would be a futile effort to fight his impeachment on the House floor or his trial in the Senate, Nixon resigned, thereby ending the constitutional crisis.

Nixon initially refused to honor the subpoena that had been issued by Judge Sirica because, in his view, executive privilege gave him complete discretion to keep executive materials (the tapes) secret, both from Congress and the courts. According to him, if a president abused this power, the only remedy was impeachment by Congress; courts had no authority to order the president to turn over the tapes, and they were not to interfere with the impeachment process. The Watergate tapes litigation (unlike *Youngstown*) therefore had a direct bearing upon the power of the judiciary. By rejecting Nixon's doctrine of executive privilege in *United States v. Nixon,* the Court was ruling in favor of its institutional power at the expense of the executive branch. Judges, not the president, were ultimately to decide in the cases that properly came before them what the president could keep secret. This decision, therefore, highlights troubling questions concerning institutional bias. Can one really expect the Court to decide against its own powers when it delineates the respective powers of the president and the judiciary? Can the Court be impartial in this kind of context?

Perhaps these kinds of questions are somewhat rhetorical. As long as judicial review is an accepted feature of American constitutionalism, judges will inevitably be defining the limits of their own powers as they define the limits of certain congressional and presidential powers. However, it is still important for American citizens to be sensitive to the potential problem of judicial bias in favor of judicial powers. Moreover, it is also arguable that in *United States v. Nixon* the Supreme Court was too eager to enter the Watergate fray. As in *Youngstown*, the Court took the very unusual step of reviewing the tapes case before the Court of Appeals had had a chance to hear or decide it. Also, it delayed its normal recess so that it could decide *Nixon* in the summer of 1974. Was all this speed really necessary?

Another concern is that some of the justices may have intensely disliked Nixon or believed that he was guilty of obstructing justice. Is it possible that these more personal factors affected what the Supreme Court did in Watergate? If so, did the Court, as Nixon insisted, unjustifiably interfere with the impeachment process? These questions are different from those concerning the way in which the Supreme Court must inevitably define the limits of its own power. Even if the Court cannot be faulted on the general ground that the Court was deciding a case that had a direct bearing on its own power, it is still possible to question the way in which the Court proceeded in *Nixon* and the conclusions it reached. Is there any reason to think that the Watergate tapes case was, as Nixon's brief to the Supreme Court argued, an example of a "great" case making "bad" law?

Certainly John Mitchell, Nixon's former attorney general and the new director of the Committee to Re-elect the President (CREEP), had absolutely no idea what was to befall the Nixon administration when he approved on March 30, 1972, among other things, G. Gordon Liddy's plan to "bug" the Watergate offices of the Democratic National Committee. Mitchell had denied authorization for the plan twice before, but on March 30, his signature initiated the events that destroyed Nixon and his administration and perhaps fundamentally altered the American presidency. The first set of wiretaps was placed over the Memorial Day weekend, but Liddy's recruits botched the job: The taps either did not work or were placed on the wrong phones. It was the second break-in on June 17, meant to rectify these problems, that proved disastrous. All the burglars were arrested, including James McCord, the security chief at CREEP, who had in his possession $100 bills that were ultimately traceable back to the same committee.

On June 19, Woodward and Bernstein broke the story that the original defendants—the five who had participated in the break-in plus E. Howard Hunt and G. Gordon Liddy—were financially linked to CREEP and the White House. Ben Bradlee, the editor of the *Washington Post,* had told his two reporters to "look for the dough," and their investigations, along with those of other newspapers, linked high officials in the Nixon administration to the Watergate coverup.[1] In early 1973, Judge Sirica, whose nickname was "Maximum John," took the next step. Convinced that the full story had not come out, he gave exceptionally harsh provisional sentences to those who pled guilty to the break-in, but he promised leniency in their final sentences if they cooperated with the prosecutors and the Senate Watergate Committee, a select committee that had already begun its investigation of the break-in and related matters. James McCord, one of the burglars who pled innocent but was convicted, came forward and implicated, among others, John Dean. At the time, Dean's official title was Counsel to the President, but his real job had been to contain the FBI investigation of the Watergate break-in. By the end of April, Dean calculated his chances and decided to talk, first to Henry Petersen, head of the Criminal Division at the Justice Department, but later to the Special Prosecutor and to Ervin's Watergate Committee.

Dean's revelations triggered the avalanche that eventually brought down the Nixon administration. In five days of numbing testimony before the Senate Watergate Committee, he told the American people (in a remarkably deliberate, if not monotonous, style) that the president was an active participant in the coverup. According to Dean's recollection, on March 21, 1973, he had explicitly warned Nixon that the Watergate coverup was a "cancer growing on the Presidency," but Nixon nonetheless decided to continue to engage in activities that in Dean's view constituted obstruction of justice—a felony. (See Box 5.1.) In addition, Dean corroborated the testimony of others that described the administration's involvement in a number of other illegal, abusive, and offensive activities. The list included illegal wiretaps, burglaries, illegal campaign contributions, and disquieting political tricks that were played on the Democrats during the campaign of 1972.

In response to Dean's testimony, John Mitchell, together with H. R. Haldeman, Nixon's chief of staff, and John Ehrlichman, director of the Domestic Council, all of whom had resigned from their positions because of the public pressure brought on by previous disclosures and allegations, testified before the committee that Dean was lying. Dean, they claimed, was protecting his own skin by incriminating the president. At this point, therefore, the situation was one of stalemate, with Nixon, Mitchell, Haldeman, and Ehrlichman on one side and the soft-spoken, unflappable Dean on the other. The ultimate question, as Senator Howard Baker, vice chairman of the Senate Watergate Committee, put it, was "What did the president know, and when did he know it?"

On July 16, 1973, something completely unexpected happened that fundamentally changed the situation. Alexander Butterfield, an aide to Haldeman who

---

[1]For the Woodward–Bernstein story, see their book *All the Presidents's Men* (New York: Simon and Schuster, 1974). A movie by the same title, based on the book, is also available.

BOX 5.1

JOHN DEAN REMEMBERS THE MARCH 21 MEETING

I began by telling the President that there was a cancer growing on the Presidency and that if the cancer was not removed that the President himself would be killed by it. I also told him that it was important that this cancer be removed immediately because it was growing more deadly every day. I then gave him what I told him would be a broad overview of the situation and I would come back and fill in the details and answer any questions he might have about the matter. . . .

. . . I told him that [Herbert] Kalmbach [Nixon's personal lawyer] had been used to raise funds to pay these seven individuals for their silence at the instructions of [John] Ehrlichman, [Robert] Haldeman, and [John] Mitchell and I had been the conveyor of this instruction to Kalmbach. I told him that . . . I had assisted [Jeb Stuart] Magruder [deputy director of CREEP] in preparing his false story for presentation to the grand jury. I told him that cash that had been at the White House had been funneled back to the reelection committee for the purpose of paying the seven individuals to remain silent.

I then proceeded to tell him that perjury had been committed, and for this coverup to continue it would require more perjury and more money. I told him that the demands of the convicted individuals were continually increasing and that with sentencing imminent, the demands had become specific. . . .

I then told the President that this was just typical of the type of blackmail that the White House would continue to be subjected to and I didn't know how to deal with it. I also told the President that I thought that I would as a result of my name coming out during the Gray hearings be called before the grand jury and that if I was called to testify before the grand jury or the Senate committee I would have to tell the facts the way I know them. I said I did not know if executive privilege would be applicable to any appearance I might have before the grand jury. I concluded by saying that it is going to take continued perjury and continued support of these individuals to perpetuate the coverup and that I did not believe it was possible to continue it. . . .

In the late afternoon of March 21, Haldeman and Ehrlichman and I had a second meeting with the President. . . .

The meeting with the President that afternoon with Haldeman, Ehrlichman, and myself was a tremendous disappointment to me because it was quite clear that the coverup as far as the White House was concerned was going to continue. I recall that while Haldeman, Ehrlichman, and I were sitting at a small table in front of the President in his Executive Office Building office that I for the first time said in front of the President that I thought that Haldeman, Ehrlichman, and Dean were all indictable for obstruction of justice and that was the reason I disagreed with all that was being discussed at that point in time.

I could tell both Haldeman, and particularly Ehrlichman, were very unhappy with my comments. I had let them very clearly know that I was not going to participate in the matter any further and that I thought it was time that everybody start thinking about telling the truth. . . .

Source: Presidential Campaign Activities of 1972—Phase I: Watergate Investigation, Hearings before the Select Committee on Presidential Campaign Activities, 93rd Cong., 1st Sess., Bk 3, pp. 998–1000.

kept track of official records in the Oval Office, testified before the committee that Nixon had taped all of his presidential conversations. As soon as this bombshell went off, everyone realized that the key to Nixon's guilt or innocence was the tapes; they could either clear him or expose him. The problem for the committee, however, was how to get a copy of the tapes. Nixon believed that executive privilege shielded the executive branch from "intrusive" congressional investigations. By invoking this doctrine, he thought he could keep any executive document from Congress and prevent any subordinate executive official from testifying before congressional committees. His position was most clearly stated by his then–attorney general, Richard Kleindienst, who testified before three subcommittees that were investigating secrecy in government. The senators asked Kleindienst some rather pointed questions, indicating their hostility to Nixon's wide-ranging doctrine of executive privilege. (See Box 5.2.) Nonetheless, when Ervin's Watergate Committee issued a congressional subpoena for the tapes, Nixon invoked executive privilege. The committee took Nixon to court over his refusal to honor its subpoena, but District Judge Gerhard Gesell declined to enforce the congressional subpoena.[2]

Because the Watergate Committee had run into a dead end, national attention in the summer of 1973 shifted to Archibald Cox, a prominent Harvard Law School professor of constitutional law who had earlier accepted the unusual Justice Department position of Special Watergate Prosecutor. Once the existence of the tapes became known, Cox moved quickly. In late July, he convinced Judge Sirica that nine tapes were potentially relevant to the grand jury's investigation of who authorized the Watergate break-in and participated in the attempt to cover it up. Sirica issued a subpoena *duces tecum* (a subpoena directed at specific documents) for the tapes, but Nixon appealed to the Court of Appeals in Washington, D.C. His argument once again relied heavily on the doctrine of executive privilege, but the Court of Appeals went five to two against Nixon.[3] At this point, the case could have gone to the Supreme Court, but Nixon decided to handle the

---

[2]See *Senate Select Comm. on Presidential Campaign Activities v. Nixon,* 498 F. 2d 725 (D.C. Cir. 1974).

[3]487 F.2d 700 (D.C. Cir. 1973).

BOX 5.2

SENATE DEBATE ON EXECUTIVE PRIVILEGE

SENATOR CHILES:
The President's news statement on March the 12th where he talks about not covering up embarrassing information and the privilege will only be exercised in those particular instances in which disclosures would harm the public interest; who makes that judgement?

MR. KLEINDIENST:
That judgement is made by the President of the United States and only by the President of the United States.

CHILES:
Does that not make us a country of men rather than law?

KLEINDIENST:
No, sir; because the power of the President is set forth in the Constitution. . . .

CHILES:
You think the Founding Fathers designed this document just to put absolute judgement in one man who held the office of the President at any time to determine whether he thought something was in the public interest or not?

KLEINDIENST:
Well, it gave—you have to check on that,Senator Chiles—but it gave to the President just as to the Congress a determination of what information the President and Congress were to give each other. Unlike the President, the Congress has a remedy because if the Congress feels the President is exercising this power as a monarch or tyrant you have an impeachment proceeding. You could impeach the President of the United States. You would have a Speaker of the House of Representatives becoming the President. Then you could impeach the Judiciary and appoint a new Judiciary, and if you wanted to exercise your power you could end up with a whole new Government. That is what I said a moment ago. Leaving aside the normal remedy of impeachment, which I do not think will be used but once every 300 years, it is our political process which determines the ultimate result. It is not what Congressmen or Senators should or should not do. If they abuse their powers they lose elections, and they do not come back.

✿   ✿   ✿

SENATOR MUSKIE:
I am talking about 2 $\frac{1}{2}$ million employees of the executive branch; do we or do we not have the power to command him to testify and——

Mr. Kliendienst:

You do not have the power to command President Nixon to come up here.

Muskie:

That is not my question.

Kleindienst:

That was an extension of your question which I have been trying to answer on three or four occasions, Senator Muskie.

Muskie:

You have fudged every answer.

Kleindienst:

You do not have the power to compel me to come up here if the President directs me not to and even if you would attempt to compel me, I would not come here.

Muskie:

Does that apply to every one of the employees of the Federal [executive] branch of the United States?

Kleindienst:

I think if the President directs it, logically, I would have to say that is correct.

❖   ❖   ❖

Senator Ervin:

Maybe I can sum up your testimony on executive privilege. You concede, I take it, that Congress does have the power to gather information for the purpose of enabling it to legislate wisely?

Mr. Kleindienst:

Yes, sir.

Ervin:

But you take the position that notwithstanding the fact that the Constitution impliedly gives this power to the Congress, that Congress cannot obtain any information whatsoever from anybody in the executive branch of the Government, or any document in the possession of the Government, unless the President specifically directs that it have it?. . .

Kleindienst:

Yes, sir, and you have a remedy, all kinds of remedies, cut off appropriations, impeach the President.

Ervin:

If we have no remedy, we can do what you say indirectly?

KLEINDIENST:

Logically, I would have to agree with that statement, Senator. . . .

ERVIN:

I understand that the main duty of the President under the Constitution and the main thing he ought to do under his oath of office is to "take care that the laws be faithfully executed," and I do not believe the President has the power to make sure the laws are not used.

KLEINDIENST:

If you ever found a President who abused his office you have your remedy and it is very carefully set forth, and if the new President abuses it you can get another one.

ERVIN:

That is to depend upon the executive branch of the Government. If the President forbids them to testify before the Senate, then the Senate would have no evidence with which to make adjudication.

KLEINDIENST:

You do not need evidence to impeach a President. You get the resolution passed by the House and trial by the Senate and if the Senate votes on that trial, and if the Senate agrees, he is impeached. That is the end of it.

ERVIN:

You cannot try cases without evidence, even impeachment trials. . . .

Source: Executive Privilege; Secrecy in Government; Freedom of Information, Hearings before the Subcommittees on Administrative Practice and Procedure and Separation of Powers of the Committee on the Judiciary, United States Senate and the Subcommittee on Intergovernmental Relations of the Committee on Government Operations, 93rd Cong. 1st Sess. (3 vols.), Vol. I, pp. 44–46, 51–52.

problem of the tapes in a more political fashion. On October 20, 1973, after further negotiations between the Special Prosecutor and the White House had failed, Nixon decided to fire Cox. The result was the infamous Saturday Night Massacre. (See Headline 5.1.)

The "massacre" occurred because neither Attorney General Elliot Richardson nor the deputy attorney general, William Ruckelshaus, would carry out the order to fire Cox. When he was appointed to the top job at the Justice Department, Richardson had assured Congress that he would not tamper with the Special Prosecutor's independence. He had also personally promised Cox that Cox could seek evidence from the president by way of compulsory judicial process (i.e., by way of subpoena). Therefore, rather than dismiss Cox, Richardson resigned. Ruckelshaus succeeded Richardson, but was himself fired when he refused to obey Nixon's order to fire Cox. Nixon had to go one more link down the chain of

Headline 5.1

command to find a person—Robert Bork[4]—who was willing to fire Cox. Bork, the solicitor general (the government's lawyer who represents the executive branch in the Supreme Court), was immediately appointed acting attorney general. Between eight and nine o'clock that night, the White House publicly announced Cox's dismissal and informed the press that agents from the FBI were occupying the offices of Richardson, Ruckelshaus, and Cox. The impression left by these events was that Nixon was trying to take personal control of the investigation of his own potential misdeeds.

The public's reaction was immediate and unmistakable. In response to protestors marching with signs asking drivers to "Honk for Impeachment," car horns blared in front of the White House. The heaviest volume of telegrams ever recorded poured into Washington. Newspaper editorials, TV commentators, and public interest groups condemned Cox's dismissal, demanded that the tapes be handed over, and called for Nixon's resignation or impeachment. (See Box 5.3.) Even members of his own political party refused to support Nixon's dismissal of Cox. Faced with this overwhelming public opposition, Nixon retreated and delivered the subpoenaed tapes to Sirica.

---

[4]This was the same Robert Bork whom President Ronald Reagan nominated in 1987 to a seat on the Supreme Court but who was not confirmed by the Senate because of his conception of constitutional rights (the right of privacy was rejected) and because of his theory of constitutional adjudication. His theory permitted the judicial invalidation of a law only if it conflicted with the words of the Constitution or the intent of the framers. Bork has defended his approach to constitutional adjudication in *The Tempting of America* (New York: Free Press, 1990).

BOX 5.3

Why it is necessary to impeach President Nixon. And how it can be done.

Richard Nixon has not left us in doubt. He means to function above the law. If he is allowed to continue, then the destruction of the Bill of Rights could follow. If, after all the Watergate revelations, we allow him to continue, we are accomplices to that destruction.

Consider what has already happened:

• On July 23, 1970, the President personally approved the "Huston plan" for political surveillance by such methods as burglary, wiretapping, eavesdropping, mail covers and spying on students by the CIA and other agencies. These methods were employed against dissenters, political opponents, news reporters, and government employees.

• In 1971, the President established within the White House a personal secret police (the "plumbers"), operating outside the restraints of law, and engaging in burglary, illegal wiretaps, espionage and perjury.

• While Daniel Ellsberg was facing trial, his psychiatric records were burglarized by White House aides and, at the direction of the President, a White House aide discussed the directorship of the FBI with the judge presiding over Ellsberg's trial.

• Private detectives were hired by White House aides to spy on the sex life, drinking habits and family problems of political opponents.

• Supporters of possible presidential opponents of President Nixon were marked as "enemies" on a special list, and targeted for harassment by the Internal Revenue Service.

• During three days in May 1971, over 13,000 people were illegally arrested in Washington, D.C. The dragnet arrests, unprecedented in American history, were declared unconstitutional by the courts. To justify the arrests, a White House spokesman, William Rehnquist, invented the doctrine of "qualified martial law."

• In 1973, the President bombed Cambodia, a neutral country, without the authorization of Congress. We learned later that he had been bombing Cambodia for three years and had deliberately concealed the bombing from Congress and from the people, thereby usurping the war-making powers of Congress. When the deception was revealed, the President said he would do the same thing under similar circumstances.

• The President has transformed grand juries into instruments of political surveillance and harassment, and caused politically motivated indictments to issue.

• The President has attacked the freedom of the press, and subjected news reporters to illegal wiretaps and harassing FBI investigations.

The doctrine of "inherent" power

Richard Nixon is not the first president to violate constitutional rights and he will not be the last. But no president has ever before systematically claimed that the Bill of Rights, which limits other government officials, does not limit the President or his agents.

When he wiretapped in violation of the Constitution, he claimed an "inherent" power to do so.

When he secretly bombed Cambodia, he claimed an "inherent" power to do so.

When he directed the dragnet arrests of thousands of demonstrators in Washington, he claimed an "inherent" power to do so.

If the President is permitted to use the doctrine of "inherent" power to override the Bill of Rights anytime he pleases, civil liberties can be cancelled at whim.

The President of the United States should symbolize our system of individual rights under law. He sets the precedent for future presidents. As U.S. Supreme Court Justice Louis Brandeis said in a

American Civil Liberties Union
84 Fifth Avenue, New York, N.Y. 10011
☐ Enclosed is my contribution of $___ to help the Impeachment Campaign.
☐ I am willing to write my Representative, and participate in the Impeachment Campaign. Please contact me.
☐ I want to join ACLU. Credit my contribution towards membership.
☐ $15 Individual ☐ $25 Joint ☐ More
Name___
Address___
City___ State___ Zip___

1928 wiretapping case:

In a government of laws, existence of the government will be imperiled if it fails to observe the law scrupulously. Our government is the potent, the omnipresent teacher. For good or for ill, it teaches the whole people by its example. Crime is contagious. If the government becomes a law-breaker, it breeds contempt for law; it invites every man to become a law unto himself; it invites anarchy. To declare that in the administration of law the end justifies the means... would bring terrible retribution...

To preserve and protect our system of individual rights under law, to restore the integrity of the Bill of Rights for us and our children, and to make the lesson clear to all future presidents in whose hands we place our lives, Richard Nixon must stand trial before the Senate. If he does not stand trial, what he has done will be done by others.

How to impeach President Nixon

In order to stand trial before the Senate, where a two thirds vote is necessary for conviction, the President must first be accused by a majority of the House of Representatives. This accusation by the House is called impeachment. Impeachment itself does not result in the removal of the President. Like an indictment, it merely begins a trial. Impeachment is what the House of Representatives does; the actual trial is held by the Senate. We believe such a trial must take place, however unpleasant.

The country can withstand the resignation of the Vice President.

The country can withstand the impeachment of the President.

The country cannot withstand a system of presidential power unlimited by the Bill of Rights.

If you believe that President Nixon should be brought to trial before the Senate for his violations of civil liberties, join the campaign for impeachment. Make your voice count in defense of the Bill of Rights.

Write your Representative in Congress in support of impeachment. And, if you are not yet a member of ACLU, please use the coupon to join. We need your help in this extraordinary campaign for impeachment and in the day-in day-out defense of the Bill of Rights.

Source: Reprinted by permission of the American Civil Liberties Union.

Soon thereafter, when it became known that a mysterious eighteen-minute gap existed on one of the tapes—the tape of a conversation that Nixon had had with Haldeman on June 20, 1972, just three days after the break-in—Nixon's credibility sagged. And because Congress was threatening to create by statute a special prosecutor office that would be completely independent of the president, Nixon had no choice but to appoint a new Special Prosecutor. His political tactic of firing Cox had therefore backfired. Many people in the country now thought that he was hiding something, and any notion that the new prosecutor, Leon Jaworski, would be more manageable than the first was quickly dispelled.

Jaworski, a prominent corporate lawyer from Texas who had formerly been president of the American Bar Association, took the job of Special Watergate Prosecutor only after Alexander Haig, Nixon's new chief of staff, had promised him the authority to use judicial process against the president and had assured him that he could not be discharged (unless he committed extraordinary improprieties) without a consensus of eight prominent congressional leaders. Putting aside its fear that Jaworski would suffer the same fate as Cox unless his position was established by statute, Congress contented itself with assurances from the new attorney general, William Saxbe, that he would not interfere with Jaworski's investigation in any way. The indictments that the grand jury handed up on March 1, 1974, settled once and for all any question about Jaworski's resolve. All of Nixon's top lieutenants—John Mitchell, H. R. Haldeman, and John Ehrlichman, among others—were indicted for conspiracy to obstruct justice and other crimes.

In the American judicial system, the grand jury is a group of ordinary citizens (usually from twelve to twenty-three) who decide whether there is sufficient evidence to indict someone and thereby hand that person over for trial. It is therefore very different from the petit jury, the function of which is to determine guilt or innocence. To fulfill its purpose, the grand jury meets in secret under the guidance of a prosecutor, does not require unanimity, and is empowered to subpoena witnesses and records and to compel testimony under oath. This institution arose centuries ago as a popular check against arbitrary prosecutors. Today, at least at the state level, it has largely been replaced by the "information," which gives the prosecutor the authority to bring charges at his or her own discretion. However, as the Watergate case reveals, the grand jury can still play an important role even if it no longer functions as it was originally conceived. Today the grand jury is often more of a useful investigatory tool for prosecutors than a check upon them.

On the same day that the indictments were handed up, Jaworski and the grand jury did two controversial things. First, even though they declined to indict the president for a crime, they named him as one of the Watergate conspirators. They took this step of identifying Nixon as an "unindicted co-conspirator" because Jaworski had serious reservations about whether it was constitutional for a sitting president to be indicted. Second, they sent to Judge Sirica a sealed report summarizing the evidence against Nixon. It was Jaworski's hope, which later came to fruition, that the judge would forward the report to Peter Rodino's House Judiciary Committee, which at the time was gathering evidence to consider the question of Nixon's impeachment. Jaworski wanted Nixon named as a co-conspirator because doing so laid the groundwork for another subpoena for sixty-four additional tapes. These tapes would be used in the trial (scheduled for September) of those already indicted. On April 16, after negotiations for the delivery of these additional tapes failed, Jaworski asked Judge Sirica for another subpoena *duces tecum,* arguing that these tapes might help some of the defendants or buttress the prosecution's case. After considerable legal wrangling between Jaworski and James St. Clair, an experienced trial lawyer whom Nixon had recruited from Boston, the president lost in the district court. On May 20, Sirica issued the subpoena over the president's objections, and the fact that the grand jury had named Nixon as an unindicted co-conspirator leaked out during the litigation. His public support, already badly eroded, deteriorated further.

St. Clair turned immediately to the Court of Appeals. His ultimate goal was to have Sirica's decision overturned, but any delay would have worked to the advantage of Nixon. It was now the end of May, and the Court of Appeals would take at least a few months to hear and decide the case. And because the Supreme Court went into recess over the summer, any appeals to it could not occur until October. Accordingly, the September trial of Haldeman, Ehrlichman, and the others would have to be delayed, or Jaworski would have to give up his demand for the tapes. Moreover, if the Supreme Court would not be able to render a decision until October, the House Judiciary Committee and the House itself might have to vote on impeachment without the benefit of more tapes. Clearly, time was in Nixon's favor.

Jaworski, however, did not cooperate. Invoking an exception that the Supreme Court had not permitted since *Youngstown v. Sawyer,* he tried to bypass the Court of Appeals by arguing that the case was of such "imperative public importance as to require immediate settlement." In response, St. Clair argued that the delay of a criminal trial was no reason to depart from normal procedure and that the Supreme Court, if it voted for expedited review, was thrusting itself into the impeachment process, a function that the Constitution clearly assigned to Congress. Despite these objections, six justices of the Supreme Court voted to accept the case for expedited review. The Court's normal summer recess was postponed.

Should the Court have waited for the case to come to it through normal channels? On the one side, there was the powerful argument that popular opinion was demanding a quick resolution of the Watergate affair, and the prestige of the Supreme Court would have suffered if the justices had gone into recess just at the time when the country needed them the most. A dangerous stalemate between an indecisive Congress and a cornered president was a real possibility in the summer of 1974. Despite legal technicalities, the Supreme Court had a responsibility to come to the rescue.[5] On the other side, commentators claimed that over-reliance upon the judiciary was itself part of the problem. It tended to weaken the legislature, making it more timid and impotent than it already was. It would have been far better if the impeachment process had taken its full course, with a full floor debate on the House floor, and, if necessary, a trial in the Senate. According to these commentators, representative institutions will decay if they are continually res-

---

[5]See Paul J. Mishkin, "Great Cases and Soft Law: A Comment on *United States v. Nixon,*" *UCLA Law Review* 22 (1974), pp. 77–80, 90–91. Also see Leon Jaworski, *The Right and the Power* (New York: Reader's Digest Press, 1976), pp. 163–65.

cued by politically insulated courts.[6] Which of these two views of the Supreme Court role during a crisis is the more defensible one?

According to Bob Woodward and Scott Armstrong's *The Brethren*, a controversial account of the secret workings of the Court that relies heavily upon "information" provided by the justices' law clerks, the five crucial votes in favor of expedited review came from Justices William J. Brennan, William O. Douglas, Potter Stewart, Thurgood Marshall, and Lewis F. Powell.[7] Of these justices, neither Marshall nor Douglas was sympathetic to Nixon or to his administration's policies. According to Woodward and Armstrong's account, Marshall's clerks reported that the justice took delight in the fact that Dean's testimony had implicated Nixon.[8] Whether this account is correct or not, it seems plausible that Marshall, the first African-American ever to serve on the Court and a former head of the NAACP's Legal Defense Fund, could not have been in favor of Nixon's racial policies, which were designed to endear him to Southern Democrats. Douglas had even more reason to dislike Nixon. In 1970, Republican House Minority Leader Gerald Ford had led an effort in the House of Representatives to impeach Douglas. However, Douglas was convinced that Nixon had been the "driving force" behind Ford's investigation.[9] Is it possible or likely that these factors affected Marshall's and Douglas's judgment of whether to expedite the Nixon case so that the Supreme Court could decide it before the House Judiciary Committee voted on the articles of impeachment? Supreme Court justices are, of course, only human beings, which raises the question of the degree to which their decisions are motivated by personal factors. *United States v. Nixon* puts the issue into stark focus: Were the justices impartially applying the law, or were certain of them out to "get" Nixon?

Jaworski and St. Clair filed written briefs to the Supreme Court by June 21, and oral argument was scheduled for July 8. Because of the obvious significance of the issues involved, the Court granted each side ninety minutes (an hour more than the normal thirty minutes) for oral argument. The excerpts from these briefs and the oral argument that follow can usefully be structured around six vital issues: first, was the president amenable or answerable to any judicial order, including a subpoena; second, were the issues involved justiciable ones suitable for judicial resolution; third, was executive privilege a "political question" that the Constitution assigned to the executive branch; fourth, did the ongoing impeachment proceedings bar judicial review of the case; fifth, could the grand jury

---

[6]See Gerald Gunther, "Judicial Hegemony and Legislative Autonomy: The *Nixon* Case and the Impeachment Process," *UCLA Law Review* 22 (1974), pp. 30–33. Gunther contends that the Supreme Court pushed the House Judiciary Committee off "center stage" and "short-circuited" the impeachment process.

[7](New York: Avon, 1981), pp. 345–46. According to Woodward and Armstrong, Chief Justice Warren Burger voted to expedite the case only after he saw that five other justices were in favor of granting Jaworski's request.

[8]Ibid., p. 339.

[9]James F. Simon, *Independent Journey: The Life of William O. Douglas* (New York: Harper & Row, 1974), p. 420.

constitutionally name the president as a co-conspirator; sixth, if the Court was to find a constitutional basis for executive privilege, what was the doctrine's scope? On each of these points, Jaworski and St. Clair clashed. *United States v. Nixon* was therefore not merely about executive privilege. The executive power to keep information confidential was at the heart of the litigation, but all the other issues must also be considered if an adequate understanding of the case is to be achieved.

The briefs and oral argument, however, may not in fact tell us everything we want to know about how and why the Court made up its mind the way it did. Other factors beyond the legal arguments themselves may have had an impact upon the decision. First, at the time of the decision, it was public knowledge that Nixon had been named as a co-conspirator, even though the grand jury had declined to indict him and even though the evidence itself remained secret to the American public. But because the complete record of the case, including the sealed grand jury report, was submitted to the Supreme Court, the justices had the option of reviewing the actual evidence against Nixon. They could even listen to the nine original tapes (or read transcripts of them) that the public's reaction to Cox's dismissal had forced Nixon to hand over to Sirica. Among these tapes was the infamous March 21, 1973, conversation that John Dean had recounted before the Senate Watergate Committee. The transcript of this discussion between Nixon and Dean (which was later made public) provided strong evidence that Nixon had authorized the payment of hush money to Howard Hunt, and it may have been enough to convince some of the justices that Nixon had obstructed justice. (See Box 5.4.) If so, is it possible that their approach to the legal arguments concerning presidential amenability to judicial process, justiciability, the grand jury, political questions, and the scope of executive privilege was affected by their conclusion that Nixon was guilty? In other words, is it possible or likely that some of the justices decided the case not on the merits of the constitutional principles involved but on the underlying fact of Nixon's guilt? If so, what is the implication? Did these justices decide the case inappropriately? Did they make "bad" constitutional law because they could not personally tolerate the thought that a crook was residing in the White House?

Another factor having a significant impact upon how the Court resolved the case was that Nixon in a public statement had said that he would obey only a "definitive" ruling by the Supreme Court. No one knew what constituted a "definitive" ruling, but the announcement gave the Supreme Court an unusual institutional incentive to reach a unanimous decision. Such an explicit rejection of its authority as the primary interpreter of the Constitution would undermine the Court's prestige and would thereby perhaps alter the American constitutional structure. Do you think that such a concern could have affected how some of the justices voted in *Nixon?*

The Court's decision against Nixon came down on July 24, sixteen days after oral argument, on the very day that the House Judiciary Committee began its public debate on the articles of impeachment. (See Headline 5.2.) At this point, Nixon could either disobey the Supreme Court or release tapes that incriminated him. He took the latter course, but in a few days he realized that his situation was

BOX 5.4

TRANSCRIPT OF MARCH 21 MEETING

NIXON:

How much money do you need?

DEAN:

I would say these people are going to cost a million dollars over the next two years.

NIXON:

We could get that. On the money, if you need the money you could get that. You could get a million dollars. You could get it in cash. I know where it could be gotten. It is not easy, but it could be done. But the question is who the hell would handle it? Any ideas on that?

DEAN:

That's right. Well, I think that is something that Mitchell ought to be charged with.

NIXON:

I would think so too. . . .

❁   ❁   ❁

NIXON:

Your major guy to keep under control is Hunt?

DEAN:

That is right.

NIXON:

I think. Does he know a lot?

DEAN:

He knows so much. He could sink Chuck Colson [presidential assistant to Nixon]. Apparently he is quite distressed with Colson. He thinks Colson has abandoned him. Colson was to meet with him when he was out there after, you know, he had left the White House. He met with him through his lawyer. Hunt raised the question he wanted money. Colson's lawyer told him Colson wasn't doing anything with money. Hunt took offense with that immediately, and felt Colson had abandoned him.

NIXON:

Just looking at the immediate problem, don't you think you have to handle Hunt's financial situation damn soon?

DEAN:

I think that is—I talked with Mitchell about that last night and———

NIXON:

It seems to me we have to keep the cap on the bottle that much, or we don't have any options.

DEAN:

That's right.

NIXON:

Either that or it all blows right now?. . .

Source: Transcripts of Eight Recorded Presidential Conversations, Hearings before the Committee on the Judiciary, House of Representatives, 93rd Cong., 2nd Sess., May–June 1974, pp. 94, 96.

hopeless. A tape of June 23, 1972, revealed that just a few days after the break-in Nixon had encouraged the Central Intelligence Agency (CIA) to stop the FBI investigation. The CIA was supposed to tell the FBI that the investigation was endangering ongoing national security operations. The tape therefore clearly showed that Nixon had been lying from the very beginning, which was more than the great majority of Americans could tolerate. Given the political climate, Nixon's impeachment by the House and his conviction by the Senate seemed to be inevitable. Accordingly, Nixon resigned on August 9, 1974, admitting that he had made some mistakes but claiming that he had done nothing illegal. Only later, in 1978, in an interview with David Frost, did he come close to apologizing for his actions. (See Box 5.5.)

Headline 5.2

BOX 5.5

Nixon's "Apology"

... "[My mistake] wasn't a beaut—it was a disaster. Ah ... and I recognize that it was a mistake. I made plenty of them. Ah, but ... ah ... I also insist that as far as my mistakes were concerned, ah ... they were mistakes frankly of the head and they weren't mistakes of the heart. They were not mistakes that had what I call an improper, illegal motive, ah ... in terms of obstructing justice. . . ."

❀   ❀   ❀

"I'm simply saying to you that as far as I'm concerned, I not only regret it, I indicated my own beliefs in this matter when I resigned. People didn't think it was enough to admit mistakes. Fine. If they want me to get down and grovel on the floor, no. Never. Because I don't believe I should. . . .

"I brought myself down. I gave them a sword. And they stuck it in. And they twisted it with relish. And, I guess, if I'd been in their position, I'd have done the same thing."

❀   ❀   ❀

"I let down our system of government and the dreams of all those young people that ought to get into government, but think it's all corrupt and the rest. . . .

"Yep, I . . . I, let the American people down. And I have to carry that burden with me for the rest of my life.

"My political life is over.

"I will never yet, and never again, have an opportunity to serve in any official position. Maybe I can give a little advice from time to time.

"I can only say that in answer to your questions, that while technically, I did not commit a crime, an impeachable offense . . . these are legalisms.

"As far as the handling of this matter is concerned, it was so botched up.

"I made so many bad judgments, the worst ones, mistakes of the heart rather than the head, as I pointed out.

"But, let me say, a man in that . . . top job, he's gotta have a heart.

"But his head must always rule his heart."

Source: Text excerpt: "I Gave Them a Sword" from *Behind the Scenes of the Nixon Interviews* by David Frost [1987 by David Paradine Television, Inc.] (New York: William Morrow and Co., Inc., 1978), pp. 251, 268–69, 272. Reprinted by permission of William Morrow & Co., Inc.

The unanimity achieved by the Supreme Court in *United States v. Nixon* did have its price. It produced an opinion that some thought long on generalization but short on substance.[10] For example, the opinion recognized without any explanation the constitutional status of the doctrine of executive privilege. Presidents did have the constitutional power to keep executive materials secret, but it was a qualified right, subject to judicial scrutiny on a case-by-case basis. To justify this result, which seemed to favor the judicial over the executive branch, the Court insisted that judges were the ultimate interpreters of the Constitution but never fully explained why the scope of executive privilege was not a political question assigned by the Constitution to the president's judgment, not to the judiciary's. Similar questions can be raised concerning how the Court handled the other issues involved in the case, especially the dispute as to whether the president could ever be subject to a court order. Here again, is it surprising or worrisome that the Court's ruling serves to expand judicial power at the expense of the executive's? The following excerpts from the briefs, from the oral argument, and from the Supreme Court's opinion will help to evaluate these criticisms. Perhaps the Court must define the limits of its authority if it is to define the limits of the other two branches of government, but *United States v. Nixon* is an excellent case to probe the assumptions underlying this feature of American constitutionalism.

ADDITIONAL READINGS

Ball, Howard. *"We Have A Duty": The Supreme Court and the Watergate Tapes Litigation.* New York: Greenwood, 1990.

Berger, Raoul. *Executive Privilege.* Cambridge, Mass.: Harvard University Press, 1973.

Breckenridge, Adam C. *The Executive Privilege.* Lincoln: University of Nebraska Press, 1974.

Cox, Archibald. "Presidential Privilege," *University of Pennsylvania Law Review* 122 (1974), pp. 1383–1404.

Freund, Paul. "Foreword: On Presidential Privilege," *Harvard Law Review* 88 (1974), pp. 13–39.

"Symposium: *United States v. Nixon*," *UCLA Law Review* 22 (1974).

BRIEFS

SPECIAL PROSECUTOR'S MAIN BRIEF

[1. Justiciability.] . . . In the district court, counsel for the President . . . raised for the first time the contention that the court lacked "jurisdiction to consider the Special Prosecutor's request of April 16, 1974, relating to the disclosure of certain presidential documents." . . . The basis for the President's contention that the court lacked jurisdiction to "consider" that "request" for evidence was the assertion that the subpoena involved merely a "dispute between two entities within the Executive Branch."

---

[10]See Philip B. Kurland, "*United States v. Nixon*: Who Killed Cock Robin," *UCLA Law Review* 22 (1974), pp. 68–75; Kurland, *Watergate and the Constitution* (Chicago: University of Chicago Press, 1978); Gunther, "Judicial Hegemony and Legislative Autonomy," pp. 33–39.

This litigation is not merely a dispute between two executive officers over preferred policy, or even over an interpretation of a statute. The courts have not been called upon to render an advisory opinion upon some abstract or theoretical question. Rather, in the context of the most concrete and vital kind of case—the federal criminal prosecution of former White House officials, styled *United States v. Mitchell, et al.*—the Special Prosecutor as the attorney for the United States has resorted to a traditional mechanism to procure evidence for the government's case at trial—a subpoena—in the face of the unwillingness of a distinct party or entity—the President—to furnish the evidence voluntarily. In objecting to the enforcement of the subpoena, the President has raised a classic question of law—a claim of privilege—and the United States, through its counsel, is opposing that claim. Thus, viewed in practical terms, it would be hard to imagine a controversy more appropriate for judicial resolution and more squarely within the jurisdiction of the federal courts. . . .

We begin by making the fundamental point, overlooked by counsel for the President, that federal criminal prosecutions are brought in the name of the United States of America as a sovereign nation. Despite his extensive powers and even his status as Chief Executive and Chief of State, the President, whether in his personal capacity or his official capacity, is distinct from the United States and is decidedly *not* the sovereign. Although the Constitution vests the executive power generally in the President, it expressly contemplates the establishment of executive departments which will actually discharge the executive power, with the President's function necessarily limited to "take Care that the Laws be faithfully executed" by other officers of the government. . . .

Congress has organized the Department of Justice and provided that the Attorney General is its head . . . [and] has vested in him alone the power to appoint subordinate officers to discharge his powers. Among the responsibilities given by Congress to the Attorney General is the authority to conduct the government's civil and criminal litigation. . . .

Congress frequently confers powers and duties upon subordinate executive officials, and in such situations the President's function as Chief Executive does not authorize him to displace the designated officer and to act directly in the matter himself. As long as the officer holds his position, the power to act under the law is his alone. A familiar example of this basic principle was illustrated by President Andrew Jackson's legendary battle over the Bank of the United States. Two Secretaries of the Treasury refused to obey the President's command to withdraw deposits from the Bank, a function entrusted to the Secretary by law. The President's only recourse was to seek a third, who complied with Jackson's wish. Attorney General Roger Taney gave a similar opinion to President Jackson, advising him that as long as a particular United States Attorney remained in office, he was empowered to conduct a particular litigation as he saw fit, despite the wishes of the President.

These principles, considered in light of the authority of the Special Prosecutor reviewed above, establish that, short of finding some way to accomplish the removal of the Special Prosecutor, the President has no legal right or power to limit or direct his actions in bringing prosecutions or in seeking the evidence needed for these prosecutions. Any effort to interfere in the Special Prosecutor's decisions is inadmissible and any order would be without legal effect so long as the Attorney General has not effectively rescinded the regulations creating and guaranteeing the Special Prosecutor's independence—a course he may be legally barred from taking without the Special Prosecutor's consent. Even then any order would have to come from the Attorney General to satisfy statutory requirements.

. . . [Also,] the President explicitly has ceded any right and power he may have to restrict the independence of the Special Prosecutor or effect his discharge by agreeing to the issuance of regulations precluding such action unless the "consensus" of eight specified Congressional officials concurs in that course. The regulations establishing this condition precedent to any action by the President have the force of law, and the Special Prosecutor thus stands before the Court independent of any direct control by the Attorney General or the President. . . .

Framing this controversy as a mere "intra-executive branch" dispute, as counsel for the President did below, seems to invoke the sterile conceptualism, long ago discarded, that since "no person may sue himself," suits between government officials cannot be maintained. . . . Although such litigation is relatively rare and typically involved disputes between an executive department and a "quasi-independent" regulatory agency, there is nothing in the "case and controversy" requirement of Article III that denies the federal courts the power to adjudicate concrete controversies between government officials over their respective legal powers and duties, particularly when—as in the present case—the resolution of the legal controversy has direct consequences upon them and private parties.

We do not suggest, of course, that the President or the Department of Justice could confer jurisdiction on the courts where such jurisdiction is constitutionally impermissible. What we do argue, however, is that the Court must look beyond the President's formalistic objections to the Court's jurisdiction, based as they are on a talismanic incantation of the "intra-executive" nature of the proceeding. By pointing to the mere formality of the Special Prosecutor's status as an executive officer, counsel to the President ignores the substantive concern underlying the "case and controversy" requirement of Article III. A proceeding is justiciable if it presents live, concrete issues between adverse parties that are susceptible of adjudication.

Although counsel for the President has argued that somehow the "separation of powers" principle denies to the federal courts the power to decide this controversy between the President and the prosecution in *United States v. Mitchell,* this argument will not withstand analysis. The inescapable irony of the President's position can only be appreciated by focusing on the fact that the regulations creating a Special Prosecutor's office armed with functional independence and with explicit authority to litigate against Presidential claims of privilege do not reflect a statutory regime imposed by the Legislative branch; these regulations were promulgated with the President's approval by his Attorney General. This, then, is the President's position—not that Congress has unconstitutionally invaded his sphere, but rather that the doctrine of separation of powers forecloses him from the ability to control his "own" Executive Branch in such a way as to safeguard public confidence in the integrity of the law enforcement process. . . . It simply stands the doctrine of separation of powers on its head to suggest that it precludes the Judiciary from giving full force and effect to the allocation of authority within the Executive Branch under an arrangement by the President as indispensable to forestall a further erosion of faith in the Executive Branch.

[2. Executive privilege: a political question.] Our basic submission, and the one we suggest controls this case, is a simple one—the courts, in the exercise of their jurisdiction under Article III of the Constitution, have the duty and, therefore, the power to determine all issues necessary to a lawful resolution of controversies properly before them. The duty includes resolving issues as to the admissibility of evidence in a criminal prosecution as well as the obligation to produce such evidence under subpoena. This allocation of responsibility is inherent in the constitutional duty of the federal courts, as the "neutral" branch of the government, to decide cases in accordance with the rule of law, and it supports rather than undermines the basic separation of powers conceived by the Constitution.

The principle was clear at the very outset of our constitutional history. Since 1803 there has been no question that in resolving any case or controversy within the jurisdiction of a federal court, "[i]t is emphatically the province and the duty of the judicial department to say what the law is." As *Marbury v. Madison* firmly establishes, this is true even though the controversy before the courts implicates the powers and responsibilities of a co-ordinate branch. In conformity with this principle the courts consistently have exercised final authority to determine whether even the highest executive officials are acting in accordance with the Constitution and have issued appropriate decrees to implement those judicial decisions. . . .

The courts have not retreated from this responsibility even when the most pressing and immediate needs of the Nation were at issue. President Truman directed the Secretary of Commerce to seize and operate specified steel facilities because of his judgment that a threatened work stoppage at the Nation's steel mills during the Korean War "would immediately jeopardize and imperil our national defense." Nevertheless, this Court ruled that the President had exceeded his constitutional powers and upheld a preliminary injunction enjoining the seizure. Justice Jackson's concurring opinion expresses the fundamental principle underlying the court's decision:

> With all its defects, delays and inconveniences, men have discovered no technique for long preserving free government except that the Executive Branch be under law.

Even Justice Frankfurter, one of the most ardent exponents of the separation of powers, who expressed "every desire to avoid judicial inquiry into the powers and duties of the other two branches of government," concurred in the judgement of the Court, albeit "with the utmost unwillingness." He recognized: "To deny inquiry into the President's power in a case like this, because of the damage to the public interest to be feared from upsetting its exercise by him, would in effect always preclude inquiry into challenged power. . . ."

It is too late in our history to contend that this duty and competence of the Judiciary is inconsistent with the separation of powers, either in general or as applied to questions of evidentiary privilege. As the court of appeals held in *Nixon v. Sirica,* such a claim, premised on the contention that the separation of powers prevents the court from compelling particular action from the President or from reviewing his determinations, mistakes the true nature of our constitutional system. Focusing on the "separation" of functions in our tripartite system of government obscures a crucial point: the exercise by one branch of constitutional powers within its own competence frequently requires action by another branch within its field of powers. Thus, the Legislative Branch has the power to make the laws. Its enactments bind the Judiciary—unless unconstitutional—not only in the decision of cases and controversies, but in the very procedure through which the Judiciary transacts its business. Congress, in scores of statutes, regularly imposes legal duties upon the President. The very essence of his constitutional function is the legal duty to carry out congressional mandates by taking "Care that the Laws be faithfully executed." Finally, the President may require action by the courts. The courts, for example, have a legal duty to give—and do give—effect to valid executive orders. Where the President or an appropriate official institutes a legal action in his own name or that of the United States, a judge is compelled to grant the relief requested if in accordance with the law.

. . . [A]s Mr. Justice Jackson explained in *Youngstown Sheet & Tube Co. v. Sawyer* (concurring opinion):

> While the Constitution diffuses power the better to secure liberty, it also contemplates that practice will integrate the dispersed powers into a workable government. It enjoins upon its branches separateness but interdependence, autonomy but reciprocity.

Thus, there is no room to argue that the separation of powers makes each branch an island, alone unto itself. Despite the "separation of powers implications, the separation of powers doctrine has not previously prevented this Court from reviewing the acts" of a coordinate branch of the government when placed in issue in a case within the jurisdiction of federal courts.

In applying the fundamental principle that the Judiciary, and not the Executive, has the ultimate responsibility for interpreting and applying the law in any justiciable case or controversy, the courts consistently have determined for themselves not only what evidence is admissible, but also what evidence must be produced, including whether particular materials are appropriately subject to a claim of executive privilege. This issue, like questions of the constitutionality and meaning of statutes or executive orders, is one of the matters that a court has a duty to resolve authoritatively whenever their resolution is an integral part of the outcome of a case or controversy within the court's jurisdiction.

The question was decided squarely in *United States v. Reynolds*, where the Executive Branch argued that "department heads have power to withhold any documents in their custody from justiciable view if they deem it to be in the public interest"—a position strikingly similar to the one advanced by counsel for the President. The case involved a Tort Claims Act suit arising out of the crash of a B-29 bomber testing secret electronic equipment. The plaintiffs sought discovery of the Air Force's official accident investigation report and the statements of the surviving crew members. Although this court agreed that an evidentiary privilege covers military secrets, it held that "[t]he court itself must determine whether the circumstances are appropriate for the claim of privilege. . . . Judicial control over the evidence in a case cannot be abdicated to the caprice of executive officers.". . .

The uniform precedent of allocating to the Judiciary the determination of the applicability and scope of executive claims of privilege not to produce necessary evidence is supported by compelling arguments of policy. Certainly, there are legitimate interests in secrecy. But these interests are more than adequately protected by the qualified privilege defined and applied by the courts. This Court, as we have noted, has adverted to the danger of abdicating objective judicial discernment "to the caprice of executive officers," and stated that "complete abandonment of judicial control would lead to intolerable abuses." This is necessarily true because the Executive has an inherent conflict of interest when its actions are called into question if it is to decide whether evidence is to remain in secret. . . .

We do not question the need for a qualified privilege to serve as an encouragement to the candid exchange of ideas necessary for the formation of executive policy. Indeed, as the court of appeals held in *Nixon v. Sirica,* such discussions are "presumptively privileged." But this case brings into high relief the dangers that would be posed by unbridled, absolute discretion to invoke executive privilege and underscores the wisdom of the rule vesting ultimate power in the courts to rule upon such claims when they are advanced in the context of judicial proceedings. President Nixon cannot be a proper judge of whether the greater public interest lies in disclosing the subpoenaed evidence for use at trial or in withholding it. He is now the subject of an impeachment inquiry by the Committee on the Judiciary of the House of Representatives, and the subpoenaed evidence may have material bearing on whether he is impeached, and, if impeached, whether he is convicted and removed from office. This is an issue to which he can hardly be indifferent. . . .

Counsel for the President previously argued that "in the exercise of his discretion to claim executive privilege the President is answerable to the Nation but not the courts." This assertion merely highlights the salutary effect of requiring the Executive to make its choice *after* the courts have adjudicated the relevant rights and obligations. Public responsibility cannot be fixed, however, until the alternatives are defined. Only then can the people, as the ultimate rulers, know who controlled the course of events and who took what decisions. The President cannot have it both ways: he cannot suggest that he could abort this investigation rather than comply with an order overruling his claim of privilege and use that hypothetical course to prevent the Court from ruling on the validity of the privilege claim itself. Unless and until the President attempts to exercise whatever powers he might have under the Constitution as Chief Executive to intervene directly in the conduct of this prosecution by the Department of Justice, as represented by the Special Prosecutor, and to procure the Special Prosecutor's dismissal and the countermanding of his conduct of the case, the President must allow the Special Prosecutor and the courts to conduct the prosecution in accordance with the regular processes of the law and without regard to any potential executive power to frustrate the administration of justice. . . .

[3. Amenability to judicial process.] At the heart of the court's power to issue and enforce a subpoena *duces tecum* directed to the President of the United States lies the "longstanding principle 'that the public . . . has a right to every man's evidence.'" This power, which in the context of the Watergate investigation and prosecution has proved essential to the full and impartial administration of justice, was upheld in *Nixon v. Sirica,* a decision with which President Nixon willingly complied, rather than seek review in this Court. . . .

The holding of the court in *Nixon v. Sirica* is hardly a newfound principle wrought from the exigencies of Watergate. The authority to issue a subpoena *duces tecum* to a sitting President was recognized as early as 1807 by Chief Justice Marshall in *United States v. Burr.* . . . Although Chief Justice Marshall acknowledged that the power was one to be exercised with attention both to the convenience of the President in performing his arduous duties and to the possibility that the public interest might preclude coercing particular disclosures, he utterly rejected any suggestion that the President, like the King of England, is absolutely immune from judicial process. . . .

The decisions in the *Burr* case and *Nixon v. Sirica* are premised on the theory that every citizen, no matter what his station or office, has an enforceable legal duty not to withhold evidence the production of which the courts determine to be in the public interest. Stated more broadly, and in more familiar terms, they flow from the premise that this is a government of laws and not of men. This Court summed up this fundamental precept of our republican form of government nearly a century ago in *United States v. Lee:*

> No man in this country is so high that he is above the law. No officer of the law may set that law at defiance with impunity. All the officers of the government, from the highest to the lowest, are creatures of the law and are bound to obey it. It is the only supreme power in our system of government, and every man who by accepting office participates in its functions is only the more strongly bound to submit to that supremacy, and to observe the limitations which it gives.

The Steel Seizure Case is perhaps the most celebrated instance where this Court has reviewed the assertion of Presidential power. As we noted above, President Truman concluded that a work stoppage at the Nation's steel mills during the Korean War "would immediately jeopardize and imperil our national defense." In directing the Secretary of Commerce to seize certain of the mills, the President asserted that he "was acting within the aggregate of his constitutional powers as the Nation's Chief Executive and the Commander in Chief of the Armed Forces of the United States." District Judge Holtzoff denied a temporary restraining order on the ground that what was involved was the action of the President and that the courts could not enjoin Presidential action. Judge Pine, however, granted a preliminary injunction. This Court, deciding "whether the President was acting within his constitutional power," upheld the preliminary injunction. In doing so, there was no doubt expressed that the Court would have granted relief against the president if he had directly ordered the seizure of the mills rather than acting through the Secretary of Commerce.

Although there have been a few notorious instances in our history in which Presidents have refused to give appropriate force to judicial decrees, or are re-puted to have made disdainful statements about the decisions, none involved direct disobedience of a court order. More importantly, it is the judgment of history that those were essentially lawless departures from the constitutional norm. The responsible constitutional position was expressed by President Truman—a defender of a strong Executive—in announcing that he would comply with an order of this Court in the Steel Seizure Case if it went against him, despite his claim of constitutional power to order a state seizure. . . .

The argument that the President is immune from process is sometimes rested upon a misreading of *Mississippi v. Johnson.* In that case the State of Mississippi sought leave to file an original bill to enjoin President [Andrew] Johnson from enforcing the Reconstruction Acts, which provided for reconstruction of the governments of the erstwhile Confederacy. Because the President was named as a defendant in the bill, this court heard argument upon the question of jurisdiction before the bill was filed, instead of reserving the question to a later stage. Attorney General Stanbury argued to the Court that the President is "above the process of any court," asserting that "[he] represents the majesty of the law and of the people as fully and as essentially, and with the same dignity, as does any absolute monarch or the head of any independent government in the world."

Faithful to the tradition that in the United States no man and no office are above the law, this Court refused to accept the Attorney General's claim of royal immunity for the President of the United States. Rather, it held that it had "no jurisdiction of a bill to enjoin the president in the performance of his official duties," distinguishing the power of the courts to require the president to perform a simple ministerial act from an attempt to control the exercise of his broad constitutional discretion:

> In each of these cases [involving ministerial duties] nothing was left to discretion. There was no room for the exercise of judgment. The law required the performance of a single specific act; and that performance, it was held, might be required by mandamus.
>
> Very different is the duty of a President in the exercise of the power to see that the laws are faithfully executed, and among these laws the acts named in the bill. . . . The duty thus imposed on the President is in no just sense ministerial. It is purely executive and political.

Mississippi v. Johnson arose shortly after the Civil War, when there was bitter political conflict over the proper national policy to be followed in dealing with the secessionist States. In declining to exercise its original jurisdiction over an equitable suit brought by a State seeking to enjoin the President from enforcing congressional policy, the Court had no occasion to decide that no federal court could ever issue any order to the President, and the Court was careful to leave open the question of the President's amenability to the judicial process where only a clear legal duty, rather than the exercise of discretionary political judgment, is involved, as in the present case. . . .

. . . The Judiciary, of course, must be circumspect in issuing process against the President to avoid interference with the proper discharge of his executive functions. For example, it might not be proper, in the absence of strong necessity, to require the President to appear personally before a court if that appearance would interfere with his schedule or the performance of his duties. Similarly, the courts should not saddle the Chief Executive with requests that are administratively burdensome. The Court's discretionary power to control its own process and grant protective orders provides adequate safeguard against undue imposition on the President's time. Beyond that, there may be some Presidential acts that are beyond the court's ken entirely, such as his exercise of discretionary constitutional powers that implicate "political questions."

But the question here is very different. The Court is called upon to adjudicate the obligation of the President, as a citizen of the United States, to cooperate with a criminal prosecution by performing the solely ministerial task of producing specified recordings and documentary evidence. This Court has defined "ministerial duty" as "one in respect to which nothing is left to discretion. It is a simple, definite duty, arising under conditions admitted or proved to exist, and imposed by law.". . . As we have shown above, the courts, and not the Executive, must decide the existence *vel non* [or not] of a privilege for evidence material to a criminal prosecution. A decision overruling the claim will be as fully binding on the President as it would be upon a subordinate executive officer who had custody or control of the subpoenaed evidence. . . .

[4. Grand jury finding.] . . . [T]here can be no valid public policy affording the protection of executive privilege where there is a *prima facie* showing that the officials participating in the deliberations did so as part of a continuing criminal plan. In this case, where the grand jury has voted the Special Prosecutor the authority to identify the President himself as an unindicted co-conspirator in the events charged in the indictment and covered by the government's subpoena, there is such a *prima facie* showing and the President is foreclosed from invoking a privilege that exists only to protect and promote the legitimate conduct of the Nation's affairs.

. . . The privilege . . . cannot serve as a cloak to protect those charged with criminal wrong-doing. Executive privilege is granted "for the benefit of the public, not of executive who may happen to then hold office."

This is a familiar principle in the law of evidentiary privileges generally. For example, a client may not hide behind the attorney–client privilege and prevent his attorney from being required to disclose plans of continuing criminal activity even though told to him in confidence. Similarly, the courts have refused to recognize any privilege not to disclose communications by a patient which were not for the legitimate purpose of enabling the physician to prescribe treatment. Even the privilege against disclosing marital communications or jury deliberations has been overruled when such communications were in the furtherance of fraud or crime. . . .

The Speech or Debate Clause provides a compelling illustration of this principle. That clause confers an explicit constitutional privilege on members of Congress in order to promote candid and vigorous deliberations in the Legislative Branch. Like executive privilege, which is based upon the same underlying policies and interests, "[t]he immunities of the Speech or Debate Clause were not written into the Constitution simply for the personal or private benefit of Members of Congress, but to protect the integrity of the legislative process." . . . But even though the Clause protects a legislator in the performance of legislative acts, "it does not privilege either Senator or aide to violate an otherwise valid criminal law in preparing for or implementing legislative acts.". . .

Justice Cardozo gave an eloquent statement of why this is not the law in *Clark v. United States,* an analogous case dealing with the secrecy normally attaching to a jury's deliberations. Speaking for a unanimous Court, he recognized . . . that such a privilege, like other privileges based on the desirability of encouraging candid discourse and interplay, is subject to "conditions and exceptions" when there are other policies "competing for supremacy. It is then the function of the court to mediate between them." The Court then held that where there is a "showing of a *prima facie* case" that the relation has been tainted by criminal misconduct, the interest in confidentiality must yield. The Court held that the jury's privilege of confidentiality is dissipated if there is "evidence, direct or circumstantial, that money has been paid to a juror in consideration of his vote." Justice Cardozo reasoned:

> The privilege takes as its postulate a genuine relation, honestly created and honestly maintained. If that condition is not satisfied. . . , [the] juror may not invoke a relation dishonestly assumed as a cover and cloak for the concealment of the truth.

The Court then drew an analogy to the attorney–client privilege, one of the most venerable privileges in the law, and emphasized: "The privilege takes flight if the relation is abused.". . .

Each of the principal participants in the subpoenaed conversations has been identified by the grand jury as a co-conspirator, and . . . it is probable that each of the subpoenaed conversations includes discussions in furtherance of the conspiracy charged in the indictment. Thus, there is no room to argue that the subpoenaed conversations are subject to a privilege that exists to protect the public's legitimate interests in effective representative government. The grand jury has returned an indictment charging criminal conduct by high officials in the Executive Branch, and the public interest requires no less than a trial based upon *all* relevant and material evidence relating to the charges. . . .

[5. Scope of executive privilege.] . . . [When executive] privilege is asserted in a judicial proceeding as a reason for refusing to produce evidence, the overall public interest, as determined by the Judiciary, must control. It is now settled law "that application of Executive privilege depends on a weighing of the public interest protected by the privilege against the public interests that would be served by disclosure in a particular case.". . .

It is axiomatic, of course, that once privileged communications are no longer confidential, the privilege no longer applies and the public interest no longer is served by secrecy. . . . [Therefore,] the President, as a result of . . . the recent release of transcripts of portions of forty-three Presidential conversations, has waived executive privilege with respect to any Watergate-related conversations. There simply is no confidentiality left in that subject and no justification in terms of the public interest in keeping from public scrutiny the best evidence of what transpired in Watergate-related conversations. Whether or not this Court agrees that there has been a waiver as a matter of law, the "diminished interest in maintaining the confidentiality of conversations pertinent to Watergate" is an important consideration in this case in drawing any balance.

The enforcement of the subpoena in this case marks only the most modest and measured displacement of presumptive privacy for Presidential conversations, and augurs no general assault on the legitimate scope of that privilege. This is not a civil proceeding between private parties or even between the United States and a private party, where masses of confidential communications might be arguably relevant in wide-ranging civil discovery. The more rigorous standards applicable in a criminal case have been satisfied here, and they sharply narrow the scope of possible future demands for such evidence. Nor is this one of a long history of congressional investigations seeking to expose to the glare of publicity the policies and activities of the Executive Branch. In such instances the evidence is often sought in order to probe the mental processes of the Executive Office in a review of the wisdom or rationale of official Executive action. The threat of freedom and candor in giving advice is probably at the maximum in such proceedings: they invite bringing to bear upon aides and advisors the pressures of publicity and political criticism, the fear of which may discourage candid advice and robust debate.

The charges to be prosecuted here involve high Presidential assistants and criminal conduct in the Executive Office. Such involvement is virtually unique. Because it is—hopefully—unlikely to recur, production of White House documents in this prosecution will establish no precedent to cause unwarranted fears by future Presidents and their aides or to deter them from full, frank and vigorous discussion of legitimate governmental issues. Indeed, future aides may well feel that the greatest danger they face in engaging in free and trusting discussion is the type of partial, one-sides revelations that the President has encouraged in this case. Certainly, courts should not lightly override the assertion of executive privilege. But the privilege is sufficiently protected if it yields only when the courts are left with the firm and abiding conviction that the public interest requires disclosure. The factors in this case overwhelmingly support a ruling that Watergate-related Presidential conversations are not privileged in response to a reasonable demand for use at the trial in *United States v. Mitchell, et al.* There is probable cause to believe, based upon the indictment, that high Executive officers engaged in discussions in furtherance of a criminal conspiracy in the course of their deliberations. The veil of secrecy must be lifted; the legitimate interests of the Presidency and the public demand this action. . . .

Respectfully submitted,

LEON JAWORSKI,
Special Prosecutor.

PRESIDENT NIXON'S MAIN BRIEF

[1. Judicial intrusion into impeachment process.] The extraordinary nature of this case stems partly from the issues directly presented, and partly from the coloration placed on those issues by the surrounding circumstances.

It would do justice neither to the parties nor to the issues if this were treated as just another case, or simply as an appeal from a discovery procedure in a criminal action against private individuals. It is, in fact, an extraordinary proceeding intrinsically related to the move now pending in Congress to impeach the President of the United States.

In effect, court process is being used as a discovery tool for the impeachment proceedings—proceedings which the Constitution clearly assigns to Congress, not to the courts. . . . As a result of the history of the so-called Watergate case in the district court, the Special Prosecutor is well aware that the district court feels obligated to turn over to the Judiciary Committee any information that might bear on the pending congressional action. Thus the effect, whatever the intent, of the discovery procedures being pressed by the Special Prosecutor would be to produce evidence for Congress that Congress could not obtain by its own procedures.

As a result, there has been a fusion of two entirely different proceedings; one, the criminal proceeding involving various individual defendants, and the other the impeachment proceeding involving the President. The first lies in the Courts: the second lies in Congress. The Special Prosecutor strengthens this fusion by utilizing the unsubstantiated, unprecedented and clearly unconstitutional device of naming the President as an unindicted co-conspirator in the criminal cases, with the apparent purpose of strengthening his claim to recordings of presidential conversations as potential evidence in the criminal cases.

Two processes—each with an entirely different history, function and structure—have become intertwined, and the resulting confusion, both conceptual and procedural, is manifestly unfair to the President as an individual and harmful to the relationship between his office and the legislative branch. . . .

If this procedure were allowed to go forward, inevitably affecting the impeachment inquiry, it would represent an expansion of the Court's jurisdiction into the impeachment process that the Constitution assigns solely to the House of Representatives. Whatever the combination of circumstances producing it, the result would be clear: an expansion of the Court's jurisdiction that the Constitution clearly prohibits. It follows necessarily that the courts may not be used either deliberately or inadvertently, as a back-door route to circumvent the constitutional procedures of an impeachment inquiry, and thus be intruded into the political thicket in this most solemn of political processes.

Anyone who has practiced before this Court is familiar with the observation of Justice Holmes that "(g)reat cases, like hard cases, make bad law." This is true if the pressures of the moment allow the courts to be swayed from their rigid adherence to great principles; if remedies for the perceived passing needs of the moment are allowed at the expense of those enduring constitutional doctrines that have preserved our system of ordered liberty throughout the ages. Of those doctrines, none is more fundamental to our government structure itself than the separation of powers—with all its inherent tensions, with all of its necessary inability to satisfy all people or all institutions all of the time, and yet with the relentless and saving force that it generates toward essential compromise and accommodation over the longer term even if not always in the shorter term. Often a price has to be paid in the short term to preserve the principle of separation of powers, and thereby to preserve the basic constitutional balances, in the longer term. The preservation of this principle, the maintenance of these balances, are at stake in the case now before this Court. . . .

[2. Justiciability.] The concept of separation of government powers is deeply rooted in the history of political theory, finding its early expression in the words of Aristotle who recognized the fundamental distinction between the legislative, executive and judicial functions.

Although subsequently elaborated upon by many historians and scholars, the principle of separation of the branches of government was most familiar to colonial America in the writings of Locke and Montesquieu.

In the most influential political work of its day, Montesquieu in the *Spirit of Laws* wrote:

> . . . When the legislative and executive powers are united in the same person, or in the same body of magistrates, there can be no liberty, ... Again, there is no liberty if the judicial power be not separated from the legislative and the executive. Were it joined with the legislative, the life and liberty of the subject would be exposed to arbitrary control; for the judge would then be legislator. Were it joined to the executive power, the judge might behave with violence and oppression. There would be an end of everything were the same men or the same body, whether of nobles or of the people to exercise all three powers, that of enacting laws, that of executing the public resolutions, and of trying the causes of individuals.

It was this philosophy that influenced the Framers of the Constitution as they began their task of developing a form of government that would survive change and crisis over the long future. . . .

The doctrine of separation of powers, as a vital and necessary element of our democratic form of government, has long been judicially recognized. As early as 1879, this Court stressed the integrity and independence of each branch of the government, when it stated: "One branch of the government cannot encroach on the domain of another without danger. The safety of our institutions depends in no small degree on a strict observance of this salutary rule." Since that time, the Court has continually reaffirmed this doctrine in an unbroken line of decisions. In *O'Donoghue v. United States*, Justice Sutherland speaking for the Court stated:

> If it be important thus to separate the several departments of government and restrict them to the exercise of their appointed powers, it follows, as a logical corollary, equally important, that each department should be kept completely independent of the others—independent not in the sense that they shall not co-operate to the common end of carrying into effect the purposes of the Constitution, but in the sense that the acts of each shall never be controlled by, or subjected, directly, or indirectly, to, the coercive influence of either of the other departments.

Again two years later, the Court added:

> *The fundamental necessity of maintaining each of the three general departments of government, entirely free from the control or coercive influence, direct or indirect, of either of the others, has often been stressed and is hardly open to serious question.* So much is implied in the very fact of the separation of the powers of

these departments by the Constitution; and in the rule which recognizes their essential co-equality.

It is this constitutional principle which establishes the most fundamental jurisdictional limitation on each of the three branches and prohibits each from intervening in the discretionary powers constitutionally vested in another coordinate branch. . . .

It is therefore evident that the district court had no jurisdiction to settle or to intervene in an intra-executive disagreement relating to the evidentiary material to be made available from one executive department to another. The settlement of such a dispute in all circumstances is within the exclusive jurisdiction of the chief executive officer, for as this Court stated in *Humphrey's Executor v. United States:*

> So much is implied in the very fact of separation of powers of these departments by the Constitution, and in the rule which recognizes the essential co-equality. The sound application of the principle that makes one master in his own house precludes him from imposing his control in the house of another who is master there.

The district court's lack of jurisdiction here is illustrated by a simple analogy. If two congressional committees simultaneously claim jurisdiction over a particular bill, it is unlikely that anyone would question that their sole recourse is an appeal to the congressional committee designated to resolve such disputes, or in its absence, to the Speaker of the House. It is inconceivable that any court would conclude that it had jurisdiction to resolve the matter, even if one or both of the disputants were to appeal to the Judiciary.

Similarly, within the executive branch, if an Assistant United States Attorney seeking information to bolster his case against an individual, were denied access to executive documents by either the Attorney General or the President, he could not properly seek assistance from the Judiciary, for a court would have no jurisdiction in the matter. . . .

In attempting to negate this fundamental jurisdictional limitation, the Special Prosecutor relies heavily on this Court's decision in *United States v. Interstate Commerce Commission* for the proposition that the Judiciary does have jurisdiction to intervene in this dispute. However, that case is plainly inapplicable for it did not involve an intra-branch dispute. On the contrary, there the Department of Justice, on behalf of the executive branch, brought suit against various independent railroads, and on appeal the [Interstate Commerce] Commission, a creation of the legislative branch, was joined as a party defendant. Under those circumstances, this Court had jurisdiction to resolve the dispute, for the ICC has been firmly recognized as an administrative body created by Congress to carry into effect its legislative policies and, like the Federal Trade Commission, "cannot in any proper sense be characterized as an arm or eye of the executive. Its duties are performed without executive leave and, in contemplation of the statute, must be free from executive control." Consequently, that dispute was plainly interbranch in nature, and therefore within the Court's jurisdiction to resolve controversies arising among the various branches. That case does not, however, in any way support the proposition that the court has jurisdiction to entertain a solely intra-executive dispute, for the Office of Special Prosecutor, unlike the Commission, was created by the executive branch, within the executive branch, and performs solely executive functions.

In this instance, there can be no question that under the doctrine of separation of powers, the Court lacks jurisdiction to intervene in an intra-executive dispute concerning the availability and use of executive documents to assist in the prosecution of any individual charged with criminal conduct. As the Judiciary has long recognized, . . . it is the exclusive prerogative of the executive branch, not the Judiciary, to determine whom to prosecute, on what charges, and with what evidence or information. Under the Constitution, the President, as the highest executive officer, was expressly delegated all prosecutorial authority when he alone was vested with the responsibility "to take care that the laws be faithfully executed." In *Marbury v. Madison,* Chief Justice Marshall expressed the views of the Court as to its jurisdiction to intervene in the authority constitutionally delegated to the President.

> By the Constitution of the United States, the President is invested with certain important political powers, in the exercise of which he is to use his own discretion, and is accountable only to his country in his political character and to his own conscience. To aid him in the performance of these duties, he is authorized to appoint certain officers, who act by his authority and in conformity with his orders.
>
> In such cases, their acts are his acts; and whatever opinion may be entertained of the manner in which executive discretion may be used, still there exists, and can exist, no power to control that discretion. *The subjects are political: they respect the nation, not individual rights, and being entrusted to the Executive, the decision of the Executive is conclusive.* (emphasis added).

Thus, the courts have uniformly recognized that under the Constitution, the Judiciary was given no role in determining any matters within the executive's prosecutorial discretion. As demonstrated in *United States v. Cox,* even when the executive branch determines, in the face of a grand jury finding of probable cause, that it will not prosecute a particular individual, the courts lack jurisdiction to intervene. In discussing the "absolute and exclusive discretion" of the executive branch in such matters, Judge Wisdom of the United States Court of Appeals for the Fifth Circuit stated in *United States v. Cox:*

> [W]hen, within the context of law enforcement, national policy is involved, because of national security, conduct of foreign policy, or a conflict between two branches of government, the appropriate branch to decide the matter is the executive branch. The executive is charged with carrying out national policy on law-enforcement and, generally speaking, is informed on more levels than the more specialized judicial and legislative branches. In such a situation, a decision not to prosecute is analogous to the exercise of executive privilege. The executive's absolute and exclusive discretion to prosecute may be rationalized as an illustration of the doctrine of separation of powers, but it would have evolved without the doctrine and exists in countries that do not purport to accept this doctrine.

A fortiori, if it is solely an executive decision to prosecute, it follows that the courts are equally powerless to determine what material within the executive branch must be used in the case. Such a decision is exclusively within the power delegated by the Constitution to the Chief Executive; and the right of the Chief Executive to determine what presidential material shall or shall not be used in the furtherance of this or any prosecution has not been delegated to the Special Prosecutor. . . .

[3. Executive privilege: a political question.] . . . [S]hould the Court determine that it does have jurisdiction to entertain this suit, it should of its own authority decline to do so, for a resolution of the fundamental issue as to whether it best serves the public interest to disclose presidential material, if not absolutely privileged, would require the Court to resolve a political question.

Underlying the doctrine of political question is the fundamental notion that many controversies brought before the Court are best resolved by another branch of the government which possesses the necessary familiarity and expertise. . . .

It was not until *Baker v. Carr*, however, that the Court finally succeeded in isolating and articulating a set of criteria for identifying an issue that presents a political question. The Court said:

> Prominent on the surface of any case held to involve a political question is found a textually demonstrable constitutional commitment of the issue to a coordinate political department; or a lack of judicially discoverable and manageable standards for resolving it; or the impossibility of deciding without an initial policy determination of a kind clearly for non-judicial discretion; or the impossibility of a court's undertaking independent resolution without expressing lack of the respect due coordinate branches of government; or an unusual need for unquestioning adherence to a political decision already made; or the potentiality of embarrassment from multifarious pronouncements by various departments on one question.

It is very clear that the Special Prosecutor's request that the district court overrule the legitimate invocation of executive privilege posed a nonjusticiable political question that meets the criteria established in *Baker*. There are no judicially discoverable standards or manageable criteria by which the courts could resolve this political question. The court below was asked to make an initial policy determination that the President has improperly or mistakenly invoked executive privilege against the Special Prosecutor. Such a determination by the lower court is constitutionally impermissible and violates the basic tenets of the separation of powers. . . .

Any determination concerning the disclosure of presidential documents necessarily requires the exercise of the unique discretion and expertise of the Chief Executive, for such a decision involves "considerations of policy, considerations of extreme magnitude, and certainty, entirely incompetent to the examination and decision of a court of justice." Only the President is in a position to determine which communications must be maintained in confidence, for the public interest in this matter is a judgment only the President can make. It involves a complex blend of policy, perspective, and knowledge uniquely within the province of the

President and the executive branch. Neither the courts nor Congress can claim for themselves the elements of knowledge and perspective necessary to examine and review such a decision. . . .

[4. Scope of executive privilege.] The Presidency, as the repository of the executive power of the United States, was forged out of intense controversy during the Constitutional Convention. . . . The result of these deliberations was to create an officer who is Chief of State, Chief Executive, Chief Diplomat and Commander-in-Chief. Because of the great role entrusted to the Presidency by the Constitution and because the President alone is representative of the whole country, there are important respects in which he is not treated by the law in the same fashion as are others. The President is not above the law—but he is responsible to the law in a specific fashion that the Framers, with utmost care, wrote into the Constitution. . . .

Executive privilege as claimed by this President has been asserted by Presidents beginning with George Washington, just as the legislative and judicial branches have continually asserted and jealously guarded their respective "privileges." The initial invocation occurred when in 1792, the House of Representatives passed a resolution requesting military papers pertaining to the campaign of Major General St. Clair. Although the papers were apparently produced, the consideration given to that request is illustrative:

> First, that the House was an inquest, and therefore might institute inquiries. Second that it might call for papers generally. Third, that the Executive ought to communicate such papers as the public good would permit, and ought to refuse those, the disclosure of which would injure the public: *consequently were to exercise a discretion.* Fourth, that neither the committee nor the House had a right to call on the Head of a Department, who and whose papers were under the President alone; but that the committee should instruct their chairman to move the House to address the President. (emphasis added).

Since then, Presidents and Attorneys General have asserted the privilege. Even more important is the fact that Presidents have always acted on the assumption that it is discretionary with them alone to determine whether the public interest permits production of presidential papers, and the other branches of Government have until recently accepted this position. The opinions over a long period of years by the highest legal officer in the Government cannot be lightly disregarded. . . . Uninterrupted usage continued from the early days of the Republic is weighty evidence of the proper construction of any clause of the Constitution. . . .

. . . The significance and rationale for [executive privilege] . . . are underscored by reference to the way in which the other co-equal branches of government have regarded the need for confidentiality. Chief Justice Burger, in *New York Times v. United States*, in his dissent, revealed his assessment of privilege:

> With respect to the question of inherent power of the Executive to classify papers, records, and documents as secret, or otherwise unavailable for public exposure, and to secure aid of courts for enforcement, there may be an analogy with respect to this Court. No statute gives this Court express power to establish and enforce the utmost security measures for the secrecy of our deliberations and

records. Yet I have little doubt as to the inherent power of the Court to protect the confidentiality of its internal operations by whatever judicial measures may be required.

Although Professor Arthur Selwyn Miller and a collaborator have recently argued to the contrary, it has always been recognized that judges must be able to confer with their colleagues, and with their law clerks, in circumstances of absolute confidentiality. Justice Brennan has written that Supreme Court conferences are held in "absolute secrecy for obvious reasons." Justice Frankfurter had said that the "secrecy that envelops the Court's work" is "essential to the effective functioning of the Court."

Congress, too, has seen fit to hold such a privilege. It is a long established practice of each House of Congress to regard its own private papers as privileged. No court subpoena is complied with by the Congress or its committees without a vote of the House concerned to turn over the documents. This practice is insisted on by Congress even when the result may be to deny relevant evidence in a criminal proceeding either to the prosecution or to the accused person. . . .

The considerations of public policy that required the deliberations of the Constitutional Convention to be held in confidence for half a century and made it imperative that judges and members of Congress be permitted to work under conditions of absolute confidentiality are particularly compelling when applied to presidential communications with his advisers. As stated by the President on July 6, 1973, in his letter to Senator Sam. J. Ervin:

> No President could function if the private papers of his office, prepared by his personal staff, were open to public scrutiny. Formulation of sound public policy requires that the President and his personal staff be able to communicate among themselves in complete candor, and that their tentative judgments, their exploration of alternatives, and their frank comments on issues and personalities at home and abroad remain confidential.

This has been the position of every President in our history, and it has been specifically stated by President Nixon's predecessors.

Writing his memoirs in 1955, President Truman explained that he had found it necessary to omit certain material, and said: "Some of this material cannot be made available for many years, perhaps for many generations." President Eisenhower stated the point with force on July 6, 1955, in connection with the Dixon–Yates controversy:

> But when it comes to the conversations that take place between any responsible official and his advisers or exchange of little, mere slips of this or that, expressing personal opinions on the most confidential basis, those are not subject to investigation by anybody, and if they are, will wreck the Government. There is no business that could be run if there would be exposed every single thought that an adviser might have, because in the process of reaching an agreed position, there are many, many conflicting opinions to be brought together. And if any commander is going to get the free, unprejudiced opinions of his subordinates, he had better protect what they have to say to him on a confidential basis. . . .

Of course, international relations and national defense have very special claims to secrecy, but the importance of the President being able to speak with his advisors "freely, frankly, and in confidence" is not confined to those matters. It is just as essential that the President be able to talk openly with his advisors about domestic issues as about military or foreign affairs. The wisdom that free discussion provides is as vital in fighting inflation, choosing Supreme Court Justices, deciding whether to veto a large spending bill, and dealing with a myriad other important questions that the President must confront in his roles as Chief of State and Chief Executive, as it is when he is acting as Chief Diplomat or as Commander-in Chief. Any other view would fragment the executive power vested in him and would assume that some of his constitutional responsibilities are more important than others. It is true that the President has more substantive freedom to act in foreign and military affairs than he does in domestic affairs, but his need for candid advice is no different in the one situation than in the other.

We submit, with all respect, that if the decision below were allowed to stand it could no longer fairly be contended that the President of the United States is "master of his own house." The confidences of that house would be open for disclosure to the Special Prosecutor—and thus ultimately to defendants—whenever one of 400 district judges chose not to accept the President's claim of privilege. . . .

[5. Amenability to judicial process.] The doctrine of separation of powers embodies the concept that each branch is independent of the others, except where some form of interaction flows from the regular operation of the government or where the Constitution or statutes explicitly provide to the contrary. . . . It means, in this case, that compulsory process cannot issue against the President. . . .

. . . [In the Burr cases, with Chief Justice Marshall presiding, t]hree subpoenas *duces tecum, in toto,* were sought and issued during the course of the intensely-contested trials, although only two were directed to President Jefferson. The first was requested on June 11, 1807, by Colonel Burr to obtain an October 21, 1806, letter from Colonel Wilkinson to the President, and two military orders, thought to be exculpatory on charges raised by a possible treason indictment. Following more than two days of argument on whether the Court had the right, under the circumstances of the case, to issue a subpoena against President Jefferson, the Chief Justice found that it ought to issue. The Court confined its inquiry to the narrow question of whether a subpoena should issue, and not to whether the court could or would compel actual compliance. The Chief Justice said:

> If then, as is admitted by the counsel for the United States, a subpoena may issue to the President the accused is entitled to it of course; and whatever difference may exist with respect to the power to compel the same obedience to the process, as if it had been directed to a private citizen, there exists no difference with respect to the right to obtain it. The guard, furnished to this high officer, to protect him from being harassed by vexatious and unnecessary subpoenas, is to be looked for in the conduct of a court after those subpoenas have issued; not in any circumstances which is to precede their being issued.

At best as can be determined from an ambiguous history, President Jefferson never complied with that subpoena. President Jefferson did transmit to the United States Attorney, George Hay, certain records from the offices of the Secretaries of the Army and Navy that were covered by the subpoena. This was done, however, in apparent ignorance of the fact that the subpoena had issued because his transmittal letter contains a well-stated argument why a subpoena should not issue. President Jefferson did not transmit the described letter from Colonel Wilkinson, although that document was specifically designated by the subpoena. It appears Burr was forced to trial for treason without the benefit of the letter, for on the convening of his subsequent trial for misdemeanor on September 3, 1807, he again demanded that letter, and another.

If President Jefferson did fully comply with that first subpoena, this is unknown to Marshall's biographer. The letters called for were not produced and Colonel Burr asserted that the President was in contempt of court, since a subpoena was outstanding. Jefferson was nervous about what Chief Justice Marshall might do, and threatened to use force against the execution of the process of the court. A subpoena *duces tecum* then issued against Hay, who had one of the letters Colonel Burr was seeking. Hay produced part of the letter but refused to give passages that the President deemed confidential. After Mr. Hay made his return, unsatisfactory to Mr. Burr, Chief Justice Marshall, noting that the President had not personally assigned any reasons for nonproduction of the item sought, cautiously opined that the President could not lawfully delegate to his attorney presidential discretion concerning what matters required continued secrecy and ordered that the letter be produced. Five days later, President Jefferson responded with his certificate and the letter, "excepting such parts as he deemed he ought not to permit to be made public." As Beveridge relates it:

> A second subpoenas *duces tecum* seems to have been issued against Jefferson, and he defiantly refused to "sanction a proceeding so preposterous," by "any notice" of it. And there this heated and dangerous controversy appears to have ended.

At this point Beveridge adds in a footnote:

> For some reason the matter was not again pressed. Perhaps the favorable progress of the case relieved Burr's anxiety. It is possible that the "truce" so earnestly desired by Jefferson was arranged.

Other historians have read the evidence the same way. Rossiter expresses doubt whether Jefferson was a great President but thinks that one act that remains "to his lasting credit" was his "first declaration of presidential independence in his rejection of Marshall's subpoena in the Burr trial." At another point, Rossiter says:

> Jefferson's rejection of Marshall's subpoena *duces tecum* in the Burr trial and Chase's opinion in *Mississippi v. Johnson,* which spared Andrew Johnson the necessity of answering a writ of injunction, make clear that the judiciary has no power to enjoin or mandamus or even question the President.

The Court in *Mississippi v. Johnson* refuted the state's request to enjoin President Johnson from enforcing two Reconstruction Act statutes because "the duty thus imposed on the President (to see that the laws are faithfully executed) is in no sense ministerial. It is purely executive and political." The Court noted that the "fact that no such application was ever before made in any case indicates the general judgment of the profession that no such application should be entertained," and summarized the thrust of the case in these terms:

It is true that in the instance before us the interposition of the court is not sought to enforce action by the Executive under Constitutional legislation, but to restrain such action under legislation alleged to be unconstitutional. But we are unable to perceive that this circumstance takes the case out of the general principles which forbid judicial interference with the exercise of executive discretion. . . . The Congress is the Legislative Department of the government, the President is the Executive Department. Neither can be restrained in its action by the Judicial Department; though the acts of both, when performed, are, in proper cases, subject to its cognizance. The impropriety of such interference will be clearly seen upon consideration of its possible consequences.

Without exception, the basic precedents support our contention that it is for the President to decide whether to disclose confidential presidential communications, and that his discretion is not subject to judicial review. Otherwise, the "essential co-equality" of the three branches . . . would be ended, and we would have taken a long—and probably irreversible—step toward government by Judiciary. Today it would be the Presidency that would be lessened and crippled in its ability to function. Tomorrow it could be Congress, for if presidential privacy must yield to a judicial determination, it is difficult to think of any ground on which congressional privacy could continue to stand. . . .

[6. Grand jury finding.] The necessary reason for the great concern and specificity of the Constitution in providing for a President at all times capable of fulfilling his duties is the fact that all three branches of government must have the capacity to function if the system is to work. While the capacity to function is assured to the legislative and judicial branches by the numbers of individuals who comprise them, the executive branch must depend on the personal capacity of a single individual, the President. Since the executive's responsibilities include the day-to-day administration of the government, including all emergency functions, his capacity to function at any hour is highly critical. Needless to say, if the President were indictable while in office, any prosecutor and grand jury would have within their power the ability to cripple an entire branch of the national government and hence the whole system. . . .

The constitutional policy that mandates that the President is not subject to judicial process or criminal indictment while President clearly shows that the grand jury action naming or authorizing the name of the President as an unindicted co-conspirator contravenes the constitutional power of the grand jury or any court of this country.

The implication by a grand jury on the basis of certain alleged facts that the President may have violated the law can have only one proper result. As stated above, the grand jury may with the district court's consent forward the factual material creating the implications, minus any conclusions, to the House of Representatives. That result was fulfilled when the grand jury filed with the court below its factual report and recommended that it be forwarded to the House Judiciary Committee, in March of 1974. The president made no objection to this move because the House of Representatives is the proper body, the only proper body, to impeach a President, as part of the process of removing a President from office. The grand jury's constitutionally impermissible authorization to the Special Prosecutor, permitting the President to be named or naming the President as an unindicted co-conspirator, however, attempts to subvert and prejudice the legitimate constitutional procedure of impeachment. . . .

As noted by the district court nothing could be more important to America's future than that the ongoing impeachment be "unswervingly fair." And nothing could be more clear than that the naming of the President of the United States as an unindicted co-conspirator by a secret grand jury proceeding, which was subsequently leaked to the press, is a direct and damaging assault on the fairness of the House impeachment proceeding. It is the kind of prejudice that a court would certainly be required to remedy or compensate for if it affected the rights of a criminal defendant to a trial free from the probability of prejudicial pre-trial publicity. . . .

The rigorous adversary format, with that most powerful tool for determining truth, cross-examination, is not available in the secret grand jury setting. It is now well established that the right of cross-examination is an essential element of due process in any proceeding where an individual's "property" or "reputation" may be adversely affected. The fundamental right to present evidence and to cross-examine witnesses in an impeachment proceeding is manifest. As the experience of our judicial system has demonstrated, the most effective method for establishing the truth of an accusation is to permit the respondent the right to personally cross-examine those presenting adverse testimony. . . .

The characterization of the President of the United States as an unindicted co-conspirator is nothing less than an attempt to nullify the presumption of innocence by a secret, non-adversary proceeding. The presumption of innocence is a fundamental of American justice; the grand jury's procedure is an implication of guilt which corrupts this ideal. To thus allow the Special Prosecutor to use such a constitutionally impermissible device, as an incident to an evidentiary desire, for the purpose of overcoming executive privilege, is wholly intolerable. The American legal system has never allowed the desire for evidence to go beyond the bounds of law. The President should not be made a hostage of the unwarranted pressure inherent in the grand jury's improper action.

The former Special Prosecutor, Mr. Archibald Cox, was quoted in the *New York Times* on January 5, 1974 . . . [as follows]: "Mr. Cox, in the telephone interview from his vacation home in Maine, described such a technique as 'just a backhanded way of sticking the knife in.'" . . . To base a desire for evidence on a stratagem which attempts to cripple the Presidency, and thus nullify the President's claim of executive privilege, is unprecedented, but more significantly a grotesque attempt to abuse the process of the judicial branch of government. . . .

[7. Conclusion.] It is no exaggeration to say that the revelations of Watergate have so sharpened the public appetite for more revelations that the claim of a Presidential right and responsibility under the Constitution to maintain the confidentiality of Presidential conversations must run the gamut of a broadly held popular sentiment that the claim is probably unjust and is therefore presumably unsound. The President's assertion of a right to maintain the confidentiality, a right relied on by every President since George Washington, is likened to the absolute right of kings. His stand on an important Constitutional principle is viewed in

many places with suspicion or even hostility. Despite his unprecedented cooperation with the investigations by allowing his advisers to testify about relevant portions of the conversations in question, he stands accused in some quarters of obstructing rather than facilitating the investigations.

Our submission on this appeal must acknowledge this Watergate phenomenon since it is an operative factor, though it is one that the courts, judging in calmness and not moved by the passions of the moment, should be expected to ignore.
We conceive it to be our task to demonstrate that the decision below was reached
by casting the Constitution in the mold of Watergate rather than applying Constitutional practices and restraints to the facts of Watergate. It is our further responsibility to show that what may seem inevitably just in the heat and excitement of
an unprecedented political scandal may prove inexorably corrosive to the principles and practices of a Constitution that must stand the test of a long and uncertain future and serve the needs of a changing culture and polity. . . .

Respectfully submitted,

JAMES D. ST. CLAIR,
Attorney for the President.

SPECIAL PROSECUTOR'S REPLY BRIEF

[1. Grand jury finding.] . . . Counsel for the President is simply wrong in alleging
that the naming of the President was a "stratagem" or "device" to "nullify the President's claim of executive privilege." This claim ignores the basic principle that the
grand jury's function is to return a "true bill" that fully and fairly alleges what it
believes the evidence shows. . . .

Nor is there any foundation for the insinuation that the grand jury's determination regarding President Nixon was intended to prejudice the President's position before the country or before the Judiciary Committee. As noted above, when
the grand jury transmitted the material evidence concerning the President to the
Judiciary Committee, it . . . abstained from offering the House its view on the
thrust of the evidence. . . .

When, however, the President refused to comply with the instant subpoena
for evidence to be used at the trial on the indictment and on May 1, 1974, moved
to quash it, claiming "executive privilege," it became appropriate, if not obligatory,
to invoke the grand jury's finding in order to permit the court to make an informed determination whether the President could lawfully invoke that public
privilege to withhold the evidence sought. . . .

In denying the President's motion to quash, the district court's opinion was
carefully guarded in referring to the significance of the sealed material. Because
of the number of persons who were necessarily privy to this information, however,
news media were able to piece together the essentials of what had been disclosed
and litigated *in camera,* and on June 6, 1974, counsel for the President publicly
confirmed the reports about the grand jury's action. But the record shows that the
grand jury, the district court and the Special Prosecutor successfully maintained

the grand jury's determination in strict confidence for several months in order to avoid unnecessary impact upon the Judiciary Committee's inquiry. It is hardly fair to say, therefore, as counsel for the President does, that the grand jury and the Special Prosecutor were attempting "to subvert and prejudice the legitimate constitutional procedure of impeachment.". . .

While we readily concede that the naming of an incumbent President as an unindicted co-conspirator is a grave and solemn step and may cause public as well as private anguish, we submit that such action is not constitutionally proscribed. The answer to the constitutional question must be shaped by two postulates of our free society: that grand juries are ordinarily responsible and that, in the public market place of ideas, the people can be trusted to assess the worth of charges and counter-charges, particularly where the acts of a public official are in dispute. There is little reason to fear either that grand juries will accuse an incumbent President maliciously, or that, if they do, their charges will receive credit they do not deserve. . . .

[2. Executive privilege: a political question.] There is no need here to review again the history that led to the regulations establishing the Office of the Watergate Special Prosecution Force or the exclusive authority that the Special Prosecutor has to maintain prosecutions within his jurisdiction. What is important to note here, however, is that counsel for the President, by accepting the proposition that the President and Attorney General can delegate certain Executive functions to subordinate officers, implicitly has conceded the validity of the regulations, promulgated with the President's consent, delegating specific prosecutorial duties and powers to the Special Prosecutor.

There can be no question that the Attorney General, with the concurrence of the President, has delegated to the Special Prosecutor "full authority" to prosecute the present criminal case and "full authority" to contest claims of executive privilege made during that prosecution. In exercising this authority, the Special Prosecutor has the "greatest degree of independence that is consistent with the Attorney General's statutory accountability." More specifically, the regulations provide that the "Attorney General will not countermand or interfere with the Special Prosecutor's decisions or actions." The only control the Attorney General retains is to dismiss the Special Prosecutor for "extraordinary improprieties."

Thus, it wholly misses the point for counsel to the President to say that the separation of powers precludes the courts from entertaining this action because "it is the exclusive prerogative of the executive branch, not the Judiciary, to determine whom to prosecute, on what charges, and with what evidence." To the extent this prerogative is exclusively Executive, it now lies with the Special Prosecutor with respect to the prosecution of *United States v. Mitchell, et al.,* not with the Attorney General or the President. In a very real sense, therefore, the office of the Watergate Special Prosecution Force is a quasi-independent agency. It is an agency intended and designed to be "independent of executive authority, except in its selection, and free to exercise its judgment without the leave or hindrance of any other official or any department of the government.". . .

Counsel for the President repeatedly stresses that the President has not delegated to the Special Prosecutor his "duty" to claim executive privilege when he sees fit, suggesting that his retention of that power somehow deprives the courts of jurisdiction. We fully agree that the President's power to assert a claim of privilege for presidential papers has not been delegated to the Special Prosecutor. Indeed, it is precisely that power, when it comes into conflict with the independent power of the Special Prosecutor in the context of a pending criminal prosecution to contest the claim of privilege, that creates the live, concrete controversy before the courts. . . .

[3. Scope of executive privilege.] We share the desire of counsel for the President to maintain a strong and viable Executive. And we do not deny that wholesale access to evidence of confidential governmental deliberations by every congressional committee and by every private litigant, no matter what the context of the requests for information or the need for information, might "chill" the interchange of ideas necessary for the successful administration of the Executive Branch. But this Court is not confronted with the alternatives seemingly posed by counsel for the President: this case does not present a choice between recognizing an absolute privilege on the one hand, or exposing the Executive to repeated unwarranted intrusions on its confidentiality on the other hand. . . .

We emphasize at this point that we are not concerned in this case with the "sovereign prerogative" of the Executive "to protect the confidentiality necessary to carry out its responsibilities in the fields of international relations and national defense." There has been no claim that any of the subpoenaed conversations involves "state secrets" or that disclosure of any of them will "result in direct, immediate, and irreparable damage to our Nation or its people." We deal instead solely with deliberations regarding a domestic crime. . . .

. . . While counsel for the President apparently rejects the notion that the courts are equipped to protect the Executive Branch against burdensome and oppressive subpoenas, there is no evidence that the courts have failed in this duty. Indeed, the expectation that the courts are incapable of protecting the legitimate interests of the Executive strikes at the very core of the concept of principled adjudication. . . . The plain fact is that, as far as we are aware, with the exception of a few subpoenas issued to the President at the request of his former aides who are now awaiting criminal trial, all of the other subpoenas to which counsel refers have been quashed by the courts, including several quashed at the Special Prosecutor's urging. Thus, just as with subpoenas to cabinet officers, the courts should be solicitous to avoid unwarranted interference with the performance of executive functions, but it is for the courts to decide whether enforcement of process is necessary in each particular case. . . .

In support of an absolute executive privilege, counsel for the president analogizes to the secrecy of internal court deliberations and refusals by Congress to afford evidence for criminal prosecutions. Certainly, we do not question the views of either the Chief Justice or Justice Brennan, quoted in the President's brief, that as a general rule the deliberations of judges, either among themselves or with their law clerks, must be kept secret. But nowhere has there been the suggestion that the secrecy is impenetrable, regardless of the reasons mandating in favor of disclosure. For example, consider the Manton case, where Circuit Judge Manton was convicted of a conspiracy to obstruct justice and defraud the United States arising out of bribes Manton accepted to influence his decision of cases. We cannot believe that if judicial colleagues of Judge Manton or his law clerk had been in a position to give material testimony on the elements of the crimes charged that they would have been excused because of general notions of confidentiality. . . .

If there is anything to be learned from the congressional refusals to produce evidence, it is that they are justified from the explicit privileges accorded Congress. . . . Unlike Congress, the President has no explicit privileges, and if any inference is to be drawn, it is that the Framers intended that he have none. Accordingly, examples of congressional refusals to provide evidence in no way imply that the "separation of powers" doctrine would otherwise have justified an absolute congressional privilege and certainly do not support the creation of an absolute executive privilege in the face of the silence of the Constitution on the subject. . . .

Respectfully submitted,

LEON JAWORSKI,
Special Prosecutor.

PRESIDENT NIXON'S REPLY BRIEF

[1. Justiciability.] . . . In an attempt to negate the intra-executive nature of this dispute, the Special Prosecutor repeatedly asserts that he, as the alter-ego of the Attorney General, does not represent the President or the executive branch in a criminal proceeding but rather the United States as a distinct sovereign entity. Such an argument is without merit for there is no sovereign entity distinct from the three recognized branches of the government. Nor, as a practical matter, is the Attorney General unique in his capacity to act in the name of the United States, for most, if not all federal actions are performed in the name of "the United States," the ultimate symbol of this nation's sovereignty. To suggest that a governmental action is not a judicial, executive, or legislative action, simply because it is taken in the name of the United States, is to confuse the basic symbol of the government with the functional divisions of its authority. The term "United States" does not refer to a separate entity but is a composite description of the three independent and co-equal branches of the government. Within their respective roles, each coordinate branch acts in the name of the United States. Thus, it is of no distinguishing consequence that the Attorney General or the Special Prosecutor invokes the name of the United States in conducting a criminal prosecution. Nor does this invocation divest the Attorney General or the Special Prosecutor of their status as subordinate officers within the executive branch of government.

To accept the Special Prosecutor's position that there is, in essence, an independent branch of the government known as the United States would make meaningless the delegation of authority and balance of power existing between the three branches, and destroy the tripartite form of government established by the Framers. It would create an additional fourth branch of government with its own representation in court and responsible to none of the other branches. Such a proposition is without logic or constitutional merit.

Alternatively, by tracing the statutory authority of the Attorney General, the Special Prosecutor appears to be suggesting to this court that there may be some legislative basis for his authority akin to a legislative regulatory agency, which would nullify the claim that the present dispute is intra-executive in nature. He summarizes his position as follows; in discharging his responsibilities, "the Special Prosecutor does not act as a mere agent-at-will of the President. He enjoys an independent authority derived from constitutional delegations of authority by the Congress to the Attorney General and from the Attorney General to him. . . ."

We do not contest the Special Prosecutor's assertion that his authority is derived from the Attorney General, but it is precisely this derivation of authority that conclusively establishes the executive nature of the office he holds. The Attorney General can only delegate to a subordinate officer the same authority and status he himself possesses. Thus, even as the alter ego of the Attorney General in a particular matter, the Special Prosecutor is necessarily vested with the same executive status, and no more. To assert that either the Attorney General, an executive cabinet member, or any subordinate officer within the Department of Justice, acts in a legislative or even quasi-legislative capacity when conducting a criminal prosecution is so contrary to the settled law as not to warrant further comment. It remains only to be said that all executive departments exist with some statutory basis, but this does not in any way alter the exclusively executive nature of their duties and responsibilities. As we point out at the beginning, "the President is the Executive Department." The Attorney General is but "the hand of the President." He is the agent of the president, and any direction given by him is but a direction of the President. . . . Thus, neither under the legislative theory nor the sovereign entity theory proposed by the Special prosecutor has he demonstrated that the present dispute is anything more than an intra-executive dispute beyond the jurisdiction of the district court.

Finally, the Special Prosecutor alleges that the delegation of authority to him by Acting Attorney General Bork, combined with the repeated assurances that he would be free to carry out his responsibilities, confers jurisdiction upon the court to resolve the instant dispute. Such an argument fails for three fundamental reasons. First, the Judiciary has never had jurisdiction to review or determine what evidence the executive branch shall or shall not use in the furtherance of its own case in a criminal proceeding. The responsibility for making this determination has always been within the executive branch, and includes the power to balance and determine what confidential governmental materials would, if disclosed, be detrimental to the public interest. A decision by the executive branch not to use a particular document, even one which tends to support its own burden of proof in a criminal prosecution, has not been and is not a proper subject for judicial review. Second, such a decision is exclusively within the duties and responsibilities delegated by the Constitution to the Chief Executive, for he alone was vested with the obligation to see "that the Laws be faithfully executed." Unless the President has delegated his authority to a subordinate officer, the President's decision in such matters is final, and an improper subject for judicial review.

Third, there has been no delegation of this responsibility by the President to the Attorney General or the Special Prosecutor in the instant case. Nor has the Attorney General attempted to delegate this authority to the Special Prosecutor. This conclusion is fully supported by the brief filed by the Special Prosecutor before this Court, for there is a notable absence of any claim by the Special Prosecutor that he was, in fact, delegated the President's responsibility to weigh the public interest in determining what presidential material shall or shall not be used in this proceeding. Since this responsibility was retained by the President, there can be no basis for a claim that the President acted beyond the scope of his constitutional authority in determining not to use certain presidential material in this case. In doing so, as Professor Bickel pointed out, he is simply "exercising the lawful powers of his office, which he may do until removed upon impeachment and conviction." Because this decision is clearly within the prosecutorial discretion vested in the executive branch, and in particular in the Chief Executive, the district court is without jurisdiction to review this determination.

The district court's lack of jurisdiction was not altered, as the Special Prosecutor suggests, merely because he may "determine whether or not to contest the assertions of executive privilege or any other testimonial privilege." In this suit, the Special Prosecutor is merely asking this Court to determine whether the Executive was correct in determining that certain executive materials should not, in the public interest, be used to further this prosecution. However, neither the President, the Attorney General, nor the Special Prosecutor, by agreement or otherwise, can foist upon the courts the executive branch's own responsibility for determining the advisability of using certain executive materials in the furtherance of its own case. . . .

[2. Executive privilege: a political question.] We deem it important to emphasize . . . [that t]he issue at stake is presidential privilege, founded in the Constitution, relating to conversations of the President with his closest advisors, not the concept of executive privilege as it may be generally applicable to persons in the executive branch and under other circumstances. . . .

All that we have said on this point was succinctly put by a distinguished constitutional lawyer, Charles L. Black, Jr., who has observed that refusal to disclose communications of the kind involved in this litigation is not only the President's lawful privilege

> but his duty as well, for it is a measure necessary to the protection of the proper conduct of this office, not only by him but, much more importantly, by his successors for all time to come. . . . It is hard for me to see how any person of common sense could think that those consultative and decisional processes that are the essence of the Presidency could be carried on to any good effect, if every participant spoke or wrote in continual awareness that at any moment any Congressional committee, or any prosecutor working with a grand jury, could at will command the production of the verbatim record of every word written or spoken.

Although the Presidency will survive if the lower court's decision is allowed to stand, it will be different from the office contemplated by the Framers and occupied by Presidents, from George Washington through today. . . .

[3. Amenability to judicial process and the grand jury finding.] The Special Prosecutor states an obvious and important truth when he reminds us that "in our system *even the President* is under the law." A fundamental error that permeates his brief, however, is his failure to recognize the extraordinary nature of the Presidency in our system and that the Framers, who fully understood this, provided an extraordinary mechanism for making a President subject to the law.

The President is not merely an individual, to be treated in the same way as any other person who has information that may be relevant in a criminal prosecution. He is not, as the Special Prosecutor erroneously suggests, merely "the *head* of the executive Branch." Instead, . . . it was announced by this court more than a century ago, and since reiterated, that "the President is the Executive Department.". . .

. . . [I]t follows *a fortiori* from the non-indictability of an incumbent President that he cannot be named as an unindicted co-conspirator, and that the action of the grand jury in this case must be ordered expunged. The ability of a President to function is severely crippled if a grand jury, an official part of the judicial branch, can make a finding that a President has been party to a criminal conspiracy and make this in a form that does not allow that finding to be reviewed or contested and disproved. To allow this would be a mockery of due process and would deny to Presidents of the United States even those minimal protections that the Constitution extends to prison inmates subject to disciplinary proceedings. . . .

The Special Prosecutor would have the Court believe that the discretion about the production of documents, which it has always been recognized that Presidents have, shrinks to a mere ministerial duty to produce what is demanded whenever a court disagrees with the Chief Executive's assessment of what the public interest requires. The argument seems little more than a play on words, intended to avoid the decisions, from *Marbury* on, that the courts may compel ministerial acts but that they cannot interfere with discretionary decisions of high executive officers.

Nothing can be clearer than that the decision to disclose or to withhold the most intimate conversations of the president with his chief advisors involves the gravest and most far-reaching possible considerations of public policy. Who can say what the long term, or even short term, public effects of the president's decision to make public transcripts of tapes of his conversations about Watergate will be? It was a difficult and monumental decision, and no man living can predict with assurance how ultimately the history of this country, and indeed of the world, may be influenced by it. It was a discretionary decision in the most important sense, and it is nonsense to call such a disclosure "ministerial" simply because the final action of disclosure can be accomplished by a messenger. . . .

[4. Conclusion.] In this setting the terminal question is: What decision best defends the constitutional structure of American government? What decision lifts the resolution of this case above the passions of this moment in history and safeguards the strengths and integrity of the Constitution against the exigencies of an unknown and unknowable future? There is no doubt about the power, indeed the responsibility, of the Court to answer justiciable questions that are appropriately posed about the meaning of the Constitution. Nor, in our submission, is there any question but that the central ideal of the Constitution is the distribution of power among the separate branches and the resolution of controversy and disagreement by accommodation rather than confrontation. A constitution is a way of governing, not a set of codified specification for the resolution of disputes among the sovereign branches. There are blank spaces on the constitutional canvas that must be left untouched if the Constitution is to bear the same creative relation to our future that it has to our past. . . .

Respectfully submitted,

JAMES D. ST. CLAIR,
Attorney for the President.

ORAL ARGUMENT

❖   ❖   ❖

JUSTICE BRENNAN: Let me understand this, Mr. Jaworski. You don't suggest that your right to this evidence depends upon the President having been named as an unindicted co-conspirator.

MR. JAWORSKI: No, sir.

BRENNAN: And so for the purposes of our decision, we can just lay that fact aside, could we?

JAWORSKI: What I was really doing in pointing to that————

BRENNAN: Well, could we?

JAWORSKI: Yes.

❖   ❖   ❖

MR. JAWORSKI: Now, the President may be right in how he reads the Constitution. But he may also be wrong. And if he is wrong, who is there to tell him so? And if there is no one, then the President, of course, is free to pursue his course of erroneous interpretations. What then becomes of our constitutional form of government?

So when counsel for the president in his brief states that this case goes to the heart of our basic constitutional system, we agree. Because in our view, this nation's constitutional form of government is in serious jeopardy if the President, any President, is to say that the Constitution means what he says it does, and that there is no one, not even the Supreme Court, to tell him otherwise.

JUSTICE STEWART: Mr. Jaworski, the President went to a court. He went to the district court with his motion to quash. And then he filed a cross-petition here. He is asking the Court to say that his position is correct as a matter of law, is he not?

JAWORSKI: He is saying his position is correct because he interprets the Constitution that way.

STEWART: Right. He is submitting his position to the Court and asking us to agree with it. He went first to the district court, and then he has petitioned in this Court. He has himself invoked the judicial process. And he has submitted to it.

JAWORSKI: Well, that is not entirely correct, Mr. Justice.

STEWART: Didn't he file a motion to quash the subpoenas in the district court of the United States?

JAWORSKI: Sir, he has also taken the position that we have no standing in this Court to have this issue heard.

STEWART: As a matter of law—he is making that argument to a court; that as a matter of constitutional law he is correct.

JAWORSKI: So that of course this Court could then not pass upon the constitutional question of how he interprets the constitution, if his position were correct. But I———

STEWART: As a matter of law—his position is that he is the sole judge. And he is asking this Court to agree with that proposition, as a matter of constitutional law.

JAWORSKI: What I am saying is that if he is the sole judge, and if he is to be considered the sole judge, and he is in error in his interpretation, then he goes on being in error in his interpretation.

STEWART: Then this Court will tell him so. That is what this case is about, isn't it?

JAWORSKI: Well, that is what I think the case is about, yes, sir.

✿   ✿   ✿

QUESTION: Are you now arguing that there is no such thing as executive privilege?

MR. JAWORSKI: No, sir.

QUESTION: I didn't think so.

JAWORSKI: No, sir. Because I say there is no basis for it in the Constitution.

QUESTION: You think if anything it's a common law privilege? Is that your point?

JAWORSKI: Yes, sir. And it has been traditionally recognized and appropriately so in a number of cases as we see it. We do not think it is an appropriate one in this case. But we certainly do not for a moment feel that it has any constitutional base.

✿   ✿   ✿

QUESTION: Didn't this Court say that it did have constitutional overtones?

MR. JAWORSKI: It said it had constitutional overtones. And I don't know in what case it may have been used. But———

QUESTION: That was in the Court of Claims, I think.

JAWORSKI: Yes, sir. But it certainly has never placed it in the Constitution so far as I am aware of, and President's counsel who have carefully examined the authorities.

QUESTION: Right.

QUESTION: That was in *Kaiser Aluminum and Chemical Corporation* case in the Court of Claims that phrase was used.

QUESTION: That is judicially tailored?

JAWORSKI: Yes, sir.

JUSTICE POWELL: Is it your view that there are not influences to be derived from the doctrine of separation of powers? Are you saying this is purely an evidentiary privilege?

JAWORSKI: That the privilege as recognized judicially may have been tied into a separation of powers doctrine we don't deny. What we say is that the separation of powers doctrine in the exercise of and calling for executive privilege has not been applied in a number of instances involving both Congress and involving also the Executive—despite the fact that even in the congressional situations the speech and debate clause is there.

What I am saying is that the separation of powers doctrine, as was pointed to in the *Doe v. McMillan* case, has not been permitted to stand in the way of this Court examining it from a standpoint of whether the executive privilege should be permitted or not.

QUESTION: In *Reynolds* the Court ended up treating the assertion of privilege there as an evidentiary privilege but it did allude to the fact that there was a constitutional question, and it said the Court wasn't reaching it, as I recall.

❊   ❊   ❊

QUESTION: Now, just a moment. I understood Mr. Jaworski to tell us this morning, very unambiguously and explicitly, that the fact that the President was named as an unindicted co-conspirator was not conveyed to the grand jury—I mean to the House of Representatives.

MR. ST. CLAIR: No it was not. The material was sent to the House of Representatives in the belief that it was non-accusatory in nature—it was simply a recital of facts.

QUESTION: Exactly. And that is what Mr. Jaworski has represented again to us this morning, was the fact of the matter.

St. Clair: Mr. Jaworski had available to him, unknown to the Judge, and unknown to counsel for the President, a secret indictment naming the President as a co-conspirator. The accusatory part followed later.

Question: Followed in what form?

St. Clair: By a newspaper leak.

Question: It wasn't sent from the court over to the House.

St. Clair: It didn't have to be. All they had to do was read the newspaper. There can be no question about it. And therefore I say this case has to be viewed realistically in the context that it is now being heard.

Chief Justice Burger: I am not sure—perhaps you can help me—are you suggesting that there was some duty on the part of the Special Prosecutor to disclose to the district Judge that there was this secret indictment before the Judge passed on whether the material should be sent to the House.

St. Clair: I think it would have been quite appropriate, because the Judge's decision was based on the proposition there was nothing accusatory; that under the circumstances absolute fairness was appropriate and required insofar as the President was concerned. No one could argue that the indictment as a co-conspirator, naming him as a co-conspirator, does anything but impair the President's position before the House of Representatives. That should, in my judgment, have been made known to the Judge. I don't know what he would have done under those circumstances. His decision was based solidly on the proposition there was nothing accusatory in the material.

Now, my brother [Mr. Jaworski] says in his brief that this material he now seeks of course will be available to the House Committee and will be used to determine whether or not the President should be impeached. So this fusion is now going to continue. And under the Constitution, as we view it, only the legislature has the right to conduct impeachment proceedings. The courts have been, from the history involved and from the language of the provisions, excluded from that function. And yet the Special Prosecutor is drawing the Court into those proceedings, inevitably, and inexorably.

✻   ✻   ✻

Justice Brennan: You have not convinced me that we are drawn into it by deciding this case. How are we drawn into the impeachment proceedings by deciding this case?

Mr. St. Clair: The impact of a decision in this case undeniably, Mr. Justice Brennan, in my view, cannot have—will not be overlooked.

Brennan: Any decision of this Court has ripples.

St. Clair: I think it would be an inappropriate thing at this time because there is pending———

QUESTION: Well, that's a different thing. You've been arguing we have absolutely no authority constitutionally to decide this case.

ST. CLAIR: I will argue that in a moment. But I am arguing now only that you should not. I am arguing now, sir, only that you should not—because it would involve this Court inexorably in a political process which has been determined by the Constitution to be solely the function of the legislative branch. And it cannot be that the impact of this Court's decision in this matter, which is one of the principled matters now pending before the House, would be overlooked. It would certainly as a matter of realistic fact have a significant impact.

JUSTICE DOUGLAS: But as I said before, we have—the beneficiaries here are six defendants being tried for criminal charges. And what the President has may free them completely. Is that true? Theoretically.

ST. CLAIR: Mr. Justice Douglas—it may.

✿   ✿   ✿

QUESTION: The difference between ignoring and filing a motion to quash is what?

MR. ST. CLAIR: Well, if Your Honor please, we are submitting the matter———

JUSTICE STEWART: You are submitting the matter to this Court———

ST. CLAIR: To this Court under a special showing on behalf of the President———

STEWART: And you are still leaving it up to this Court to decide it.

ST. CLAIR: Yes, in a sense.

STEWART: In what sense?

ST. CLAIR: In the sense that this Court has the obligation to determine the law. The President also has an obligation to carry out his constitutional duties.

STEWART: You are submitting it for us to decide whether or not executive privilege is available in this case.

CLAIR: Well, the problem is the question is even more limited than that. Is the executive privilege, which my brother concedes, absolute or conditional.

STEWART: I said "in this case." Can you make it any narrower than that?

ST. CLAIR: No, sir.

STEWART: Well, do you agree that that is what is before this Court, and you are submitting it to this Court for decision?

ST. CLAIR: This is being submitted to this Court for its guidance and judgment with respect to the law. The President, on the other hand, has his obligations under the Constitution.

STEWART: Are you submitting it to this Court for decision?

ST. CLAIR: As to what the law is, yes.

STEWART: If that were not so, you would not be here.

ST. CLAIR: I would not be here.

✿   ✿   ✿

JUSTICE STEWART: Your argument is a very good one as a matter of political science, and would be a very fine one as a matter of constitutional and probably statutory law—except hasn't your client dealt himself out of that argument by what has been done in the creation of the Special Prosecutor? You have just pointed out that the Special Prosecutor is quite different from the United States Attorney.

MR. ST. CLAIR: Right. Perhaps with respect to everything except—the President did not delegate to the Special Prosecutor the right to tell him whether or not his confidential communications should be made available as evidence. So that within the package of executive power normally represented by the executive department as to who shall be prosecuted, that has been delegated to this gentleman and he has exercised that power. When—he has done that. With what evidence—he has done that, as we will deal with in a few moments. But not with that portion of the evidence that is available that constitutes Presidential confidential communications. And the special Prosecutor cannot, and even if the President did give him that authority, probably could not, as a constitutional matter, delegate that. But in any event——

QUESTION: Delegate what? He probably would not and could not delegate what?

ST. CLAIR: The right to order the President to give up confidential communications. That was not delegated.

QUESTION: Not the unfettered right to get it, but the right to go to court and ask a court to decide whether or not he is entitled to it.

ST. CLAIR: Right. And the President, under no circumstances, gave up any of his defenses with respect to that.

QUESTION: And you are making those defenses here and now.

ST. CLAIR: Making them right now.

QUESTION: No question about that.

QUESTION: You are living testimony to the fact that he did not give up his right to defend his position in court.

St. Clair: And my brother concedes that.

Question: The fact that the delegation to Mr. Jaworski gave him the right to contest the President's claim of executive privilege presupposed that the President had a right to assert the privilege—not the right to assert it necessarily with complete finality. That is what we are really arguing about here today, isn't it?

St. Clair: If we get beyond the subject matter situation.

❊   ❊   ❊

Justice White: You wouldn't suggest that every conversation the President has had while he's in office would be subject to executive privilege?

Mr. St. Clair: No. It would have to be a confidential communication.

White: Well, it has to be in the course of his duties as President.

St. Clair: Yes, sir.

White: Now, I don't suppose if he was talking with one of his aides, Mr. Haldeman, Mr. Ehrlichman, about an investment of his out in California, you know, or some other place———

St. Clair: Or a tennis game or whatever.

White: Yes. You wouldn't suggest that that———

St. Clair: My brother doesn't suggest that that is what he wants either.

White: Well, how about conversations about a campaign, about the Nixon campaign?

St. Clair: That's getting a little closer.

White: It isn't closer to the executing of the laws of the United States, is it, running of a political campaign?

St. Clair: I don't think it is very close, no.

White: Conversations about that subject matter.

St. Clair: My brother isn't seeking any such conversations.

White: I know. But shouldn't the President have to say at least, even if the privilege is as absolute as you say it is, shouldn't he at least have to say I believe or assert that the executive privilege applies to this tape because this conversation is in the course of his performance of his duties as President?

St. Clair: As I read some of———

Question: You haven't done that either, have you?

St. Clair: We have not done that. We have simply responded to an assertion that these all relate to Watergate. Assuming that to be the facts———

QUESTION: Would you automatically say that every conversation about Watergate is in the course of the performance of the duties of the President of the United States?

ST. CLAIR: I would think it would be, yes, sir.

QUESTION: Why is that, Mr. St. Clair?

ST. CLAIR: Because he has the duty, (a) to enforce the laws; that is, to prosecute these cases; and (b) he has to take care to see that the laws are enforced; that is, to investigate.

❖   ❖   ❖

QUESTION: What is the public interest in keeping that [i.e., conversations of a conspiracy] secret?

MR. ST. CLAIR: To avail the President, if Your Honor please, of a free and untrammeled source of information, and advice, without the thought or fear that it may be reviewed at some later time, when some grand jury in this case, or some other reason, suggests there is criminality. For example————

QUESTION: But you————

ST. CLAIR: ————it's very important—I'm sorry.

QUESTION: You did release them for the grand jury in this case.

ST. CLAIR: Yes. In the President's discretion, he did that. And it's a discretionary matter. But, for example, the simple matter of appointments, if I may, an appointment of a judge, it's very important to, the judiciary to have good judges. It's not at all unheard of for lawyers to be asked their opinion about a nominee. Now, if that lawyer wants to be sure that he's going to be protected in giving candid opinions regarding a nominee for the bench, it's absolutely essential that that be protected. Otherwise, you're not going to get candid advice. Now, this isn't a State secret, it isn't national defense; I suggest it's more important, because that judge may sit on that bench for thirty years.

QUESTION: Well, don't you think it would be important if the judge and the President were discussing how they were going to make appointments for money?

ST. CLAIR: I'm sorry, sir, I didn't understand your question.

QUESTION: Don't you think it would be important in a hypothetical case if an about-to-be appointed judge was making a deal with the President for money?

ST. CLAIR: Absolutely.

QUESTION: But under yours it couldn't be. In public interest you couldn't release that.

St. Clair: I would think that that could not be released, if it were a confidential communication. If the President did appoint such an individual, the remedy is clear, the remedy is he should be impeached. Let me give you an example———

Justice Marshall: How are you going to impeach him if you don't know about it?

St. Clair: Well, if you know about it, then you can state the case. If you don't know about it, you don't have it.

Marshall: So there you are. You're on the prongs of a dilemma, huh?

St. Clair: No, I don't think so.

Marshall: If you know the President is doing something wrong, you can impeach him, but the only way you can find out is this way; you can't impeach him, so you don't impeach him. You lose me some place along there. . . .

THE OPINION

Mr. Chief Justice Burger delivered the opinion of the Court. . . .

[1. Justiciability.] The mere assertion of a claim of an "intra-branch dispute," without more, has never operated to defeat federal jurisdiction; justiciability does not depend on such a surface inquiry. In *United States v. ICC*, the Court observed, "courts must look beyond names that symbolized the parties to determine whether a justiciable case or controversy is presented."

Our starting point is the nature of the proceeding for which the evidence is sought—here a pending criminal prosecution. It is a judicial proceeding in a federal court alleging violation of federal laws and is brought in the name of the United States as a sovereign. . . . Congress has vested in the Attorney General the power to conduct the criminal litigation of the United States Government. It has also vested in him the power to appoint subordinate officers to assist him in the discharge of his duties. Acting pursuant to those statutes, the Attorney General has delegated the authority to represent the United States in these particular matters to a Special Prosecutor with unique authority and tenure. The regulation gives the Special Prosecutor explicit power to contest the invocation of executive privilege in the process of seeking evidence deemed relevant to the performance of these specially delegated duties.

So long as this regulation is extant it has the force of law. . . .

. . . [I]t is theoretically possible for the Attorney General to amend or revoke the regulation defining the Special Prosecutor's Authority. But he has not done so. So long as this regulation remains in force the Executive Branch is bound by it, and indeed the United States as the sovereign composed of the three branches is bound to respect and enforce it. Moreover, the delegation of authority to the Special Prosecutor in this case is not an ordinary delegation by the Attorney General to a subordinate officer: with the authorization of the President, the Acting Attorney General provided in the regulation that the Special Prosecutor was not to be removed without the "consensus" of the eight designated leaders of Congress. . . .

In light of the uniqueness of the setting in which the conflict arises, the fact that both parties are officers of the Executive Branch cannot be viewed as a barrier to justiciability. It would be inconsistent with the applicable law and regulation, and the unique facts of this case, to conclude other than that the Special Prosecutor has standing to bring this action and that a justiciable controversy is presented for decision. . . .

[2. Executive privilege: a political question.] . . . [W]e turn to the claim that the subpoena should be quashed because it demands "confidential conversations between a President and his close advisors that it would be inconsistent with the public interest to produce." The first contention is a broad claim that the separation of powers doctrine precludes judicial review of a President's claim of privilege. The second contention is that if he does not prevail on the claim of absolute privilege, the court should hold as a matter of constitutional law that the privilege prevails over the subpoenas *duces tecum.*

In the performance of assigned constitutional duties each branch of the Government must initially interpret the Constitution, and the interpretation of its powers by any branch is due great respect from the others. The President's counsel, as we have noted, reads the Constitution as providing an absolute privilege of confidentiality for all presidential communications. Many decisions of this Court, however, have unequivocally reaffirmed the holding of *Marbury v. Madison,* that "it is emphatically the province and the duty of the judicial department to say what the law is."

. . . Notwithstanding the deference each branch must accord the others, the "judicial power of the United States" . . . can no more be shared with the Executive Branch than the Chief Executive, for example, can share with the Judiciary the veto power, or the Congress share with the Judiciary the power to override a presidential veto. Any other conclusion would be contrary to the basic concept of separation of powers and the checks and balances that flow from the scheme of a tripartite government. We therefore reaffirm that it is "emphatically the province and the duty" of this Court "to say what the law is" with respect to the claim of privilege presented in this case. . . .

[3. Amenability to judicial process.] . . . In support of his claim of absolute privilege, the President's counsel urges two grounds, one of which is common to all governments and one of which is peculiar to our system of separation of powers. The first ground is the valid need for protection of communications between high government officials and those who advise and assist them in the performance of their manifold duties; the importance of this confidentiality is too plain to require further discussion. Human experience teaches that those who expect public dissemination of their remarks may well temper candor with a concern for appearances and for their own interests to the detriment of the decision making process. . . .

The second ground asserted by the President's counsel in support of the claim of absolute privilege rests on the doctrine of separation of powers. Here it is argued that the independence of the Executive Branch within its own sphere insulates a president from a judicial subpoena in an ongoing criminal prosecution, and thereby protects confidential presidential communications.

However, neither the doctrine of separation of powers, nor the need for confidentiality of high level communications, without more, can sustain an absolute, unqualified presidential privilege of immunity from judicial process under all circumstances. The President's need for complete candor and objectivity from advisers calls for great deference from the courts. However, when the privilege depends solely on the broad, undifferentiated claim of public interest in the confidentiality of such conversations, a confrontation with other values arises. Absent a claim of need to protect military, diplomatic or sensitive national security secrets, we find it difficult to accept the argument that even the very important interest in confidentiality of presidential communications is significantly diminished by production of such material for *in camera* inspection with all the protection that a district court will be obliged to provide.

The impediment that an absolute, unqualified privilege would place in the way of the primary constitutional duty of the Judicial Branch to do justice in criminal prosecutions would plainly conflict with the function of the courts under Article III. In designing the structure of our Government and dividing and allocating the sovereign power among three coequal branches, the Framers of the Constitution sought to provide a comprehensive system, but the separate powers were not intended to operate with absolute independence.

> While the Constitution diffuses power the better to secure liberty, it also contemplates that practice will integrate the dispersed powers into a workable government. It enjoins upon its branches separateness but interdependence, autonomy but reciprocity.

To read the Art. II powers of the President as providing an absolute privilege as against a subpoena essential to enforcement of criminal statutes on no more than a generalized claim of the public interest in confidentiality of nonmilitary and nondiplomatic discussions would upset the constitutional balance of a "workable government" and gravely impair the role of the courts under Art. III.

[4. Scope of executive privilege.] Since we conclude that the legitimate needs of the judicial process may outweigh presidential privilege, it is necessary to resolve those competing interests in a manner that preserves the essential functions of each branch. The right and indeed the duty to resolve that question does not free the judiciary from according high respect to the representations made on behalf of the President.

The expectations of a President to the confidentiality of his conversations and correspondence, like the claim of confidentiality of judicial deliberations, for example, has all the values to which we accord deference for the privacy of all citizens and added to those values the necessity for protection of the public interest in candid, objective, and even blunt or harsh opinions in presidential decision making. A President and those who assist him must be free to explore alternatives in the process of shaping policies and making decisions to do so in a way that many would be unwilling to express except privately. These are the considerations justifying a presumptive privilege for presidential communications. The privilege is fundamental to the operation of government and inextricably rooted in the separation of powers under the Constitution. In *Nixon v. Sirica,* the Court of Appeals held that such presidential communications are "presumptively privileged," and this position is accepted by both parties in the present litigation. We agree with Chief Justice Marshall's observation, therefore, that "in no case of this kind would a court be required to proceed against the President as against an ordinary individual."

But this presumptive privilege must be considered in light of our historic commitment to the rule of law. This is nowhere more profoundly manifest than in our view that "the twofold aim [of criminal justice] is that guilt shall not escape or innocence suffer." We have elected to employ an adversary system of criminal justice in which the parties contest all issues before a court of law. The need to develop all relevant facts in the adversary system is both fundamental and comprehensive. The ends of criminal justice would be defeated if judgments were to be founded on a partial or speculative presentation of the facts. The very integrity of the judicial system and public confidence in the system depend on full disclosure of all the facts, within the framework of the rules of evidence. To ensure that justice is done, it is imperative to the function of the courts that compulsory process be available for the production of evidence needed either by the prosecution or by the defense.

Only recently the Court restated the ancient proposition of law, albeit in the context of a grand jury inquiry rather than a trial, "'that the public . . . has a right to every man's evidence' except for those persons protected by a constitutional, common law, or statutory privilege." The privileges referred to by the Court are designed to protect weighty and legitimate competing interests. Thus, the Fifth Amendment to the Constitution provides that no man "shall be compelled in any criminal case to be a witness against himself." And, generally, an attorney or a priest may not be required to disclose what has been revealed in professional confidence. These and other interests are recognized in law by privileges against forced disclosure, established in the Constitution, by statute, or at common law. Whatever their origins, these exceptions to the demand for every man's evidence are not lightly created nor expansively construed, for they are in derogation of the search for truth. . . .

In this case we must weigh the importance of the general privilege of confidentiality of presidential communications in performance of his responsibilities against the inroads of such a privilege on the fair administration of criminal justice. The interest in preserving confidentiality is weighty indeed and entitled to great respect. However, we cannot conclude that advisers will be moved to temper the candor of their remarks by the infrequent occasions of disclosure because of the possibility that such conversations will be called for in the context of a criminal prosecution.

On the other hand, the allowance of the privilege to withhold evidence that is demonstrably relevant in a criminal trial would cut deeply into the guarantee of due process of law and gravely impair the basic function of the courts. A President's acknowledged need for confidentiality in the communications of his office is general in nature, whereas the constitutional need for the production of relevant evidence in a criminal proceeding is specific and central to the fair adjudication of a particular criminal case in the administration of justice. Without access to specific facts a criminal prosecution may be totally frustrated. The President's broad interest in confidentiality of communications will not be vitiated by disclosure of a limited number of conversations preliminarily shown to have some bearing on the pending criminal cases.

We conclude that when the ground for asserting privilege as to subpoenaed materials sought for use in a criminal trial is based only on the generalized interest in confidentiality, it cannot prevail over the fundamental demands of due process of law in the fair administration of criminal justice. The generalized assertion of privilege must yield to the demonstrated, specific need for evidence in a pending criminal trial. . . .

. . . It is elementary that *in camera* inspection of evidence is always a procedure calling for scrupulous protection against any release or publication of material not found by the court, at that stage, probably admissible in evidence and relevant to the issues of the trial for which it is sought. That being true of an ordinary situation, it is obvious that the District Court has a very heavy responsibility to see to it that presidential conversations, which are either not relevant or not admissible, are accorded that high degree of respect due to the President of the United States. . . . The need for confidentiality even as to idle conversations with associates in which casual reference might be made concerning political leaders within the country or foreign statesmen is too obvious to call for further treatment. We have no doubt that the District Judge will at all times accord to presidential records that high degree of deference suggested in *United States v. Burr,* and will discharge his responsibility to see to it that until released to the Special Prosecutor no *in camera* material is revealed to anyone.

POSTSCRIPT

In the years following Nixon's resignation, Congress enacted a number of statutes to remedy some of the problems uncovered during the Watergate era. Two of these statutes addressed the specific issues raised in *United States v. Nixon:* what information should be available to what kind of prosecutor so that high executive officials can be punished for their criminal activities. In 1978, Congress passed the Ethics in Government Act, which defined the procedures for appointing independent counsels to investigate and prosecute executive wrongdoing, and in 1980 it enacted the Classified Information Procedures Act, which regulated how classified information should be used in criminal trials. The goals of these laws were to ensure prosecutorial independence from executive control (e.g., Cox's firing) in cases involving high executive officials, to protect properly classified information from disclosure at trial, and to increase the likelihood that improperly classified information could be declassified and used to convict high executive officials of their criminal acts. Formal procedures for evaluating executive privilege in criminal trials and a formal prosecutorial independence, both now based upon statutes, replaced the more ad hoc procedures used in the Watergate tapes litigation and the informal independence of the Watergate special prosecutors.

Title VI of the Ethics in Government Act sets forth the following procedures for appointing an independent counsel: First, the attorney general conducts a preliminary investigation of the allegations; second, within 90 (or 120) days the attorney general must file a report with a special court—the "Special Division" of the U.S. Court of Appeals for the District of Columbia; third, if the attorney general reports that there are "reasonable grounds" to believe that further investigation is warranted, he or she applies to this court for the appointment of an independent counsel; and fourth, the "Special Division" appoints the independent counsel and defines the jurisdiction in which he or she will have complete authority over all aspects of the investigation and prosection. According to Title VI, an independent counsel can be removed by the attorney general only for "good cause," physical disability, mental incapacity, or any other condition that substantially impairs his or her ability to prosecute. If the prosecutor is removed in this manner, the attorney general must justify the dismissal to the "Special Division" and to the Judiciary Committees of the House and Senate. Finally, rather than removal, the "Special Division" can terminate the independent counsel's office when it finds that all of the matters within the prosecutor's jurisdiction have been investigated.

In 1988, despite three major objections leveled against Title VI, the Supreme Court upheld its constitutionality in *Morrison v. Olson*.[11] The first objection was that the judicial appointment of the prosecutor violated the Appointments Clause, which requires that all "Officers of the United States" be nominated by the president and confirmed by the Senate (Art. II, Sect. 2). In his majority opinion, Chief Justice William H. Rehnquist responded by observing that the same clause authorized Congress to vest the appointment of "inferior officers" in "the President alone, in the Courts of Law, or in the Heads of Departments." The key issue, therefore, was whether an independent counsel was an "Officer of the United States" or an "inferior officer." Rehnquist decided in favor of the latter description because the counsel could be removed by the attorney general and because the office itself was limited: Its duties, jurisdiction, and tenure were all narrowly circumscribed. Accordingly, in the Court's judgment, it did not violate the Appointments Clause if Congress gave courts the power to appoint independent counsels.

The second objection centered on the "Special Division's" role in defining the jurisdiction of an independent counsel. The judiciary, it was argued, could not

---

[11]487 U.S. 654 (1988).

perform this function because it was not a judicial one of deciding "cases" and "controversies." Rehnquist answered this charge by once again referring to the Appointments Clause. Though it was true that the powers granted to the judiciary by Article III were limited to those of adjudication, the Appointments Clause of Article II was an additional grant of power to the judiciary, giving it the constitutional authority, if Congress enacted appropriate legislation, to define the jurisdiction of an "inferior officer" whom it had appointed. The other "miscellaneous" powers assigned to the judiciary by Title VI, Rehnquist continued, were also constitutionally acceptable according to this analysis. Granting extensions, receiving reports, even terminating the office of an independent counsel—these were not, in a strict sense, judicial powers, but they were "ministerial" in character and therefore not "a significant judicial encroachment upon executive power or upon the prosecutorial discretion of the independent counsel."[12]

The last objection was that the conditions imposed upon the attorney general's authority to remove the independent counsel violated the principle of separation of powers by depriving the president of his constitutional power to dismiss all executive subordinates. In his reply to this issue, Rehnquist acknowledged that the function of the independent counsel was "executive," but he insisted that the restrictions on removal did not "sufficiently" deprive "the President of control over the independent counsel to interfere impermissibly with his constitutional obligation to ensure the faithful execution of the laws."[13] After all, Title VI did not, at the expense of the executive, increase the power of Congress or permit the judiciary to usurp "properly executive functions."[14] The removal restrictions limited only the executive's power to dismiss an independent counsel. In the Court's opinion, these kinds of restrictions were constitutional because they did not compromise the president's fundamental duty to enforce the law.

Justice Antonin E. Scalia wrote a strong and vehement dissent, arguing that Article II, Section 1 vested *all* executive power in the president and that criminal investigation and prosecution was "a quintessentially executive function."[15] Accordingly, the statute was unconstitutional because it deprived the president of complete control of a function that the Constitution assigned to him. It was unconstitutional for the judiciary to appoint such an executive officer and for the Congress to limit the president's power to remove a subordinate who exercised "purely" executive powers. Nonetheless, despite Scalia's objections, the seven-to-one decision settled the issue of Title VI's constitutionality. In *Morrison v. Olson,* the Court had thus concluded that a statutorily based independent counsel was a constitutional means of addressing the serious problem of high executive wrongdoing.

However, Title VI expired on December 15, 1992, leaving the country somewhat adrift in regard to the way officials should respond to allegations of wrongdo-

---

[12]*Id.* at 682.

[13]*Id.* at 693.

[14]*Id.* at 695.

[15]*Id.* at 706.

ing by high executive officials. Were in-house investigations by the Justice Department sufficient? Should the attorney general appoint special counsels similar to those that played such important roles during the Watergate crisis? Or should Congress reenact a statutorily defined procedure and office that would guarantee investigative and prosecutional independence in the event of a new instance of executive wrongdoing? These sorts of questions have most recently reappeared in 1993 in the light of published allegations that President Bill Clinton, while he was governor of Arkansas, and his wife, Hillary, may have had, through their partnership in the Whitewater land development company, illicit dealings with a failing savings and loan institution. For some months, Janet Reno, Clinton's attorney general, maintained that the Justice Department could be relied upon to conduct an adequate investigation, but in late January 1994, under pressure from a president worried about public perceptions, she appointed Robert Fiske, a Republican, as special counsel to investigate "the Whitewater Affair." Clearly, the problems of investigating and prosecuting high executive officials for wrongdoing, a problem particularly highlighted in the Watergate era, have not yet been resolved.[16]

"Graymail" refers to the situation in which criminal defendants, often former government employees, demand that the government produce at trial (and thereby publicly disclose) classified information, claiming that it will exonerate them or show that their actions were authorized by their superiors. In such cases, the government must either disclose the information or (thereby accomplishing the defendant's goal) dismiss the prosecution. This kind of tactic is similar to the one that Nixon pursued in the tapes litigation. Even though the tapes were not formally classified, Nixon insisted that they were protected by executive privilege. Accordingly, Nixon argued, if Jaworski did not think he could obtain convictions without the tapes, he should dismiss the indictments. Nixon, in short, believed that he was empowered to decide if keeping the tapes secret was more important than convicting high executive officials. The Supreme Court, of course, disagreed. As long as military and diplomatic secrets were not involved, judges were to make the determination as to whether the claim of executive privilege was to be honored or not. The loophole of military and diplomatic secrets, however, was potentially a large one. What if a defendant claimed that he could not receive a fair trial unless he could introduce classified information at his trial? *United States v. Nixon* never purported to answer this question.

On October 15, 1980, Congress enacted the Classified Information Procedures Act (CIPA) to try to solve this problem. It set up an elaborate, secret pretrial procedure by which the government and the defendant inform the judge of what classified information they will use. The judge then makes rulings on whether the evidence that the defendant has requested is *relevant* to the charges and *admissible* in a court of law. The government is obliged to produce all the classified evidence that the judge thinks is relevant and admissible, or it must, subject to the judge's approval, substitute either a summary of the classified infor-

---

[16]For further commentary and criticism of *Morrison v. Olson* and Title VI, see Terry Eastland, *Ethics, Politics and the Independent Counsel: Executive Power, Executive Vice, 1789–1989* (Washington: National Legal Center for the Public Interest, 1989); Stephen L. Carter, "The Independent Counsel Mess," *Harvard Law Review* 102 (1988), pp. 105–41.

mation or a statement admitting the relevant facts. If the judge rules that certain pieces of classified information must be disclosed to ensure a fair trial, the attorney general, acting upon the advice of relevant intelligence agencies, may still refuse to provide the information. However, at this point, if the needed classified information is refused, the court can dismiss specific indictments against the accused.[17] In other words, CIPA places the ultimate responsibility for what classified information should be used in public courtrooms in the hands of the executive branch, ultimately subject to the president's direction, not in the hands of the courts.

Although Title VI and CIPA have helped to solve some of the problems implicit in a Watergate-type prosecution of high executive officials, the Iran-*contra* affair shows that there are still some troubling, perhaps irresoluble, issues. By the procedure outlined in Title VI, Lawrence Walsh was appointed independent counsel with full authority to investigate and prosecute all illegal actions pertaining to the Reagan administration's resupply of the Nicaraguan *contras* that was financed by the profits made from arms sales to Iran. Walsh's investigation resulted in indictments against Oliver North, John Poindexter, and Joseph Fernandez, charging each with at least one of the following types of misconduct: (1) obstruction of a congressional investigation; (2) diversion of monies from the Iranian arm sales to the *contras;* and (3) a conspiracy to conduct an illegal covert action in Nicaragua. However, specific indictments had to be dismissed against these defendants because the intelligence agencies convinced Attorney General Richard Thornburgh that crucial classified information should not be disclosed. In regard to one of these cases, Lawrence Walsh has claimed that the relevant classified information was not disclosed even though it was publicly known. The government, in other words, did not want to publicly acknowledge what everyone knew to be true—the fact that certain American facilities existed in Latin America.[18]

Therefore, it seems that the problem of how to prosecute high executive officials continues to perplex us. Because the executive branch controls what information is classified, and thereby what information is subject to CIPA, it has the ability to obstruct independent prosecutions of executive criminal wrongdoing by refusing to disclose information that the defendant and the judge believe is necessary for a fair trial. In this kind of context, a former government employee subject to indictment might still successfully practice the art of "graymail," especially if those in charge of classified information are sympathetic to the defendant's plight.

But problems arising from CIPA were not the only ones that Walsh had to confront in his effort to investigate and prosecute high executive officials implicated in the Iran-*contra* affair. In 1990 Walsh's one major success—the conviction of Colonel Oliver North—was undermined when a federal appeals court overturned the conviction on the grounds that the evidence the prosecution had used at the trial had been tainted by North's immunized testimony before Congress.

---

[17]This is only the briefest sketch of the procedures of CIPA. For a more thorough account, see Richard Salgado, "Government Secrets, Fair Trials, and the Classified Information Procedures Act," *Yale Law Journal* 98 (1988), pp. 427–46.

[18]See Lawrence E. Walsh, "Secrecy and the Rule of Law," *Oklahoma Law Review* 43 (1990), p. 587.

Then, in an act that to some was reminiscent of President Gerald Ford's pardon of Richard Nixon, President George Bush on December 24, 1992, a few weeks before leaving office, pardoned Caspar W. Weinberger, Ronald Reagan's secretary of defense, who had been indicted for lying to Congress about the facts of the Iran-*contra* affair. Five other participants in the affair also received pardons.[19] An incensed Walsh condemned what Bush had done, claiming that "the Iran-*contra* cover-up, which had continued for more than six years, has now been completed."[20]

Following these pardons, Walsh shifted the investigation to Bush, arguing that the former president had engaged in "misconduct" by failing to turn over to the prosecutors his 1986 campaign diary. However, nothing came of Walsh's last effort. His seven-year (and $35 million) effort to bring charges against those who had "covered up" up the Iran-contra affair ended in failure. On January 17, 1994, Walsh presented his final report. Congressional grants of immunity, presidential pardons, and the particular provisions of the Classified Information Procedures Act made it impossible for him to accomplish successfully his job as independent prosecutor. In the end, Walsh's report suggests that the problem of bringing high executive officials to justice for criminal wrongdoing, especially when classified information is involved, largely remains an unresolved problem of American constitutionalism.

---

[19]Duane R. Clarridge, Clair E. George, Elliot Abrams, Alan G. Flors, Jr., and Robert C. McFarlane.

[20]*New York Times,* December 25, 1992, p. A1.

Index

◆